Nations under God
The Geopolitics of Faith in the Twenty-First Century

EDITED BY
LUKE M. HERRINGTON
ALASDAIR MCKAY & JEFFREY HAYNES

E-INTERNATIONAL
RELATIONS
PUBLISHING

E-IR Edited Collections
Series Editors: Stephen McGlinchey, Marianna Karakoulaki and Robert Oprisko

E-IR's Edited Collections are open access scholarly books presented in a format that preferences brevity and accessibility while retaining academic conventions. Each book is available in print and e-book, and is published under a Creative Commons CC BY-NC 4.0 license. As E-International Relations is committed to open access in the fullest sense, free electronic versions of all of our books, including this one, are available on the E-International Relations website.

Find out more at: http://www.e-ir.info/publications

Recent titles
Popular Culture and World Politics: Theories, Methods, Pedagogies
Ukraine and Russia: People, Politics, Propaganda and Perspectives
Caliphates and Islamic Global Politics

Forthcoming
Restoring Indigenous Self-Determination (New edition)
System, Society & the World: Exploring the English School (2nd Edition)

About the E-International Relations website
E-International Relations (www.E-IR.info) is the world's leading open access website for students and scholars of international politics. E-IR's daily publications feature expert articles, blogs, reviews and interviews – as well as a range of high quality student contributions. The website was established in November 2007 and now reaches over 200,000 unique visitors a month. E-IR is run by a registered non-profit organisation based in Bristol, England and staffed with an all-volunteer team.

E-International Relations
www.E-IR.info
Bristol, England
Published 2015 (e-book and print)

Copy Editing: Gill Gairdner
Production: Ran Xiao
Cover Image: Iryna_Rasko

ISBN 978-1-910814-04-8 (paperback)
ISBN 978-1-910814-06-2 (e-book)

A catalogue record for this book is available from the British Library

Acknowledgments

The editors would first like to thank Stephen McGlinchey who agreed to green light this ambitious project for E-International Relations. The contributors to the book must also be thanked for taking the time to produce their pieces.

Some of the content in the editors' introduction to this volume was adapted from Luke M. Herrington's MA thesis written for the University of Kansas. As such, he would like to extend his gratitude to Hal Elliott Wert, Brent J. Steele and Eric A. Hanley for their thoughtful encouragement and feedback on that embryonic work. He would also like to thank Dan G. Cox, Hal Elliott Wert and Brent J. Steele for the professional guidance and mentorship they have provided through the years.

Abstract

Nations under God: The Geopolitics of Faith in the Twenty-first Century is a timely contribution to the ongoing discussion on religion and global politics. The volume brings together over thirty leading scholars from a variety of disciplines such as political science, international relations theory, sociology, theology, anthropology and geography. Utilising case studies, empirical investigations and theoretical examinations, this book focuses on the complex roles that religions play in world affairs. It seeks to move beyond the simplistic narratives and overly impassioned polemics which swamp the discourse on the subject in the media, on the internet and in popular nonfiction by acting as a vessel for scholarly research on religion. Overall, the book presents a more balanced analysis of the multifaceted roles taken on by religions (and religious actors) in global politics.

Luke M. Herrington is an editor-at-large at E-International Relations and Assistant Reviews Editor for *Special Operations Journal*. He is a PhD student in the Department of Political Science at the University of Kansas where he previously earned an MA in Global and International Studies. His interests include the role(s) of religion in international politics, hegemonic stability theory and ontological security.

Alasdair McKay is an editor-at-large at E-International Relations. He holds undergraduate and postgraduate degrees in politics from the universities of Manchester and Aberystwyth. He has worked for an African human rights NGO and in the parliamentary office of an MP. His research interests include intrastate conflict, African politics, Islamism, political anthropology, religion and violence, and IR theory.

Jeffrey Haynes is Associate Dean of Faculty (Research and Postgraduate Studies) and Director of the Centre for the Study of Religion, Conflict and Cooperation, London Metropolitan University. He is recognised as an international authority in five separate areas: religion and international relations; religion and politics; democracy and democratisation; development studies; and comparative politics and globalisation. He has written many books, journal articles and book chapters, totalling around 160 such publications since 1986. His most recent book is *Faith-Based Organizations at the United Nations* (Palgrave Macmillan, 2014).

Contents

'Le vingt et un siècle sera religieux ou ne sera pas'

(The twenty-first century will be religious or it will not)

-- André Malraux

Introduction

'The World is the Mighty Temple of the Gods'

LUKE M. HERRINGTON & ALASDAIR McKAY
E-INTERNATIONAL RELATIONS

This introductory chapter is divided into five parts. The opening section provides a brief overview of why religion matters in today's world. Considering various polling data and demographic studies, the section demonstrates how levels of religiosity are increasing in the world and consequently that the world as a whole is becoming a more religious place. The next section presents a discussion of the secularisation debate and the global religious resurgence. Section three examines the popular literature concerning religion and global politics since the 9/11 attacks and looks at some problems with the current discourse. The penultimate section problematises some of the terminology used in this book and considers the meaning of specific terms, like religion. The concluding section introduces the contents of the book.

'The Mighty Temple of the Gods'

Throughout human history, politics and religions have engaged in a complicated dance. On the one hand, religions, in their various forms, have been involved in some of the bloodiest and most brutal episodes in human history. Yet, at various points in time and space, religions have also been linked to periods of scientific discovery, campaigns for human rights and freedoms, and periods of artistic and cultural creativity. As Scott Atran remarks, 'it [religion] has done everything you can imagine, and its contrary'. [1]

Today, the dance between religious belief and global politics appears to be as noticeable as ever, with religion now occupying a core position in contemporary political discourse. Indeed, it is difficult to read a newspaper article or watch a television report without bearing witness to a story with some religious colouring to it, and the twenty-first century certainly seems to feel like it is, to use the terminology of Toft, Philpott and Shah, 'God's

Century'.[2] Commenting on the contemporary global environment, the renowned sociologist Peter Berger—who had previously predicted that by the twenty-first century, communities of faith would likely be huddled in small groups in an effort to resist a global culture of secularism—declared: 'The world today, with some exceptions ... is as furiously religious as it ever was, and in some places more so than ever.'[3] Following suit but with a greater degree of elaboration, the political scientists Pippa Norris and Ronald Inglehart argue that 'The publics of virtually all advanced industrial societies have been moving towards more secular orientations during the past fifty years. Nevertheless, the world as a whole now has more people with traditional religious views than ever before—and they constitute a growing proportion of the world's population.'[4]

These are not hollow claims. The evidence suggests that while it is true that general religious ceremonial attendance and the authority of religious figures have declined in most developed countries, developing nations show significant levels of religious commitment and they possess a continually rising portion of the world's population. Pew survey data shows that more than eight in ten people throughout the world identify with a religious group. A comprehensive demographic study by the Pew Research Center's Forum on Religion & Public Life of more than 230 countries and territories estimates that there are 5.8 billion religiously affiliated adults and children around the globe, which represents 84 per cent of the 2010 world population of 6.9 billion.[5]

In 2003, Professor Assaf Moghadam assembled a comprehensive dataset on the global trends of religious adherence and found that, with a few exceptions, religious followers were growing at a faster rate than that of any other segment of the world's population.[6] In fact, Pew's 2012 data confirm that atheism and non-religious self-identification are the categories with the smallest growth rates, well below the rate of overall population growth.[7] Even more recent data compiled by Boston University's World Religion Database, which is considered to be the largest online religious demographic data source available to scholars, confirms that these trends in religious adherence persist today.[8] The 2014 Yearbook of International Religious Demography shows that the global number of those who identify as religious is still on the rise, meaning that the world, as a whole, is becoming more, rather than less, religious.[9] Consequently, the world today is, to an extent, as the Roman Stoic philosopher Seneca described it 2000 years ago: 'the mighty temple of the gods'.[10]

Secularisation and the Return of Religion

The general rise in global religiosity is understood to be part of an evolving phenomenon dubbed the resurgence of religion. Scott Thomas summarises this development as 'the increasing importance of religious beliefs, practices, and discourses in personal and public life, and the growing role of religious or religiously-related individuals, non-state groups, political parties, and communities, and organisations in domestic politics, and this is occurring in ways that have significant implications for international politics'.[11] So whether one likes it or not, religion is here to stay in both the near and the distant future and it seems that the dance between religions and world politics will continue for some time.

For many, it simply wasn't supposed to be this way; as Thomas puts it, 'We live in a world that is not supposed to exist'.[12] Since the sixteenth century and the dawn of the European Enlightenment, secular-minded people have been predicting the decline and slow death of religion. Though they expressed their hypotheses in different ways, significant thinkers such as Marx, Comte, Spencer, Durkheim, Kierkegaard, Cortes, Solzhenitsyn, Nietzsche and Weber believed that religion would gradually fade in importance and cease to be significant via modernity's seemingly unyielding forces. This line of thinking gradually grew into the secularisation thesis, which describes 'the process by which sectors of society and culture are removed from the domination of religious institutions and symbols'.[13] This thesis is essentially a corollary of modernisation theory; together, the two theories suggest that social modernisation marginalises religion as a consequence of the shifting sources of legitimacy invoked by the modern nation-state. Secularisation and modernisation theorists see the fact that the nation-state no longer derives is legitimacy solely or primarily from the gods, God, or any other supernatural force as a consequence of this process. Instead, its foundation in rational thought, bureaucracy and legalistic principles encourages the state to search out the will of the people and scientific discovery for its legitimacy.[14] Thus, the indiscriminate relegation of religion to the private sphere of human life is said to be a by-product of this social change.[15]

As the influence of religion over public life did, over time, seem to diminish significantly as forecasted, the secularisation thesis gained traction and, by the 1960s, gained acceptance as a social scientific law of sorts. With attendance at religious services declining, religion legitimately appeared to be in global retreat from secularisation. Indeed, the zeitgeist of secularisation was perhaps best encapsulated by a 1966 Time magazine cover asking: 'Is God Dead?'[16]

However, a series of events eventually cast doubt on the accuracy of the secularisation thesis and rumours of religion's death began to seem somewhat exaggerated. In 1979, the world witnessed the Islamic Revolution in Iran and the war of the Islamic mujahidin against the Soviet occupation of Afghanistan. The following year, Ronald Reagan was elected president of the United States with the support of highly politicised evangelical Christians, Jews and Mormons. In Eastern Europe, the Polish Solidarity trade union successfully challenged the Communist state, with the backing of Pope John Paul II and the Roman Catholic Church. Later in the 1980s, India saw Sikh separatists challenge the secular state in the form of the Khalistan movement; and the violent conquest of the 'Golden Temple' in Amritsar. Sikh bodyguards assassinated Indira Gandhi, and the 1980s also saw the rise of the Hindu-nationalist Bharatiya Janata Party. Towards the end of the decade, religious nationalists challenged secular Zionism in Israel as the first Intifada shifted power from secular nationalists to Islamist groups in neighbouring Palestine.[17]

The epitaphs for religion, composed from the 1960s on, were starting to feel a little premature. Religion, it seemed, was proving remarkably resilient in the face of the forces of secularisation, weathering the storm, rising from its deathbed resurgent. As ever, history was not without its sense of irony; the forces driving religion's resurgence were the very forces that many believed would trigger its demise—mainly globalisation, but also its companions: technological modernisation, democratisation, economic development, industrialisation and urbanisation. Of course, as the world moved into a new millennium, one event would punctuate this resurgence more than any other: the terrorist attacks of 11 September 2001 would sharply illustrate that religion was back on the map.

9/11, Religion and the 'Scholars of Opportunity'

The 9/11 attacks violently marked the inception of the new century. On that day, four airplanes were hijacked by members of the sub-national Islamic terrorist organisation, Al-Qaeda, and turned into weapons that would inflict more than 3,000 casualties on the US. The images of smoke billowing from the Twin Towers in New York City were met not only with horror by the general public throughout the West and beyond but also with shock by scholars and policymakers. Many experts were unable to fathom that an event like the terrorist attacks of 11 September 2001 could have occurred at any point, let alone on that day. The failure to forecast the catastrophe raised serious doubts about the direction of International Relations experts and practitioners and how they understood religion in world politics. Subsequently, it is arguable that one of the most significant impacts of the attacks—at least for International Relations scholars—has been the questions generated about the role of religions in the world. To paraphrase Philpott, 9/11 emphasised, possibly more than any other recent historical occurrence, that religion continues to be a potent force in global politics, and one whose influence is only partly understood by scholars and practitioners.[18]

Since 9/11, greater attention has been paid to religion and its role in the world, and many have taken note of Peter Berger's warning that 'Those who neglect *religion* in *their* analyses of contemporary affairs *do so* at great *peril.*'[19] Indeed, former US secretary of state Madeleine Albright even remarked: 'Like many other foreign policy professionals, I have had to adjust the lens through which I view the world, comprehending something that seemed to be a new reality but that had actually been evident for some time.'[20]

Yet much of the writing on religion and its role in world politics is problematical. Many of the works on religion that have been published since 9/11—and many from before—unfortunately illustrate a distinct lack of understanding of religion and politics by focusing disproportionately on the issues of violence associated with just one religion: Islam. Samuel Huntington's influential 'Clash of Civilizations' thesis deserves particular mention here. Stemming from his 1993 Foreign Affairs article, Huntington's thesis states that

> [t]he fundamental source of conflict in this new world will not be primarily ideological or primarily economic. The great divisions among humankind and the dominating source of conflict will be cultural. Nation states will remain the most powerful actors in world affairs, but the principal conflicts of global politics will occur between nations and groups of different civilizations. The clash of civilizations will dominate global politics. The fault lines between civilizations will be the battle lines of the future.[21]

Following arguments put forward by Bernard Lewis, Huntington suggests that civilisational conflicts are more frequent between Muslims and non-Muslims. Believing Islam to have 'bloody borders', Huntington argues that future conflicts between the West and Islam are inevitable.[22] Comprehensive critiques of Huntington's work are located elsewhere,[23] but it is important to note that, in spite of its errors, Huntington's thesis injected several ideas into the popular understanding of religion that prevail to this day.[24] Most significantly, Huntington's depiction of religion—namely Islam—as inherently conflict-prone helped perpetuate the belief that religion is essentially as a source of violence in the world. Together with the events of 9/11, Huntington's thesis is largely responsible for the ubiquitous focus on Islam and violence that persists among many thinkers on religion and politics today.

Studies confirm the myopia of the literature. According to the online catalogue at the Library of Congress (LOC), there were only 19 books published on the subjects of religion and IR between 1991 and 2001, while there were 16 published on religion and violence with an additional 23 on religion and war.[25] Using similar LOC data, Ron Hassner finds that half the books published on religion and international politics after 1973 were not published until after 9/11, but what is more staggering is that publications on religion in war have skyrocketed from an average of two or three a year to an average of 14 since 2001. Meanwhile, in the decade after 9/11, more books were published about Islam and war (155) than were published from the invention of the printing press in the fifteenth century to 2001 (154).[26]

Hassner laments that the need for reliable information on, and analyses of, religion in the aftermath of 9/11 has been in large part poorly met by authors he calls 'scholars of opportunity', who lack the credible expertise and 'substantive knowledge' to adequately address these topics.[27] These concerns are certainly warranted. Arguably, much of the current discussion on religion and politics is dominated by those with not only limited knowledge of politics, history, and religion but also a considerable set of political biases. The New Atheists are one of the most easily discernible of such groups.

The 'New Atheists' is a term used to describe a collective of modern anti-theistic writers and activists who gained greater popularity after 9/11. The leading figures are biologist Richard Dawkins, neuroscientist Sam Harris, philosopher Daniel Dennett and the late journalist, Christopher Hitchens. Their work is frequently distributed by major publishers, ending up on best-seller lists and read by millions. Moreover, the so-called 'Four Horseman' of the movement enjoy a considerable presence on television as experts on religion and politics and command high-figure speaking fees at public events.

Despite their popularity, the key figures of the group have been subjected to a fair amount of criticism by more than just theologians and religious figures. Many have scrutinised the New Atheists for engaging in overly simplistic analyses of a number of complex socio-political issues involving conflict, and engaging in lazy generalisations and 'straw man' criticisms of religion. Scott Atran describes the approach of individuals such as Harris and those he identifies with as 'scientifically baseless, psychologically uninformed, politically naïve, and counterproductive for goals we share'.[28] Atran even accuses Harris and his followers of ignoring the increasingly rich body of scientific research on religion—and religion and terrorism in particular.[29]

Likewise, Jonathan Haidt and David Sloan Wilson criticise the New Atheists' analysis concerning the sociological role of religion in society. Contrary to the New Atheists' slogan, coined by Hitchens, that 'religion poisons everything', the two believe that religion can act as a force for both good and bad in the world.[30] On similar grounds, Hassner points out that the New Atheists habitually emphasise correlations between religion and violence while ignoring or dismissing any relationship between religion and 'the promotion of morality, science, or art'.[31] Ken R. Dark has even highlighted the inconsistencies of the New Atheist claim that atheism will naturally lead to tolerance, peace and greater freedoms, and he highlights that the only polities historically responsible for promoting 'state-sponsored atheism' have persecuted 'not only religious believers but other sections of the public as well'. Indeed, Dark argues that human rights and personal freedom in general have been subject to heavy restriction in officially atheist states.[32]

The politics of the New Atheism have also been called into question, particularly regarding what many criticise as an anti-Muslim bias and a willingness to defend and exercise double standards when it comes to Western aggression. Critics have also argued that the group only understands religion through the prism of Huntington's flawed 'Clash of Civilizations' thesis, i.e. that the New Atheists exhibit similar Islamophobic tendencies in their attitudes towards Muslims.[33] In this way, the New Atheists are not entirely dissimilar from the anti-Catholic polemicists who were prominent in the early twentieth century, including the likes of Paul Blanchard and Avro Manhattan. Manhattan, for example, once attempted to absolve the West for the war in Vietnam by placing blame on a vast conspiracy orchestrated by the Holy See and Catholic interest groups.[34]

Regardless of whether one fully endorses all the allegations of anti-Muslim 'animus' against the New Atheists, however, the general increase in anti-Muslim polemical writings which have found a growing space during the war on terror is a serious problem. Indeed, since 9/11, the internet has become awash with anti-Muslim websites, which portray themselves as reliable sources of information on Islam and Muslims but largely consist of half-truths, conspiracy theories and misleading conclusions. These counter-jihad sites are animated by several traits:

> A far-right, anti-Islamic ideology that accuses Europe of wilfully subjugating its power to Muslim extremists is being taken increasingly seriously in certain political circles. Counter-jihad discourse mixes valid concerns about jihad-inspired terrorism with far more complex political issues about immigration to Europe from predominantly Muslim countries. It suggests that there is a threat not just from terrorism carried out by Islamic

extremists but from Islam itself. Therefore, by extension, all European Muslims are a threat.[35]

John Esposito describes this anti-Muslim movement as

> a cottage industry that has been meticulously cultivated by anti-Muslim polemicists and their resourceful funders, who master the domain of the internet with dozens of highly visible blogs and websites supported by hundreds of user blogs to which they link.[36]

If the New Atheists represent relatively 'respectable' instances of Hassner's scholars of opportunity, then the leading figures of this collective—which has become known as the counter-jihad movement—are more extreme and objectionable examples of the phenomenon.

But unlike the New Atheists, the counter-jihad movement typically identifies as religious; the movement is comprised primarily of hard-right Christians and Zionists. However, the latter certainly represent the intellectual disciples of the former, and the New Atheists sometimes stray rather close to the claims of the counter-jihad movement's conspiracy wing. For instance, the counter-jihadist Robert Spencer frequently endorses Sam Harris, who has himself flirted with the discredited 'Eurabia' conspiracy theory in claiming that France will become a majority Muslim country by 2025.[37]

The problem with these modern scholars of opportunity and the popular discussions of religion and politics they inspire is that many people too often confuse these individuals with proper authorities and their works with legitimate academic research, which limns another important parallel between modern Islamophobia and previous anti-Catholic polemic. Consider Manhattan again; throughout much of the early-to mid-twentieth century he was counted as the leading expert on the role of the Catholic Church in world politics, despite there being little evidence to suggest that he was ever more than an anti-Catholic conspiracy theorist. Manhattan's avowed atheism notwithstanding, many right-wing anti-Catholics continue to treat him as the authority on the foreign policy of the Holy See and the global activities of the Catholic Church writ large. For example, Chick Publications, a publishing house owned by the Christian fundamentalist Jack T. Chick, produces anti-Catholic and anti-Muslim hate-speech, including new editions of Manhattan's previously out-of-print books.[38]

Unfortunately, as the study of religion in International Relations deepens, there is a real danger that otherwise well-informed individuals, including legitimate scholars and students, could believe such opportunists as Manhattan, the counter-jihadis or the New Atheists (among others) to be proper sources of information on religion and politics, demonstrating if nothing else that there is certainly a pedagogical need for a more scholarly approach to religion and world affairs.

To be sure, there is a rich body of scholarly literature on the subject, but the need to better communicate such research seems to be growing every day, especially given, for example, the activities associated with relatively new threats like the Islamic State in Syria and Iraq—or even the recent attack at the Charlie Hebdo editorial office in Paris. This attack, which took the lives of 12 people, together with the series of subsequent attacks that took the lives of five more have been counted as the worst instance of terrorism on French soil in decades. Regrettably, the attacks have spawned violent outbursts against French Muslims and fanned the anti-Muslim flames previously tended by far-right politicians and members of the counter-jihad movement. This stands in stark contrast to the Australian response to the hostage crisis in Sydney in December. The social media hashtag, #IllRideWithYou, was prompted by many Australians' concerns for the well-being of their local Islamic community in the wake of the crisis. Given this book's aim to highlight more than just the polemical 'dangers' of religion, such violent episodes should not be considered in a vacuum. The very real need to better communicate our findings also stems from the other end of the spectrum; the diplomatic activities of Pope Francis, who, among other things, recently helped facilitate the warming of US–Cuban relations, serve as a case in point.[39]

Problematic Terminology

Nations Under God: The Geopolitics of Faith in the Twenty-First Century is a publication from E-International Relations that aims to contribute to the very necessary discourse concerning religion in global politics. It seeks to move beyond the simplistic narratives and overly impassioned polemics that swamp the popular discourse and act as a vessel for the scholarly research on this subject. Utilising case studies, empirical investigations and theoretical examinations, this text examines the complex roles religions play in world affairs. The book also seeks to bring an interdisciplinary perspective to the subject matter. Indeed, it seems a truism to suggest that religion is a subject that transcends the scope of a single discipline; this book thus brings together leading scholars from schools of thought as diverse as political science, international relations, sociology, theology, anthropology and geography. While paying attention, of course, to religion's role in pressing global issues such as conflict, the book also examines the complex relationship between religion and other key issues affecting the globe today such as peace-building, human rights, nationalist politics, the status of the modern nation-states, European integration and international co-operation. Thus, the book's overall aim is to present a more balanced analysis of religion in the world today.

But before proceeding further and discussing the content of the book, some cards should be placed on the table; we must concede that the title was chosen primarily for attention-seeking reasons. While students and scholars represent the key target audience for the publication, it is hoped that the book's ostentatious title will foster interest in other spheres, especially as its title is also read online. Entitling the book Nations under God: The Geopolitics of Faith in the Twenty-First Century also seeks to highlight some of the major problems with the current discourse on religion and politics discussed above, by mimicking, and to a certain extent parodying, the popular polemical, anti-religious screeds of the time, such as The God Delusion, God is Not Great and The End of Faith.[40] Indeed, some may see problems with the title. The idea that religion can be equated with one god, particularly the God of Judeo-Christian (-Islamic) tradition, is deeply questionable, as is the notion that it can be equated with 'faith'. Both assumptions are generally associated with a very specific Christian (and Protestant) understanding of religion, which views religion from a Western vantage point. Evoking the concept of nations also yields problems as it makes several assumptions about states as the key actors in politics and inadvertently precludes analysis of non-state actors. The use of the term geopolitics is troublesome as it is somewhat difficult to define. However, one should note that the problematisation of these concepts was intentional, and importantly, remember that Timothy Fitzgerald discusses these issues (and others) in greater depth in the concluding chapter.

Nevertheless, concepts like 'religion' remain highly problematic; religious studies scholars, anthropologists and sociologists have struggled to define the term for more than a century. Indeed, Christian theologians have wrestled with 'religion' for thousands of years. Saint James, for example, once described true religion as the care of orphans and widows and the act of maintaining one's purity (James 1: 27). However, such a Christo-centric conception of religion evokes Western notions of 'true' religion, the likes of which led Christopher Columbus and other European colonisers in the so-called New World to treat the Native American Indians they encountered as barbarians subject to Aristotle's natural law of slavery some 1,500 years later.[41] Such prejudices are easy to elicit from normative definitions of true religion, like the one promoted by James, and it took some time for scholars and theologians to break away from an understanding of religion rooted in these ideas. By the early modern period, most definitions of religion still used a fourfold classification system that could only understand religions as Jewish, Christian, Islamic or Pagan, and failed to recognise the religious tendencies of less advanced societies. By 1901, however, E. Ritchie observed that (mis)characterising 'savages' as having 'no religion', as Columbus and his contemporaries had done with the Native Americans, trod dangerously close to dogmatic pronouncements of 'true' religion versus 'false' religion. Though his own definition still sought to identify the 'essence' of 'religion',[42] which might have been too narrow to encompass, for example, the Confucian tradition of East Asia, attitudes like Ritchie's would eventually permeate the discourse, inspiring new notions of 'world religion' and 'new religious movements'. Though these newer concepts are themselves imperfect in that (if nothing else) they remain susceptible to criticisms of Christo-centrism, this helps explain how scholars have come to understand religion today.[43]

The problem is, however, that these terms do not necessarily foster an understanding of 'religion' itself, and while religious studies scholars still debate its meaning, few IR scholars have accepted the challenge of defining the term for the sake of their own work. Perhaps defining religion represents too cumbersome an epistemological exercise for IR scholars, though some have gleaned important lessons from the religious studies literature. Michael Barnett, for instance, cautions against the kind of essentialisation of religion pursued by scholars like Ritchie, preferring instead to view religions as social constructs built on historically and culturally situated relationships,[44] an observation which is actually quite interesting since it may help students and scholars (if not policymakers or the general public) understand why defining religion is such an arduous task. That is, some scholars, notes Bruce Lincoln, aver 'that no universal definition of 'religion' is possible, since all such definitions are themselves the historical product of culturally specific discursive processes'.[45]

Toft, Philpott and Shah are among a small chorus of IR scholars who have reflected on the meaning of religion, but the exercise seems too burdensome even for them, as they prefer to uncritically defer to the analytic philosopher William P. Alston's definition. In doing so, however, they compensate for the problem identified by Lincoln by taking a 'dimensional' approach to the definition of religion, similar to the one identified by Ninian Smart or Martin E. Marty, which sees religion as possessing some elements from a list of several. Alston identifies seven elements of religion, including: (1) a belief in the supernatural; (2) the ability to communicate with the supernatural; (3) a belief in some form of transcendent reality; (4) a distinction between the profane and sacred; (5) a worldview articulating the human role in relation to the world; (6) a code of conduct; and finally, (7) a temporal community bound by adherence to the preceding elements. Alston's dimensional definition recognises that while no religion may be characterised by all seven elements, many religions will be characterised by most of them.[46]

The problem with adopting this approach is not with the definition per se but with the general lack of conceptualisation among IR scholars. Though political comparativists and methodologists have sounded the alarm about the uncritical importation of concepts and ideas from other disciplines (and theoretical approaches) for some time,[47] IR scholars interested in religion have yet to reflect deeply on the meaning of their subject, choosing instead to defer to scholars like Alston. They may be forgiven, though, since defining religion represents a cumbersome epistemological exercise, as noted above. As a matter of fact, such important conceptual work may be worthy of a full-length article in its own right, so work remains. Future research must pick up the mantle of (re)conceptualising religion in International Relations. For the meantime, given these considerations and due to space constraints, readers will note the absence of a uniform definition of religion guiding the contributions to this book. Instead, we defer to the authors to define the concept in their own work if necessary, and we trust our readers to keep the problematic meaning(s) of this ineffable term in their own minds as they read on, because, as the late W. Richard Comstock observes, 'Augustine's famous observation about time applies with equal force to religion; if not asked, we know what it is; if asked, we do not know.'[48]

The Book

The collection is divided into four parts. The first section examines various ways of theoretically comprehending religion in contemporary global politics. Stephen Dawson opens with a discussion of the resurgence of religion. In this chapter, Dawson examines the phenomenon known as the religious resurgence and then highlights the problems and opportunities for IR theorists yielded by the phenomenon. Dawson argues that, above all else, scholars must meet the challenges posed by examining religion in the world critically.

As something of a warning for scholars, Jodok Troy explores how not to theorise religion in world politics. Troy reflects on the ongoing trend of 'de-marginalising' the topic and point outs grievances with secularisation theorising. He then considers the shortcomings when talking about religion as a variable, pointing out how the Western understanding of religion shapes and limits our theorising. Finally, he discusses some of the alternative and complementary approaches of addressing religion in IR.

Gertjan Dijkink's article presents an approach to the issue of religion and geopolitics which draws attention to the changing territorial orders that control the geopolitical game as territorial orders are dominant ways of linking authority to geographic distinctions.

John Rees calls for four analytical categories that together constitute a framework to assist policymakers better understand the complex dynamics of religion relevant to particular foreign policy decisions. Rees suggests that the four dynamics described in his chapter are useful 'policy optics' that strategists can apply when trying to understand the political culture of states and regions where their foreign policy interests are located. Rees moves on to suggest that once these categories have been deduced, the work of policy will be twofold: first, to establish the relative weightings of identified dynamics in a specific geopolitical context, and, second, to situate the weighted dynamics of religion into the broader strategic imperatives of defence, diplomacy and development. Rees then applies the four analytical categories to the case study of Egypt (2011–2014).

Mark Cladis urges that we learn from the past, notes the limits of past theories of secularisation as applied to Romanticism and suggests some helpful ways to rethink religion and the secular in the twenty-first century. Cladis believes that by applying an interpretive lens that acknowledges the religious traditions that permeated British Romanticism, we gain insight into not only its dynamic religious dimensions but also its political, economic and environmental dimensions.

In the final article of the section, Fabio Petito argues that the resurgence of religions in world politics has to be read in the context of civilisations, which are defined in a fundamentally culturalist sense that reassert themselves as strategic frames of references, not as direct protagonists, of international politics. He proceeds to argue that this development has also to be understood as part of a longer-term process of challenge to Western dominance—what Hedley Bull called the 'cultural revolt against the West'—that intensified after the Second World War.

Part II examines the relationship of religion with the nation-state and society. The section begins with the chapter by Linda Woodhead, in which she discusses the dramatic change in global religions since 1989 and their relationship to the nation-state. Woodhead explores how an emerging new paradigm or new style of religion has become dominant over the last 25 years and how an older style of religion has declined. What Woodhead refers to as 'old-style religion' dates back to the sixteenth century and was forged in the crucible of emerging nation-states. 'New-style religion' dates from the late nineteenth century and has burgeoned in the context of the globalised, market-based societies of the post-Cold War era.

Jonathan Fox's article assesses the competition between secular and religious actors, a relationship which is complicated by several additional relationships and phenomena. In this chapter, Fox focuses on three particular phenomena: competition within the religion camp, competition within the secular camp, and the complex relationship between supporting and restricting religion.

Brendan Sweetman's philosophical chapter contributes to the broader discussion of religion, the state and secularism. Sweetman explores the pressing question of whether religion should be a private matter in contemporary secular democracies.

The next article by anthropologist Don Handelman examines the complex relationship between holism, religion and geopolitics. Handelman argues that values of holism underlie and infuse a wide variety of religions, including the monotheisms. Handelman then argues that the actualisation of holism is accomplished through the potentiality of religion to encompass and orientate social units of varying scale including the nation and the nation-state. In the concluding section, he briefly orientates the discussion to modern Israel.

Scott Hibbard's chapter explores why conservative renderings of religious tradition remained politically influential in certain secular nation-states. Using the examples of Egypt, India and the United States, Hibbard argues that religion remains relevant to modern politics because it continues to define collective—and particularly national—identities and is uniquely able to provide a moral framework for political action.

Utilising Angola as a case study, anthropologist Ruy Blanes explores the country's relationship between the state and religious institutions. Blanes argues that in Angola there are two seemingly contradictory yet correlated phenomena concerning religious practice: the opening up of the local landscape for transnational religious circulation, mostly in its capital, Luanda; and the process of 'nationalisation' or 'Angolanisation' of religious activity.

In another case study, Fang-long Shih explores the Taiwanisation movement, focusing on how the god Nazha represents the struggle of Taiwanese identity against Chinese identity. Fang-long discusses how religion in Taiwan has, since the 1980s, reflected the transformation of politics, i.e. the shift from the local rivalries of political factions to island-wide campaigns on the strategic importance of its geopolitical entity. Fang-long looks at the god Nazha and how it has become a vehicle for the formation of a new Taiwanisation discourse.

Kaarina Aitamurto explores the strong alliance between the state and the Russian Orthodox Church and the role this relationship plays in Russian nationalist politics. The article draws our attention to the Rodnoverie movement and how this illustrates the versatility of nationalism in contemporary Russia and the difficulties of constructing clear national identities in modern societies, where people have more choices and more overlapping identities, many of which transcend national boundaries.

Part III examines the role of religions in both violence and peace. The section opens with a chapter by Mona Kanwal Sheikh that examines sociotheology— a concept she developed with Mark Juergensmeyer—as a template for understanding religious worldviews. The chapter concentrates on how sociotheology can help us understand religious violence but also discusses the applicability of the framework in a broader context. Sheikh argues for the development of a more nuanced understanding of the dynamics between epistemic worldviews and their social location and also a more systematic research programme for the archaeological reconstruction of epistemic worldviews in their social milieus.

Continuing the discussion on the theme of conflict, Lee Marsden's chapter analyses the casual influence of religion on violence and considers the claims of religious actors themselves and how policymakers have sought to work with alternative religious actors in the battle for hearts and minds in a conflictual international order.

Shireen Hunter explores sectarian tensions in the Middle East and South Asia. Through examining various geopolitical situations, Hunter challenges the widely held belief that religion is the primary cause of the tensions in the region. While acknowledging that the existence of religious differences creates a receptive environment for the emergence of such conflicts, Hunter argues that politics and conflicting security and other interests of international and regional actors—and their competition for power and influence—are the principal culprits.

Nilay Saiya discusses the effect of religious factors, including religious liberty, on conflict and political stability. The chapter challenges the conventional wisdom that treats religious liberty as normatively a good idea but not an issue centrally related to power politics. Saiya shows that religious liberty is connected to political stability in profound ways. Using the example of Iraq, the article demonstrates that where religious liberty is threatened, the chances of a state experiencing sectarian violence increases, as does the likelihood that violence will spread to neighbouring countries.

Drawing upon his previous empirical studies, Dan G. Cox discusses what he describes as a religious diversity peace dividend in international affairs. Cox argues that religious tolerance and respect for religious freedoms should approximate a peace dividend, as he and his colleagues observed, with terrorism rates declining in states with greater levels of religious (and ethnic) pluralism. He concludes that more research is needed to ascertain if the effects of religious freedom are as strong as the religious diversity peace dividend he originally observed.

Pauline Kollontai's chapter focuses on the work of the inter-religious transnational organisation, Religions for Peace, and examines its peace-building work under the aegis of globalisation. She shows that one important aspect of these transnational actors is that they are already modelling ways of working together across religions to manifest the principles and values associated with peace and justice present in the fabric of all religious teachings.

Section IV focuses on the relationship between religion, transnational institutions and human rights. Jeffrey Haynes looks into the motives behind faith-based organisations (FBOs) at the United Nations. This article focuses on the activities of selected FBOs at the UN, the most significant inter-governmental organisation with a global public policy role.

François Foret's article discusses the role of religion in European integration. Presenting several levels of analysis, the chapter argues that European integration interacts with the contemporary evolution of religion but does not command it.

James L. Guth and Brent F. Nelsen continue the discussion on religion and European integration. The authors observe that the major approaches to explaining the remarkable success of the European project usually stress economic interests, strategic motivations, or institutional forces in the growth of continental unity since 1945, while few have said very much about religion. Guth and Nelsen then suggest that despite the purported secularisation of European politics, the religious 'confessional culture' has affected and continues to affect the movement towards European unity.

Paul Rowe examines the expanded influence of religious actors in global civil society. Rowe suggests that the influence of religion in the world is viewed by many as a dangerous development. This then reflects the way that the anti-social activities of radical religious movements dominate media headlines. He points out that when the day-to-day activities of global religious movements are assessed, one finds a wide array of actors involved in development, peace advocacy and the cultural vitality of global society. Rowe concludes that the normative power of religious movements to shape global civil society is an important theme of inquiry for political scientists to investigate in the future.

J. Paul Martin's chapter formulates a human rights-based approach to religion. He argues that secularism has become too amorphous and culture-bound a concept to guide religion-related policies in contemporary domestic and international affairs. He then suggests that secularism needs to be replaced by the more widely accepted and tested standards and institutions of the modern international human rights regime that define substantial legal obligations and practices developed and accepted through treaties by the world's states. Martin concludes that the human rights framework calls for not only state neutrality but also state engagement with religion, and thus for national and international institutions able to protect the rights associated with the freedom of religion by working to minimise inter-religious discrimination and conflict.

Allen D. Hertzke explores the role that many Christian networks play on the global stage in human rights advocacy, humanitarian succour and peacemaking. Hertzke argues that a genuine global system, in which a theological ideal serves as a central organising principle, is emerging. Unlike governmental structures or even UN institutions, this system is more organic and nimble in upholding human dignity. This system links local actors and congregations with international mission, development and denominational structures that magnify the collective Christian witness in policy circles.

Ishtiaq Ahmed's chapter sheds light on the relationship between human rights and religion in Pakistan. Given the sectarian divisions within the Pakistani Muslim community and social segregation between men and women among Muslims in general, Ahmed explores the implications and ramifications for the human rights of not only conventionally defined non-Muslims such as Christians, Hindus and so on but also a number of groups that, prior to the partition of India, had been subsumed within the general category of Muslims.

Continuing the discussion of Islam, Jonathan Benthall looks at the demands for Islam to undergo a 'renaissance' or 'reformation'. He suggests that although there have been many progressive Muslim individuals over the last century and longer, they have not consolidated themselves into durable institutions, contributing to the crisis of authority in Islam. Looking to historical reform movements, Benthall argues that something could be learnt from the Reform movement in nineteenth century Judaism, when rabbis and synagogues in Germany and the USA realised they had common interests and began to correspond and coordinate.

Elizabeth Shakman Hurd's chapter looks at religion liberty and tolerance. Hurd examines the 'two faces of religion' discourse, a concept which originated in a Tony Blair speech on religion. Hurd investigates how the concept is operationalised in a specific context, one of many in which the global dynamics of good religion/bad religion have come to life. Hurd introduces an alternative approach to religion and world politics, developed in her forthcoming book, that builds on the distinction between religion as construed by those in power (including the good religion/bad religion framing) and religion as lived by local inhabitants. This conceptual lens developed by Hurd allows us to see 'beyond religious freedom' by revealing the mixed political consequences for Sahwahi refugees of the representation of their camps as 'ideal spaces' occupied by tolerant refugees who support religious freedom and interfaith dialogue.

In the conclusion chapter, Timothy Fitzgerald deconstructs some of the common Anglophone categories of everyday public life that appear in this collection's title, attempting to indicate how they conceal (largely unconscious) rhetorical devices that allow abstract and rather empty terms to appear persuasive, objectively real and inevitable. Fitzgerald then argues that when examining religion in contemporary world affairs we need general categories to think with.

Notes

1. Scott Atran ,'Discussion of Beyond Belief: Science, Religion, Reason and Survival', *The Edge*, 29 November 2006. Retrieved 28 December 2014 from http://www.edge.org/discourse/bb.html#atran
2. Monica Duffy Toft, Daniel Philpott, Timothy Samuel Shah, *God's Century: Resurgent Religion and Global Politics* (New York: W.W. Norton and Co., 2011).
3. Peter L. Berger, 'Secularism in Retreat', *The National Interest*, 46 (1996/7): 5.
4. Norris, P. and R. Inglehart, *Sacred and Secular: Religion and Politics Worldwide* (Cambridge, UK: Cambridge University Press, 2004), 5.
5. 'The Global Religious Landscape', Pew Research Center, 18 December 2012; available online at http://www.pewforum.org/global-religious-landscape-exec.aspx (accessed 19 November 2014).
6. Assaf Moghadam, 'A Global Resurgence of Religion?' (unpublished paper, Weatherhead Initiative Project on 'Religion and Global Politics', August 2003), Table: 'Global Trends in Religious Adherence, 1900–2025, by Religion'. See also Michael C. Desch, 'The Coming Reformation of Religion in International Affairs? The Demise of the Secularization Thesis and the Rise of New Thinking About Religion,' in *Religion and International Relations: A Primer for Research*, The Report of the Working Group on International Relations and Religion, p.22. Available at:<http://rmellon.nd.edu/assets/101872/religion_and_international_relations_report.pdf> First accessed August 8, 2015.
7. Laurie Goodstein, 'Study Finds One in 6 Follows No Religion', The New York Times, 18 December 2012) reports the results of a recent Pew Survey of Americans which

despite the growth of this category still finds that over 83 per cent identify with some religion. See http://www.nytimes.com/2012/12/18/world/pew-study-finds-one-in-6-follows-no-religion.html?_r=0.

8. The International Religious Demography Project, The World Religion Database; available online at http://www.worldreligiondatabase.org/wrd_default.asp

9. Brian Grim, *Yearbook of International Religious Demography 2014* (Brill, 2014).

10. Seneca, *Epistulae morales ad Lucilium*. Quoted from Jon R. Stone, ed., *The Routledge Dictionary of Latin Quotations: The Illiterati's Guide to Latin Maxims, Mottoes, Proverbs, and Sayings* (New York: Routledge, 2005).

11. Scott M. Thomas, *The Global Resurgence of Religion and the Transformation of International Relations* (New York: Palgrave Macmillan, 2005).

12. Scott M Thomas, 'Outwitting the Developed Countries? Existential Insecurity and the Global Resurgence of Religion', *Journal of International Affairs*, 61:1 (2007), 21.

13. Peter L. Berger, *The Sacred Canopy: Elements of a Sociological theory of Religion* (Garden City: Doubleday, 1967), 107. Similarly, Bryan Wilson defines secularisation as 'the process whereby religious thinking, practice and institutions lose their social significance', in *Religion in Secular Society: A Sociological Comment* (London: C.A. Watts, 1966), 14.

14. Jonathan Fox and Timothy Samuel Sandler, *Bringing Religion into International Relations* (New York: Palgrave Macmillan, 2004), 10-11.

15. Jeffrey Haynes, *An Introduction to International Relations and Religion* (Harlow, UK: Pearson Longman, 2007), 8.

16. *Time Magazine*, 'Is God Dead?' (5 April 1966).

17. Martin Riesebrodt, 'Religion in the Modern World: Between Secularization and Resurgence', Max Weber Lecture, 15 January 2014.

18. Daniel Philpott, 'The Challenge of September 11 to Secularism in International Relations' *World Politics*, 55:1 (2002), 66-95. See also Erin K. Wilson, *After Secularism: Rethinking Religion in Global Politics* (Basingstoke, UK, Palgrave Macmillan, 2012), p. 1.

19. Peter L. Berger, 'Secularism in Retreat', *The National Interest*, 46 (Winter 1996/7), 3.

20. Madeleine Albright, *The Mighty and the Almighty: Reflections on America, God, and World Affairs* (New York: Harper Perennial, 2007).

21. Samuel Huntington 'The Clash of Civilizations?', *Foreign Affairs*, 72:3 (1993).

22. Samuel Huntington, *The Clash of Civilizations and the Remaking of World Order* (New York, Simon & Schuster, 1996).

23. J. Paul Barker (ed.) *The Clash of Civilizations: Twenty Years On* (E-International Relations, 2013).

24. Samuel Huntington, *The Clash of Civilizations and the Remaking of World Order* (New York, Simon & Schuster, 1996).

25. The Library of Congress, 'Library of Congress Online Catalogue', 19 September 2012; available online at http://catalog.loc.gov/ (accessed September 2014).

26. Ron E. Hassner, 'Religion and International Affairs: The State of the Art', in *Religion, Identity, and Global Governance: Ideas, Evidence, and Practice*, edited by Patrick James (Toronto: University of Toronto Press, 2011), 37-56.

27. Ibid., 39

28. Scott Atran, (2006, November 29). 'Discussion of Beyond Belief: Science, religion, reason and survival', *The Edge*. Retrieved 5 April 2010 from http://www.edge.org/discourse/bb.html#atran

29. Ibid.

30. David Sloan Wilson, *Darwin's Cathedral: Evolution, Religion, and the Nature of Society* (Chicago: University of Chicago Press, 2002); David Sloan Wilson 'Beyond Demonic Memes: Why Richard Dawkins is Wrong about Religion', *Skeptic* (4 July 2007). Retrieved 5 December 2014 from http://www.skeptic.com/eskeptic/07-07-04/#feature; Jonathen Haidt, Patrick Seder and S. Elin Kesebir, (2008), 'Hive Psychology, Happiness, and Public Policy', *Journal of Legal Studies*, 37, 133-156; J. Graham, B.A. Nosek, J. Haidt, R. Iyer, S. Koleva and P.H. Ditto, (2010), 'Mapping the Moral Domain', *Journal of Personality and Social Psychology*.

31. Hassner, 'Religion and International Affairs', 39.

32. Ken R. Dark, 'Large-Scale Religious Change and World Politics', in *Religion and International Relations*, edited by Ken R. Dark (New York: Palgrave MacMillan, 2001), 50-82.

33. See Wade Jacoby and Hakan Yavuz, 'Modernization, Identity and Integration: An Introduction to the Special Issue on Islam and Europe', *Journal of Muslim Minority Affairs,* 28:1 (2008), 2; 'Glenn Greenwald, Sam Harris, the New Atheists, and anti-Muslim animus', *The Guardian*, 3 April 2013; Chris Hedges, *I Don't Believe in Atheists: The Dangerous Rise of the Secular Fundamentalist*, (New Continuum International Publishing Group, 2008); Jesse Singal, 'Reza Aslan on What the New Atheists Get Wrong About Islam', *New York Magazine*, 14 October 2014.

34. Avro Manhattan, *Vietnam... Why Did We Go? The Shocking Story of the Catholic Church's Role in Starting the Vietnam War* (Chino, CA: Chick Publications, 1987).

35. Toby Archer, 'Countering the counter-jihad', RUSI, 15 August 2008; available at https://www.rusi.org/publications/monitor/rss/ref:A48A5851376CB9/#.VaKbL7e06V4 (accessed 28 December 2014).

36. 'Islam in the Public Square' by John L. Esposito, American Academy of Religion Presidential Address.

37. Robert Spencer, 'Sam Harris: "My Criticism of Islam is a Criticism of Beliefs... but My Fellow Liberals Reflexively View it as an Expression of Intolerance"', *Jihad Watch*, 8 October 2014, available from http://www.jihadwatch.org/2014/10/sam-harris-my-criticism-of-islam-is-a-criticism-of-beliefs-but-my-fellow-liberals-reflexively-view-it-as-an-expression-of-intolerance (accessed 20 January 2015); and Sam Harris, 'On the Reality of Islam,' *Truth Dig*, 7 February 2006, available at http://www.truthdig.com/report/item/20060207_reality_islam (accessed 20 January 2015).

38. Thom Burnett, ed., *Conspiracy Encyclopaedia: The Encyclopaedia of Conspiracy Theories* (New York: Chamberlain Brothers, 2005), 255. Also see Avro Manhattan, 'The Vatican's Holocaust' (Springfield, MI: Ozark Books, 1986); available at http://www.chick.com/information/religions/catholicism/vaticanholocaust.asp (accessed 20 January 2015).

39. Colum Lynch and Keith Johnson, 'Mosque Attacks Spark Fears of Blowback After "Charlie Hebdo"', *Foreign Policy*, 8 January 2015, available from http://foreignpolicy.com/2015/01/08/mosque-attacks-spark-fears-of-blowback-after-charlie-hebdo/ (accessed 20 January 2015); Adam Chandler, 'The Roots of #IllRideWithYou', *The Atlantic*, 15 December 2014, available from http://www.theatlantic.com/international/archive/2014/12/illridewithyou-hashtag-sydney-siege-anti-islam-australia/383765/ (accessed 20 January 2015); and Gregory Korte and Oren Dorell, 'Pope Francis played key role in US-Cuba deal', *USA Today*, 18 December 2014, available from http://www.usatoday.com/story/news/world/2014/12/17/pope-key-role-in-us-cuba-deal/20533525/ (accessed 6 January 2015).

40. See Christopher Hitchens, *God is Not Great: How Religion Poisons Everything*

(Atlantic Books; 2007); Richard Dawkins, *The God Delusion* (Bantam Books; London 2006); Sam Harris, *The End of Faith: Religion, Terror, and the Future of Reason* (W.W. Norton 2004).

41. Sam D. Gill, *Native American Religions: An Introduction* (Australia: Thomson Wadsworth, 2005), 5-8; and Benjamin Keen and Keith Haynes, *A History of Latin America: Ancient America to 1900* (Boston, MA: Houghton Mifflin Company, 2004), 58-60, 76-78, 101-104.

42. Leigh Eric Schmidt, 'Review of The Invention of World Religions: Or, How European Universalism was Preserved in the Language of Pluralism by Tomoko Masuzawa', *Journal of the American Academy of Religion* 74:1 (2006), 230.

43. Schmidt, 'Review of *The Invention of World Religions*', 230; and Peter Beyer, 'Globalization and the Institutional Modeling of Religions', in *Religion, Globalization, and Culture*, eds, Peter Beyer and Lori Beaman (Boston, MA: Brill, 2007), 169. Also see Timothy Fitzgerald, 'Hinduism and the "World Religion" Fallacy', *Religion*, 20:2 (1990), 101-109.

44. Michael Barnett, 'Another Great Awakening?: International Relations Theory and Religion', in *Religion and International Relations Theory*, ed. Jack Snyder (New York: Columbia University Press, 2011), 106.

45. Bruce Lincoln, 'Review of *Genealogies of Religion: Discipline and Reasons of Power in Christianity and Islam* by Talal Asad', *History of Religions*, 35:1 (1995), 83-84.

46. Toft, Philpott, and Shah, *God's Century*, 20-21. Also see Ninian Smart, *Secular Education and the Logic of Religion* (London: Faber, 1968); and Martin E. Marty with Jonathan Moore, *Politics, Religion, and the Common Good: Advancing a Distinctly American Conversation About Religion's Role in Our Shared Life* (San Francisco, CA: Jossey-Bass). Toft, Philpott, and Shah are joined by Jeffrey Haynes in adopting the dimensional approach to defining religion. Haynes is counted among the few IR scholars to have considered this definitional dilemma, but instead of engaging in the necessary conceptual exercise, he defers to Marty's definition. See Jeffrey Haynes, *An Introduction to International Relations and Religion* (Harlow, UK: Pearson Longman, 2007), 11-12.

47. See, for example, James Johnson, 'How Conceptual Problems Migrate: Rational Choice, Interpretation, and the Hazards of Pluralism', *Annual Review of Political Science*, 5 (June 2002), 223-248; and Nathaniel L. Beck, 'Political Methodology: A Welcoming Discipline', *Journal of the American Statistical Association*, 95:450 (June 2000): 651-654.

48. W. Richard Comstock, 'Toward Open Definitions of Religion', *Journal of the American Academy of Religion*, 52:3 (September 1984), 499; emphasis added.

Part One

Understanding Religion(s) in the World Today

1

The Religious Resurgence: Problems and Opportunities for International Relations Theory

STEPHEN DAWSON

LYNCHBURG COLLEGE, VIRGINIA, USA

A number of books have been published in the past ten years on the conviction widely shared by scholars across a variety of disciplines that we are currently experiencing a worldwide religious resurgence. In this chapter I examine more closely the very notion of a 'religious resurgence' and its theoretical implications for International Relations (IR). There are two points I wish to make. First, one way to understand the religious resurgence is in terms of a theoretical shift: as IR scholars move beyond the secularisation thesis, religion becomes more obvious as a variable in global politics. Second, the return of religion qua theoretical shift requires rethinking the fundamental idea of religion, as making sense of the religious resurgence requires a critical concept of religion.

The Religious Resurgence and the Secularisation Thesis

In the mid-1990s, when Peter L. Berger declared that a religious resurgence was underway, scholars took notice.[1] Since the 1960s, Berger was renowned as one of the leading proponents of the secularisation thesis. Briefly, secularisation describes three interrelated social processes: first, the differentiation of secular institutions (the state and the free market, for example) from religious institutions (such as the church); second, the decline of religious beliefs; and third, the privatisation of religious belief and practice.[2] In short, secularisation describes a process of social change. It is a hypothesis that attempts to explain what is unique about modernity. For this reason, secularisation is 'twinned', as it were, to the process of modernisation. With respect to traditional religion (and traditional ways of life, for that matter), modernisation acts like a solvent. As a society modernises, religion loses its distinctive features—for instance, the public prominence and influence of religious institutions and leaders, the social utility of religion (as, say, a source of moral value), and epistemic claims to revelatory authority. Religion recedes from public life into the private. Its universal claims to truth are transmuted as deeply felt personal convictions.[3]

As a process of social change, secularisation and its effects were thought to be irreversible. In a phrase indelibly linked with Max Weber, secularisation would end in a 'disenchanted' world, or a world largely free of religion. Throughout the twentieth century, the 'disenchantment of the world' acquired the status of a general law among social scientists. This is why Berger, in a 1968 interview in the New York Times, confidently predicted that, by 'the twenty-first century, religious believers are likely to be found only in small sects, huddled together to resist a world-wide secular culture'. Berger allowed that this prognosis was based on his reading of the current situation, which 'could be changed by a third world war or some other upheaval'.[4]

Such upheaval was soon provided by real-life events, such as the election of the evangelical Christian Jimmy Carter to the White House, the mobilisation of conservative fundamentalists under the banner of the Moral Majority, the Islamic Revolution in Iran, and the rise of the Solidarity movement in Poland. The cumulating effect of these events was not unlike that of the iceberg and the Titanic: empirical reality punched a hole in what was seemingly an unsinkable hypothesis. Scholarly mea culpas followed. Berger retracted his earlier prediction and admitted that the 'world today ... is as furiously religious as it ever was ... [the] body of literature by historians and social scientists loosely labelled 'secularisation theory' is essentially mistaken'.[5] The events of 11 September 2001 emphatically punctuated Berger's claim that the world is as 'furiously religious' as ever.

Furiously is perhaps the operative word here. The concept of secularisation does not simply describe a historical process. It is also a normative claim about the proper relationship between religion and politics. This normative claim is founded on two political myths. The first, dubbed the 'myth of religious violence' by William T. Cavanaugh, claims that religion is a universal component of human culture, honeycombed with irrationality, divisiveness, an inability to compromise and tendencies towards authoritarianism.[6] The only hope for lasting peace is to separate the religious sphere from the secular sphere (politics, the economy and public life, generally). This in turn leads to the second, labelled by Scott M. Thomas the 'myth of liberalism'.[7] According to this myth, the hazards of religious violence can only be controlled by the imposition of the modern liberal state in which politics becomes secular and religion is privatised. In short, religion (and, in particular, its propensity for violence and disorder) is the problem, and the order fostered by the secular liberal state is the solution.

These two myths worked together (though colluded might be a better word) not only to separate politics from religion but also to make the particular historical terms of that separation normative for both politics and religion, generally. In other words, the collusive effect of these two myths charged the descriptive concepts 'religion' and 'politics' with normative authority. These two concepts no longer simply describe human phenomena; rather, they distinguish normal and abnormal varieties. For example, secularism becomes the new normal for politics. Thus, widely utilised theories of International Relations, such as realism and liberalism, presume the absence of religion from the outset simply because religion is supposed to be outside politics. In this respect, both realism and liberalism can be described as secularising theories insofar as 'religion' and 'politics' are separated prior to analysis.[8] Religion asserting itself politically (as in the case of the Moral Majority in the United States or the Islamic Revolution in Iran) is seen as an anomaly. In the 1990s, politically active religion was thought to be, perhaps, a new type of religion altogether.[9] Fundamentalism, for example, was envisioned as a new form of religion, the primary characteristic of which was opposition to modernity.

Two empirical examples can be offered to demonstrate the extent to which religion has been excluded from International Relations theory and analysis. Both are provided by Timothy Samuel Shah. The first comes from the American Political Science Review.[10] For the 100th anniversary issue (2006), Kenneth D. Wald and Clyde Wilcox surveyed the APSR archives and found that 'prior to 1960 only a single APSR article sought to use religion as a variable to explain empirical phenomena'. The situation did not noticeably improve with the rise of politically active religion in the 1970s. The years following 1980 are devoid of articles focused on religious factors, save one essay on American Government and two in Comparative Politics. Shah's second example cites a similar study undertaken by Daniel Philpott, who reviewed the leading journals in International Relations.[11] Philpott discovered that 'only six or so out of a total of about sixteen hundred [articles published in leading IR journals] featured religion as an important influence'. [12]

The religious resurgence challenges conventional assumptions on two levels. Empirically, as Berger and many other social scientists have observed, religion is alive and well in the modern world. It's not exactly clear, however, what this observation means. Is the world more religious than it ever has been before? Is it more religious than it was at an earlier time? Answering either one of those questions is difficult. Not only is religiosity difficult to measure, it is also difficult to express conceptually. Perhaps these are not the best questions to ask. It's quite possible that the world looks different simply because social scientists and other scholars have removed their secularisation goggles. In other words, the world hasn't changed so much as the way in which scholars look at it has. The theoretical shift presumed by the religious resurgence speaks to the second challenge: integrating religion into existing theories of International Relations. The easiest way to do this would be, to use a cooking analogy, add and stir: add religion and stir it into already existing theories. The key question begged by this strategy is, of course, whether religion is the sort of concept one can simply add and stir.

Theorising Religion in International Relations

At first glance the word 'religion' seems relatively straightforward. Most people use words like 'religion' and 'religious' in everyday speech. Problems arise, however, when we try to define 'religion'. It's not that 'religion' is indefinable; rather, 'religion' suffers from a sort of definitional satyriasis: no matter how many suitors there are, 'religion' is ready to accept another. Beneath the sheer variety of competing definitions, however, two fundamental marks characteristic of the specifically modern category of religion can be discerned. First, religion is something that is ontologically unique—that is, religion is a transhistorical, transcultural object. While it takes empirical form in a dizzying variety of ways, its core or essence can be concisely expressed in different systems of propositions and beliefs about reality. Second, in order to be known, religion requires the epistemological contrast of 'not-religion', or the secular. Religion and the secular together form a binary opposition, which is a pair of related concepts that are mutually exclusive in meaning. A simple example would be the binary opposition 'up' and 'down'. Secular and religion are likewise connected. An important point to keep in mind is that both religion and the secular are historically located in European Latin Christendom. Not only is religion identified with Christianity, but the secular is originally a theological category unique to Western Christendom.[13] In short, the roots of the religion–secular binary run deep in the Western tradition.

Problems with the modern category of religion become apparent when scholars attempt to use religion as an analytic or descriptive category. In sorting 'religious' and 'non-religious' phenomena, we simply reproduce the normative claims specific to the category of modern religion—that is, religion is something sui generis standing in binary opposition to the secular. More generally, the normative claims projected by the modern category of religion electrify descriptive treatments of 'religious' phenomena with a prescriptive charge. This leads to what I have called going rogue—when an ostensibly descriptive or analytic term becomes charged with normative authority, which causes analysis to slice (in the golfing sense) west, as in the direction of Western civilisation.[14] What is more, rogue concepts have a strong tendency to enfold normative assumptions and commitments into scholarly analysis by continued uncritical application. The power of rogue concepts is their protean ability to mimic 'normal' concepts and, once insinuated within analyses, metastasise. Once that happens, the analysis is, in a manner of speaking, possessed. Analysis of global politics, which aims to produce knowledge, becomes instead the re-inscription of normative claims about 'religion' and 'politics' and the normal relationship between the two. Scholars in the field of Religious Studies have recognised this problem, and some advocate dispensing with the concept 'religion' altogether.[15] While sympathetic with this argument, ultimately I think it goes too far—it's a utopian gesture rather than a methodological strategy. The word 'religion' is too finely woven into the fabric of our thinking to be simply cast aside. What we can do, however, is rethink the way that we critically understand and deploy the concept of religion.[16]

I hope it is clear at this juncture that religion is not the sort of concept that can be added and stirred into established theories. There are other ways, however, to integrate religion into IR theory and analysis. Some of these attempts clear new ground; others succumb to a variety of problems. [17] Many of these problems can be traced back to insufficient theorising or a tendency to rely uncritically on the conventional understanding of the word 'religion' (frequently the two are combined). Concepts of religion can be too closely identified with a particular religious tradition (many concepts of religion, for example, amount in practice to a generalised description of Protestant Christianity). Concepts can be reified—that is, they are insufficiently sensitive to the historical and social contexts in which particular religions develop. Concepts can become ensnared in theological disputes over whether God, the gods, or transcendent reality are necessary criteria for determining the category of religion. Any of these problems, unchecked, allow concepts of religion to go rogue.

The religious resurgence is at once a return of religion to global politics as well as to International Relations theory. While a number of theoretical challenges arise, opportunities open up as well. When IR theorists stalk religion, they should do so critically. They should keep in mind Jonathan Z. Smith's admonition that 'religion is solely the creation of the scholar's study. It is created for the scholar's analytic purposes by his imaginative acts of comparison and generalisation. Religion has no independent existence apart from the academy.'[18] The upshot of Smith's remark is that the concept of religion used as a scholarly term of art should be carefully distinguished from the notion of religion we use in everyday speech. Religion in everyday speech depends on the secular for its meaning. In analysing religious phenomena we want to be critically aware of differences in history, society and culture, both with regard to the phenomena being studied and the concepts we are utilising. A critical or self-aware concept of religion is thus necessary for scholars to understand the religious resurgence.

Notes

1. Peter L. Berger, "Secularism in Retreat," *The National Interest* 46 (1996/97): 3–12.
2. My presentation of secularization as three interrelated social processes is indebted to Jose Casanova. For discussion, see his "The Secular, Secularizations, Secularisms," *Rethinking Secularism* (New York: Oxford University Press, 2011), 54–74, as well as his *Public Religions in the Modern World* (Chicago: The University of Chicago Press, 1994)
3. There is a great amount of material on secularism and secularization. For a short version of the narrative of secularism, see Charles Taylor, "Western Secularity," *Rethinking Secularism*, 31–53; for the longer version, see Charles Taylor. *A Secular Age* (Cambridge, Mass.: The Belknap Press of Harvard University Press, 2007). For discussion of the secularization thesis, see Steve Bruce, *Secularization: In Defense of an Unfashionable Theory* (New York: Oxford University Press, 2013), and Rob Warner, *Secularization and Its Discontents* (London and New York: Continuum International Publishing Group, 2010).
4. 'A Bleak Outlook is Seen for Religion', *New York Times*, 25 February 1968.
5. Berger, "Secularism in Retreat," 3.
6. For discussion, see William T. Cavanaugh, *The Myth of Religious Violence* (New York: Oxford University Press, 1999), passim.
7. For discussion, see Scott M. Thomas, *The Global Resurgence of Religion and the Transformation of International Relations* (New York: Palgrave Macmillan, 2005), 21–69.
8. Daniel Philpott and Timothy Samuel Shah argue that the secularism of international relations theory is the product of the same historical transformation that created the modern world of sovereign states. See their 'The Fall and Rise of Religion in International Relations: History and Theory', *Religion and International Relations Theory* (New York: Columbia University Press, 2011), 34–37.
9. A good example of this is provided by the Fundamentalist Project, a well-funded, multi-year research project under the direction of Martin Marty that examined the phenomena of "fundamentalism" across religious traditions. Five thick volumes issued from the Project before it ended in 1995.
10. Kenneth D. Wald and Clyde Wilcox, 'Getting Religion: Has Political Science Rediscovered the Faith Factor?' *American Political Science Review* 100:4 (2006), 523–29.
11. Daniel Philpott, 'The Challenge of September 11 to Secularism in International Relations', *World Politics* 55.1 (2002), 66–95.
12. Quoted in Timothy Samuel Shah, 'Religion and World Affairs: Blurring the Boundaries', *Rethinking Religion and World Affairs* (New York: Oxford University Press, 2012), 4.
13. Casanova, 'The Secular, Secularizations, Secularisms', *Rethinking Secularism*, 56.
14. I have discussed the notions of 'going rogue' and 'rogue concepts' elsewhere. See

my 'The Religious Resurgence and International Relations Theory', *Religious Studies Review* 39.4 (2013), 201–21.

15. For one well-known argument in support of this position, see Timothy Fitzgerald, *The Ideology of Religious Studies* (New York: Oxford University Press, 2000).

16. Since the 1980s, no scholar has been more influential in critically rethinking the concept of religion than Talal Asad. See his *Formations of the Secular: Christianity, Islam, Modernity. Cultural Memory in the Present* (Stanford: Stanford University Press, 2003); ibid, *Genealogies of Religion: Discipline and Reasons of Power in Christianity and Islam* (Baltimore: The Johns Hopkins University Press, 1993); and ibid, 'Reading a Modern Classic: W.C. Smith's *The Meaning and End of Religion*', History of Religions 40.3 (2001), 205–222. Some other scholars have built on Asad's work. Some provide genealogies of religion: Peter Harrison, *'Religion' and the Religions in the English Enlightenment* (Cambridge: Cambridge University Press, 2002 [1990]); Brent Nongbri, *Before Religion: A History of a Modern Concept* (New Haven: Yale University Press, 2013); Guy G. Stroumsa, *A New Science: The Discovery of Religion in the Age of Reason* (Cambridge, Mass: Harvard University Press, 2010). Still others study the intersection of religion and politics (and the ways in which "religion" obscures the terms of that intersection): William E. Arnal and Russell T. McCutcheon, *The Sacred Is the Profane: The Political Nature of "Religion"* (New York: Oxford University Press, 2013); Russell T. McCutcheon, *Critics Not Caretakers: Redescribing the Public Study of Religion* (Albany: State University of New York Press, 2001); and ibid, *Manufacturing Religion: The Discourse on Sui Generis Religion and the Politics of Nostalgia* (New York: Oxford University Press, 1997). Scholars have also examined the construction of "religion" in the context of the rise of Religious Studies: Daniel Dubuisson, *The Western Construction of Religion: Myths, Knowledge, and Ideology*, trans. William Sayers (Baltimore: The Johns Hopkins University Press, 2003); and Tomoko Masuzawa, *The Invention of World Religions: Or, How European Universalism was Preserved in the Language of Pluralism* (Chicago: University of Chicago Press, 2005).

17. For three examples of the skilful integration of religion into International Relations analysis, see Elizabeth Shakman Hurd, *The Politics of Secularism in International Politics* (Princeton: Princeton University Press, 2007); Daniel H. Nexon, 'Religion and International Relations: No Leap of Faith Required', *Religion and International Relations Theory*; and Thomas, *The Global Resurgence of Religion and the Transformation of International Relations*.

18. Jonathan Z. Smith, *Imagining Religion: From Babylon to Jonestown* (Chicago: The University of Chicago Press, 1982), xi.

2

'Little do they know …' How (Not) to Theorise Religion and International Relations

JODOK TROY
UNIVERSITY OF INNSBRUCK, AUSTRIA

Introduction[1]

One example of the many fluctuating academic 'working groups on religion and International Relations' eloquently summarises the *agreement* of scholars in International Relations (IR) when it comes to the intersection of religious 'issues' and IR: (1) the marginalisation of religion in the subject, which is, (2), due to the thinking of secularisation theory is, finally, (3), unwarranted.[2] It is by now also commonplace to understand 'secularisation' as a more nuanced term—and therefore to make a distinction between secularisation (as an empirical phenomena) and secularism (as, more or less, an ideology; an 'ism'). However warranted those claims may be, and no matter how much consensus they achieve in the academic community, they nevertheless at the same time point to complications in theorising religion and IR.

I will outline how, and how not, to theorise on the topic from a classical Realist point of view, seeing IR primarily as practical philosophy, relying in its analysis on interpretative methods, normative theory and anthropological insights. I do this along the following steps. First, I reflect for a moment on the ongoing trend of 'de-marginalising' the topic and, at the same time, point out grievances when it comes to secularisation theorising. Second, I reflect on shortcomings when talking about 'religion as religion', i.e. to categorise religion as a 'variable', therefore pointing out how the Western understanding of religion shapes and limits theorising. Finally, I reflect on some of the alternative and complementary approaches of addressing religion in IR.

De-marginalising the Topic

Charles Taylor's *A Secular Age is* a prominent study dealing with religion and politics with great impact.[3] His central concept is the 'immanent frame', an attempt based on a liberal agenda to exclude anything metaphysical from the public (i.e. political) sphere.[4] This is certainly useful and contributes to philosophical problems and understandings of many current issues.[5] The central thesis, that we live in a secular age, however, cannot hold up to reality.[6] In other words, what is missing in theorising on the topic are (empirical) insights from the sociology of religion.[7] When it comes to the agreement over the shortcomings of secularisation theory, we therefore encounter two phenomena that are relevant for matters of religion and IR. As Elizabeth Shakman Hurd's *The Politics of Secularism in International Relations* outlines, there is a difference between the actual *practice* of *secularisation* (i.e. separation of church and state) and belief in the *concept* of *secularism* (i.e. secularisation leads to modernisation).[8] It is a matter of constructing what both terms actually mean. Hence, one problem is the misunderstanding of inter-disciplinary (or at least trans-disciplinary) research; the other is the absence of it. 'How to cite a sacred text',[9] for example, can be a tricky business.

9/11 shed light on religion for IR, encouraging more mainstream engagement with the subject. Whereas studies on religion and IR written before 9/11 focused on religion and violence, nowadays many focus on one particular religion: Islam. The problem is not the fixation on one particular religion. The problem, in terms of scientific analysis, is the dualism in which it is framed.[10] This dualism is either the framing that religion is about peace and that problems are only posed by misguided fanatics or lunatics who just don't get it right (i.e. the 'proper' religion). On the other side, there are the well-known, often atheistic criticisms trying to point out that religion as such is a problem no matter how it is interpreted. Another problem is the categorising of religions as cultural forces opposing each other, most famously argued for by Samuel Huntington.[11] What likely follows is that different religious traditions are differently developed in terms of modernity. Hence the assumption that what is necessary for those religions and cultures is to start a process like the European Enlightenment. The problems here described build on the understanding of 'religion' as a modern, Western *construction*,[12] but this leads to some subsequent epistemological shortcomings.[13]

Go, Measure Faith

The above-mentioned selection of problems and disputes on religion and IR are caused by one prevailing problem of social science epistemology: the desire to *code* religion as a *variable*. This is based on a 'Protestant' understanding of religion: to characterise religion as a *set of beliefs*, effectively reducing religion to theology—and, for that matter in IR, to political theology. The more extensive theoretical underpinning of this discussion is the differentiation between functionalistic (not what but *how* people believe; i.e. the 'doing') and substantive (what people believe; i.e. a set of beliefs or doctrines; i.e. the 'being') approaches to religion.[14] Again, Huntington's work is illustrative for this point. If we understand the set of beliefs of a given actor, we will be able to deduce that actor's behaviour. This is the belief that faith can be measured, based on the assumption that a certain set of beliefs can influence political behaviour or political choices and can therefore be categorised just like any other variable in the standard rational actor model. This understanding of religion leads to several theoretical and practical problems.

First, it underestimates what Scott Atran in the case of terrorism and religion research terms the 'devoted actor'. This is a type of actor, 'regardless of utilitarian calculations', willing 'to make extreme sacrifices based on a deontological evaluation of "appropriateness" rather than an instrumental calculus'.[15] Second, as outlined above, it leads to the desire to code and measure religion (i.e. particular believers). The resulting studies are valuable for IR theorising. However, and primarily, they are just that: coding faith according to the certain set of beliefs to which a group of people adheres. What follows is most often a confusion of correlation and causation. Most causal claims in IR studies relying on such research are nothing other than (assumed) claims.[16] Simply put, if two actors with two different coded identities are engaged in conflict, it is easy (and alluring) to jump to the conclusion that the reason for the conflict is their respective identities.

Third, it resembles the social science fixation on the 'why' question. Why does religion cause violence—that is, why does religion lead to violent political actions? What social sciences tend to ignore is that there is a considerable difference between *abstract* ideas (e.g. just war, jihad, pacifism, etc.) and 'informal religious ideas, practices, symbols, or social structures',[17] as Ron Hassner outlined. Thus, it is said to be necessary to explain *identities* in order to make statements on religious influence on political behaviour.[18] Identities are defined as 'a person's conception of which of his characteristics make him distinct from others according to his social role: is he a Lutheran, a Catholic, a German nationalist? Identities are made up in part of ideas, which people hold stably over the long term. A person with a Protestant identity, for instance, persists in holding Protestant ideas'. However, 'identities can change and do so when people come to hold new ideas and self-conceptions'.[19] Going further, Michael Oakeshott reminds us that identity 'is nothing more than an unbroken rehearsal of contingencies, each at the mercy of circumstance and each significant in proportion to its familiarity. It is not a fortress into which we may retire.'[20] 'Measuring' faith while following their research agenda is what many social scientists can certainly do very well. Nevertheless, the question remains whether we are not just measuring a certain set of beliefs and habits and expected practices which do not, in the end, provide much insight and is prone to lead to hasty conclusions.

The fourth problem arising from this understanding of religion and IR, after the desire to frame religion as a variable, is the general desire to 'integrate' religion into IR theory along the lines of Liberalism–Realism–Constructivism. This, of course, goes beyond the above-mentioned attempts and problems caused by attempts to explain and understand research puzzles where traditional IR and religion intersect. It resembles the will to integrate religion into IR theory. This can even lead to outcomes such as integrating religion into Neorealism.[21] One laudable outcome of this kind of research is that there are some textbooks on the topic available.[22] Nevertheless, the outcomes are inevitably reductive and sometimes idiosyncratic readings and interpretations of the already existing theoretical framework. Take, for example, Realism: 'Little do they know that they meet under an empty sky from which the gods have departed'—so Hans Morgenthau concedes for the universalistic aspirations of foreign policy.[23] This phrase and other selected phrases from Morgenthau and other Realists have often been taken to argue that in and for Realism, religion and ethical principles do not matter, or are at least of secondary importance.[24] However, it can also be understood as: 'whether Morgenthau's sky is empty of gods or not, what people believe about it matter.[25]

The 'new' nationalism, detached from religion, was, in Morgenthau's eyes, the main problem in the international sphere. 'The state has become indeed a "mortal God", and for an age that believes no longer in an immortal God, the state becomes the only God there is'[26] is therefore a very easily misunderstood phrase. Nicolas Guilhot aptly pointed out that Morgenthau's Realism was a criticism of the secularising tendencies that nationalism unleashes.[27] 'Little do they know …' indeed that critique was—at least *also*—directed against liberal internationalism as the new (secular) paradigm unleashed from the national interest (which, for classical Realism, is itself more of an epistemological category than an ontological one). This episode on Realism illustrates two things. First, it shows there are many ways of reading the historiography of theoretical traditions. Along those ways we tend to confuse the theoretical and philosophical assumptions of theories. Second, it illustrates that there are beneficial engagements of IR thinking with political theology.[28] Most obviously they concern our understanding of particular terms and concepts such as the political, the state, sovereignty and many more.[29]

Pure and Unseparated: Additional Approaches

Making sense of religion and IR in epistemological terms seems a bit like overcoming the distinction between oil in water: pure and at the same time unseparated, as already outlined in my examination of the problematic concepts and terms of 'religion' and 'secularism'. To illustrate this point more comprehensively, I revisit, via the work of three authors, the practicability of the statement that religion and politics are not genuinely distinct from each other: René Girard, William Cavanaugh and Michael Walzer.

Girard's mimetic theory illustrates how a theory of the origins of culture and religion remains apt for explaining modern politics: human behaviour is shaped by the imitation of the desire of others.[30] Thus, we end up in a competition imitating the other's desires.[31] It is sameness that is a problem in the social sphere, not difference. People fight because they are the same; they fight over the same goods. Where difference and differentiation vanishes, the 'narcissism of the minor difference', as Sigmund Freud called it,[32] becomes overwhelming. In quantitative and qualitative terms, the most violent conflicts take place not between but within groups. Religions have been aware of this dynamic and in the past solved mimetic crises by sacrificing an innocent victim. It is, according to mimetic theory, no coincidence that the founding moment of religious traditions is most often a murder or human sacrifice—a scapegoat. The purpose of this is not least to canalise violence. Similar mechanisms are at work within the political sphere. The modern excess of responsibility, seeking to bring individuals to justice, is arguably a tendency that confirms some of the basic assumptions of mimetic theory, such as the scapegoat mechanism. 'Blaming and shaming' individuals, i.e. bringing them (e.g. warlords) to justice, is certainly a legitimate liberal achievement. At the same time, however, this tendency largely ignores the social conditions that led to the outcomes (e.g. mass murder).[33] More generally, mimetic theory illustrates that our modern judicial system and the arising international criminal law rests on scapegoating.[34]

In *The Myth of Religious Violence,* Cavanaugh argues not that religion is peaceful but that its opposed secular outputs (such as ideologies).[35] Further, and in line with Daniel Philpot's conclusions,[36] Cavanaugh argues against the popular IR narrative that the Protestant Reformation 'divided Christendom along religious lines' and that the 'wars of religion … demonstrated to the West the inherent danger of public religion. The solution to the problem lay in the rise of the modern state'. Henceforward, the story gained foundational importance for the secular West, because it explains the origin of its way of life and its system of governance. It is a creation myth for modernity.[37] Consequently, a good question to ask is, 'what's so "religious" about "religious terrorism"?'[38]—and, for that matter, 'religious violence', since 'the dominant narrative is that religion caused the bloodshed of the Thirty Years' War, which European nation-states finally resolved through widespread adoption of secular forms of government'.[39]

Finally, the communitarian Walzer pointed out that 'Drawing the Line', i.e. between the 'twin toleration'[40] of religion and politics, does not make much sense, even for a liberal understanding of politics:

> So long as there are different ideas, no realisation can be definitive. On the religious or ideological side of the line, the good society can have an absolute form; on the political side, it is always provisional... It doesn't matter whether the conceptions are religious or secular; their protagonists have exactly the same right to join the competition.[41]

What is important here is not the way of managing the politics that Walzer defends in his argument. What is important is that the 'religious' and 'secular' spheres are not two absolutely distinct configurations of *power*. 'What counts as religious, secular or political in any given context is not only socially constructed; it is a function of different configurations of power surrounding the construction of the categories the religious, the secular and the political— and the boundaries between them.'[42]

Conclusion

During the course and aftermath of the so-called 'Salman Rushdie Affair', some early attempts at interpretive research and narrative theory on religion and politics were conducted. They can be summarised with the statement that '[w]hereas the Western liberal tradition places priority on individual autonomy, the Islamic tradition presents a communitarian view in which the concept of the self is realised collectively in the community of Islam and is defined through traditions and concepts of honour'.[43] 'Because' as Cecelia Lynch concludes, 'no religious doctrine can guide believers to appropriate action in all contexts, what should be done must be *interpreted*'.[44]

Less *theology* (i.e. understanding religion in substantial terms), therefore, and more religious *sociology* (i.e. understanding religion in functional terms) along with the study of *political* theory (i.e. in understanding what constitutes the political sphere) would constitute better research conduct and contribute a more nuanced understanding of 'Nations under God'. At the same time, theology remains a necessary part of the analysis and the essentialist–functionalist gap is a narrow one. In a 'spiritual' age, however, formalised and measurable (patterns and systems of) belief may no longer matter that much.[45]

Notes

1. Acknowledgements: Austrian Science Fund (FWF) project P 25198-G16 *Which Structure, Whose Virtue? Realism's Premises on Men and Power.*

2. Working Group on International Relations and Religion, 'Conclusion', in *Religion and International Relations: A Primer for Research*, 184–6, 184. http://rmellon.nd.edu/assets/101872/religion_and_international_relations_report.pdf.

3. Charles Taylor, *A Secular Age* (Cambridge, Mass.: Belknap Press of Harvard University Press, 2007).

4. Interestingly enough, Taylor set out as a genuine liberal Philosopher and eventually became one of the foremost Catholic ones in recent years.

5. See, for example, already John W. Meyer et al., 'World Society and the Nation□ State', *American Journal of Sociology* 103, no. 1 (1997): 144–181.

6. Peter L. Berger, 'The Desecularization of the World: A global overview', in *Religion and foreign affairs: Essential readings*, ed. Dennis Hoover and Douglas Johnston (Waco, Tex: Baylor University Press, 2012), 21–32.

7. For that matter the work of sociologists of religion such as Peter L. Berger, Robert Wuthnow, Brian Grim, or Rodger Finke may be recalled. Peter L. Berger, 'Secularization Falsified', *First Things*, February 2008; Robert Wuthnow, 'Understanding Religion and Politics', *Daedalus* 120, no. 3 (Summer 1991); Brian J. Grim and Rodger Finke, 'Religious Persecution in Cross-National Context: Clashing Civilizations or Regulated Religious Economies', *American Sociological Review* 72, no. 4 (2007).

8. Elizabeth Shakman Hurd, *The Politics of Secularism in International Relations* (Princeton: Princeton University Press, 2008).

9. Ron E. Hassner, 'How to Cite a Sacred Text', *Politics and Religion* 6, no. 04 (2013).

10. Jonathan Fox, 'Multiple Impacts of Religion on International Relations: Perceptions and Reality', http://www.ifri.org/files/politique_etrangere/4_2006_Fox.pdf.

11. Samuel P. Huntington, *The Clash of Civilizations and the Remaking of World Order* (New York, NY: Simon & Schuster, 2003).

12. Brent Nongbri, *Before Religion: A history of a modern concept* (New Haven Conn. u.a: Yale Univ. Press, 2013). Concerning IR see also Timothy Fitzgerald, *Religion and Politics in International Relations: The Modern Myth* (New York: Continuum, 2011).

13. Cecelia Lynch, *Interpreting international politics* (New York, NY: Routledge, 2014), 88-91.

14. Mona K. Sheikh, 'How does religion matter? Pathways to religion in International Relations' *Review of International Studies* 38, no. 02 (2012).

15. Jeremy Ginges and Scott Atran, 'Sacred Values and Cultural Conflict', in *Advances in Culture and Psychology, Volume 4*, ed. Michele J. Gelfand, Chi-yue Chiu and Ying-yi Hong, Advances in Culture and Psychology (Oxford: Oxford University Press USA, 2013), 273–301, 276.

16. See, for example, Monica Duffy Toft, Daniel Philpott and Timothy Samuel Shah, *God's Century: Resurgent Religion and Global Politics* (New York: W.W. Norton, 2011); Jonathan Fox, *A World Survey of Religion and the State* (Cambridge: Cambridge University Press, 2008); Pippa Norris and Ronald Ingelhart, *Sacred and Secular: Religion and Politics Worldwide* (Cambridge: Cambridge University Press, 2004).

17. Ron E. Hassner, 'Religion as a Variable', in *Religion and International Relations: A Primer for Research*, 68–86; Ron Hassner, *Religion on the Battlefield* (Cornell University Press, forthcoming).

18. Sebastian Rosato, 'The Sufficiency of secular International Relations Theory', in *Religion and International Relations: A Primer for Research*, 176–83. For examples of the mentioned research see, for instance, Jonathan Fox, 'State Failure and the Clash of Civilisations: An Examination of the Magnitude and Extent of Domestic Civilizational Conflict from 1950 to 1996', *Australian Journal of Political Science* 38, no. 2 (July 2003); Fox, *A World Survey of Religion and the State.*, Jonathan Fox, *An Introduction to Religion and Politics: Theory & Practice* (New York: Routledge, 2013).

19. Daniel Philpott, 'The Religious Roots of Modern International Relations', *World Politics* 52, no. 2 (January 2000): 217. Philpott, at the example of the Protestant Revolution's impact on the Westphalian (states) system, illustrated that ideas which shape identities, in this case religious ideas, indeed alter the social role. Philpott, 'The Religious Roots of Modern International Relations', Daniel Philpott, *Revolutions in Sovereignty: How Ideas shaped Modern International Relations* (Princeton: Princeton University Press, 2001). Still, this example reflects the prevailing acceptance and promoted thinking that a certain "set of ideas", a belief-system, is the reason for a certain kind of action.

20. Michael Oakeshott, *Rationalism in Politics and Other Essays* (London: Methnen, 1962), 170–1.

21. See, for example, Nukhet A. Sandal and Jonathan Fox, *Religion in international relations theory: Interactions and possibilities,* Routledge studies in religion and politics (London: Routledge, 2013).

22. See, for example, Fox, *An Introduction to Religion and Politics;* Sandal and Fox, *Religion in international relations theory.* For another, and perhaps the very first of its kind, see particularly Jeffrey Haynes, *An Introduction to International Relations and Religion*, 2nd ed. (Harlow: Pearson Education, 2013).

23. Hans J. Morgenthau, *Politics among Nations: The Struggle for Power and Peace*, 2nd ed. (New York: Alfred A. Knopf, 1956), 233–4.

24. See, for example, Sandal and Fox, *Religion in international relations theory*, 32–3. Counter evidence quotations are easily found but such a selective engagement provide first of all historiographical insights to Realism.

25. Rebecca A. Glazier, Religion and realism: Charting a middle path for International Relations theory', in *Religion and the realist tradition: From political theology to international relations theory and back*, ed. Jodok Troy, Routledge studies in religion and politics (London and New York: Routledge), 176–84, 176.

26. Hans J. Morgenthau, The Evil of Politics and the Ethics of Evil', *Ethics* 56, no. 1 (October 1945): 15.

27. Nicolas Guilhot, 'American Katechon: When Political Theology Became International Relations Theory', *Constellations* 17, no. 2 (2010). Some even claim a genuine religious heritage for Morgenthau's Realism. Ben Mollov, *Power and Transcendence: Hans J. Morgenthau and the Jewish Experience* (Lanham, Md: Lexington, 2002).

28. See, for example, Nicolas. Rengger, 'On theology and international relations: World

politics beyond the empty sky', *International Relations* 27, no. 2 (2013).

29. Jean Bethke Elshtain, *Sovereignty: God, state, and self; the Gifford lectures* (New York: Basic Books, 2008); Vendulka Kubálková, "Towards an International Political Theology," *Millennium - Journal of International Studies* 29, no. 3 (2000); Péter Losonczi, Mika Luoma-aho and Aakash Singh, eds., *The future of political theology: Religious and theological perspectives* (Farnham, Surrey, England;, Burlington, VT: Ashgate, 2011).

30. René Girard, *The Scapegoat* (Baltimore Md.: John Hopkins University Press, 1986); René Girard, *Violence and the Sacred* (London: Athlone Press, 1988), translated by Patrick Gregory.

31. For a recent primary source on mimetic theory see, for example, René Girard and Benoît Chantre, *Battling to the End: Conversations with Benoît Chantre* (East Lansing: Michigan State University Press, 2010).

32. Anton Blok, 'The Narcissism of Minor Differences', *European Journal of Social Theory* 1, no. 1 (1998).

33. Kirsten Ainley, 'Individual Agency and Responsibility for Atrocity', In *Confronting evil in international relations: Ethical responses to problems of moral agency*. Edited by Renée Jeffery, 37–60 (New York, N.Y: Palgrave Macmillan, 2008).

34. Nathan Kensey, 'Scapegoating the Guilty: Girad and International Criminal Law', In *Violence, Desire, and the Sacred: René Girard and Sacrifice in Life, Love, and Literature*. Edited by Scott Cowdell, Fleming Chris and Joel Hodge, 67–80 (London: Bloomsbury, 2014).

35. William T. Cavanaugh, *The Myth of Religious Violence: Secular Ideology and the Roots of Modern Conflict* (Oxford: Oxford University Press, 2009).

36. Philpott, *Revolutions in Sovereignty*.

37. Cavanaugh, *The Myth of Religious Violence*, 123.

38. Jeroen Gunning and Richard Jackson, 'What's so "religious" about "religious terrorism"?', *Critical Studies on Terrorism* 4, no. 3 (2011).

39. Cecelia Lynch, *Interpreting international politics* (New York, NY: Routledge, 2014), 89.

40. Alfred Stepan, 'Religion, Democracy, and the "Twin Tolerations"', *Journal of Democracy* 11, no. 4 (October 2000).

41. Michael Walzer, *Thinking Politically: Essays in Political Theory* (New Haven: Yale University Press, 2007), Selected, edited, and with an introduction by D. Miller, 159–60.

42. Scott M Thomas, 'Culture, Religion and Violence: Rene Girard's Mimetic Theory', *Millennium - Journal of International Studies* 43, no. 1 (2014): 308–327, 317.

43. M. M. Slaughter, 'The Salman Rushdie Affair: Apostasy, Honor, and Freedom of Speech', *Virginia Law Review* 79, no. 1 (1993): 153–204, 155.

44. Cecelia Lynch, *Interpreting international politics* (New York, NY: Routledge, 2014), 91. Talad Asad, 'The Idea of an Anthropology of Islam', *Qui Parle* 17, no. 2 (2009): 1–30.

45. Harvey Cox and others see the world after an age of faith (i.e. understood as confidence) and an age of belief (e.g. opinion) in a spiritual era where traditional (hierarchical and structural sets and structures) of beliefs are on the retreat. Harvey Gallagher Cox, *The future of faith*, (New York, NY: HarperOne, 2009).

3

Shifting Territorial Orders and Religion

GERTJAN DIJKINK
UNIVERSITY OF AMSTERDAM, THE NETHERLANDS

Geopolitics and Human Feelings

For those who follow world news, the statement that religion and geopolitics are narrowly related is quite obvious and perhaps more so than ever. If we define geopolitics as the propensity of states or localised groups to optimise their territorial assets at the expense of other localised actors, there is a lot of contemporary geopolitics that seems to resonate with religion. In view of the violent campaigns in which Islamic groups try to gain control over states in Africa and the Middle East with the explicit aim of constituting a moral regime or new caliphate (Islamic State), the link between geopolitics and religion seems undeniable. Yet we should be aware that systematic analysis of international conflict data covering a long period does not provide statistical evidence of the effect of religious difference on the *outbreak of war* between states or groups.[1] Nor, despite what the 'Clash of Civilizations' thesis would have us believe, could such a thing be proved for the more recent historical period. Nonetheless, a mass of publications report how religious arguments have been used by groups to rationalise their territorial independence and bolster national morale in the prelude to war. The Exodus story from the Bible was used in early modern European (Protestant) states like England and the Dutch Republic to suggest that they had found their promised land like the wandering Israelites or even as descendants of a lost Jewish tribe.[2] Islamic tribes have used their religion in rivalry with other tribes by claiming a special link with the Prophet—even if their main ancestor was only his barber. Such examples impel us to account for the fact that religion is often embedded in a national identity complex (always relevant in international conflict[3]) and that religious difference is difficult to define.

Here I will follow a different approach to the issue of religion and geopolitics by drawing attention to the changing territorial orders that control the geopolitical game. Territorial orders are dominant ways of linking authority to geographic distinctions. One such territorial order is the current process of globalisation while another was the formation of states in Europe at the end of the Middle Ages. Such shifts in the geography of power upturn established interests and human feelings of security and therefore demand a legitimating philosophy that might acquire the status of religion. There are of course other options for people faced with a changing territorial order, such as ignorance or violent resistance. In Hirschmann's terms the options are *exit*, *voice* or *loyalty*.[4] In a globalising world *exit* is a characteristic resistance against the ideal of the 'open society'. As Chechen guerrilla fighter Noukhaev once remarked, 'I am against the open society ... because it wants to turn my closed, barbarian, world into a citizen's world.' Such attitudes easily turn into violent resistance, as exemplified by tribal Islam and Al Qaeda.[5] The other option, *voice*, can be associated with attempts to endow the new order with a vision that makes the world meaningful again rather than with changing its structure. This is the more affirmative role of religion, answering to human feelings that are injured by a new power configuration.

Religion as a Response to Some Major Territorial Events in History

One of the most familiar examples of a religion that may have owed its origin to the mental struggle with an inconvenient territorial order is Christianity. Its message of love, even across ethnic lines, fitted the transnational imperial order of Rome better than the Jewish emphasis on one God favouring one (Jewish) people. Of course, the brutal unifying power of Rome had to be balanced by a mighty vision of an all-encompassing Kingdom in Heaven reigning through love or the 'Holy Spirit' rather than war, but the new transnational order and opportunities for mobility could still be saved. The Christian religious innovation was an act of reconstruction rather than deconstruction. Crossan and Reed assert: 'both Jesus and the apostle Paul are not so much trapped in a negation of global imperialism as establishing its positive alternative here upon earth.'[6] How much the Roman world order was a reference point in Jesus's message also revealed itself in his designation, 'son of God'. As Showalter remarks, 'Many of those who referred to Jesus as "son of God" knew perfectly well that a Latin form of the phrase was among the most frequent descriptions for Augustus and his successors.'[7] Two years after his death in 44 BC, the Roman Senate proclaimed Julius Caesar 'God'. His successor, Augustus, who ruled when Jesus was a youngster, consequently used the title 'son of God' (*divi filius*).

While Christianity more or less embraced an imperial order, the rise of Islam can be attributed to a downright attack on such order. Due to the complex social conditions that offer a breeding ground for religion, we should acknowledge that it is difficult to achieve unequivocal causal explanations. Even if we ignore the particular explanations given by believers there remains a vigorous debate among scholars about the origins of Islam. Nevertheless, widely accepted explanations pointing to social tensions in the Arab heartland due to the rise of trade have been convincingly refuted. Patricia Crone has shown that they were not fundamental enough or sufficiently specific in time and space to explain such a deep shift in people's way of life and outlook.[8] She suggested that the only event with sufficient impact in the late sixth and early seventh century was the imperial threat to the Arab world from two sides: the Byzantine Empire from the West and the Persian Sassanid Empire in the East. The power of these giants (versus the Arab tribes) was accentuated by their state-like qualities and monotheistic religion. Where a direct political unification of the Arab tribes was unfeasible, they 'responded' with religious means: a monotheistic belief that matched, so to speak, the power of worldly empires by eliminating multiple and manipulable Arab gods. It helped achieve geopolitical aims, with the Umayyad Caliphate, hardly a century later, ruling over a territory that extended from the Indus to the Atlantic Ocean.

The geopolitical significance of the Reformation in early modern Europe is usually explained as an impetus for territories like the Low Countries to secede from the Catholic Habsburg Empire and for religious wars that haunted the German Länder in the late sixteenth century. Yet there is also a conceivable reverse influence, with the rise of sovereign states pushing the new religious conception. When Europe could still be imagined as a unified Christian Empire governed by a twofold Emperor-Pope, it was also possible to believe in a direct link between 'earthly' governance and the realm of the 'divine'. Actually people were accustomed to see real-world events as direct manifestations of God's presence and intervention. The disunity created by kings that pretended to be 'Emperors in their own realm' seemed to desecrate authority and involve ordinary people in an immoral or Godless pursuit.[9] How could so many different rulers pretend to represent the divine? The problem could only be solved by dismissing any claim to represent God on Earth and carry out His aims—even the Pope's. Luther's message did not deny the possibility of a good government ruling in accordance with God's will, but this could only be judged by intimate knowledge of the Scriptures. The distancing between the divine realm and a world ruled by earthly powers that occurred in the sixteenth century has been nicely illustrated in Kirstin Zapalac's study of the paintings that decorated the town hall of Regensburg (Germany) in the sixteenth century.[10] In a painting from 1536 on the wall of the council chamber, the Last Judgment is shown as an event happening on Earth. Almost a hundred years later it was replaced by a painting that depicts the virtues of good government in allegorical style, with a small zone in the upper part referring to the Last Judgment, clearly separated from the earthly events.

Globalisation as a Territorial Impetus for Religious Revival

The age of globalisation has many characteristics, such as time–space compression[11] and the erosion of local values (in the wake of a spreading capitalism) that upset people all over the world.[12] Here, I conceive of globalisation solely as a changing territorial order, a new geography of authority. This has only recently received the systematic attention that transcends the stock remark that the state is fading away. The observations of authors on this subject mainly concern two transformations of the established international order. First, the emergence of transnational regimes that transcend national sovereignty with rules such as those issued by the WTO, the UN Human Rights Council, arbitration in commercial conflict or the issuing of quality certificates for eco-friendly production (MSC, FSC, etc.). The second is the creation of extraterritorial authority by states that create transboundary regimes among neighbouring states or special (industrial or agricultural) zones within states that are withdrawn from national control or democratic supervision. Saskia Sassen has applied herself for more than a decade in explaining that these forms of globalisation are not imposed on states by forces coming from the outside but are a logical consequence of the political and economic dynamics within states. While originally particularly interested in transnational regimes, she has recently shifted attention to the second category of 'the disassembling of national territory'.[13] We should acknowledge, however, that discussion persists on the capability of states to withdraw from transnational regimes or carve out special privileges. For example, the certification of eco-friendly practices has been discredited by countries of the (global) South as a neo-colonial Northern strategy and some of them have subsequently introduced their own standards or insisted on involvement in the way such certificates are issued.[14] While states are still able to enforce their rules with violent means, the only power that an international regime can wield is exclusion (which may anyway be an effective disciplining force).

All ingredients for a religious revival identified in the historic examples given above are obviously just as present in the current era: the experience of imperial threat (or opportunity) and a change in the spatial configuration of authority. The challenges may be different in the North and the South but they are unlikely to be solved by a nineteenth-century 'belief' in the state as 'saviour' given the corruption that characterises many contemporary authoritarian states (like Russia[15]). While political Islam seems to opt for re-establishing the historic caliphates, contemporary Christianity has distanced itself from external authority in its charismatic movements, which emphasise individual ability to cope with the absence of a territorial protective shield. The success of Pentecostal groups in Latin America depends on what Fer has called 'the Pentecostal paradigm of mobility', which gives its members the feeling of upward mobility and self-worth, something fitting a world-city rather than nation-state.[16] Conversely, Muslim fundamentalism, propagated by cultural shock[17] and territorial shock,[18] has elected for the *exit* option—or rather the revolutionary choice to remake the world according to its own image. In attracting people with divergent ethnic and geographic origins it shows itself a truly globalised movement, though lacking a religious 'toolkit' to make the geopolitical reality more palatable.

None of these movements can really be described as religious innovation in the same class as the birth of Christianity or even the Reformation. Change of this sort of magnitude cannot be detected (yet) in our age, although there are many spiritual movements ('New Age' religions) that aim to reinforce individual abilities to cope with a world in which it has become more difficult to feel represented. This aspect of the emerging territorial order is the main driver in a new human search for religious meaning.

Notes

1. Errol A. Henderson, 'Not Letting Evidence Get in the Way of Assumptions: Testing the Clash of Civilization Thesis with More Recent Data', *International Studies* 42 (2005) 458-69

2. Howard, D. Weinbrot, *Britannia's Issue: The Rise of British Literature from Dryden to Ossian* (Cambridge: Cambridge University Press, 2007). John K. Hale, 'England as Israel in Milton's writings', *Early Modern Literary Studies* 2.2 (1996) 3.1-54. http://purl.oclc.org/emls/02-2/halemil2.html

3. Gertjan Dijkink, *National Identity and Geopolitical Visions: Maps of Pride and Pain* (London: Routledge, 1996)

4. Albert O. Hirschmann, *Exit, Voice and Loyalty: Responses to Decline in Firms, Organizations and States.* (Cambridge MA : Harvard university Press, 1970)

5. Akbar Ahmed, *The Thistle and the Drone. How America's War on Terror Became a Global War on Tribal Islam.* (Washington: The Brookings Institution, 2013).

6. John D. Crossan and Jonathan L. Reed, *In Search of Paul. How Jesus's Apostle Opposed Rome's Empire with God's Kingdom* (New York: HarperCollins, 2004) 409.

7. Daniel N. Showalter, "Churches in Context: The Jesus Movement in the Roman World" in *The Oxford History of the Biblical World,* ed. Michael D. Coogan (New York: Oxford University Press, 1998) 388-419.

8. Patricia Crone, *Meccan Trade and the Rise of Islam* (Princeton: Princeton University Press, 1987)

9. See Stuart Elden for an extensive discussion on the changes in juridical and political conceptions of territory in this period. Stuart Elden, *The Birth of Territory* (Chicago: University of Chicago Press, 2013).

10. Kirstin Zapalac, 'In His Image and Likeness': Political Iconography and Religious Change in Regensburg, 1500-1600 (Ithaca: Cornell University Press, 1990).

11. David Harvey, The Condition of Postmodernity: An Enquiry into the Origins of

Cultural Change (Oxford: Blackwell, 1989)

12. See Daniel Golebiewski, 'Religion and Globalization: New Possibilities, Furthering Challenges', *E-International Relations* accessed August 1, 2014 http://www.e-ir. info/2014/07/16/religion-and-globalization-new-possibilities-furthering-challenges/.

13. Saskia Sassen, *Territory, Authority, Rights: From Medieval to Global Assemblages* (Princeton NJ: Princeton University Press, 2006). Saskia Sassen, 'When Territory Deborders Territoriality', *Territory, Politics, Governance* 1 (2013) 21-45. Saskia Sassen, "Land Grabs Today: Feeding the Disassembling of National Territory," *Globalizations* 10 (2013) 25-46.

14. Peter Vandergeest, and Anusorn Unno, 'A New Extraterritoriality? Aquaculture Certification, Sovereignty, and Empire', *Political Geography* 31 (2012) 358-67.

15. The term corruption insufficiently characterizes the Russian political system which suffers from a structural dissolution of central political authority that is itself an echo of globalization rather than isolation See: Johan Engvall, 'The State as Investment Market: a Framework for Interpreting the Post-Soviet State in Eurasia', *Governance: An International Journal of Policy, Administration and Institutions* (2013), accessed May 20, 2014 doi: 10.1111/gove.12064

16. Yannick Fer , "Pentecôtisme et Modernité Urbaine: Entre Déterritorialisation des Identités et Réinvestissement Symbolique de l'Espace Urbain," *Social Compass* 54 (2007) 201-10

17. Olivier Roy, *Globalized Islam: The Search for a New Ummah* (New York: Columbia University Press, 2004)

18. Ahmed, *The Thistle And the Drone* (2013)

4

The Four Religions of Foreign Policy

JOHN A. REES
UNIVERSITY OF NOTRE DAME, AUSTRALIA

Religion was once discounted as a primary factor in the strategic thinking of states. To be sure, religious traditions did influence the cultural interpretation of 'national interest' in many contexts (in this, and other important ways, religion has been a constant in international politics[1]) but only on rare occasions were faith traditions consciously deployed as the drivers of state policy. The main priorities were instead ideological, as state actors measured success against military and economic capabilities in the service of one prevailing political vision or another.[2] Such priorities clearly remain, yet analysts of foreign policy increasingly understand traditional state motivations interacting with religio-cultural elements now considered to be as important as they are enduring. These changes in foreign policy reflect what some scholars see as a larger 'postsecular turn' in IR.[3] In this context, the present chapter enters an important debate on current state approaches towards religion and sketches an alternative policy framework that incorporates the nuances of religion at play in the international sphere.

Faith and Foreign Policy

Explanations for a shift in international policy towards religion are complex and varied, including the following: the emergence of 'soft power' diplomacy allowed cultural, and in specific cases religious, authorities a seat at the negotiating table;[4] Third World nations began to prioritise 'authenticity' alongside economics as important for nation building, providing a foundational role for religion in some contexts;[5] international organisations recognised religious NGOs and communities as key development agents;[6] emphases on 'civilisations'[7] and 'strategic culture'[8] grafted religion onto important discussions of global security; the multifarious importance of

Muslim-majority politics worldwide has raised important debates about pluralism in international society; [9] and the post-Cold War outbreak of nationalism has at times been inspired by religion and can be conceived as a form of political religion itself.[10]

Foreign policy—understood as the sovereign interest of states exercised in the international realm—is the latest domain of world affairs to focus on religion as a primary resource for political activity. Perhaps the most notable development is the strategy by the US State Department to 'engage' religious leaders and faith communities in the areas of humanitarian assistance, advancement of democratic norms, and conflict prevention and security.[11] For the West more generally, the theme of religious freedom now links issues of democracy, development and security into a single foreign policy agenda.[12] Globally, religion emerges at the forefront of central policy dialogues between state diplomats and global institutions of religion, notably on issues of peace and stability.[13] This high-level uptake has attracted the scrutiny of analysts who have begun to raise important ideological and practical questions about the current embrace of religion in the international policy sphere. It is to these that we briefly turn.

Religion and International Policy: Are We Still Caught in a Binary?

Several scholars have responded to the rise of religion in foreign policy by querying whether these initiatives bring new agendas or simply reinforce existing interests.[14] One way to approach the question is to read emerging policy initiatives against prior 'new agenda' arguments on religion in the wider discourse of IR. For instance, Martin E. Marty reconceptualised the world as 'religio-secular' and in so doing has helped a new generation of scholars move beyond a secular-versus-sacred binary towards a more incorporative model.[15] Are the recent foreign policy initiatives on religion an expression of this more integrated understanding? Further to this, do states now engage religion as partners in policy making, and what interests set the agenda for doing so?

In a seminal article on the place of religion in international policy,[16] Elizabeth Shakman Hurd offers a detailed critique of the current international 'drive to operationalise religion',[17] arguing that such initiatives remain predicated on a binarian approach. According to Hurd, state actors adopt a split view of religion itself, releasing the resources of what *states themselves* consider to be 'peaceful religion' as a counter to the destabilising influence of what *they* determine to be 'dangerous religion'.[18] In an ISIS-age of religious extremism, where so-called 'moderate' religion is being enlisted to counter the extremist threat, the logic of such a policy framework indeed seems compelling.

However, Hurd convincingly argues that this 'two faces of faith' approach[19] actually limits the full potential of religious engagement in international policy because it still 'relies on an institutional "secular versus religious" landscape'.[20] In other words, the construction of religion by states to fulfil 'special' state interests remains the dominant characteristic of foreign policy. Thus, what looks like a new policy engagement with religious actors and interests is actually the containment of religion via traditional state agendas.

Towards an Alternative Policy Framework

Hurd then takes us beyond the binary by arguing that, irrespective of latter-day realisations about the utility of religion in international affairs, religion has always 'assumed different forms and occupied different spaces under modern regimes of governance'.[21] Such a view echoes Talal Asad's cogent insight that traditions of faith have 'always [been] involved in the world of power'.[22] How might this view impact the making of foreign policy? In the first instance, it would require new policy models that were less concerned with the special inclusion of religion in policy thinking and more focused on *the nuances of religion that regularly inhabit policy spaces*. Such a refocus is reflected in Peter Mandaville's astute comment on the Department of State religion initiative:

> the single greatest contribution such an office could make is to help foreign affairs officers and diplomats across all regional and functional bureaus understand that engagement with religion and religious actors needs to become a routine and standard part of the diplomatic toolkit.[23]

This is important because reframing religion as a regular feature of foreign policy activity offers state policy makers more strategic options for engaging religious actors and interests in any given context. Yet how can the complexities of religion be incorporated into a strategic framework regularly applied by foreign policy makers who, for the most part, will not be religion specialists?[24] We now begin to sketch a new framework that potentially recognises more of the nuances of religion while respecting the logics that policy makers still operate within.

The Four Religions of Foreign Policy

States must strategise. Accordingly, state actors would profit from regular attempts to understand the nuanced ways religion features in the power arrangements of countries and regions where their strategic interests lie. That is to say, and in keeping with Mandaville's comment above, thinking about religion should be a regular habit of mind for foreign policy makers. This is most effectively done via a stable set of categories that can be consistently applied to multiple contexts.

While the peace/danger framework is easy to understand and implement, it arguably misrepresents how religious actors and interests operate on the ground. As an alternative approach, the four categories introduced below constitute a new diagnostic grid designed to assist policy makers better understand these complexities in their foreign policy deliberations. The first two categories repurpose concepts originally applied in the foundational work of Jose Casanova.[25] All four categories are constantly interacting at the global level and are thus more precisely described as 'dynamics'.

a. The dynamic of collision – when secular and religious spheres are formally separated in the building of a modern political order. The dynamic of collision has its roots in the Westphalian notion of the separation of church and state.[26] Religion becomes subordinate to, and contained by, state sovereignty in the formation of a secular society in the service of civic life.

b. The dynamic of collusion (combination) – when secular and religious resources combine in the creation of a political culture. In contrast to the European experience of collision and partition, in the United States the resources of religion and state each contribute to the creation of a durable Enlightenment secularism.[27] Religion becomes an expression of citizen freedom and a form of social capital for nation and community building.

c. The dynamic of coercion – when religious actors are targeted and expelled from the public sphere by the threat and practice of state violence. This dynamic has its modern roots in communist and developing world contexts where muscular secularism repressed religion as an imperative for rapid modernisation. Contrasting the political cultures of Western Europe and North America, in contexts of coercion secularism is carried via political autocracy and military control. Religion can be used by these regimes, but more significantly, becomes a resource for grassroots identity and resistance against secularist oppression.[28]

d. The dynamic of co-option – when political culture is established upon the concepts, institutions and laws of a single religious tradition. The dynamic of co-option can be seen as the corollary to coercion, though arguably more representative and therefore less predicated on the necessity for political violence. Numerous states, notably in the Islamic world, utilise strong majority religious traditions in the development of national and cultural unity, producing a variety of political cultures from absolute monarchy (Saudi

Arabia) to clerical oligarchy (Iran) and democracy (Indonesia).[29]

I suggest that the dynamics described above have the potential to be used as 'policy optics' by foreign policy makers trying to understand the political culture of states and regions where their foreign policy interests are located. Single categories are not intended to describe an entire context, as most will feature at least two—and likely more—dynamics of religion at play in the same geopolitical space. Moreover, changes in political circumstance will likely re-order the characterisation of religion from a political perspective. The 'four religions' framework thus provides analysts with an efficient mechanism for understanding how these issues might be important in the policy-making process without examining religion under the constraints of a false binary. I shall attempt to illustrate this via a very brief consideration of religious dynamics in the recent political upheavals in Egypt.

The Example of Egypt (2011–2014)

Situating the influence of religion in the politics of Egypt is as important as it is difficult. What follows is an introductory application of the 'four religions' framework as a means to assist foreign policy makers better understand the role of religion in the Egyptian context.

Egypt is the most populace nation in the Middle East and North Africa (est. 86 million), over 90 per cent of whom are Muslim (the vast majority Sunni).[30] A minority Christian community (mainly Coptic) has also played a significant role in Egyptian political and economic life.[31] Egypt has been pivotal in the formation of modern political identity across the MENA region. Aspects of such influence began, according to Asad, via the importation of European legal codes in the nineteenth century.[32] It is contested, however, whether this represented an imperial effect or was built upon a more complex interaction with existing religious law and tradition.[33] In the post-war period, Gamal Abdul Nasser's efforts to modernise Egypt and unite the region under the banner of Arab nationalism had an equally complex connection to religion as both a marginalised element of culture and a vital force of political identity.[34] Once a regional leader in post-colonial politics of the 1950s and 1960s, Egypt again became the central theatre of political change via the democratic revolutions of 2011, with religious actors and interests playing a major role in the unfolding drama. What religious dynamics have characterised the Egyptian political landscape over time, and how do they influence our thinking at the level of foreign policy?

Coercion and Co-option: Religion under Autocracy (1954–2011)

Prior to 2011, religion and politics in Egypt was shaped by a complex interplay of *coercion* (the autocratic control of religious actors by the state) and *co-option* (the use of religious tradition in governance and law). The targets of coercion were the Muslim Brotherhood, who sought political reform and resistance to colonial influence based on the introduction of Islamic laws and traditions, and an overlapping network of militant groups seeking political and cultural change via more extremist violence.[35] While Egypt's three military rulers—Nasser (1954–1970), Sadat (1970–1981) and Mubarak (1981–2011)—actively opposed the militant threat, they also had varying regard for the Brotherhood. Sadat, for example, helped to revive the Brotherhood after it was driven underground by Nasser, as a way to counter the interests of the Soviet-inspired Egyptian left.[36] Mubarak by contrast, ruling in an emerging post-Cold War world order, feared the grassroots legitimacy that the Brotherhood had achieved among Egyptians as both a social development and political entity.[37] In Mubarak's view, movement towards democracy would seek to further empower the Brotherhood.[38]

Egyptian politics was also shaped by the central *co-option* of religion within the structures and protocols of government. For instance, Article 2 of the 1971 Constitution declared Islam as the state religion and Islamic jurisprudence the principal source of legislation.[39] (This remains essentially unchanged in the 2012 Constitution.) Yet the central legal embrace of Islam coincided with the regulation of Islamic associations. For example, writing in 2008, Jonathan Fox notes: 'All mosques require licenses and the government appoints and pays the salaries of their prayer leaders. The government recently began to bring under its control unofficial mosques located in residential buildings. Religious political parties are illegal. The Muslim Brotherhood, a fundamentalist Islamic organization, is banned.'[40] Thus, while *co-option* is an embedded characteristic of Egyptian politics in this period, the overarching dynamic is that of autocratic *coercion* exercised against the freedom of religious association.[41]

Collusion: Religion in Revolution (2011)

Revolutions that swept the MENA region, beginning in Tunisia in 2010, were embodied in Egypt by a broad-based religious and secular coalition that *colluded* and *combined* its energies to form a movement for change that helped remove the Mubarak regime from power in early 2011. A dynamic of *collusion*—whereby the resources of religion and state contribute to the creation of a durable politics—can be seen in the 'al-Azhar document' of June 2011, named after Egypt's pre-eminent mosque and university. According to

Nathan Brown, the document was negotiated by 'leading religious scholars and prominent intellectuals' who were able to agree to 'a set of lofty principles, generally interpreting Islamic teachings in a manner very consistent with liberal values and democratic practice'.[42] Thus, the al-Azhar document 'represents not only a laudable search for common ground but also a measure of a political bargain'[43] where some sort of postsecular democratic accommodation could be achieved. Yet at the more illiberal end of the spectrum, Brown also notes that 'talk of "collusion" and a "bargain" between the Brotherhood and Egypt's military rulers soon passed from the realm of rumour and allegation to accepted fact without any serious evidence'.[44] What was more certain was that the Brotherhood's wide social operations stood it in good stead to contend as the major force in democratic elections. In a closely fought multi-round campaign, Mohammed Morsi of the Brotherhood became Egypt's elected president (2012), potentially beginning a period where the majority religious identity would *combine* more explicitly with secular standards in the democratic governance of the nation. This was not to be.

[Co-option] and Coercion: Fear and the Return of Autocracy

What dramatically entered Egyptian politics was not a new dynamic of religion so much as the fear of one. As with many incoming national administrations, Michael Wahid Hanna reports that 'the Brotherhood-led government floundered and squandered much of its goodwill', overreaching with 'a single-minded focus on factional gain and power all but ignoring the crushing economic burdens that Egyptian society was forced to bear every day'.[45] This context, together with the miscalculation by Morsi of granting himself sweeping powers to overcome parliamentary gridlock, made secular democrats and the military establishment fear that a Brotherhood-led Egypt would be *co-opted* by an autocratic style of Islamism, even though alternative political outcomes were possible. How the Brotherhood would have managed its newfound democratic legitimacy over time will never be known. As a consequence of the fear of Islamist co-option—represented here as [co-option]—the Morsi administration was overthrown in 2013 via a military coup, subjecting the religious politics of the nation to the rule of *coercion* once more—where religious actors are targeted and expelled from the public sphere by the threat and practice of state violence—under the new presidency of former general President Abdel Fattah al-Sisi. Indeed, in a salient commentary on the evolution of coercive power in Egypt's 'crystallizing dictatorship', Dalia Fahmy can write of a deepening crisis characterised by 'the closing of political space, the elimination of public dissent, and the removal of the trappings of democracy'.[46]

In sum, applying the four religions of foreign policy to the Egyptian context, policy makers can deduce a shift from the dynamic of coercion (as military control), to collusion (as revolution and renewal), to the fear of co-option (the rationale for *coup d'état*), and the return of coercion (as autocracy). The absence of collision (producing a civic religion in service to a democratic secular state) is understood given the religio-demographics of the people, and certainly not to be confused with coercion, which is characterised by a lack of representation in favour of a reliance on force.

Conclusion

Whatever points of debate exist regarding the Egyptian situation, applying the 'four dynamics' approach arguably holds more potential and offers more insight for foreign policy makers to engage religion in this complex political space than the peace/danger model currently in vogue as a policy perspective. Indeed, it is arguable that a peace/danger logic is partly responsible for returning Egypt to quasi-military control, resisting as it does modes of accommodation between religion and politics that existed in the hard fought hopes of the 2011 revolution.

Beyond the example of Egypt, once the dynamics of religion have been deduced in any given policy context, the work of foreign policy would then be to situate the dynamics of religion within a state's own strategic priorities. In this way, the present chapter has begun to sketch a way that foreign policy makers can first understand the landscape of power where religion readily resides before deciding how to prioritise religious interests in the foreign policy process.

Notes

[1] For example, on the dynamics of the Cold War - a period assumed to have had little religious influence - see Muehlenbeck, P., ed. (2012) *Religion and the Cold War: A Global Perspective*, Nashville: Vanderbilt University Press, and Kirby, D., ed. (2003) *Religion and the Cold War*, Hampshire: Palgrave MacMillan.

[2] Periods of US foreign policy may have been the exception, notably under Eisenhower who saw a religious foundation to the ideological conflicts with the Soviet Union. See Herzog, J.P. (2011) *The Spiritual-Industrial Complex: America's Religious Battle against Communism in the Early Cold War*, Oxford & New York: Oxford University Press. Though Third-Worldism drew at times from deep religio-cultural wells, the common drivers were politico-economic. See Berger, M. (2004) 'After the Third World? History, destiny and the fate of Third Worldism', *Third World Quarterly*, 25(1): 9-39. Religion, never completely dismissed in the Soviet Union, was a tool used at times by the Communist elite for domestic and international purposes. e.g. see Kenez, P. (2006) *The History of the Soviet Union from Beginning to End. New York*, Cambridge University Press, pp.152-154.

3. E.g. see 'Special Issue: The Religious as Political and the Political as Religious: the blurring of sacred and secular in contemporary International Relations', *Politics, Religion and Ideology*, 15(3), 2014; and 'Special Issue: The Postsecular in International Relations', *Review of International Studies*, 38(5), 2012.

4. Haynes, J. (2012) *Religious Transnational Actors and Soft Power*, Surrey: Ashgate; Johnston, D., ed. (2003) *Faith-Based Diplomacy: Trumping Realpolitik*, Oxford & New York: Oxford University Press.

5. Thomas, S.M. (2000) 'Taking religious and cultural pluralism seriously: the global resurgence of religion and the transformation of international society', *Millennium: Journal of International Studies*, 29(3): 815-841

6. Belshaw, D., Calderisi, R., Sugden, C., eds. (2001) *Faith in Development: partnership between the World Bank and the Churches of Africa* (Oxford: Regnum); Marshall, K. & Keough, L. (2004) *Mind, Heart and Soul in the Fight Against Poverty*, Washington, D.C.: The World Bank; Clarke, M., ed. (2013) *Handbook of Research on Development and Religion*, Cheltenham, UK: Edward Elgar.

7. Huntington, S.P. (1996) *The Clash of Civilizations and the Remaking of World Order*, New York: Simon and Schuster.

8. Johnston, A. (1995) 'Thinking About Strategic Culture', *International Security*, 19(4): 32-64; Booth, K. & Trood, R. (1999) Strategic Cultures in the Asia-Pacific. Auckland: Macmillan.

9. Esposito, J.L. & Voll, J.O. (1996) *Islam and Democracy*, Oxford: Oxford University Press; Nasr, V. (2006) *The Shia Revival: how conflicts within Islam will shape the future*, New York & London: W.W. Norton; Cesari, J. (2014) *The Awakening of Muslim Democracy: religion, modernity and the state*, Cambridge: Cambridge University Press.

10. Smith, A.D. (2000) 'The "sacred" dimension of nationalism', *Millennium*, 29(3): 791-814.

11. US Department of State, "US Strategy on Religious Leader and Faith Community Engagement" http://www.state.gov/s/fbci/strategy/ (accessed 14/8/2014)

12. Eg: Canadian International Council, 'Religion and Foreign Policy', http://opencanada.org/indepth/religion-and-foreign-policy/ (accessed 18/8/2014). For media commentary on the EU guidelines regarding religious freedom see The Economist, 'The EU and Faith: A religious policy by stealth', www.economist.com/blogs/erasmus/2013/07/eu-and-faith (accessed 26/8/2014)

13. E.g. 'At Vatican, Shimon Peres Proposes "United Nations of Religions"', The Algemeiner, 4 September, 2014 http://www.algemeiner.com/2014/09/04/at-vatican-shimon-peres-proposes- per centE2 per cent80 per cent98united-nations-of-religions per centE2 per cent80 per cent99/ (accessed 10 September, 2014). On religious international organisations and world politics see Marshall, K. (2012) *Global Institutions of Religion*, London and New York: Routledge.

14. For a discussion on the US Department of State initiative see The Immanent Frame, 'Off the Cuff: Engaging religion at the Department of State', 30 July, 2013 http://blogs.ssrc.org/tif/2013/07/30/engaging-religion-at-the-department-of-state/ (accessed (14/8/2014)

15. Marty, M.E. (2003) 'Our Religio-Secular World', *Daedalus* 132(3): 42-48

16. E. Shakman Hurd, 'International Politics after Secularism', *Review of International Studies*, 38:5 (2012), pp. 943–961

17. Hurd, p.945

18. Hurd, p.947.

19. The phrase can be linked to Toy Blair and the work of the tony Blair Faith

Foundation. See Tony Blair, 'Taking Faith Seriously', New Europe Online (2 January 2012) http://www.neurope.eu/blog/taking-faith-seriously.

20. Hurd, p.953

21. Hurd, p.953

22. 'If the secularisation thesis seems increasingly implausible to some of us this is not simply because religion is now playing a more vibrant part in the modern world of nations. In a sense, what many would anachronistically call "religion" was always involved in the world of power.' Asad, T. (2003) Formations of the Secular: Christianity, Islam, Modernity. Stanford, CA: Stanford University Press. p.200. Italics original.

23. The Immanent Frame, 'Off the Cuff: Engaging religion at the Department of State', 30 July, 2013 http://blogs.ssrc.org/tif/2013/07/30/engaging-religion-at-the-department-of-state/ (accessed (14/8/2014)

24. Consultation with religious stakeholders is understood to be equally important. The present concern is the regular 'habits of mind' undertaken by policy makers alongside the consultation process.

25. Casanova, J. (2006) 'Rethinking Secularisation', The Hedgehog Review, 8(1-2): 7-22

26. 'As a result of this protracted clash, the Enlightenment critique of religion found here ample resonance; the secularist genealogy of modernity was constructed as a triumphant emancipation of reason, freedom, and worldly pursuits from the constraints of religion; and practically every "progressive" European social movement from the time of the French Revolution to the present was informed by secularism.' Casanova, p.11

27. '...the triumph of 'the secular' came aided by religion rather than at its expense, and the boundaries themselves became so diffused that, at least by European ecclesiastical standards, it is not clear where the secular ends and religion begins. Casanova, p.12

28. Perhaps most prominent in a European context is Catholic resistance to Soviet control in Poland in the 1980s. See Thomas, S.M. (2005) The Global Resurgence of Religion and the Transformation of International Relations. New York: Palgrave MacMillan. pp. 3-7. Beyond Europe coercion can be seen in varied contexts in recent political history including Buddhist resistance to the junta in Burma, the challenge of the Falun Dafa movement to displays of religion in the public domain in China, and Islamist democracy movements opposing military dictatorship in the Maghreb prior to the 2011 revolutions. On the latter see Tamimi, A.S. (2001) Rachid Ghannouchi: A Democrat with Islamism. New York: Oxford University Press, pp.105-124.

29. See Rahnema, S & Moghissi, H, (2001) 'Clerical Oligarchy and the Question of "Democracy" in Iran', Iran Chamber Society. Found at: www.iranchamber.com/government/articles/clerical_oligarchy_democracy_iran.php. (accessed May 4, 2013); Gu, Man-Li & Bomhoff, Eduard J. (2012) 'Religion and Support for Democracy: A Comparative Study for Catholic and Muslim Countries', Politics and Religion, 5(2): 280-316; Volpi, F. (2004) 'Pseudo-Democracy in the Muslim World', Third World Quarterly 25 (6): 1061-1078

30. Pew Forum on Religion and Public Life, Mapping the Global Muslim Population, Washington DC: Pew Research Centre, October 2009, pp.16-17

31. Palmer, M. (2007) The Politics of the Modern Middle East. Belmont, CA: Wadsworth Cengage, p.74. The small indigenous Jewish community was largely expelled in 1956.

32. Asad, pp.252-253

33. See Asad, pp.205-256

34. E.g. 'Nominally secular-patriotic in outlook and socialist by creed, Arab nationalism

was the secularisation of Sunni political identity in the Arab world.' Nasr, p.92

35. Palmer, pp.78-79

36. Palmer, p.55. The Brotherhood had tried to assassinate Nasser in 1954. The aftermath of this event led to the diversification of Islamist resistance against the state into reformist and militant schools.

37. al-Awadi, H. (2009) 'A struggle for legitimacy: the Muslim Brotherhood and Mubarak, 1982–2009', Contemporary Arab Affairs 2(2): 214–228

38. Palmer, p.58

39. Fox, J. (2008) A World Survey of Religion and the State (New York: Cambridge University Press) p.237

40. Fox, p.237

41. Importantly, this control was also exercised for the protection by the state of religious minorities such as Coptic Christians.

42. Brown, N.J. (2012) 'Contention in Religion and State in Postrevolutionary Egypt', Social Research, 79(2):540

43. Brown, p.541

44. Brown, p.544

45. Hanna, M.W. (2014) 'God and State in Egypt', World Policy Journal, 31(2):68

46. D. Fahmy, 'This is Not Mubarak-lite: The New Face of Authoritarianism', The Immanent Frame, 19 May 2014. http://blogs.ssrc.org/tif/2014/05/19/this-is-not-mubarak-lite-the-new-face-of-authoritarianism (accessed 20 May 2014).

5

Looking Back to See Forward: Romanticism, Religion and the Secular in Modernity

MARK S. CLADIS
BROWN UNIVERSITY, USA

Introduction: Lessons from the Romantics

Santayana famously warned, 'Those who cannot remember the past are condemned to repeat it.' What of those who cannot learn from the past failures of theories of secularisation? In this article, I urge that we learn from the past, note the limits of past theories of secularisation as applied to Romanticism, and suggest some helpful way to rethink religion and the secular in the twenty-first century.

As a scholar in the academic study of religion, I often investigate the largely unexamined religious backgrounds, perspectives and practices of what are otherwise considered secular thinkers, discourse and institutions. My current research focuses on the central democratic, religious and environmental perspectives and practices that informed one another in eighteen and nineteenth-century British Romantic literature and its subsequent and sustained legacies in America. This investigation employs a triscopic approach: a methodology that involves careful attention to the three-way intersection of democracy, religion and the environment. In most accounts of British Romanticism, the religious aspects of Romanticism (Protestant and Catholic, orthodox and heterodox, deistic and panentheistic) are neglected, or, if included, are narrativised as belonging to a process of secularisation. Romantic portrayals of religion are either belittled or privatised. While it is expedient to claim that British Romanticists eschewed religion in lieu of secularised thought, it is more accurate to say that they often dissociated religion—here understood as normative beliefs, practices and perspectives about the divine—from strictly denominational church dogmatics and politics, and engaged religion, broadly understood, in the service of progressive social and environmental aims—both national and global. By applying an interpretive lens that acknowledges the religious traditions that in fact permeated British Romanticism, we gain insight into not only its dynamic religious dimensions but also its political, economic and environmental dimensions.

Although scholars, highly influenced by secularisation theories, routinely assumed that religion was waning during the height of British Romanticism (roughly 1800–1860), it turns out that participation in religious institutions was actually increasing during this time. More importantly, close readings of the salient texts of many if not most of the Romantic authors manifest powerful religious images and themes. Only an opaque lens, such as a prior interpretive commitment to secularisation and its worldview, would obscure sight of such palpable religiosity. This is not to claim, of course, that all Romantic texts look alike or have the same commitment to or notion of religion. It is to claim, however, that our theories of secularisation have often prevented more nuanced readings. Not only did scholars neglect the (often radically progressive) religious beliefs and commitments that were evident in many texts; they also failed to note how Romantic literary production was itself understood as a religious *practice*. Wordsworth's *Prelude*, for example, or Coleridge's 'Religious Musings' were understood as a form of religious (and political) practice that shaped author and reader alike. The early compositions of Wordsworth and Coleridge were religiously, politically and environmentally progressive, and the three—the religious, the political and the ecological—augmented and supported each other.

Religion, then, contributed importantly to both the content and the expression of many Romantic *public* visions. Many Romantic authors identified with dissenting, Christian traditions that put them at odds with the religious and political establishment of the day. The expression of their radical religious views was understood as political stances and practices and hence they were frequently deemed enemies of the state and suffered accordingly. Theologically, they tended to advance a theology that was part panentheistic, part Christian orthodoxy. Spirit, it was commonly held, is infused throughout nature, and to such an extent that it becomes practically impossible to know where 'spirit' ends and nature begins. And social protest, as I have said, was understood as a religious practice. The poetic, religious task of many Romantic authors was to offer vivid, detailed descriptions of the horrors of war, poverty and various unjust social policies, thereby inspiring the appropriate human emotions and sympathy in otherwise prejudicial hearts.

Secularism in Modernity

'Religion', as a category, was certainly being transformed during the Romantic era, as was the concept of 'the secular' and the active, democratic 'citizen'. Religion, politics and the secular were not (and are not) stagnant terms. This article is not the place to give a detailed account of such changes during the Romantic era, but I hope that I have said enough about religion and Romanticism to show that our past theories of secularisation have not served us well and that our current discussions of religion and the secular in modernity could benefit from more nuanced accounts of each of the key terms, religion and the secular. In the remainder of this chapter, then, I wish to reflect broadly on these key terms, especially on 'the secular'. For the sake of expedience and candour, I will identify what I consider to be the good, the bad and the ugly notions of 'the secular'. The context for my reflections is my own political and cultural home, namely, that of the US: a deeply and diversely religious society that struggles with how to navigate differences, religious, political and otherwise. I believe that my reflections, however contextualised, can be usefully extrapolated to other, similar cultural, political contexts.

Secularism: Good Sense

Secularism in the good sense is characterised by three ideal features: 1) when participating in the public and political realms, citizens do not normally assume that others necessarily share their religious perspectives or perspectives on religion; 2) citizens do not treat religious perspectives in public debate as a special case subject to special exclusion or special privilege; and 3) government neither officially sponsors nor hinders religion, upholding the First Amendment. The first two features of secularism (in the good sense) pertain to constraints on citizens, and the third on government.

The first constraint on citizens amounts to an acknowledgment that we live in a pluralistic society and that we therefore should not assume that everyone shares our perspectives, whether, for example, those perspectives be religious or anti-religious.[1] The second constraint acknowledges that fellow citizens are free to bring to democratic deliberation whatever perspectives they deem appropriate, provided that they do so in such a way so as to honour the first constraint. A premise here is that all voices are to be heard and none are initially to be treated as special, subject to exclusion or privilege. I add the qualifier, initially, to indicate that over time a particularly insightful voice can gain authority and hence in some sense be deemed 'special'—that is, especially knowledgeable and helpful. Conversely, a consistently unreasonable or foolish voice can eventually be deemed poorly informed or worse. Religious perspectives, then, are treated just like any other more or less comprehensive views—such as those of Marxism, pragmatism, secular humanism or hedonism.

When a perspective (religious or otherwise) is offered in public debate, citizens speak and listen—or write and read—in a distinct manner that acknowledges the constraints of secularism. This distinctive manner entails, among other things, the principle of non-privileging and the principle of focused attention. The first principle pertains primarily to the speaker, the second to the listener.

The speaker, understanding that no assumptions can be made about the comprehensive views of her fellow citizens, will not privilege her speech—that is to say, will not expect all to deem it self-evidently true and without need of justification. Rather, she will attempt to offer arguments and reasons in such a way that will garner some support from or will appeal to a diverse audience. Due to no fault of her own or her audience, she may not be successful. Persuasion, even when advancing good ideas, is not guaranteed because 'public reason' or an overlapping consensus does not always favour every good perspective or idea.

Secularism in the good sense, then, admits but does not privilege religious perspectives or reasons into democratic deliberation. In practice, this principle of non-privileging often amounts to a constraint on the interlocutor offering the religious reason or perspective. The *principle of focused attention*, in contrast, applies primarily to the listeners. When religious reasons are offered in democratic debate, listeners ought to focus on the particular issue at hand and avoid introducing negative global judgments on religion in general or on a particular religion associated with the offered religious reason. This recommendation to avoid negative global judgments is not a form of religious apologetics. Such global judgments are rarely productive or satisfying. To disparage or to dismiss out of hand an entire tradition such as Hinduism or Christianity (or Marxism or pragmatism, for that matter) entails caricatures or at the very least essentialising. The principle of focused attention does not, of course, require that one accepts as compelling any offered religious reasons or the religious traditions to which the reasons may be connected. It simply requires that, whenever possible, the focus of the conversation or debate remain on the specific issues at hand. This principle of focused attention safeguards against dismissing or deriding an interlocutor simply on the basis of his or her religious identity.

Both principles are supported by and belong to a larger set of skills and virtues associated with excellence in the practice of democratic, public engagement. Such virtues include but are not limited to attentiveness, discretion, humility and sensitivity to audience, as well as courage, honesty and judgment.[2] Religious perspectives in public debate do not uniquely or especially call for the need of public engagement virtues. These skills and virtues would dissuade throwing dogmatically one's beliefs into the faces of others. But here the vice and the corresponding virtue do not necessarily run along religious versus nonreligious lines. A non-religious Marxist, feminist or environmentalist may be as likely to fail to exhibit the appropriate virtues as, say, a Christian or a Buddhist.

Secularism seeks to uphold both the Establishment Clause and the Free Exercise Clause of the First Amendment: to prohibit government from officially funding or otherwise sponsoring religion and to guarantee the free exercise of religion. This commitment to the First Amendment is the third ideal feature of secularism in the good sense. Secularism seeks to protect citizens from all manner of theocracy (the imposition of religion) as well as to safeguard citizens' liberty of conscience (including the free exercise of religion or atheism). The First Amendment is a legal expression of a central cultural aspiration of secularism, namely, that each citizen be treated with dignity and respect regardless of their religious perspectives and perspectives on religion. To treat a fellow citizen with dignity and respect does not require agreement with a citizen's views, but it does require that one assumes (at least initially) that the citizen, whether religious or non-religious, is reasonable and deserves a 'hearing'. The First Amendment, then, grants rights with respect to religion (the prohibition of religious coercion and protection of religious expression); and secularism, in turn, envisions and aspires to cultural practices that are informed by and that support the First Amendment.

Secularism: Bad Sense

Secularism in the bad sense is characterised by three positions: it holds that 1) religion is a discrete, sui generis phenomenon; 2) religion is not self-critical or open to critique and exchange (because, it is held, religion is radically subjective or based on dogmatic authority or both); and therefore 3) religious citizens can and should accept the privatisation of religion, that is, they should keep their religion out of politics. These three positions presuppose a narrow, parochial view of religion that is unconvincing in the face of actual, lived religion. Generally speaking, religion is a culturally complex, historical institution that cannot be separated easily or radically from other institutions, whether they be moral, aesthetic, economic or political. Generally, religions are dynamic and change in response to and in dialogue with individuals, communities, events and developments both within and outside a given religious tradition. Generally, religion is a pervasive aspect of a person's identity, an aspect that both informs and is informed by other aspects of one's identity, including one's various beliefs, ideals, authorities, attitudes and practices—all of which are embedded in and respond to local, national and global sociohistorical and physical circumstances.

The good and useful ways that religion can be generalised, then, undermine the narrow, parochial way that religion is understood by secularism in the bad sense. The social history of the narrow, parochial view is complex. One explanatory narrative points to various eighteenth and nineteenth-century German, French, and British Enlightenment and Romantic thinkers who (supposedly) promoted the view that religion is ultimately inward, subjective, and private. Another explanatory narrative argues that the narrow, parochial way of conceiving religion was (supposedly) strategically forged at a time when it was tactical for European nations to conceive of religion as a discrete, private arena separate from the state and from science. Jointly, these explanatory narratives suggest that in modernity it was convenient for many European constituencies to establish a pact of nonaggression between 'religion' and 'the secular'—the new emerging privatised view of religion would not interfere with politics and science, and the new emerging laicised view of the secular would not interfere with religion.

Insofar as these accounts are correct, secularism in the bad sense fails to be self-reflective and investigate the ways in which it operates with (and helped to create) a concept of religion that has little traction with actual lived religion. This is bad enough. But secularism in the bad sense becomes all the worse when governments attempt to enforce the narrow, parochial view of religion. It can be plausibly argued that US foreign policy sponsors good religion abroad, namely, religion that has been suitably reformed—that is, privatised.[3] Secularism in the bad sense, then, has fashioned a notion of religion that has little relation to how most religion is lived, and now governments such as the US are attempting to impose and normalise this fanciful view of religion.

Secularism: Ugly Sense

It is one thing to attempt to privatise religion for the sake of a pact of non-aggression; some among the religious themselves have contributed to the pact. It is another thing to promote aggressively the view that religion is a destructive, superstitious relic of the past that has no place in modernity. In this view, secularism is the modern age of humans enlightened and freed from the shackles of religion. Secularism is the essence of modernity and religion is the antithesis of all that is modern. This is the ugly sense of secularism.

Its origins may be innocent enough, but its continuing effects are menacing. Theories of secularisation supported the view that religion was increasingly an anomaly in modernity and was hence retrograde; proponents of secularisation wished to protect progress and save the world from backsliding into an inferior, religious state. The declension theories, however, turned out to be largely wrong, and yet the hope for secularisation persisted among many. Secularists of this sort continue to maintain that religion is the antithesis of modernity and enlightened humanity. They would like to keep religion not only out of politics but off the planet as well. And if you object to their view, you yourself risk being branded as a sympathiser with the unenlightened barbarians. In the meantime, the world's abundant and diverse religious populations are doing the things that everyone else in modernity is doing—building skyscrapers, farming, investing in the market, designing computers, raising children, writing books, cooking, and teaching in universities. Their very presence in the world poses a mystery to these secularists. For, given the unmitigated evil that (in their view) accompanies religion, how can religion persist in modernity? Even if Marx, Freud, Tylor and Durkheim provided suitable explanations for the *origin* of religion, there appears to be no accounting for its *persistence*. Perhaps cognitive science will do better. Meanwhile, the religious populations are stigmatised—implicitly or explicitly—by these secularists, and religious resentment is growing all around us.

Religion, the Secular and Modernity

My hope is that having identified secularism in the good, bad, and ugly senses, we can approach more judiciously issues pertaining to religion, politics and the secular in the twenty-first century. At the heart of my *normative view* of secularism in the good sense is a commitment to honour diversity in our public and political life and a reasonable hope that from such diversity comes promising outcomes. This commitment and hope evinces J. S. Mill's conviction that 'only through diversity of opinion is there, in the existing state of human intellect, a chance of fair play to all sides of the truth'.[4]

In addition to this normative conclusion, I also hope that my reflections have suggested that we revise our *empirical narratives* of the birth of modernity. At the beginning of modernity we see not the absence of religion but its abundance—and an abundance of modern developments for how to accommodate it, even while those very developments were often being informed by religion. This should tell us something of significance about ourselves and about contemporary struggles to achieve democratic societies. Modernity—for all its multiplicity—has for the most part engaged with, wrestled with and been informed by religion, in one form or another. My initial comments on religion and Romanticism were intended to illustrate this point. The pervasive religious aspects of Romanticism demonstrate the failure of previous theories of secularisation. Modernity has never been a monolithic intellectual, cultural force antithetical to religious belief and practice. Religion informed a central chapter of modernity, namely the Romantic era, and to this day religion continues to shape the identity of individuals in their public and their private lives. It is, then, not much of a stretch to claim that religion continues to shape modernity. Our theories of the secular and our democratic institutions need to acknowledge this pervasive religious presence.

Notes

1. On this feature of secularism, see Jeffrey Stout, *Democracy and Tradition* (Princeton: Princeton University Press, 2004), pp. 93 and 98.
2. For an excellent discussion on democratic virtues—'practical wisdom and tact'— in public engagement, see Stout, *Democracy and Tradition*, pp. 85-86.
3. For a convincing version of this argument, see Saba Mahmood's 'Religious Reasons and Secular Affect: An Incommensurable Divide?' *Is Critique Secular? Blasphemy, Injury, and Free Speech* (Berkeley: University of California Press, 2009), pp 64-100.
4. J. S. Mill, *'On Liberty' and Other Writings*, ed. Stefan Collini (Cambridge: Cambridge University Press, 1989), p. 49.

6

The Contemporary Ambiguities of Religions as a Source of Civilisational Identity

FABIO PETITO

UNIVERSITY OF SUSSEX, UK

Against the prediction of the theorists of modernisation on the inescapable withering away of religion, it is back at the centre stage of international politics. Furthermore, this return appears to be antagonistic and does not seem to be for the (common) good. But how can we explain this visible resurgence of religion in world politics in the post-Cold War era? What can we say about the logic—if there is just one—by which religions interact, infuse or even 'sacralise' international politics today? These are questions of great topicality, especially in the light of how religion and politics have been recently interacting in both the Islamic and the Western world as well as in their precarious relationship. In this chapter, my starting point is that the resurgence of religion as a central factor in contemporary international relations is linked to the renewed visibility of the concept of civilisation in post-Cold War political discourses. More specifically, drawing on Johann P. Arnason's recent work—and in this regard Samuel Huntington's argument retains part of its validity—I want to argue that the resurgence of religions in world politics has to be read in the context of civilisations, defined in a fundamentally *culturalist* sense, reasserting themselves as *strategic frames of references*, not as direct protagonists, of international politics. This development also has to be read as part of a longer-term process of challenge to Western dominance that has intensified since the Second World War and which Hedley Bull called the 'cultural revolt against the West'.

But does such a 'civilisational' reading of politicised religions necessarily reinforce the influence of the 'culture talk' approach, with its essentialised and polarised tendencies? Or can this interpretation actually help to problematise the predominant reading of religion in IR as the ultimate threat to international order and stability (especially, in the forms of the identity politics of the 'new wars', the terrorist attacks of religious fundamentalists or the 'Clash of Civilizations' thesis)? What does such a civilisational reading tells us about the status of the relationship between religion and politics both in the Islamic and the Western world as well as in their precarious relationship?

The Post-Cold War World and the Global Resurgence of Religion

For the predominant academic and public discourse following the end of the Cold War, the return of religion in international politics has primarily come in the form of a militant and violent-prone form of politics, almost as a God-sent plague or punishment on the earth, or 'the revenge of God', as the title of one of the first books that focussed on this resurgence seemed to evoke (G. Kepel). The examples are many: the conflicts in Bosnia, Algeria, Kashmir, Palestine, Sudan; but also the rise of worldwide Islamism and Hindu Nationalism or the growing role of the Christian Right on America foreign policy or of Orthodoxy on the Russian state; and of course, the events of 11 September came as a seal to unequivocally confirm such a worrying and destabilising trend. More generally, I think that there are three, possibly four, ways in which this resurgence of religion in international politics has been apprehended/read by the discipline of International Relations: 1) in the context of the so-called 'new wars' where political violence is often manifested within 'failed' states and driven by a politics of identity and irregular warfare designed along religious lines; 2) in the context of religious fundamentalism and international terrorism; 3) within the context and fears of a forthcoming 'Clash of Civilizations'; and possibly, 4) in the context of the growing attention to the role of religious domestic interests and agendas in the more assertive foreign policies of some states.[1]

Unfortunately, when the resurgence and relevance of religious identities in post-Cold War international relations has been acknowledged in one of the above-mentioned four modalities, it has been detected and interpreted within the framework of what Scott Thomas has called the 'Westphalian presumption', that is, the notion that religious (and cultural) pluralism cannot be accommodated in international society but must be privatised or overcome by a cosmopolitan ethics, if there is to be international order.[2] In other words, according to this view, politics with reference to religious identity comes to the fore only *qua* ultimate threat to order, security and civility, and its politicisation is always an inescapable threat to security, inimical to 'modernity' and to the resolution of conflicts—as, for example, the 'new wars' driven by the politics of identity and the terrorist attacks of religious fundamentalists would show.

Religion and IR: The Biases of the Predominant Understanding

This view, which is very strong in Western academia and political circles, is based on the assumption that politicised religion is always about political instability, a disordered state of international affairs, fundamentalist politics and terrorism. As a result, it overlooks the positive role politicised religion can play (in a qualified way) in the modernisation, democratisation and even peace-building in several countries of the so-called Western and non-Western world as well as in the construction of a new normative structure adequate for a more *pluralist* and multicultural future world order. There are two reasons which can explain this biased approach of the predominant political analysis: the first has to do with the way we have traditionally thought about international politics and its European experience and what, as I mentioned, could be called the 'Westphalian presumption'; the second has to do with the implicit bias of the social sciences against religion rooted in Enlightenment and Positivism self-understanding vis-à-vis religion.

This is why I have argued that the rejection of religion seems inscribed in the genetic code of the discipline of IR. Arguably, this is because the main constitutive elements of the practice of international relations were purposely established in early modern Europe to end the wars of religion. At that point in history—paraphrasing the powerful words of Thomas Hobbes—God made space for the great Leviathan (the sovereign state), that mortal god to which the *new modern man* owes his peace and security; religion was privatised, and through the principle of *'Cuius region, eius religio'* (the ruler determines the religion of his realm), pluralism among states and non-interference were born and worshipped as the new sacred principles of the emerging Westphalian order. As a consequence, politics with reference to religion becomes the ultimate threat to order, security and civility and must not inhabit the practice of international relations or, subsequently, the discipline of IR.

The second 'bias' lies, it seems to me, in International Relations' self-understanding as a party to the Enlightenment project, and in its self-conception as a social science that holds a privileged access to knowledge of social phenomena. First, and more broadly, it should not come as a major revelation that religion and the Enlightenment have not always been on 'very good terms' either theoretically or politically. Rather, the Enlightenment project envisages as its central mission the supersession of those traditional religious-based *worlds* into a universal, individually based and rationally justified *modern world*.[3] Second, and more specifically, we have to remember that modern international law, arguably the predecessor of the discipline of International Relations, was born under the auspices of Alberico Gentili's celebrated cry, *'Silete theologi in munere alieno!'*—let theologians keep silent about matters outside their province!—which symbolically marked the end of the scholastic world and the advent of a new epoch, the Westphalian era, in which international politics would be examined from a secular rather than a theological standpoint.

An Alternative Reading: Religions and Civilisations in a Post-Western World

This problematic and biased assumption/presumption precludes a different understanding of the resurgence of religions in world politics. I want to argue that if many philosophers and sociologists have interpreted this return as 'the end of modernity' or the 'de-secularisation of the world', what is more relevant from the perspective of politics and international relations is that in the post-Cold War era religion has become a critical source of civilisational identity in a context where civilisations, defined in a fundamentally *culturalist* sense, are reasserting themselves as *strategic frames of references*, not direct protagonists, of international politics.

This development is in a sense a typical post-Cold War fact to the extent that as Arnason has pointed out, 'civilizational claims and references now play a more important role in the global ideological context then they did when the rival universalisms of the Cold War era dominated the scene'.[4] It has, however, also been read as part of a longer-term process of challenge to Western dominance, intensifying since the Second World War, that Hedley Bull called the 'revolt against the West'. According to Bull, the revolt against Western dominance comprised five waves: first, what he calls the struggle for equal sovereignty; second, the anti-colonial revolution; third, the struggle for racial equality; fourth, the struggle for economic justice; finally, the struggle for what he calls the cultural liberation.[5] This last stage of the revolt against the West, which is also often referred to as the search for cultural authenticity of the non-Western world or the fight against its cultural neo-imperialism, had its most politically visible example in the Iranian Islamic revolution of 1979 and the worldwide emergence of political Islam, but it can also be seen in the new assertiveness of Asian countries in the name of so-called 'Asian values'.[6] It is my contention that we are in large part still living today within this process of cultural revolt, which has arguably intensified since the end of the Cold War implied the political necessity of a common (political, economic and social) liberal (Western) model for the whole planet.

Religion in this new context has become one of the major voices of resistance and provided the frame for a radical critique against the globalisation of a Western-centric and liberal order. To use the effective words of Regis Debray, 'religion turns out after all not to be the opium of the people, but the vitamin of the weak'[7] and becomes one of the key vectors of political resistance and struggle in the name of the social ethics of 'really existing communities' and of arguments which resonate in the everyday life of people. This process of the cultural revolt against the West is, it seems to me, relevant to understanding the new centrality of civilisational politics in the post-Cold War era—and in this regard Samuel Huntington's argument retains part of its validity.

Finally, in my view this development is made even more clear and pressing by the new centrality acquired by the issue of democracy and democratisation in the post-Cold War international agenda and in particular in the post-9/11 context. Contrary to what many supporters of democracy-promotion have been arguing, the spreading of democracy will not necessarily reduce the growing contestation of the Western-dominated nature of contemporary international society but might rather reinforce it: there seems to be growing evidence that the most recent successful cases of democratisation in the non-Western world are ones driven by the indigenisation and cultural re-interpretation of democracy.[8] This process, which, borrowing from a notion developed in Christian theology, I call 'democratic inculturation',[9] seems to be the most appropriate way to root democratic institutions and forms of political participation into stable and lasting regimes—and definitively more likely to succeed than an externally promoted (if not coercively imposed) strategy of liberal-democracy promotion. Such processes of 'democratic inculturation', which can be thought of as examples of the 'multiple modernities' paradigm, would arguably reveal even more clearly the political bias of contemporary international society by removing the criticism of the concrete impossibility of merging 'modern' political values and practices with 'traditional' cultures and ways of living.

Civilisational Politics in a Post-Secular World: An Epoch-Making Transformation of the International Society

In conclusion, our hypothesis is that the post-Cold War resurgence of religion in world politics is taking place through the reassertion of civilisation, defined in a fundamentally *culturalist* (and therefore religious) sense, as a strategic frame for world politics. What is at stake in this context is neither what the most theoretically appropriate definition of civilisation is nor how we can better develop a civilisational analytical framework; it is rather the recognition—which Huntington has wrongly transferred into the realm of the academic debate on the definition of civilisation—that the current political understanding of civilisations is significantly shaped by religious traditions. In other words, the predominant contemporary political understanding of civilisation has naturalised the still-important academic thesis that sees in 'religious cores the most constitutive elements of whole civilizations',[10] which is based on the insight that 'The moral and spiritual architecture of every civilisation is grounded, more than any other factor, in religious commitments that point to a source of normative meaning beyond the political, economic, and cultural structure themselves'.[11]

Civilisational politics is the way in which religion infuses or even 'sacralises' international politics today. Civilisational politics is neither new nor unchanging. However, the contemporary civilisational politics seems to have very clear culturalist/religious connotations, which were less relevant, for example, during the Cold War when civilisational politics was defined in a fundamentally ideological/political way. It is enough to think of the political transformation that the notion of the West has gone through, from the political community of the Free World which included, for example, Japan and Turkey, to the culturalist-religious notion of a Judeo-Christian legacy which in the post-1989 context makes it much more difficult to refer to Japan and Turkey as part of the West, even if the old strategic and security alliances still prevail.

Of course, other definitions of civilisations are possible and therefore different kinds of civilisational politics can be imagined: for example, we can think of civilisations as material cultures, as Fernand Braudel has done with the Mediterranean; civilisations defined in this way could then become a strategic frame of reference for a civilisational politics of regional integration, as has been modestly attempted by a number of political justifications for a Mediterranean-centred regional political initiative.

Today, the international society is experiencing an epoch-making process of transformation: the economic shift towards the East, the emergence of the BRICS countries, the further spreading of democracy. The global resurgence of religion is not unrelated to these structural changes. We need the pragmatism to recognise the emergence of a new multipolar world of 'multiple modernities', whereby the merging of 'modern' political values and practices with traditional local references and ways of living, often rooted in religious traditions, will be the rule rather than the exception. I have also called these developments a movement towards a post-secular international politics. This is the result not only of how Western and non-Western societies alike are living through times of social transformation and political crisis, in which the established ways of conceiving the role of religion in politics and in the secular public sphere are being criticised and challenged, but also of the broader epoch-making process of slow, but ineluctable, transformation of the normative structure of international society beyond its Eurocentric civilisational origin and liberal ideological configuration. In this context, we need an intellectual move towards a post-secular international thinking, which is not only a self-conscious reflexive thematisation of these momentous challenges but also an attempt to chart a viable path towards the construction of global peace and justice.

Notes

1. Examples of this approach are Mark Juergensmeyer, *Terror in the Mind of God: The Global Rise of Religious Violence* (Berkeley, CA: University of California Press, 2000) and Mary Kaldor, *New and Old Wars: Organised Violence in a Global Era* (Cambridge: Polity Press, 1999). For a very insightful research that problematises some of the predominant views on 'religious fundamentalism' see, Martin E. Marty and R. Scott Appleby, eds., *The Fundamentalism Project*, vols. 1-5 (Chicago: The University of Chicago Press, 1991-1995).

2. Scott Thomas, 'Taking Religious and Cultural Pluralism Seriously: The Global Resurgence of Religion and the Transformation of International Society', *Religion in International Relations*, 21-53.

3. Alasdair MacIntyre, *Whose Justice? Which Rationality?* (London: Duckworth, 1988), see in particular ch. XVII entitled 'Liberalism Transformed into a Tradition'

4. Arnason, *Civilisations in Dispute*, 6.

5. Hedley Bull, 'The Revolt Against the West', in *The Expansion of International Society*, 220-24. See also Andrew Linklater, 'Rationalism', in *Theories of International Relations*, 2nd ed., ed. Scott Burchill et al. (Palgrave, 2001), 103-28 and Robert H. Jackson, *Quasi-States: Sovereignity, International Relations and the Third World* (Cambridge: Cambridge University Press, 1991), esp. ch. 4.

6. See for example, Robert Lee, *Overcoming Tradition and Modernity: The Search for Islamic Authenticity* (Boulder, CO: Westview Press, 1997). For the so-called 'Asian values' debate, see Fareed Zakaria, "Culture is Destiny: A Conversation with Lee Kuan Yew", *Foreign Affairs* 73, no. 2 (1994): 109-26 and Daniel A. Bell, *East Meets West: Human Rights and Democracy in East Asia* (Princeton, N.J.: Princeton University Press, 2000).

7. NPP, 2008, vol 25, no. 4, 35

8. As a telling example since Islam is often represented as incompatible with democracy, I want to point to the growing role that mainstream Political Islamic parties have been playing in advancing the cause of democracy in countries such as Turkey, Jordan and Indonesia, see for example John L. Esposito and John Voll, *Makers of Contemporary Islam* (New York: Oxford University Press, 2001) and Graham E. Fuller, *The Future of Political Islam* (New York, Palgrave Macmillan: 2006).

9. The term 'inculturation' is used in Christian theology to refer to the adaptation of the Gospel in native cultures and also the introduction of these cultures into the life of the Church. The term was popularized by the encyclical *Redemptoris Misssio* of Pope John Paul II (1990), but predates that encyclical. See Peter Schineller, *A Handbook of Inculturation* (New York: Paulist Press, 1990) and Aylward Shorter, *Toward a Theology of Inculturation* (Maryknoll, New York: Orbis Books, 1988). In *Redemptoris Misssio* Pope John Paul II consistently talks of inculturation as a bi-directional dialogical process, the ongoing dialogue between faith and culture. Such an idea, it seems to me, could also be productively applied to our contemporary understanding of democracy which could well be enriched by contributions of non-western cultures. For *Redemptoris Misssio*, see http://www.vatican.va/holy_father/john_paul_ii/encyclicals/documents/ hf_jp-ii_enc_07121990_redemptoris-missio_en.html accessed on 15/1/2007.

10. Arnason, *Civilisations in Dispute*, 233. Of course here the locus classicus is Max Weber's analysis of the religious pre-conditions for Western modernity and capitalism, see *The Protestant Ethics and the Spirit of Capitalism* (London, Unwin, 1968)

11. Max L. Stackhouse, 'Introduction', *God and Globalization*, vol. 3, eds. Max L. Stackhouse and Diane B. Obenchain (Harrisburg, PA: Trinity Press International, 2002), 11.

Part Two

The Nation-State and Society

7

Religion's Changing Form and Relation to the State since 1989

LINDA WOODHEAD
LANCASTER UNIVERSITY, UK

There is no longer any doubt that religion needs to be taken seriously as a factor in international relations. But a great deal of the discussion and representation of religion—including that in the media and politics—remains stuck in an outdated understanding of religion.

The argument I develop here and in other work is that the global religious landscape has changed dramatically since around 1989, at which point an emerging new paradigm or new style of religion became dominant and an older style of religion recessive.[1] What I refer to as 'old-style religion' dates back to the sixteenth century and was forged in the crucible of emerging nation-states. 'New-style religion' dates back to the late nineteenth century and has burgeoned in the context of the globalised market-based societies of the post-Cold War era.

I will outline some headline features of this transformation, and reflect briefly on factors facilitating and obstructing it. It is important to be clear that the transition I identify is not necessarily one from existing traditions of religion (like Islam or Christianity) to new and post-traditional forms (like New Age spirituality), but often a re-configuration existing religions traditions (from old to new styles of Islam, Christianity, etc.). The outcome is a complex contemporary landscape in which old and new styles co-exist and compete.

Old-Style Religion and the Crucible of the Nation-State

It is generally accepted, but often forgotten, that state and religion were historically co-formed as inseparable parts of nation-state-building projects.

Thus, in the West from the sixteenth century, new forms of church-based religion, both Catholic and Protestant, came into being which had the same set of defining characteristics as the emerging states they were so closely tied to.[2] Codification and 'confessionlisation', the development of legal systems and constitutions, the textual statement of core beliefs, the consolidation of hierarchies of male power, the systematisation of religion-state relations and the organization of centralised bureaucracies were all part and parcel of the process. Superstitious 'accretions', popular practices, unsystematic and inefficient elements, appeals to tradition-as-authority, and overly feminised elements were excised in a process of purification and rationalisation.[3]

In this 'reformation' of religion and politics, religion sometimes had a leading role in the consolidation and control of national territory; the imposition of unity and uniformity of belief, values and language; economic rationalisation; the development of educational and legal systems. There were many struggles and confrontations between religion and state, but even more by way of the common pursuit of mutual interest. In the process, religious and political leaders came to resemble one another ever more closely, sitting in the same political chambers, rubbing shoulders in the same corridors of power and socialising in the same networks.

Indeed, as Michael Mann demonstrates in volume two of and I argued more summarily in, it was only through imitating and appropriating many aspects of religion, including wealth, that nation-states were able to grow and eventually vie with or eclipse religious bodies in power and influence.[4] The process was most definitive in relation to Protestant state churches, but even the supranational Roman Catholic and Orthodox churches eventually came to be state-regulated within national territories by control of property, creation of parallel systems of civil law, establishment of concordats and so on—though only definitively so in the second half of the twentieth century.

In this long process, religion formed in slightly but significantly different ways along with the differences between national and national-colonial contexts. Thus, 'Irish Catholicism', 'US Catholicism', 'Filipino Catholicism' and 'Mexican Catholicism', for example, developed as distinct variants. Non-Western religions rationalised in analogous ways, often under the impetus of internal reform movements. Some of these religio-national differences remain so significant that they still need to be referred to in order to make sense of, for example, different welfare-state regimes across Europe and different public and political stances towards resident Muslim populations.[5]

The Reason Why a Secularisation Perspective Became Dominant

By the latter part of the twentieth century, however, old-style religion had been so comprehensively domesticated by various nation-state constitutional arrangements that it was possible for political, academic and even religious elites to believe that it had been permanently privatised and denuded of political significance. Thus, as late as 1994 Henry Kissinger could write a book on that contains not a single entry for 'religion' in the index. A secularisation perspective became dominant.[6]

Brilliant men like Kissinger or Habermas could ignore religion because they stood at the end of the era in which state control of religion reached its apogee. They were able to overlook the continuing role of religion in the provision of welfare, healthcare, education and value-solidarities because these services had become so established and domesticated in the post-Second World War context that they had become invisible as religion. It is only when things don't fit in and won't lie down that they get noticed. In relation to religion, that is what has happened increasingly since 1989. In the process, a new style of religion has started to eclipse the old.

De-compartmentalisation

The striking feature of new-style religion with regard to its social location is its social de-differentiation or 'de-compartmentalisation'.[7] Religion has come out of the box. It has emerged again in public life in both old and new ways— across spheres of welfare, education, dispute settlement, healthcare, healing, entertainment, etc. This de-privatisation of religion has taken place in the context of ever-deepening urbanisation and ever-expanding commerc-ialisation and marketisation/growth of consumer capitalism.[8]

This changed location and context of operation explains the eclipse of old- by new-style religion. Like other parts of the public sector, the latter is governed by committees and due process. Its pace is dictated by complex and slow decision-making procedures. It finds it hard to change course, be entrepreneurial and adapt to new opportunities. By contrast, new-style religion is more like a business enterprise or many start-up firms. It often develops from the grassroots (including from socially marginal groups), is fuelled by new spiritual resources and ideals, throws up new leaders all the time and is quickly adaptive to new opportunities. It draws on the unregulated energies of any number of women and men, who often act individually and unaccountably, taking advantage of the low start-up costs of religious enterprises and of opportunities provided by processes of globalisation and new media.

Even in a country like the UK where there is still an extensive and mainly well-functioning state-supervised healthcare and welfare system, there are many spaces for such religion to operate within. In relation to healthcare, for example, the growth of alternative and complementary forms of medicine that often have an explicitly spiritual dimension has been remarkable.[9] It is estimated that around 40 per cent of the population participate at some point in their lifetime.[10] This sphere has grown since the 1980s to constitute a major and indispensable part of the current health landscape today, without which the state-based National Health System would not be able to cope and which the latter increasingly acknowledges, despite some vociferous critics.

This example shows that there are opportunities for new-style religion even where the state is relatively well-functioning and extensive. But where this is not the case, and where post-war dreams of reconstructed, newly independent secular national utopias have crashed, as in parts of North Africa and the Middle East, the opportunities are even greater. Consider, for example, the growth of mega-churches worldwide, many of which have de-compartmentalised to provide services which secular states have failed to provide as effectively—welfare, healthcare, old-age provision, childcare, counselling, legal advice, education and even housing. I have recently seen mega-churches in the Philippines building their own residential and worshipping communities on a vast scale—which they provide on market principles. This succeeds because more trust is placed in the market and these communities than in the state.

Such post-secular-utopian religious projects often ignore the state and grow in the context of the market. Many have few state-related political ambitions or claims to make. They neither go to the state for favours nor seek the alliances which characterised old-style religion. Indeed, what has recently been happening in countries like Nigeria and the Philippines is that government and politicians have had to turn to for help and favours – whether securing votes and endorsements or finance, or using them to provide services for which the 'big state' was once thought responsible.[11]

Changing Religious Authority and Leadership

New-style religion is also bound up with the rise of new religious actors and authorities and the decline of old. Secularisation theory needs to be recast to take account of the fact that what we have been witnessing is not so much a as a decline in traditional forms of, including traditional leaderships, scriptures and traditions. To imagine religion as defined by a founder, a set of scriptures, a hierarchical priestly leadership and a bounded set of traditions and rituals is now disastrously out of date.

In relation to leadership, striking confirmation is provided by the large surveys of adults aged 18+ in the UK that I carried out with survey company YouGov in 2014.[12] When asked where they take guidance from in living their life and making decisions, 0 per cent of people say 'religious leaders, local and national' (the figure rises to just 2 per cent if you allow the option of selecting four different authorities). Moreover, the figure is not necessarily higher amongst actively religious people: for example, 0 per cent of church-going Catholics say they take most guidance from their religious leaders.[13]

But the conditions which make it so hard for old religious authorities—priests, bishops, imams, rabbis, etc.—to retain their power are the perfect conditions for new religious actors. In a context of increased consumer and democratic choice, more extensive education and greater personal responsibility, many people are no longer willing to defer to higher authorities. Scandals and failures amongst traditional leaders do not help. New leaders have to be much more approachable, skilful and facilitating,

Invoking Max Weber, we can say that both traditional and bureaucratic modes of religious authority have been declining, whilst charismatic styles have been growing—while also insisting that the kind of spiritual charisma which succeeds today is one which facilitates and empowers others, rather than being authoritarian.[14] Such leadership is now eclipsing the older style, despite the fact that politicians prefer to have their photos taken with the latter. Their value has become symbolic.

Under the heading of changing authority, there is also more than can be explored here about the way in which religious structures and institutions have been changing. Suffice to say that the religious landscape since the 1980s has been characterised by the rise of new local, national and transnational religious networks that are closely related not only to migration and mobility but also to virtual social networks. The latter also connect people face to face on an occasional basis by way of large gatherings, festivals and pilgrimages—to Mecca, the Ganges, Lourdes and so on (all growing in popularity). Thus old-style national, territorialised and local neighbourhood-based forms of religion tend to decline, while globalised and partially virtual forms flourish. In terms of religious institutions, the maxi and the mini appear to be more successful than the midi.

Thus, the most vital contemporary forms of religion grow in the context of the global market—or rather, many segmented markets. In religion, one size can no longer fit all. Universalising agendas like those of national churches that tried to impose common rituals and beliefs and create a commonwealth of resources are receding fast. In their place there is diversification into market niches that often run across nations or even continents.

This explains many recent developments, including the success of many forms of religion that are conservative in relation to gender roles and sexual ethics. They appeal to the vastly expanding global middle classes and speak to their concerns: blessing and supporting the pursuit of prosperity, helping people achieve it by building local and global networks of connection and support, upholding a stable nuclear family unit with male dominance along with growing female independence and respect for the dignity of children, encouraging consumption, and allowing for a great deal of direct personal religious participation without the mediation of old religious leaderships—hence concentration on personal relations with the divine and the experiences and benefits it brings.[15]

In this diversified religious world, however, progressive and radical forms of religion also flourish alongside more conservative ones. Thus, the decades since the 1980s have also witnessed the transnational growth and expansion of various forms of neo-pagan spirituality, often with strong feminist, egalitarian and ecological emphases. They have spawned a diversity of transnational networks, connections, literatures, and festivals, and they depend on local and personal initiatives and leaderships that often rise and fall rather rapidly.

These various kinds of niche religion do not just grow and promote themselves by their own efforts but are strengthened by marketing initiatives directed at them. Thus Reina Lewis, for example, shows how new entrants into the fashion target a global market of orthodox religious women from across different religious traditions who are all interested in modest forms of dress.[16] New religious publics are sustained and defined by being targeted as niche consumer groups.

Religious Diversity

A key feature of the contemporary religious landscape is therefore its sheer diversity. There is no one kind of religion that is doing well, and no overall trend—and no single theory can explain it all. Even in a nation-state context, there is now a bewildering proliferation and complexity, with rapid growth and decline of various religious leaders, groups, churches, networks, ideas, fashions, movements and so on.

Novelty becomes more important than ever before—just as in any other kind of consumer market. So new religious movements, phenomena and 'revivals' spring up and die down rapidly. A phenomenon like the Toronto blessing can spread like wildfire in charismatic Christian circles worldwide before fading away after only a few years. There then has to be an attempt by its sponsoring agency to replace it with something new – in this case the more New Age-influenced practice of 'soaking prayer'.[17]

Competition is a major driver. Rival religious leaders and entrepreneurs keep religion vital by innovating and diversifying and by identifying new consumer groups. Even the old-style religious institutions, alarmed by falling numbers and support, try to get in on the act—branding themselves with logos, carrying out market research, trying to get in touch with the views and needs of their potential audiences and investing in growth research and programmes. They begin to behave more like businesses than bureaucracies, albeit a bit late in the game.[18]

New-style religion does not replace old but exists side by side or in different sediments. And we are starting to witness a fightback of some old-style religious authorities. Their strategies include selective borrowing from new-style religions, attempts to protect and extend alliances with political power, and renewed efforts to attract members and funding. Some forms of old-style religion are also currently active in defending their interests under various slogans and initiatives (such as 'religious freedom' and 'inter-faith dialogue') and by attempts to defend the display of their symbols in public.[19] A consequence of this co-existence and competition of old- and new-style religion is a sharp and often aggressive tone in parts of the religious marketplace as various competing groups vie with one another.

Conclusion: Realities versus Representations of Religion

This sketch of religious transformation must end with a paradox that I can only indicate and not explore. I have suggested that, since 1989, old-style religion has become recessive and new-style dominant. The irony is that most media and political representations of religion remain stuck in the old paradigm and blind to or dismissive of the new. The effect is to artificially support the former despite the fact that its support, vitality and political significance is dwindling. As a result, the full impact of the religious revolution that has been taking place is yet to be felt.

I would like to acknowledge the invaluable assistance of Tuomas Martikainen, Francois Gauthier and Erin Wilson.

Notes

1.   Linda Woodhead and Rebecca Catto, *Religion and Change in Modern Britain*

(London: Routledge, 2012).

2.   Peter Beyer, '2011 Association for the Sociology of Religion Presidential Address. Socially Engaged Religion in a Post-Westphalian Global Context: Remodeling the Secular/Religious Distinction', *Sociology of Religion* 73:2 (2012), 109-129.

3.   Max Weber, *From Max Weber: Essays in Sociology*. Edited and translated by Hans Gerth and C.Wright Mills (New York: Oxford University Press, 1958).

4.   Michael Mann, *The Sources of Social Power: Volume 2. The Rise of Classes and Nation States 1760-1914*. 2nd edition. (Cambridge: Cambridge University Press, 2012). Linda Woodhead, *An Introduction to Christianity* (Cambridge: Cambridge University Press, 2004).

5.   Gosta Esping-Andersen, *The Three Worlds of Welfare Capitalism* (Princeton: Princeton University Press, 1990). J. Fetzer and C.Soper, *Muslims and the State in Britain, France, and Germany*, (Cambridge: Cambridge University Press, 2005).

6.   Grace Davie, *The Sociology of Religion* (London: Sage, 2013).

7.   Jose Casanova, *Public Religions in a Modern World* (Chicago: University of Chicago Press, 1994).

8.   Gauthier, Francois, Tuomas Martikainen and Linda Woodhead (eds) (2011) *Social Compass* 58(3) Special issue: *Religion in Consumer Society*. Francois Gauthier and Tuomas Martikainen, eds, *Religion in the Neoliberal Age: Modes of Governance and New Political Economy* (Farnham: Ashgate, 2013). Francois Gauthier and Tuomas Martikainen, (eds), *Religion in Consumer Society: Brands, Consumers, Markets* (Farnham: Ashgate, 2013).

9.   Paul Heelas and Linda Woodhead, *The Spiritual Revolution: Why Religion is Giving Way to Spirituality* (Oxford, UK and Malden, USA: Blackwell, 2005).

10.   Eeva Sointu and Linda Woodhead, "Holistic Spirituality, Gender, and Expressive Selfhood," *Journal for the Scientific Study of Religion* 47: 2 (2008), 259-276.

11.   Nancy Davis and Robert Robertson, *Claiming Society for God. Religious Movements & Social Welfare* (Bloomington and Indianapolis: Indiana University Press, 2012).

12.   Linda Woodhead (2014) http://faithdebates.org.uk/research/

13.   Linda Woodhead (2014) http://faithdebates.org.uk/wp-content/uploads/2013/11/WFD-Catholics-press-release.pdf

14.   Max Weber, 'The Sociology of Charismatic Authority', in Gerth and Wright Mills, *Max Weber*, 245-252. See also Alp Arat, *Spiritual Charisma. Embodiment and Facilitation in Contemporary Practices of Meditation* (University of Lancaster, unpublished PhD thesis, 2013).

15.   See, for example, Özlem Sandikci, 'Researching Islamic marketing: past and future perspectives', *Journal of Islamic Marketing* 2:3 (2011), 246 – 258.

16.   Reina Lewis, *Modest Fashion. Styling Bodies, Mediating Faith* (London: I.B.Tauris, 2013).

17.   Michael Wilkinson and Peter Althouse, 'Pentecostal-Charismatic Prayer and Social Engagement', in Giuseppe Giordan and Linda Woodhead (eds), *Prayer in Religion and Spirituality. Vol 4, Annual Review of the Sociology of Religion*. (Leiden, Boston: Brill, 2014) 221-242.

18.   Mara Einstein, *Brands of Faith: Marketing Religion in a Commercial Age* (London: Routledge, 2008).

19.   Lori Beaman, 'Battles over Symbols: The "Religion" of the Minority Versus the "Culture" of the Majority', *Journal of Law and Religion* 28:1 (2012), 67-104.

8

The Secular–Religious Competition Perspective

JONATHAN FOX
BAR-ILAN UNIVERSITY, ISRAEL

While it can be said that the study of religion in world politics has deep roots, many of those roots stem from what has come to be known as secularisation theory. This body of theory predicted that modern phenomena such as urbanisation, mass literacy and education, science, technology, rationalism, the increasing power of the modern state, mass participation in politics, and geographical mobility, among others, would lead to the demise of religion worldwide.[1] In the 1960s, prominent social scholars such as Anthony F. Wallace confidently predicted that the 'evolutionary future of religion is extinction . . . . Belief in supernatural powers is doomed to die out, all over the world.'[2] While Wallace's predictions were extreme, though by no means unique, the sentiment that religion was at the very least in significant decline was the dominant social science view on religion in the 1960s and well thereafter.[3]

Interestingly, international relations theory ignored religion on a more profound level. Rather than addressing why religion would become less important, until recently it simply did not address religion. Before 2001, international relations scholarship that addressed religion as a significant causal factor in world politics was rare.[4]

Clearly, the prediction of religion's demise as a significant political force was inaccurate. How could social scientists have gotten it so wrong? I posit that, in a sense, they did not. All of the modern factors predicted to undermine and challenge religion are real and, in fact, do undermine and challenge religion. The failure was not in the perception of the nature of these modern challenges to religion but in the belief that religion would succumb to these challenges. I posit that religious actors remain active and important in world politics because they have effectively responded to these challenges.

Specifically, these factors led to the rise of a family of ideologies that are today called secularism. Secularists, the adherents of this family of ideologies, seek to at the very least reduce religion's public role. I define political secularism as *an ideology or set of beliefs which advocates that religion ought to be separate from all or some aspects of politics and/or public life*. This definition focuses on secularism as a political ideology. Though it does not deny that secularism can also have non-political manifestations, my focus here is on politics.

This insight is key to what I call the *secular–political competition perspective* (or for short, the *competition perspective*), which, I posit, explains much of religious politics worldwide. Political secularists seek to at the very least reduce religions' public role. At the same time, however, religious actors seek to increase the public role of religion. Put differently, no matter how strongly a state supports religion, there are people who feel that it does not support religion strongly enough; and no matter how secular a state, there are those who feel it is not secular enough. These actors compete in the political arena to influence state religion policy.

This insight is necessary to understand a key aspect of religious (and anti-religious) politics. It is also necessary to understand why secularisation theory remains an important source of understanding. The *inevitability* of religion's demise is so central to secularisation theory that, arguably, removing it removes the heart and soul of the theory to the extent that what remains can no longer be called secularisation theory. However, when religion's inevitable demise is removed from the equation, this body of theory becomes an important source of insight on the origins, nature, and motivation of religion's opposition in this worldwide political competition.

The *competition perspective* is the central theoretical argument that I outline in my forthcoming book, *Political Secularism, Religion and the State*, which is part of my larger *Religion and State* (RAS) project.[5] In the book I examine 111 types of government religion policy for 177 countries between 1990 and 2008. In this chapter I refer to some of the basic findings from this larger study.

While the competition between religious and secular actors is present in multiple political, social and even economic venues, in this chapter I focus on one specific political venue, government religion policy. A government policy can include laws, decisions by government officials, both national and local, as well as court decisions. Religious and secular actors compete to influence policy with religious actors seeking to get the government more involved in supporting religion, or at least their version of religion, while secular actors seek to separate government from religion and get the government to limit religion in the public sphere.

Among the 111 types of religion policy included in my study, 51 involve state support for religion. This type of policy is in flux but there is a clear trend. Thirty-seven of these types of policy have become more common between 1990 and 2008, with six becoming less common and eight remaining the same. Examining the same information by country shows that 72 (40.7 per cent) countries increased their overall levels of support while 20 (11.3 per cent) decreased their levels of support. Thus, a bit over half of the world has changed its policy of support towards religion, with some supporting religion more and some supporting it less. This is clearly consistent with the competition perspective, but there is also a clear trend during this time period as religious actors have had more success in this competition than their secular counterparts.

A Complex Competition

The *competition perspective's* view of religious politics as a competition between religious and secular actors, while important, only depicts part of a complex set of relationships. The competition between secular and religious actors is complicated by several additional relationships and phenomena. In this chapter, I focus on three of them: competition within the religion camp, competition within the secular camp, and the complex relationship between supporting and restricting religion.

Both the religious and secular camps are complex. Obviously, there is no single religion that the world's religious population agrees upon. Furthermore, religious traditions are often divided into competing denominations and even within a single denomination there are usually diverse views on both how the religion should be interpreted and practised and the extent and nature of that religion's proper influence on politics. Thus, within the religious camp there is competition both between and within religious traditions. Put simply, at the same time as religious actors compete with secular actors in the political arena they also compete with each other.

One manifestation of this competition between religions is religious discrimination. I define religious discrimination as restrictions placed on the religious practices or institutions of minority religions that are not placed on the majority religion. This is different from the restrictions placed on all religions, including the majority religion, in that restrictions placed on all religions usually represent hostility towards, or fear of, religion in general. Or, at least, restrictions placed on all religions reflect a desire to control religion or limit its political power. Resections that focus specifically on minority religions effectively give those religions left untargeted an advantage over the former. Thus, they represent, among other things, government intervention in the religious economy on behalf of the favoured religion or religions.

Religious discrimination is quite common and increasing. In 1990,[6] 136 countries (76.8 per cent) engaged in religious discrimination against at least some minorities. By 2008 this had increased to 146 (82.5 per cent). Of the 30 types of religious discrimination tracked by the RAS project, 28 became more common between 1990 and 2008 while only the remaining two remained stable. Also, 86 (46.9 per cent) states increased levels of religious discrimination during this period, while only 23 (13.0 per cent) lowered levels of religious discrimination. Thus, in this arena of government policy, the competition within the religion camp is strong and getting stronger. Types of religious discrimination which were particularly common in 2008 include restrictions on proselytising and missionaries (92 countries), the requirement of minority religions to register with the state (73 countries), restrictions on the building, maintaining or repairing of places of worship (65 countries), and restrictions on the public observance of religious practices (43 countries).

There is also considerable competition within the secular camp. While political secularists agree that governments should become less involved in religion, philosophies differ considerably on what this means and how it should be accomplished. By limiting the discussion to philosophies found only in democratic states, I have identified three categories of secularist ideology. These ideologies are defined by how they answer the following questions: 1) May the state support religion? (2) May the state restrict religion? (3) May the state restrict religious discourse and expression appropriate in the political speech? (4) May the religious ideals of a specific tradition influence public policy?

The most extreme of these ideologies is the *secularist-laicist* conception that views religion as undermining democracy. Accordingly, religion is banned from the public sphere but allowed in the private sphere. This means that the state may not support religion and restrictions on religion are not only allowed as long as they are limited to the public sphere and applied equally to all religions. Also, religion is not appropriate for political expression and should not influence state policy.[7] France's 2004 law that bans overt religious symbols in public schools, including traditional Islamic head coverings, is a classic example of this model. Unlike most other European restrictions on religious clothing and symbols, this law explicitly includes all religions rather than focusing only on the head coverings worn by Muslim women. While someone from another tradition of secularism might consider this policy a restriction on religious liberty, from the French perspective, religious symbols constitute an aggressive encroachment of religion—something that should be a private matter—on the public sphere.

The second model, the *absolute separation of religion and state* model, bans all government support for religion as well as all government interference in religion. In relation to the four questions I outline above, this model clearly bans any support for religion as well as any restrictions on religion, but there is some debate within this philosophy over the proper role of religion in public political discourse and in influencing public policy. In the US, most believe that religion has a place in public life, but there is debate over the exact role religion should play in society. More specifically, a majority believe that the use of religious language in political speech is acceptable and that religious input into policy is allowed as long as it does not lead to advantaging any religions over others or restrictions on religious minorities. However, a minority believe that the Jeffersonian wall of separation between church and state should extend to religious motivations for policy decisions and even religion's intrusion into political discourse.[8]

The final model, the *neutralist* model, requires that the government treat all religions equally. States may become involved in religion as long as this principle of equality is maintained.[9] Thus, in relation to the four questions I list above, both support for religion and limitations placed upon it are allowed as long as these policies are applied equally to all religions. This concept of equal application also applies to political discourse and religious influence on policymaking.

These three models have important implications for day-to-day policy. Take, for example, religion in public schools. Under the secular-laicist model, any public expression of religion, including wearing overt religious symbols such as crosses, Jewish yarmekahs and Muslim head coverings, can be banned; and there would certainly be no religious education. Under the absolute separation doctrine, the wearing of religious symbols can be allowed but there would be no state-supported religious education in public schools. Under the neutralist doctrine, even religious education in public schools would be allowed as long as it was provided equally to all religions for which there are a significant number of students and it was not mandatory. Thus, there are serious divisions within the secularist camp. Outside of the liberal school of thought these divisions deepen, as there are even more extreme forms of secularism, though they are less common today than they have been in the past. For example, most communist and some fascist regimes ban religion from government, the public sphere *and the private sphere*. Thus, these extreme secular ideologies severely limit religion in all aspects of public and private life, or they attempt to ban it altogether.

The final complexity in government religion policy stems from the tension between supporting religion and restricting it. Supporting religions is inexorably intertwined with control. When a government supports a religion, that religion becomes, to some degree, dependent upon the government and susceptible to control even if control was not the original intent. In fact, one of the best ways to control religion is to support it while tying that support to some form of government control.[10] For example, when a government supports religious education it can influence what is taught in those classes as well as who teaches them. Similarly, a government that supports a religious institution, perhaps by establishing an official religion, can control aspects of that institution's inner workings through the appointment of religious officials.[11]

Both restricting and supporting religion are common. In 1990,[12] 132 (74.4 per cent) states restricted their majority religion, and usually all other religions, in some way. By 2008 this increased to 146 (82.5 per cent). Twenty of the 29 types of restrictions on all religion in a country tracked by the RAS project became more common during this period while only five became less common. Sixty-eight (38.4 per cent) countries enacted more restrictions in 2008 than they did in 1990, while only 20 (11.3 per cent) enacted fewer. Some of the most common types of restrictions in 2008 included restrictions on religious political parties (63 countries), government harassment or arrest of religious officials (43 countries), and government monitoring or restrictions on clerical sermons (41 countries).

Perhaps the best indication of the overlap between control and support is that every single country which restricts religion also engages in at least a few of the 51 types of support for religion tracked by the RAS project. Even more interestingly, setting aside countries which are generally hostile to religion, the countries which regulate and control religion the most are those that support it most strongly. In fact, levels of regulation and control of religion— and this includes regulation and control of the state's majority religion—are on average over twice as high in states with official religion as they are in states which generally maintain separation of religion and state. Thus, this complexity in state motivation is clearly present not only in theory but also in practice.

This means that when we objectively see a state supporting a religion this does not necessarily mean that the government looks favourably upon religion. It can also mean that the state seeks to limit or control religion. Often this control is focused on religion's political influence, with governments supporting religion in society but limiting its political influence. The 63 countries which limit religious political parties are a good example of this phenomenon. However, whether the intent is to support or control religion, the increasing levels of religious support and the fact that in 2008 all countries other than South Africa engaged in at least a few of the 51 types of religious support tracked by the RAS project mean that religion certainly remains relevant across the world.

Conclusions

Given all of this, the *competition perspective* depicts a complex relationship between religion and politics. While the religious and secular camps compete for political influence, there is at the same time competition within each of these camps. Also, while it is possible to identify a government's policy towards religion, it is often difficult to fully know the complex motivations behind that policy.

That being said, two things are clear. First, religion policy across the world is in a state of flux. Second, governments are becoming more involved in religion than they were in the past. Looking at three types of policy—support for religion, restrictions on the majority or all religions, and discrimination against religious minorities—98 of 177 countries tracked by the RAS project increased their involvement in at least one of these factors without decreasing it on any of the others. By contrast, only 22 lowered their overall involvement and 28 increased some aspects while lowering others. Only 29 experienced no changes at all.

Thus, between 1990 and 2008, religious actors have had more victories in their competition with secular actors, but secular actors are still active and successful in many cases. Just as secular actors did not succeed in eliminating religion at the peak of secularism's influence in the mid-twentieth century, it is unlikely that religious actors will succeed in eliminating secularism. While in recent years religious actors have learned how to successfully counter secular political actors, it is likely that in time, secular actors will also adjust tactics and strategies to more successfully compete. Thus, the competition between the two, which is the central insight of the *secular–religious competition perspective*, will likely continue for the foreseeable future.

Notes

1. Jonathan Fox, *An Introduction to Religion and Politics: Theory and Practice* (London: Routledge, 2013); and Bryan R. Wilson, *Religion in Sociological Perspective* (Oxford: Oxford University Press, 1982).

2. Anthony F. Wallace, *Religion: An Anthropological View* (New York: Random House, 1966): 266-267.

3. Jose Casanova, *Public Religions in the Modern World* (Chicago, Il: University of Chicago Press, 1994): 17; Phillip S. Gorski and Ates Altinordu, 'After Secularization', *Annual Review of Sociology* 24, (2008): 55-85; and Monica D. Toft, Daniel Philpott, & Timothy S. Shah, *God's Century: Resurgent Religion and Global Politics*, (New York: W. W. Norton & Company, 2011).

4. Scott M. Thomas, *The Global Resurgence of Religion and the Transformation of International Relations: The Struggle for the Soul of the Twenty-First Century* (New York: Palgrave-Macmillan, 2005); Nukhet Sandal and Jonathan Fox, *Religion in International Relations Theory: Interactions and Possibilities* (New York: Routledge, 2013); and Daniel Philpott, 'The Challenge of September 11 to Secularism in International Relations', *World Politics* 55 (1) (2002): 66-95.

5. Jonathan Fox, *Political Secularism, Religion and the State* (Cambridge: Cambridge University Press, forthcoming); also see Jonathan Fox, *The Religion and State* (RAS) *Project*; available from www.religionandstate.org.

6. This includes several countries which did not become independent until after 1990. In these cases I include the first year of available data.

7. Ahmet T. Kuru, *Secularism and State Policies Toward Religion: The United States, France and Turkey* (Cambridge: Cambridge University Press, 2009).

8. Ibid.; also see Carl H. Esbeck, 'A Typology of Church-State Relations in American Thought', *Religion and Public Education* 15 (1) (1988): 43-50.

9. John T. S. Madeley, 'A Framework for the Comparative Analysis of Church-State Relations in Europe', *West European Politics* 26 (1) (2003): 23-50.

10. Metin Cosgel and Thomas J. Miceli, 'State and Religion', *Journal of Comparative Economics* 37(2) (2009): 403; N. J. Demerath, III, *Crossing the Gods: World Religions and Worldly Politics* (New Jersey: Rutgers University Press, 2001): 204; and Brian J Grim and Roger Finke, *The Price of Freedom Denied* (New York: Cambridge University Press, 2011): 207.

11. Kuru, *Secularism and State Policies Toward Religion*, 8, 166-167; and Oliver Roy, *Secularism Confronts Islam* (New York: Columbia University Press, 2007): 27–28

12. This includes several countries which did not become independent until after 1990. In these cases I include the first year of available data.

9

Church, State and Culture: Should Religion Be a Private Matter?

BRENDAN SWEETMAN
ROCKHURST UNIVERSITY, USA

A type of a secular liberalism has become an influential, even dominant worldview among sections of what might be broadly described as the intellectual class in many Western societies. Without needing to go into the content of this view in detail, its advocates generally hold that the physical realm is all there is (and will be studied by science), and so we need secularist accounts of politics and morality, and indeed eventually of all areas of life. A secularist account would be one that explains its subject matter (including human existence) in terms of physical stuff, like matter and energy, and that, consequently, makes no appeal to the supernatural. Needless to say, advocates of this general approach to the nature of life and the universe do not, by any means, always agree among themselves concerning the details of such a view; yet there would be quite broad agreement on the general foundational beliefs of this worldview. This worldview is also sometimes referred to as naturalism, or philosophical atheism, or, as (my own preferred term) secularism.

Secularism

We can make a few general points about this view. First, its proponents often regard themselves as 'enlightened' about matters of culture, society, law and politics. They see themselves as being in the vanguard of the progress of modern civilisation; a consequence of this is that a significant number of secularism's adherents adopt a superior, even supercilious attitude (almost as a matter of policy) towards the worldviews with which they disagree, particularly the religious ones, and their advocates. The perception that one is 'enlightened' also sometimes makes proponents of secularism impatient with their naysayers, and is often the cause of their failure to consistently apply the principles they profess to otherwise support, e.g. on free speech.

A second significant feature of secularism is the way its advocates respond to the fact that the vast majority of people reject this view of reality and human life and adopt a religious view instead; this response involves promoting the pragmatic argument that the religious worldview should be relegated to a private sphere. Secularists are fond of claiming that one can practise a religious view in one's private life and circle of family and friends, but that it should have no influence on matters of public policy where it would have an effect on everyone, including those who do not accept it. This view is sometimes defended by appeal to a particular interpretation of an important democratic principle, the principle of the separation of church and state. The view that religion should be relegated to a private realm now permeates modern culture in the West to a very significant extent, even though it is often inconsistently applied. As a result, one might often see the secularist media quote a religious leader approvingly if they agree with what he or she says, while criticising him or her when they don't. This is also why one can see the principle of the separation of church and state selectively applied, so that it often appears less as a principle and more as a tactic in a political debate, as when various political interest groups in the United States, for example, police conservative churches for their involvement in political issues, while ignoring the political activity of liberal churches.

Although secularism is an increasingly influential worldview in certain circles, it faces one very large, indeed fatal, problem: it is rejected by many, who believe it to be untrue! Now, it is not my intention here to argue for the merits of either secularism or religion. Rather, I want to consider what society should do when it has a fundamental disagreement of this nature, at the level of worldview, which in turn brings out various problems with the secularist position on these matters. But first we should make a few preliminary qualifications. I am assuming a democratic society as a backdrop—that we must settle our disagreements within the context of a democratic system. While the same general issues could obviously arise in other political systems as well, democracy places us in a distinctive context that we must take into account when considering these general philosophical questions. Second, we must also recognise that we are working within a context of pluralism. Pluralism here means that we have several different worldviews present in the same state, and that advocates of each think their worldview should have some influence on political, moral, social and cultural debates. Sometimes this is called *the problem* of pluralism: the problem of what to do when there are different worldviews that are significant players in the same state, especially at the political and moral level. Third, I am not assuming that all secularists hold the exact same worldview, nor am I assuming that all religious believers share the same beliefs. We must recognise that there will be different visions of secularism just as there are different visions of religion; that not all secularists agree among themselves, and also, perhaps, that a religious position might overlap with a secular viewpoint on some issues. We just need to keep before our minds the general orientation of each worldview; specific differences are not that significant when we are considering foundational philosophical questions.

Should Secularism be Presumptive?

What arguments might one advance to support the position that whenever there is a disagreement between a religious worldview and a secularist worldview, the religious worldview should be confined to the 'private realm' while we defer to the secularist worldview? What arguments suggest that we should appeal to the secularist worldview in making political arguments, for example, but cannot appeal to a religious worldview when, say, discussing issues of social justice, abortion, social welfare policies or any of the issues of the day? I do not believe there are any arguments supporting this conclusion that do not involve special pleading or that are not based upon a prior commitment to the superiority of secularism. Nevertheless, two arguments are popular. The first is the argument that secularist worldviews and religious worldviews are in two different categories, and this fact allows us to treat them differently. This is a way of arguing that secularism is in some superior category that allows us to discriminate in its favour. It is often hard to specify the nature of this special category that confers a powerful advantage on certain worldviews, but one version of this first argument is that secularist views appeal to reason (and perhaps science) to support their claims, but religious views do not. Religious beliefs, it is claimed, are based on 'faith', understood in the sense of believing without evidence or without regard to the evidence, often accompanied by the belief that faith is not subject to reason, or perhaps that faith is higher than (or outside of) reason.

I agree that when advancing a new moral or political view, especially one with the potential to reshape society, one should ideally try to frame as best one can these views in a way that might have some appeal to those who hold different worldviews. Religious believers frequently do this, and can do it for many or most of their moral and political beliefs. It is just too simplistic to argue that all religious beliefs are based on 'faith'—understood in the pejorative sense that they disregard evidence—while the opposite is somehow true of all secularist beliefs. Of course, for some of our beliefs we may be incapable of expressing them in totally neutral, rational terms. But this is just as true for many secularist beliefs as it is for religious beliefs. For example, suppose I argue that job applications should be examined randomly because of my secularist assumption that the origin of life on Earth was a chance event stemming from totally natural causes; I should then also be able to argue for evaluating all applications equally if I believe that everyone has the same basic set of human rights because God created all people equally. It is hard to see why a religious believer cannot appeal to his belief in the truth of certain religious claims if a secularist is allowed to appeal to his belief in the truth of certain secularist claims. Moreover, there is a significant element of *faith* involved in both sets of beliefs in the key sense that all worldviews make claims that go beyond what any rational argument or evidence could prove definitively. So, the most society can hope for, indeed, what it should strive for, are *reasonable* beliefs—beliefs that can be backed up through reason (and, perhaps, as much evidence as possible). The secularist view simply ignores the long tradition of reason in religion and plays to stereotypes that believers ignore evidence because such stereotypes are easier to dismiss—it's a straw man argument!

Engaging with many of the great thinkers in religious history (and in contemporary times) would necessitate that secularist approaches become involved in a serious debate, one they could quite possibly lose. This is why advocates of the so-called 'new atheism', for example, are afraid to engage in detailed discussions of actual arguments, preferring instead to rely on rhetoric and superficial appeals to emotion and stereotypes. My position on the rationality of worldviews is that all worldviews are 'faiths' to some extent, that a faith must be rational in order to be taken seriously, especially in politics, and that the religious view of the world in general is a rational faith, perhaps even more so than secularism.

Secularism vs. Religion in a Democratic State

This brings us to a second line of argument for keeping religion out of politics. One might be inclined to believe that secularism is a better (more correct, more true) worldview in terms of content. Although they may not always admit it, secularists believe their worldview is superior because it is correct on the major issues. They are free to believe this, of course, but this is where the background assumption of democracy is important. Suppose you are convinced that religious belief is not as rational as I think it is and are prepared to offer a robust defence of the superior rationality of secularism. The problem is that this does not help us with the issue of the role of religion in public life. This is because it is crucial to recognise that it is not necessary for me to convince the secularist that religious belief is rational in order for religious beliefs to have a role in politics; all that is necessary is that I hold them to be rational. And, we might add, I do not need to convince a significant number of people of this fact. If we are to compare the two general positions in terms of numbers, a significant number of people (indeed billions more) are already convinced of this fact.

We should not forget the fact that we are actually discussing the rationality of religious belief vis-à-vis the rationality of secular beliefs; we are discussing whether religious beliefs can be introduced into the political arena in a democratic society. We should also acknowledge that the question about the reasonableness of a particular belief, and whether it can play a role in public and social policy debates, is itself a matter for debate in the public square. This is a key point frequently overlooked by secularists who sometimes seem to think that theirs should be the default position if they disagree with a religious believer on certain issues! But any type of suppression of a view *before* a public debate is held violates the basic principles of democracy itself, especially freedom and equality.

This is why the problem of pluralism is a very difficult problem and why one might be tempted to engineer an end run around the democratic process to advance one's worldview. The problem arises because once one accepts a democratic form of government as the backdrop of a debate and then says, 'I believe that X is objectively true and should shape society', one must recognise that, however much he or she may not like it, one is only speaking for *oneself* on the matter and others may have different views. Part of the meaning of freedom in a democratic context is that an individual cannot speak for someone else on these matters. Moreover, democracy in theory supports the expression of different views on various matters (though it does not always work out this way in practice).

The best solution to the problem of pluralism then is to have an open, full and honest public square debate on the issues of the day, and then to vote on them. This is not a perfect solution because we must accept that sometimes the majority can get things wrong, and logically, just because a consensus emerges on a certain issue does not mean that the consensus is correct. However, this is a better solution than the two main alternatives. One is to appeal to the High Court in various countries to settle various contentious issues in society. This approach is very popular in the United States, where the most controversial issues in contemporary culture have been settled not democratically but by decisions of the US Supreme Court, even so serious an issue as abortion. But the problem with this approach is that it turns the courts into yet more political bodies, which people try to manipulate for their own ends—hence the big political fights every time a vacancy occurs on the US Supreme Court and the reason justices are described as 'liberal' or 'conservative'.

Another possible way to solve the problem of pluralism is to appoint some smaller (elite) group to deal with contentious matters, say, by recommending policy decisions or options to the government. But the problem with this approach is obvious: the make-up of the group will be susceptible to political influence and, from a philosophical point of view, it would involve a minority deciding key issues for the majority. How can this be better than the majority deciding? One might argue that the minority is somehow more 'enlightened', but this argument simply raises again the problems we have already considered.

Is the State Neutral between Worldviews?

This brings us by way of conclusion to the question of whether the state is neutral between worldviews, i.e. promotes no worldview itself, as liberal political philosophers claim. It should be obvious that the state is not neutral and cannot be neutral. This is because many of the laws of the state embody moral values, and these moral values enshrine in law key beliefs that are held by various worldviews, for example, beliefs about justice, equality, peace, freedom and the common good. These values clearly appeal to those three general areas of belief that form the substance of a worldview, the nature of reality, the nature of the human person, and the nature of moral and political values, and they are among the foundational beliefs of various worldviews. In addition, those who do not agree with these values (or more usually with specific interpretations of these values) are excluded from *practising* their worldview on these matters by the state. For instance, those who believe that some people are not equal to others cannot practise this view in hiring for a job. As Richard John Neuhaus has noted, 'the public square will not and cannot remain naked. If it is not clothed with the "meanings" borne by religion, new "meanings" will be imposed by virtue of the ambitions of the modern state.' Political philosopher Charles Larmore admits that the liberal state does not aim at *complete* moral neutrality. It tends to be neutral only with regard to controversial conceptions of the good life but *not to all values or norms whatsoever*. The problem is that the norms and values it is not neutral towards will be used to *restrict* various versions of the good life that the liberal political philosopher does not approve of, and so Larmore's point begs the very question at issue. In short, the liberal political philosopher is never totally neutral towards key values in the philosophical, moral and political debate concerning how society should be organised politically—there are always some values that are not doubted and that are then, more crucially, used to *restrict* other views.

It is important to recognise that *coercion is always going on in political society*, and it is impossible to find an individual or worldview that does not try to impose at least some beliefs on others. And values that become the basis of law always influence the society as a whole, especially when their effect is considered over time. We must recognise, however, that not all views can be accommodated, so some people will be profoundly disappointed, and disgruntled. This disagreement must be handled with the utmost care. One of the reasons debates in modern democratic states have become more contentious is that, as more worldviews gain prominence, many of them conflicting with others, a difficult transition has been required from a monolithic-leaning society to a pluralist one. This transition has not been handled well, and the result is increasing polarisation of worldviews and a growing belief that reasonable disagreement is no longer possible on some questions. This can lead to a tendency to regard one's opponent as morally wrong, even morally evil, leading to a tendency to vilify or demonise them.

Lastly, it is possible to take an optimistic or a pessimistic approach to the problem of pluralism; the optimistic approach holds that dialogue can be fruitful; the pessimistic approach is motivated by the view that dialogue is no longer possible, so we are engaged in a political fight rather than a philosophical argument. Even considering all of the issues very carefully, in what is quite a complicated topic, it is hard to predict which one of these approaches will prove closer to the truth in the future in the modern democratic state.

Further Reading

Francis Canavan, *The Pluralist Game* (Rowman and Littlefield, 1995).

Kent Greenawalt, *Private Consciences and Public Reasons* (Oxford U.P., 1995).

Robert Kraynak, *Christian Faith and Modern Democracy* (University of Notre Dame Press, 2001).

Richard John Neuhaus, *The Naked Public Square* (Eerdman's, 1984).

Charles Larmore, *Patterns of Moral Complexity* (Cambridge U.P., 1987).

Brendan Sweetman, *Why Politics Needs Religion: The Place of Religious Arguments in the Public Square* (InterVarsity, 2006).

Charles Taylor, *Philosophical Arguments* (Harvard U.P., 1995).

10

Holism, Religion and Geopolitics

DON HANDELMAN
HEBREW UNIVERSITY OF JERUSALEM, ISRAEL

During the latter half of the twentieth century, distinguished Western scholars and radical theologians announced the 'Death of God', the precipitous decline (according to polls and surveys) of explicit religious affiliation and observance. In a world becoming globalised and transnational, God was no longer counted among the players making a difference; religion could be counted out in comprehending geopolitics. At the turn of the twenty-first century, the 'God is Dead' formulation appears an unwelcome apparition, one now dead and deeply interred. The effects of religion in the geopolitics of North Africa, the Middle East, the Indian subcontinent and indeed in the USA and Russia are undeniable and profound. What is it that occurred in the brief span of a few decades? Did Westerners and others quite suddenly find religion again? Were the survey-takers simply off the mark? Did the rush to judgement and speedy conclusions—no less an affliction of today's academic researchers than of political pundits—supersede cultural common-sense? Today's students of geopolitics must take into account the burgeoning religiosities in numerous global conflicts. But just what is it that must be taken into account? What is it that makes 'religion' special in its effects on populations from the small to the huge? Is there something to religion that demands taking on a different perspective, one of longer range and one that for good reason is resistant to the kind of narrow analysis—like that of game theory and other theories of strategic analysis—that severely restricts broader perspectives?

My response is that the most critical aspect of religion is the constitution of a vision and value of holism. Religion is the prime conveyor of values of holism (of whatever scale) in a world continuously fragmenting and reworking through politics and economics. I claim further that this understanding of religion in the abstract stands the tests of time from the ancient through the present. Yet what do I intend through the idea of holism? And why should a vision of holism be important in considering the effects of religion in geopolitics in a very wide variety of social and political orders?

Holism and Religion

Anthropologist Louis Dumont understood holism as value (that he phrased as ideology) through which social order is organised.[1] Holism is the most inclusive of values in that in part, 'Holism entails the *integrity* of the *entirety*, where the entirety may be any kind of human unit—cosmos, group, and even the individual in certain instances—of differing scales, complexities, and consequences'.[2] In this usage the emphasis within an entirety is on integrity, in the senses of entireness, completeness, soundness with their implications of integration. However, *integration* refers more to parts added together to make a whole, so that in the first instance the connections between parts is additive, while the intention here is that integrity refer more to synergetic relationships within and among the parts of a whole. Thus, the connections between parts must be *relational*. Given the relational-ness that is carried by values of holism, one should be concerned with the logics of how cultural and social wholes hold together with the clear intimation that this 'holding together' is in the first instance dynamical rather than structural.[3] Moreover, holism is not restricted to particular sizes of human organisation. Rather, values of holism may be embedded in human units from the large scale of entire groups and peoples to the tiny scale of the individual (when the search, say, for self-actualisation is significant). One must emphasise that holism is *not* an 'essence'—rather, holism indexes how people and things (indeed, cosmos) are, are not, or are partially put together. And, so, that which constitutes holism varies historically, contextually. Nonetheless, the propensities towards holism in the human condition were and are profound.

Given that holism takes shape and lodges in vastly different scales of human existence, it then has a very broad cachet in the organisation of human existence. One way of thinking on 'religion' is that *it takes everything into itself*, without needing to specify just what 'everything' might be. Potentially, 'religion' is just that, everything. As such, cosmos and 'religion' in the ancient sense are isomorphic to a high degree. And of all forms of organisation invented by human beings throughout history, it is 'religion' that most closely encompasses that which I am calling here holism and that postulates holism as a basic value of the practice of faith. It is questionable whether in ancient times one could separate 'religion' from other domains of existence, apart from doing this as an analytical exercise. The reason for this is that the organisation of religion (as the cosmos, as metaphysically the entirety of what there is) encompassed all other domains of living, and therefore needed no separate name. Among historians of the European Middle Ages, Aaron Gurevich argues powerfully that this period in everyday popular culture was characterised by holism and, so, by the realism of the close presence of God in the daily lives of human beings.[4] Louis Dumont maintains that this holism fragmented with the Enlightenment, the Reformation and the rise of individualism; and that from this breakup of cosmos there emerged distinct native categories and domains of living like 'religion', along with 'economy', 'polity', 'family' and so forth.[5]

This broad cachet enables the search for the presence and power of holism in a variety of phenomena, especially those of the political (the civil, the totalitarian) that have been termed 'religions' by political scientists and others, yet rarely recognising the most powerful quality of all—holism—that these phenomena share with religion. The propensity for holism in human cultures never disappeared. Given the intimate relationship between holism and religion, one can state unequivocally as a rule of thumb that when values of holism are present, religion is close by (even if invisible); and, correspondingly, when a political system is called a 'religion' this implies that the value of holism is paramount. Unsurprisingly, then, values of holism revive relatively easily in relation to various local and global conditions (including those of secularism), whether through nationalisms, civil religions, new religions, trans-local migrations, and on.

Even as Western mindfulness, schooled in the scientific ethos of liberal democracy, seeks to keep politics and religion apart, over and again to the chagrin of heirs of the Enlightenment, political communities that are themselves submerged and schooled in ideologies of peoplehood and nationhood take on attributes of holism. If we understand the profound affinity between holism and religion—and to a serious degree between holism and modern nationalism—then the entanglement of religion and politics comes into clearer focus. The states that arose in the latter period of the modern era commonly insisted that their nationalisms—often keyed to peoplehood and nation—were holistic; thereby ensuring the ongoing entwinements between holisms of politics, nationhood and religion clashing and converging. Therefore, for religion and nationalism to be strongly related, there is no necessity to argue, for example, that nationalism is the religion of the modern state.[6] Whether or not a 'religion' is an 'invented tradition', a newly created phenomenon with, consequently, little or no historical depth, does not matter in my argument.[7] What matters are values of holism and the ways in which they are embedded, organised and practised in social orders. In this regard one must not overlook that, of the surviving world religions, it is the monotheisms that generally have given especial importance to their own historical depths as validating their significance in the world. Monotheistic holisms insist that (historical) time (both past and future) is integral to their own existence and organisation, thereby encompassing both 'history' and its end-time, the transcendental End Time of linear time-reckoning. The generative connection between monotheism and modern nationalism is clear. As political philosopher John Gray states succinctly, 'Secular thinking is a legacy of Christianity and has no meaning except in a context of monotheism'.[8] Modern secular nationalisms grew from the premise of monotheism that time is evolutional through processes of perfecting the human (and therefore the significance of historical depth to the monotheisms) together with the monotheistic stress on absolute difference in identity as perhaps *the* criterion of membership, which the modern nation-states and nationalisms utterly naturalised in the mundane world and made their own.[9]

During the nineteenth and twentieth centuries, nationalisms flourished through a multitude of great and little wars and other conflicts. Values of holism were and are critical to the birth and cohesion of Western nations and nation-states, even those that appeared secular. How does this square with my argument that when values of holism are present then religion is nearby? A useful case in point is that of the juridical and political theorist, Carl Schmitt, a highly influential thinker in Germany during the Weimar Republic and Nazi rule. The prominent sociologist Zygmunt Bauman has called him, 'arguably the most clear-headed, illusion-free anatomist of the modern state and its in-built totalitarian inclination'.[10] Schmitt's thinking demonstrates the synergistic relationship of nationalism and religion in modernity.

Secular Nationalism and Religious Theology: The Case of Carl Schmitt

Schmitt's concern lay with the sovereignty, indeed the holism, of the German state, that for him was the treasury of being German, of German-ness. Interestingly, Schmitt gave little import to the native German conception of nation, the holistic *volk*, rejecting this as romantic organicism that was incapable of taking action to save the sovereignty of the state-in-crisis.[11] Yet in fact he went one better than the *volk* as the basis of national holism by embracing an even more essentialist and very twentieth-century conception, that of race. Schmitt maintained that true Germans share essential qualities of race-as-being, so that the category of race and that of cultural homogeneity were isomorphic, that is, one and the same. Members of the German race shared the same homogeneous, cultural qualities of upbringing (*erziehung*), of character building (*bildung*), of values and perceptions. In order for the national to flourish, these 'natural', cultural particularities that were based in race had to be sovereign. Values of holism were paramount in this racial-cultural formation that was threatened by the 'general political will' on which democratic political processes were based. Therefore, the 'people' had to distinguish between 'friends', those who shared in the natural qualities of the race, and 'enemies', those who were different and therefore divided and threatened the holism of the natural national. Only if enemies were destroyed would national sovereignty true to itself emerge and triumph. Thus, after the Nazi rise to power, Schmitt strongly advocated the ethnic cleansing of Jewish jurists from the German courts because only those jurists who were 'participants in a racially determined type [*artbestimmsten Weise*] of legal community to which they existentially belong' could comprehend a German legal case in the right way.[12]

All of this sounds as if Schmitt simply was a straightforward secular racist. Yet religion, Christianity, was deeply embedded in Schmitt's conception of how the holistic, modern, sovereign state had to protect itself, since the inevitable confrontation between friend and enemy had to 'take place at the metaphysical level—the level of one faith against another. For this reason the confrontation is one of "political theology"',[13] with its more distant echoes of monotheistic Christian Kingship in Europe. Another scholar of Schmitt goes so far as to argue that Schmitt's vision 'would interpret the present in light of a Christian conception of history'—theistic, salvational, holding off the coming of the Antichrist[14]: another instance of religion close by, with values of holism invoked as the bottom line of a state holding itself together. Schmitt's conception of the geopolitics of the elementary friend/enemy confrontation was that the state composed of members sharing essentialist, constitutive qualities (the friends) had to become authoritarian and totalitarian to protect its sovereignty. The state and its rulers become a 'state of exception', one that encompasses the state and that, in turn, cannot be encompassed.[15] Schmitt draws a direct line between (political) jurisprudence and the miracle, which he likened to an 'exception': 'The exception in jurisprudence [one that breaks all of its rules] is analogous to the miracle in theology'[16] and it is within the space-time of the essentialist exception, the 'miracle': that order made is saved from chaos.

Yet how does the 'miracle of the exception' come about? Schmitt states that he who decides on the exception is sovereign.[17] In other words, the sovereign is the one who takes transcendence on himself and in the process encompasses the whole of the state. Yet it is no less the space-time of the exception that itself is transcendent, for Schmitt argues that 'The exception is that which cannot be subsumed; it defies general codification [and is] the [juridical] decision in absolute purity.'[18] If the exception cannot be subsumed, then the exception itself is encompassing. And, so, it is the exception in the person of the sovereign that encompasses the entirety of the state. This is the exception and the sovereign as pure miracle.[19] This view of political sovereignty powerfully resonates with Christianity, since the sovereign not only occupies the place of God but is no less the miracle of Christ, the God-man who is indeed the exception who orders cosmic chaos and promises salvation.

Entering the Twenty-First Century

Is there reason to expect any radical shift in the relationship between values of holism in political setups and religion in the twenty-first century? All three monotheisms are flexing their faiths in powerful though different ways. As Olivier Roy puts it, we are facing 'the sudden emergence in all Western monotheistic religions of new forms of religiosity, all of them communitarian (but of a purely religious community), exclusive (a clear dividing line separates the saved from the damned), and inclusive (all aspects of life must be placed by the believer under the aegis of religion'.[20] Evangelical and Charismatic Christianity in their numerous strands have become a successful global missionary religion, calling 'upon the faithful to submit to the [holistic] totalising authority of divine agency' and actively competing for converts with Islam.[21] Islam is taking diverging paths, including the eruption of religious movements whose holisms relate to interpretations of the nation of Islam, the *ummah*. Another pathway turns towards 'a radical individuation ... that is ... divorced from modes of collective solidarity and action', yet an individuation that relocates much of 'collective responsibility' within the holistic, ethical obligations of the individual.[22] From this perspective, self-sacrifice and martyrdom may also be understood as a holistic, ethical act through which the individual transcends himself or herself.[23] Israel, a majority of whose citizens define it as the Jewish state, is a latecomer nation-state that takes its shaping from holistic European nationalisms of the nineteenth and twentieth centuries. Israel is nurturing religious nationalism that is expansive territorially and culturally, in terms of which state and nation (defined in Judaic religious terms) are vying with one another for supremacy as to which holistically will encompass the other. In this emerging contest, one that may turn into a comprehensive *kulturkampf*, the elephant in the room is Israel's reputed (and virtually certain) stockpiling of nuclear weaponry and the potentiality of its use.

Perhaps one of the great tragedies of modernity (and no less its greatest irony) is that any attempt to put things together, to keep things together in holistic ways, will have intimations of religion which continually challenge any geopolitics based on liberal values or game theoretical premises. The pursuit of holism continues, from that of the 'whole' individual to that of the 'whole' community, the 'whole' nation and the 'whole' state. From the perspective taken here, the bottom line is that if values of holism are here to stay during the foreseeable future (and there is no evidence that they are not) then so is religion. And religions carry their own baggage as to why and how the world is put together ultimately and transcendentally and how this impacts on human social orders. The twenty-first century looks to be a more God-fearing time for international geopolitics.

Notes

1. Louis Dumont, *Essays on Individualism: Modern Ideology in Anthropological Perspective* (Chicago: University of Chicago Press, 1986), 279.
2. Don Handelman and Galina Lindquist, 'Religion, Politics and Globalization: The Long Past Foregrounding the Short Present - Prologue and Introduction', *Religion, Politics and Globalization: Anthropological Approaches* (New York: Berghahn Books, 2011), 20. Parts of this chapter are taken from that essay.
3. Two kinds of 'holding together' are discussed in Don Handelman, 'Inter-gration and intra-gration in cosmology', in *Framing Cosmologies: The Anthropology of Worlds* (Manchester: Manchester University Press, 2014), 95-115.
4. Aaron I. Gurevich, *Categories of Medieval Culture* (London: Routledge & Kegan Paul, 1985); and, Gurevich, *Medieval Popular Culture* (Cambridge: Cambridge University Press, 1988).
5. Louis Dumont, *From Mandeville to Marx: The Genesis and Triumph of Economic Ideology* (Chicago: University of Chicago Press, 1977).
6. As does, for example, Carleton Hayes in his, *The Historical Evolution of Modern Nationalism* (New York: Russell and Russell, 1968); and see the critique of Talal Asad, *Genealogies of Religion* (Baltimore: Johns Hopkins University Press, 1993), 189.
7. Eric Hobsbawm and Terence Ranger, ed., *The Invention of Tradition* (Cambridge: Cambridge University Press, 1983).
8. John Gray, *Black Mass: Apocalyptic Religion and the Death of Utopia* (London: Allen Lane, 2007), 191.
9. Keep in mind that of all the world religions, only the three monotheisms demand that membership be only in one faith: absolutely inclusive and exclusive.
10. Zygmunt Bauman, 'Seeking in modern Athens: an answer to the ancient Jerusalem question', *Theory, Culture & Society*, 26 (2009), 76.
11. Carl Schmitt, *Political Theology: Four Chapters on the Concept of Sovereignty* (Chicago, University of Chicago Press, 1995), 49.
12. Schmitt, quoted in William E. Scheuerman, 'Down on law: The complicated legacy of the authoritarian jurist Carl Schmitt', *Boston Review*. Accessed at: http:bostonreview.net/BR26.2/scheuerman.html (February 2009).
13. Tracy B. Strong, 'Foreword' to, *Political Theology* (Chicago: University of Chicago Press, 2005), xxviii.
14. Martti Koskenniemi, 'International law as political theology: How to read Nomos der Erde?' *Constellations*, Vol.11, no. 4, 2004, 501.
15. Carl Schmitt, *Political Theology: Four Chapters on the Concept of Sovereignty* (Cambridge MA: MIT Press, 1985), 12-13. Here I am not going into how Schmitt's theory of the 'exception' should be understood as foundational for today's much better known conception of the 'exception' of Georgio Agamben.
16. Schmitt, *Political Theology*, 36, 12.
17. Schmitt, *Political Theology*, 5.
18. Schmitt, *Political Theology*, 13.
19. One must consider that the state of exception can become self-generating, becoming its own grounds for decision-making.
20. Olivier Roy, *Secularism Confronts Islam* (New York: Columbia University Press, 2007).
21. Omri Elisha, 'Faith beyond belief: Evangelical Protestant conceptions of faith and

the resonance of anti-humanism', *Social Analysis* 52 (2008), 56; and Mira Z. Amiras, 'Amazaghite, Arab/Islamic hegemony, and the Christian Evangelical challenge', *Religion, Politics and Globalization: Anthropological Approaches* (New York: Berghahn Books, 2011), 209-230.

22. Faisal Devji, *Landscapes of the Jihad: Militancy, Morality, Modernity* (London: Hurst, 2005), 42.

23. Devji, *Landscapes of the Jihad*, 120. See, too, Olivier Roy, *Globalised Islam: The Search for a New Ummah* (London: Hurst, 2004), and Don Handelman, 'Self-exploders, Self-sacrifice, and the rhizomic organization of terrorism', *Religion, Politics and Globalization*, 231-262.

11

Religious Politics and the Rise of Illiberal Religion

SCOTT W. HIBBARD
DEPAUL UNIVERSITY, USA

It has been argued that the twenty-first century will be 'God's Century'.[1] By this it is meant that religion—not God, but religion—will remain a central feature of both international and domestic politics for the next several decades. The basis for this claim can be found in the recent past. Over the last twenty-five years, the world has witnessed an increased level of political activism by religious individuals and organisations. This resurgence of religious politics is evident in the violent sectarianism and exclusive religious identities of the contemporary Middle East, the persistent communalism in South Asia and the continued salience of an illiberal religious politics in the United States and elsewhere. Conceptually, the trend is interesting given the assumptions of secularisation theory, which predicted that the influence of traditional belief systems would diminish with the onset of economic and political development. The persistence of religious politics has also given rise to the view that diplomats, politicians and political scientists all need to better understand religion if they are going to understand contemporary international politics.[2]

While there are a variety of explanations for the post-Cold War resurgence of religious politics—and a voluminous literature—what is missing from much of the debate is an understanding of precisely *how* religion relates to modern politics, and, more to the point, *which type* of religion one is in fact talking about. Religion is neither as monolithic nor as undifferentiated as many assume. On the contrary, religion is a multi-faceted phenomenon, which—in its more benign moments—manifests as ethical teachings that counsel peace and reconciliation, while at other moments informs the religious communalisms (i.e. sectarianisms) that are at the heart of so much war and conflict. These different interpretations of religion vie with one another for influence, inform competing visions of social life and frequently define the political fault lines within society.

This chapter will address these issues by asking the question: *Why have conservative renderings of religious tradition remained so politically influential in secular societies as Egypt, India and the US?* This question is the basis of my 2010 publication *Religious Politics and Secular States*.[3] The following pages offer a brief summation of the larger study. The answer to the aforementioned question, which will be elaborated below, is that religion remains relevant to modern politics because it continues to define collective—and particularly national—identities, and, second, because religion is uniquely able to provide a moral framework for political action. As a result, political actors of all stripes invoke religion in pursuit of their various political ends. While these three issues help to explain the continuing relevance of religion to modern politics, the question remains why a conservative or illiberal rendering of religious tradition has been so prominent, and not a more inclusive or liberal interpretation.[4] This last aspect of contemporary religious politics is perhaps the most interesting because it highlights the internal divisions within religion, and captures what Scott Appleby has referred to as religion's fundamental ambiguity: the continuing tension between competing interpretations of a given religious tradition and the pattern of social life that each envisions.[5]

Religion and Politics Reconsidered

One of the defining features of the post-Cold War era has been the resurgence of religious politics. By this we mean the increased politicisation of individuals and groups that are defined by their faith tradition. This trend is surprising, in part, because it contradicts the widely held assumptions of modernisation theory, and its corollary, the secularisation thesis. Modernisation theory predicted that religion would become less relevant as modern states and market capitalism displaced the church (or other formal religious organisations) as the dominant institutions of public life. It was also assumed that personal belief would decline as religious myths lost their hold on the popular imagination. Just as markets and states marginalised the church, it was believed that science and reason would displace religious belief as a means of explaining the world. Insofar as religion remained, it would be a personal affair and limited to individual matters of conscience. Modernity subsequently came to be defined by a differentiation of social life into a variety of spheres: secular and religious, on the one hand, and public and private on the other.[6]

The proliferation of religious politics in the post-Cold War era has forced a re-evaluation of these assumptions. One explanation for the resurgence of religious politics has focused on the material context, arguing that the rise of religious politics has less to do with religion than with issues such as economic disparity, social justice and political grievances.[7] The issue, in short, is politics, not religion. The basis for this argument is the perceived failure of the modern state to address basic human needs. This failure creates the popular discontent that subsequently finds expression in religious terms. While such political movements may articulate their grievances in a religious and cultural idiom, the underlying impetus is argued to be economic and political. It is a mistake, then, to interpret contemporary activism as 'religious' since the source of grievance lies in a material context. Religious fundamentalisms, then, ought to be seen as a by-product of a rapidly changing economic, social and political environment, not as a 'return' to religion per se.

An alternative perspective views the trend as a genuinely religious phenomenon, reflecting a resurgence of faith traditions in an increasingly atomised and secular world. From this view, the religious politics of recent years embodies a popular rejection of secularism and secular norms. This 'deprivatisation of religion', it is argued, is attributed to a deep desire by religious populations to 're-normativise' the public sphere and otherwise assert themselves within an overtly secular (or atheistic) society.[8] From this perspective, religious mobilisation in the post-Cold War era embodies a rebellion of religious populations against secular elites and pits those who seek to infuse public life with the 'traditional values' of religion against a state that embodies the irreligious values of secular modernity.[9] The revivalism of recent years simply reflects a shift in popular attitudes towards religion, and this is seen as an organic expression of traditional populations who seek to re-shape the political life of their countries.[10] Religion, from this perspective, is the causal variable emanating from the realm of civil society and driving modern politics.

While each of these explanations has their merit, a third approach seeks to integrate the insights of both and argues that the larger trend is *both* religious and political. It is this third alternative that informs the views of this chapter. While the driving impetus for much religious activism may, indeed, be socio-economic and political in nature, it is significant that it is religion to which political actors appeal, and not some other ideological resource. This is indicative of the continued salience of religion in speaking to fundamental questions of human existence: life, death and moral purpose. While science and reason help to explain the mechanical operations of the world, they are less able to address the normative questions faced by both individuals and society. Moreover, religion provides a language to articulate moral purpose, sanction the exercise of power, and otherwise situate contemporary political issues in a wider, normative framework. Hence, even if there is a formal separation of church and state—that is, a separation of religious authority from political authority—religious ideas and beliefs continue to provide a basis for social cohesion and a language for contemporary politics.

It is for these reasons that even ostensibly secular states have invoked religious narratives to sanction their authority. This last point warrants elaboration. A key failing of modernisation theory was the assumption that modern states were invariably hostile to religious belief of all sorts. This assumption was incorrect. While some states tried to eradicate religion—or greatly restrict it—this was by no means universal. More commonly, states sought to control, regulate or otherwise use religion to their own ends. As I discuss in the larger study, religion was (and remains) a central feature of the nationalist project, and nationalist narratives provide a new means by which religion enters the public sphere. As Anthony Marx has argued:

> [Within the European context,] religious fanaticism was the basis for popular engagement with—for or against—centralising state authority ... . Nationalism emerged when the masses were invited onto the political stage or invited themselves in. But that invitation did not come inclusively from books, enrichment, or schooling, but rather from sectarian conflicts, enraging sermons and callings. The passions of faith were the stuff of which the passions for the state were built.[11]

Part of the explanation for the contemporary resurgence of religion, then, is that religion never went away. Even if religious *institutions* are less central to modern social life, religious ideas, imagery and symbolism remain enormously influential in the construction and mobilisation of collective identities. Nationalist and sectarian ideologies, for example, commonly draw upon religious motifs and symbols in order to reinforce social solidarity and motivate political action.[12] The religious dimensions of nationalism also offer a narrative within which individual sacrifice is given transcendent meaning, associating it with both a mythic past and an ostensibly better future. Similarly, the moral language inherent within religious tradition is used to legitimise political authority or claims to such authority. By linking human existence to a transcendent realm, religion provides a framework for interpreting political events and articulating moral purpose. Even within a tradition of secular nationalism religion is able to lend a universal, and sacred, quality to what is, in essence, a particular set of political arrangements.[13]

It is for these reasons that religion is so readily invoked for political purposes. Religion is used by opposition groups to critique the status quo (in what is called the 'prophetic' function of religion) and articulate an alternative political program that recognises the opposition as the legitimate authority. Similarly, state elites have never been reluctant to appropriate religion for their own purposes. On the contrary, state actors have long used religion to sanctify political power and imbue relationships of dominance with the aura of natural right. In either instance—prophetic or priestly—the ultimate goal of such instrumental manipulation is to link the narrow political interests of a particular group to that of moral, national and religious purpose.

What is most interesting about the post-Cold War resurgence, however, involves the type of religion with which it is associated. What defined this latter era was not a resurgence of religion, per se, but, rather, a resurgence of *illiberal* visions of religion at the expense of *liberal* ones. In the mid-twentieth century, the type of religion that was dominant in public life was liberal and modernist—i.e. interpretations that eschewed a literalist reading of scripture for metaphorical and emphasised tolerance and ecumenical co-existence. These liberal interpretations of religion were consistent with secular norms of neutrality and informed a vision of society that was (theoretically) inclusive. Modernist religion was also associated with the political left, the promotion of social justice and the eradication of poverty. On the other hand, illiberal religion—i.e. interpretations that held monopolistic claims on truth, placed an emphasis upon scriptural literalism and tended to be intolerant of alternative beliefs—were commonly associated with the political right and traditional patterns of social and political hierarchy.

In the mid-twentieth century, illiberal or 'fundamentalist' forms of religion (and the organisations which espoused them) were politically marginalised and commonly repressed. This marginalisation was perceived as a harbinger of religion's future, and it is this trend that informed the secularisation thesis. However, the relative influence of these competing interpretations of religion began to change in the 1970s and early 1980s. During this latter period, mainstream political actors came to see religious fundamentalisms as a bulwark against socialism and a useful carrier of a patriotic majoritarianism. In the Cold War context, such religious activists gained support on a variety of continents from state actors who had come to see illiberal religious movements as a constituency to be courted, not a threat to be marginalised. It ought not to be surprising, then, that with the end of the Cold War—and the discrediting of the political left—that conservative religious groups would emerge as a forceful presence in these societies.

This trend is evident in each of the case studies examined in *Religious Politics and Secular States*. In all three cases—Egypt, India and the United

States—the post-World War II period was defined by a commitment to a secular vision of modernity. State actors throughout the 1950s and 1960s were the articulators of a progressive vision of national development, and sought to embed secular norms in the institutions of nation and state. Government policy during this period was commonly associated with poverty alleviation, state-led economic development, and social justice. An ecumenical (or modernist) understanding of religion was important here because it provided a moral—and non-sectarian—basis to political life. It was this historical moment that informed modernisation theory and the belief that modernity was, by definition, secular and progressive. Secularism in this context did not necessarily entail the removal of religion from the public sphere (although many advocated this alternative). Rather, secularism in the mid-twentieth century was seen as neutrality in matters of religion and belief, at least in the context of the cases under discussion. Secular norms and identities were thus perceived as an important mechanism for integrating diverse populations into a common political framework. Conservative social forces, on the other hand, and the illiberal religious ideas they espoused, were typically associated with a reactionary past and seen as an obstacle to the kind of economic and political reform promoted by modern states.

In the 1970s and 1980s, however, the commitment of state elites to social change diminished, and along with it their dedication to a secular vision of national life. State leaders and other mainstream political actors in all three cases abandoned their support for a liberal vision of religion and society in favour of conservative or illiberal religious ideologies. During this latter period, illiberal interpretations of religious traditions were used to counter leftist politics and legitimise hierarchical patterns of social order. Exclusive visions of national identity were also used to heighten communal loyalties, and appeal to a homogenised notion of group identity. This was an important means of diminishing the salience of class in national politics and generating popular support for a conservative political agenda. It was also an important part of the Cold War dynamic. In this context, state elites took either a weak stand against religious communalism—not wishing to oppose conservative cultural forces—or actively sought to co-opt such forces for their own purposes. This changing attitude of state actors towards illiberal religion marked a sharp break from previous practice and reflected a new set of priorities. Rather than serve as an agent of social change, state policy sought to reify existing patterns of social hierarchy. In this new era, state and religion would be used to maintain the status quo, not transform it.

Conclusion

There are several factors, then, that help to explain why exclusive interpretations of religion emerged so forcefully in the post-Cold War era.

Despite the common assumption that the contemporary resurgence of religious politics represents a popular rejection of state led secularisation or is the result of a failed modernity project, the aforementioned cases indicate a more nuanced explanation. On the one hand, religion was never removed from the public sphere. Rather, religion was always important in shaping identity, articulating political purpose and legitimating authority. A key variable, though, in explaining the demise of a modernist vision of religion and society—and the corresponding rise of an illiberal vision—is the changing orientation of mainstream political actors who abandoned commitments to an inclusive vision of social order, and chose instead to 'ride the tiger' of an exclusive religious politics.[14] This is not to argue that religion does not matter—nor that religion is epiphenomenonal—but it is to argue that fundamentalisms did not emerge autonomously from the realm civil society to reshape modern politics. Rather, the political fortunes of illiberal religious groups and activists changed precipitously when state actors sought to support, not repress them.

The turn towards exclusive interpretations of religion by ostensibly secular state elites raises two important and related questions. First, why was the commitment to secular norms so readily displaced, and, second, why was the attraction of exclusive (as opposed to inclusive) versions of religion so strong? In regard to the first issue, loyalty to liberal ideas—and the relegation of religion to the private sphere—proved less compelling in each of the cases during the 1970s and 1980s than was the compulsion of religious sectarianism. Some would argue that this reflects the limits of loyalty to a public sphere shorn of religious imagery, or the continuing appeal of certitude in a world defined by socio-economic change. These are important and valid points. However, there is more to the answer than just these two issues. Here, the cases are instructive. In each instance, religion was (and is) central to the construction of collective, and particularly national, identities. Hence, religion was invoked to activate or appeal to the ethnic or religious loyalties of key constituencies. In this context, religion was (and is) an important tool in providing a sense of belonging to a larger community and attachment to the institutions that govern society. Perhaps more importantly, religion provides a moral framework for contemporary politics and lends a timeless quality to institutions that are, in reality, modern social constructs. It should not be surprising, then, that both the defence and the critique of the modern state are frequently done in a religious vernacular.

This, then, leads to the second issue. It was not just religion that was being promoted, but exclusive interpretations of religion. Why was this? There are two answers indicated by the cases. One is that the inherent communalism within the very idea of the nation-state—the tendency towards a 'homogenizing ideology of unity'[15]—more readily conforms with exclusive visions of religion than do their liberal counterparts. In other words, the communalism inherent within exclusive interpretations of religion fit more readily with the ideological requirements of the modern state than does the ambiguity of liberal religion. Very much related to this is the certitude offered by illiberal religion and the utility that such an unquestioning faith can provide for modern political actors. Second, the role of state elites in promoting one vision of religion and society as opposed to the other is crucial. If the first point deals with the inherent tendencies—and tensions—within both religion and society, the second point involves human agency and choice. As the cases illustrate, the embrace of communalism was not pre-ordained, or determined, by the nature of the state. On the contrary, there was an ongoing tension between liberal and illiberal visions of the nation, and this was a defining feature of the politics of all three societies. Moreover, the active role of state elites within the debates over how to define the nation proved critical to the success of liberal renditions of religious politics in the mid-twentieth century and illiberal interpretations in the latter part of the twentieth century. This helps to explain, then, the transition from a benign expression of civil religion to a more assertive religious nationalism and the attendant refashioning of the political realm. Although both visions of society are latent within the idea of the nation-state, the actions of state leaders had an important bearing upon which of the two emerged as dominant at a given point in time.

The cases also indicate that one cannot assume that an exclusive vision of religion and society is somehow more natural, more authentic or ultimately more effective. Nor do the cases argue that the resurgence of religious politics is *simply* a matter of elite manipulation. On the contrary, what the study illustrates is the interactive and the variable nature of this entire process. Religion is a potent force and has been alternately used for both good and ill by political actors. Moreover, religion can provide an inclusive basis to social life, or justify an exclusive (and often violent) chauvinism. Implicit in this variability is an assumption about human nature and the continuing tension between man's better impulses and his/her more aggressive ones. The instrumental manipulation of illiberal visions of religion by political leaders, then, reflects a willingness to pander to the baser instincts of the majority community. Instead of appealing to a more virtuous reading of religion—one that unifies diverse communities instead of dividing them—the appeal to an illiberal rendering of religious tradition had the clear intention of polarising the population along communal lines. The intent was also to promote the interests of one community (or one section of a community) at the expense of all others. The fallout in each of the cases, moreover, has been detrimental to the larger goal of providing a cohesive—and inclusive—basis to political life.

Notes

1. Monica Duffy Toft, Daniel Philpott, Timothy Samuel Shah, *God's Century: Resurgent Religion and Global Politics* (New York: W.W. Norton and Co., 2011).

2. Doug Johnston and Cynthia Sampson, eds., *Religion: The Missing Dimension of Statecraft* (New York, Oxford University Press, 1995).

3. Scott W. Hibbard, *Religious Politics and Secular States: Egypt, India and the United States* (Baltimore: Johns Hopkins University Press, 2010).

4. By illiberal religion I am referring to interpretations of religious tradition that place an emphasis upon scriptural literalism, conservative morality and exclusive claims on religious truth. Liberal or 'modernist' understandings of religion, on the other hand, are defined by their tendency to read scripture as metaphor, employ reason as a guide for interpreting religion, and are more inclined towards religious pluralism

5. R. Scott Appleby, *The Ambivalence of the Sacred: Religion, Violence and Reconciliation* (New York; Rowman and Littlefield Publishers, Inc., 2000), p. 27.

6. For a more thorough discussion of secularism and the secularization thesis, see Scott Hibbard, 'Religion, Nationalism and the Politics of Secularism', in Scott Appleby and Atalia Omer, eds., *Oxford Handbook on Religion, Conflict and Peacebuilding* (Oxford University Press, Forthcoming).

7. See for example Mark Tessler, 'The Origins of Popular Support for Islamist Movements', in John Entelis, ed., *Islam, Democracy and the State in North Africa* (Bloomington: Indiana University Press, 1997).

8. Jose Casanova, *Public Religions in the Modern World* (Chicago: University of Chicago Press, 2004), p. 5.

9. Mark Juergensmeyer, *Global Rebellion: Religious Challenges to the Secular State, from Christian Militias to al-Qaeda* (Berkeley: University of California Press, 2008).

10. See for example John Micklethwait and Adrian Wooldridge, *God Is Back: How the Global Revival of Faith is Changing the World* (New York: The Penguin Press, 2009).

11. Anthony Marx, *Faith in Nation: Exclusionary Origins of Nationalism* (New York: Oxford University Press, 2003), p. 197.

12. See for example Anthony Smith, 'The Sacred Dimension of Nationalism', *Millennium: Journal of International Studies*, 2000. Vol. 29, No. 3, pp. 791-814. See also David Little, 'Belief, Ethnicity and Nationalism', in *Nationalism and Ethnic Politics* Vol 1, No. 2, Summer 1995 (London: Frank Cass, 1995).

13. This is evident in the notion of civil religion. See Robert Bellah, 'Civil Religion in America', in *Beyond Belief: Essays on Religion in a Post-Traditionalist World* (Berkeley: University of California Press, 1991).

14. The reference is to Zia al-Huq's efforts to co-opt Sunni fundamentalism into the service of the Pakistani state in the 1980's. See Seyyed Vali Reza Nasr, *The Islamic Leviathan: Islam and the Making of State Power* (New York: Oxford University Press, 2001), Chapter 3.

15. Zoya Hasan, 'Changing Orientation of the State and the Emergence of Majoritarianism in the 1980's', in K.N. Panniker, *Communalism in India: History, Politics and Culture* (Delhi: Manohar, 1991), p. 152.

12

Assessing State and Religious Institutions: A Comment from the Case of Angola

RUY LLERA BLANES
UNIVERSITY OF BERGEN, NORWAY

In a continent that has been recently described as the new demographic centre of Christianity and a stronghold of politically active Islamic movements,[1] Angola has become in recent years an interesting case study through which one might consider the complexities of the geopolitics of faith in the twenty-first century. As I will argue throughout this text, in Angola we observe two seemingly contradictory but nevertheless correlated phenomena in what concerns religious practice: the opening up of the local landscape for transnational religious circulation, for the most part occurring in its capital, Luanda; and the process of 'nationalisation' or 'Angolanisation' of religious activity.[2] The intersection of both dynamics has highlighted the role of the state—materialising, in the Angolan case, as the MPLA party[3] as main actor in the definition of religious activity.

Historical Dynamics

From a historical point of view, Angola has been in many ways a classic example of religious transnationalism, long before the concept became part of the academic jargon. In a sense it is a reminder of the century-old presence of Christianity in the continent, following the arrival, in the fifteenth century (1482), of the Portuguese explorer Diogo Cão in the Congo River basin, escorted by Italian missionaries. As historians such as John Thornton, Adrian Hastings, Richard Gray, Carlos Almeida and others have described,[4] the first contact was indeed one of mission and conversion, with the surprisingly successful adoption of Christian faith on behalf of the rulers and elite of the then kingdom of Kongo, which occupied a significant part of northern Angola. However, the region very soon became a stronghold of African Christianity, long before that was even a concept in the study of religions. Autochthonous expressions such as Kimpa Vita and the Antonian movement exemplified the intersection of Christian expansion from the Vatican and the theological autonomy of local expressions.[5] In the late colonial period (from, roughly, the 1885 Berlin Conference to Angolan independence in 1975) we observe two different movements developing: the increasing presence of Catholic endeavours in the Portuguese colony; and the emergence of Protestant missions of north European or North American origin—mainly Baptist, Methodist, Presbyterian, Philafrican and evangelical— in the hinterland, engaging in proselytist and educational projects.[6] Despite differences in the state–institution relationship, both Catholic and Protestant enterprises can be seen as part of the 'civilizing mission' upon which the Portuguese empire embarked, which was mostly an outcome of an economic project of exploitation.[7]

This model of the relationship between church and state would set the template for what occurred after independence in 1975. As in other newly independent African countries, Angola experienced, by the hand of the ruling party MPLA, a process of 'sovietisation of the social',[8] by which religious activity was removed from the public space and, in some specific cases, actively persecuted. This policy, sponsored mostly by the cabinet of the first Angolan president, Agostinho Neto (1975–1979), eventually subsided into a more pragmatic policy, in which the mainstream religious movements progressively re-emerged as public partners of the state, playing an important role in sectors of social welfare and education.[9] In particular, after the 1992 elections, when significant changes were made to the country's political, juridical and financial systems (i.e. the introduction of a multipartisan system and a number of economic reforms), and despite the continuation of the civil war that continued to destroy Angola, the door opened for the arrival of a number of foreign churches, some of which were iconic representatives of contemporary 'southern' religious transnational geopolitics, such as the Universal Church of the Kingdom of God[10] and the Igreja Maná. These churches soon made a significant impact in the local urban scenery, especially through the construction of cathedrals and an active role in the public sphere.[11] Today, the urban landscape of Luanda appears pervasively punctuated by landmarks of religious architecture, as well as with recurring public displays (demonstrations, concerts, services, etc.) on behalf of these churches, which compete in the public space with other local Christian movements such as the Tokoist church. In such cases, one often observes multiple engagement with government-sponsored activities, such as aiding electoral registration campaigns and promoting health awareness or public safety policies.

From this particular perspective, the emergence and implantation of Brazilian-originated churches can be understood within wider socio-economic movements that have made Angola and Brazil strong partners in the Southern Atlantic area while retaining a strong tie to the idea of Lusophony. Within this framework it has been mostly churches with an evangelical-pentecostal background that have been able to successfully establish themselves in the local sphere, as an outcome of wider movements of expansion of such branches of Christianity throughout the world.[12] However, other movements of transnational religious flux can also be detected; for instance, the increasing presence of churches of Bakongo ethnicity originating in the DRC, not only in the continuum that connects Luanda and its northern border[13] but also extending southwards. These churches tend to be characterised by their informality and lack of public visibility, working mainly in the capital's *musseques* (slums). They remain transnational in their scope, and in most cases escape the second process I wish to highlight here: state control of religious activity.

Nationalising Religion

Apart from the overarching narrative of transnational religious circulation described above, one can also observe in Angola what could be called a process of 'nationalisation' of religion, a state-promoted strategy of not allowing religious creeds to claim any kind of economic or political allegiance to territories outside of Angola. This policy, as we can already pick up from the above description, has become increasingly present since Angolan independence in 1975. The country's constitution defines the state as being laic and recognising religious freedom 'as long as [the churches] do not undermine the Constitution and public order, and conform to the law'.[14] However, although it is not specifically stated in the Law of Religious Freedom, religious institutions in Angola are inserted within the specific post-reform and post-war political and economic environment of Angola, where the MPLA government defines, supervises and centralises all sectors of business and enterprise but where capitalist models also are encouraged in what has been described as 'business Angola-style'.[15]

One particularly relevant case in point is that of the Muslim community in Angola, which has been object of intense debate in both national and international media. The Comunidade Islâmica de Angola (CISA) has existed in the country for several years[16] and has unsuccessfully tried to have its juridical status recognised by the government. Despite recurring complaints on behalf of local leaders in the media, the government has rarely, if ever, made a public statement on the issue. It was recently forced to deny its prohibition after several media reports denouncing the forceful closure of mosques.[17] However, in my conversations with people close to government or involved in religious affairs in Angola, this comment recurs: considering the Muslim allegiance to Mecca and the transnational networks and circulations with which it is composed, the government will not (or 'should not', depending on the interlocutor) recognise Islam in Angola because it would challenge the country's 'Christian identity'. This statement, although historically speaking seemingly contradictory, characterises the current sentiment in present-day Angola, where, as previously mentioned, the key word is 'partnership'. In any case, the media interventions of local Muslim leaders always point towards a narrative of integration and legitimation, which in turn is not recognised by the government.

Considering the portrait above, it appears that Christianity enjoys a situation of supremacy in Angola. And indeed, it is demographically hegemonic and intrinsically connected to the country's colonial and postcolonial history. However, a closer look will reveal complexities that distinguish between certain Christian institutions and insert other, non-religious elements into the equation beyond the nationalist imagination, i.e. economic and political/ethnic factors.

Pluralism and Competition

This last point becomes evident when we look at the evangelical and Pentecostal field in Luanda, where we can distinguish four major groups in terms of geographical origin: 1) historical evangelical movements, the outcome of nineteenth and twentieth-century missionary projects originating in Europe and North America; 2) transnational, southern Atlantic churches, mostly of Brazilian origin and frequently close to a Neo-Pentecostal model; 3) Bakongo-based 'Holy Spirit' churches, frequently originating from the Democratic Republic of Congo and loosely associated with the blending of evangelical and 'traditional' elements;[18] and finally 4) locally initiated churches, sponsored by Angolan leaders who may or may not have belonged to other, originally foreign churches.[19]

The result of such a diverse scenario is the competition of multiple, diverse perceptions concerning evangelical and Pentecostal Christianity. For instance, in my interactions with religious folk in Angola, I noticed that there is a perception of foreignness regarding Brazilian churches that combines a certain suspicion with the acknowledgement of their entrepreneurial capacities—an idea that is undoubtedly associated with ongoing south–south economic connections between Angola and Brazil, involving business interactions (in the resources and construction sectors) as well as cultural and media exchange (music, soap operas, etc.). This combination may also be a by-product of the strategic silence that these churches promote in terms of public commentary on internal political affairs, making them either 'good partners' or 'accomplices' of the state (depending on the political positioning of each interlocutor).

This view contrasts with the more ambiguous (and in any case negative) image of Bakongo churches, which are frequently accused in the local media of illicit behaviour—from witchcraft to adultery, smuggling and exploitation, etc. This, in turn, is associated with the complicated position of Bakongo ethnicity in Angolan culture, often framed as 'foreign' to Angolan interests.[20] Such an environment may explain why many such churches remain, voluntarily or involuntarily, within the informal sector and in neighbourhoods with a predominantly Bakongo ethnicity (Cazenga, Palanca, etc.). In such neighbourhoods it is a hard task to keep up with the continuous emergence of movements and institutions that emerge around prophetic and charismatic figures, some of them French-speaking—such as the famous Combat Spirituel church, led by a Congolese couple and well known for its deliverance sessions that take place in the Cazenga neighbourhood. On the other hand, many local evangelical churches—such as the Assembleia de Deus Pentecostal do Makulusso—have initiated their own processes of transnationalisation, working through the Angolan diaspora outside Angolan territory, with representations in other corners of the Lusophone Atlantic, for example Brazil and Portugal. They represent part of what we have called elsewhere 'prophetic diasporas'.[21]

Such a plurality becomes even more complicated when we attempt to make sense of the denominational histories of these churches. As noted by Angolan researchers,[22] there is a history of dissidence, proliferation and innovation within most major churches that challenges the classical distinctions between religious institutions and makes any map of their journey into a labyrinth. From this perspective, the delimitations that identify evangelical and Pentecostal churches from other Christian movements are in most cases difficult to perceive, rendering them virtually useless in many cases. The result of this is a complex mosaic of churches that respond diversely to the process of 'nationalisation' mentioned above.

Churches equipped with significant economic and infrastructural resources are able to establish fruitful partnerships with the government and collaborate with its agenda of nationalisation while establishing themselves as part of the local scenery; smaller churches seek public legitimation through a process of applying for official recognition. Other movements prefer to remain on the margins of the system, developing their own informal transnational networks.

Notes

1. See Philip Jenkins, 'The Next Christianity', *The Atlantic Monthly* (October 2002); Yushau Sodiq, 'Islam in Africa', *The Wiley-Blackwell Companion to African Religions* (Oxford: Wiley-Blackwell).

2. See Ruy Blanes, *A Prophetic Trajectory* (Oxford and New York: Berghahn Books, 2014). This text recaps and expands ideas developed in a recent chapter called 'Politics of Sovereignty: Evangelical and Pentecostal Christianity and Politics in Angola', published in Simon Coleman & Rosalind Hackett (eds), *The Anthropology of Global Pentecostalism and Evangelicalism* (New York: New York University Press, 2014).

3. The People's Movement for the Liberation of Angola (MPLA) was one of the movements that staged the liberation wars against the Portuguese colonial authorities (1961-1975) and is today the political party that has ruled Angola since its independency in 1975.

4. John Thornton, 'The Development of an African Catholic Church in the Kingdom of Kongo', *Journal of African History* 25:2 (1984), 147-167; 'African Religions and Christianity in the Atlantic World', *Africa and Africans in the Making of the Atlantic World, 1400-1800* (Cambridge: Cambridge University Press, 1998). Adrian Hastings, *The Church in Africa, 1450-1950* (Oxford: Oxford University Press, 1994). Richard Gray, 'A Kongo Princess, The Kongo, Ambassadors and the Papacy', *Journal of Religion in Africa* 29:2 (1999), 140-154. Carlos Almeida, 'Entre gente "aspra e dura" – advertências de um missionário no Congo e Angola (1713-1723)', *Revista Lusófona Ciência das Religiões* 13-14 (2008), 463-483

5. John Thornton, *The Kongolese Saint Anthony: Dona Beatriz Kimpa Vita and the Antonian Movement* (Cambridge: Cambridge University Press, 1998).

6. Didier Pëclard 1995, 'Ethos Missionaire et Esprit du Capitalisme. La Mission Philafricaine en Angola 1897-1907', *Le Fait Missionaire* (Cahier 1) (1995), 1-97; 'Religion and Politics in Angola: The Church, the Colonial State and the Emergence of Angolan Nationalism, 1940-1961', *Journal of Religion in Africa* 28:2 (May 1998), 160-186. Christine Messiant, 'Protestantismes en Situation Coloniale: Quelles Marges?' *Lusotopie* (1998), 245-256. Benedict Schubert, *A Guerra e as Igrejas. Angola 1961-1991* (Basel: P. Schlettwein Publishing, 2000). Iracema Dulley, 'Notes on a Disputed Process of Signification. The Practice of Communication in Spiritain Missions in the Central Highlands of Angola', *Vibrant* 5:2 (2008), 75-99.

7. David Birmingham, *Empire in Africa: Angola and its Neighbors* (Athens OH: Ohio University Press, 2006).

8. Ruy Blanes and Abel Paxe, 'Atheist Political Cultures in Independent Angola', *Social Analysis* 59:2 (2015), 62-80.

9. I am referring to churches such as the Catholic Church, the Methodist Church, the Angolan Baptist Church (IEBA) and, more recently, the Tokoist Church (see Blanes 2014). In some cases, such as in the IEBA, they appeared at this stage as 'national versions' of former missionary institutions.

10. See e.g. Paul Freston, Paul, *Evangelicals and Politics in Asia, Africa and Latin America* (Cambridge: Cambridge University Press, 2001); 'The Universal Church of the Kingdom of God: a Brazilian Church finds Success in Southern Africa', *Journal of Religion in Africa* 35:1 (2005), 33-65.

11. See e.g. Clara Mafra, Claudia Swatowiski and Camila Sampaio, 'O Projeto Pastoral

de Edir Macedo. Uma Igreja Benevolente para Indivíduos Ambiciosos?', *Revista Brasileira de Ciências Sociais* 27(2012), 81-96.

12. Allan Anderson, *An Introduction to Pentecostalism: Global Charismatic Christianity* (Cambridge: Cambridge University Press, 2013, 2nd Edition). Coleman & Hackett, *The Anthropology of Global Pentecostalism and Evangelicalism.*

13. Luena Pereira, 'Os Bakongo de Angola: Religião, Política e Parentesco num Bairro de Luanda', PhD diss., University of São Paulo (2004).

14. Instituto Nacional para os Assuntos Religiosos, *As Religiões em Angola. A Realidade do Período Pós-Independência (1975-2010),* (Luanda: INAR, 2010). My translation.

15. Ricardo Soares de Oliveira, 'Business Success, Angola-Style: postcolonial politics and the rise and rise of Sonangol', *Journal of Modern African Studies* 45: 4 (2007), 595-619. One exception, for historical reasons, is obviously the Catholic Church. Although it may appear somewhat subsumed in this text, the Catholic Church is a central player in Angolan post-independence history. See e.g., Tony Neves, *Angola: Justiça e Paz nas Intervenções da Igreja Católica* (Lisbon: Texto, 2012).

16. As a federation, the CISA exists formally since 2007, as a merger between several previous smaller, unrecognized associations. But there are records of Muslim presence in the territory since colonial times.

17. See e.g., Aristides Cabeche and David Smith, 'Angola accused of "banning" Islam as mosques closed', *The Guardian*, November 28, 2013. Accessed November 30, 2013. www.theguardian.com/world/2013/nov/28/angola-accused-banning-islam-mosques/.

18. These are usually referred to as *Mpeve ya Nlongo* (Holy Spirit) churches, an umbrella term that covers several different religious expressions that combine Christian beliefs with local healing practices. But there are also more 'mainstream' Pentecostal churches of Congolese origin in Angola. Perhaps the most visible and established one in Angola is the Igreja do Bom Deus (Church of the Good God), founded by pastor Simão Lutumba in Angola in 1981.

19. Within the proliferated scenario of Angolan Christianity, obviously this systematization does not encompass the totality of the evangelical and Pentecostal universe. For instance, the Assemblies of God are known to have been present in the territory for several decades. Furthermore, during my research in the past years I recorded the presence of Portuguese evangelical missions in the territory, mostly structured around NGO-type work such as the construction of schools, health posts, etc., in rural areas.

20. See e.g. Jean Michel Mabeko-Tali, 'La Chasse aux Zairois à Luanda' *Politique Africaine* 57 (1995), 71-84; Luena Pereira, 'Os Bakongo de Angola'.

21. Ramon Sarró and Ruy Blanes, 'Prophetic Diasporas. Moving Religion Across the Lusophone Atlantic', *African Diaspora* 2:1 (2009), 52-72.

22. Fátima Viegas, *Angola e as Religiões* (Luanda: Edição de Autor, 1999); *Panorama das Religiões em Angola. Dados Estatísticos 2007* (Luanda: Instituto Nacional para os Assuntos Religiosos, 2007).

13

The Geopolitics of Religious Performance in Twenty-First Century Taiwan

FANG-LONG SHIH
LONDON SCHOOL OF ECONOMICS, UK

Taiwan's status began to evolve from merely a geographical area into a geopolitical entity in the seventeenth century, when the island came under Dutch colonial control and was thus incorporated into regional and global geopolitics. However, Taiwan's position has always been marginal: on the periphery of the Chinese and then the Japanese empires, and now on the edges of the USA's current sphere of influence. This chapter examines the issues around how marginal Taiwan has been represented culturally and symbolically in the twenty-first century's new geopolitical climate. It explores the twin themes of 'religion and politics; religion and nationalism' in the Taiwanisation movement, focusing on how the god Nazha represents the struggle of Taiwanese identity in an attempt to open new political spaces for itself in the international world.

Taiwan's Liminality: Neither a State nor a Nation-State

This geopolitical marginality has intensified in recent years, with the rise of China as a global superpower. 'Marginality' has a negative connation, and Corcuff has suggested a more positive and creative perspective by using the term 'liminality'.[1] The concept of 'liminality' was first articulated by a French anthropologist, Arnold Van Gennep, who defined rituals as 'rites of passage' made up of three stages—separation, liminality and incorporation—with liminality referring to 'an in-between period during which an individual is in transition between a state of life that (s)he has not yet fully left, and a new stage into which s(he) has not fully entered'.[2] Corcuff's application of the concept of liminality to the sociological study of Taiwan's geopolitics and international relations requires analytical attention be directed to Taiwan's temporal isolation in a Cold War bubble and also the spatial connectivities at play in a given time frame.

Taiwan is indeed in a state of liminality, being neither a state nor a non-state. Between 1947 and 1949, the then-ruling government in China—the Kuomingtang (KMT, Chinese Nationalist Party)—retreated to Taiwan following the defeat of its forces on Mainland China at the end of the civil war with the Chinese Communist Party (CCP). The decision to give Taiwan to the KMT had been made by the Allies at the Cairo Conference of 1943, on the condition that the three nations (the Republic of China, the US and the UK) would fight alongside one another until Japan's surrender. However, although the Treaty of San Francisco, which Japan signed in 1951, stated that Japan renounced all right, title and claim to Formosa and the Pescadores, it did not specify what Taiwan's legal status actually was. Taiwan's status remained liminal: for the CCP's newly founded People's Republic of China, Taiwan was a place still to be brought under its control, while the KMT continued to assert its Republic of China was the sole legitimate government of all China. The KMT regarded itself as in temporary exile on Taiwan, and the island was imagined as a mere province of an imagined territory of China that was even larger than that of the PRC; it even included Outer Mongolia, which the PRC had recognised as independent in 1949.[3]

The KMT at first enjoyed international recognition but, with the Sino-Soviet split in the late 1960s, ideological opposition to communism in the West lost ground to pragmatic political calculation. The US, along with many other Western countries, used relations with China strategically against the Soviet Union. The CCP's PRC began to replace the KMT's ROC as the internationally recognised government of China. In 1971, the ROC lost its seat in the General Assembly of the Security Council of the United Nations, and this was followed by the loss of diplomatic recognition by the UK in 1972 and by the USA in 1979.[4] The ROC/Taiwan has since become even more politically isolated, with the PRC undergoing a process of neo-liberal capitalist transition from the 1980s and increasing its interaction with the rest of the world from the 1990s. It is indeed from such a socio-economic perspective, as Sung-sheng Chang points out, that 'greater penetration of global capitalism in the post-Cold War era has hiked the stakes of symbolic wars ... these factors have come increasingly to determine the condition of possibility for culturally representing Taiwan.'[5]

God Nazha and Taiwan's Visibility

Religion in Taiwan since the 1980s has reflected the transformation of politics; a shift from local rivalries of territorial deities to island-wide Mazu pilgrimages 'constituting a ritual of pan-Taiwaneseness'[6] and further linked to a growing sense of Taiwanisation. Taiwanisation in the new mobile digital era has further evolved into an imagined relation between people who might never meet, mediated by social media. In particular, the god Nazha has become an actor for the formation of a new Taiwanisation discourse, seeking to connect Taiwan with the rest of the world and thus to create a political space for Taiwan. No other deity generates as much enthusiasm among young Taiwanese as Nazha. This is perhaps because of Nazha's unruly nature: many young people in Taiwan today identify with him, an unruly god, in contrast to other gods/goddesses, who are upright but distant—especially when they feel frustrated at being unjustly treated.

Nazha is also known as the Third Prince, in reference to the third son of General Li Jing. The Third Prince Nazha has the position of Marshal in the Centre of the Heavenly Altar, also known as 'Marshal of the Centre of the Altar', commanding the five 'camps': of the North, of the South, of the East, of the West, and of the Centre.[7] This is signified by the five flags carried behind Nazha while on tour. In religious processional troupes, Nazha takes the lead when deities of higher rank go on inspection tours in their own territory or visiting tours to other temples. Along with dancing, performances normally involve singing, martial arts and trances or spirit-possession, and the whole ensemble is known as 'troupe culture'. The young performers, like other young people, often go to discotheques and nightclubs, and they have incorporated elements from the nightclubs they love into the Nazha performance for which they are trained. The Nazha act has therefore undergone a transformation: while bearing giant Nazha body puppets and retaining certain rigid gestures associated with the god, the young performers now dress in modern fashions, wearing sun glasses as they dance to techno music and follow disco beats. This adaptation is known as 'the Techno Nazha the Third Prince'.

The turning point in Nazha's popularity was a performance at the opening ceremony of the 2009 World Games in Kaohsiung. About twenty giant Nazha body puppets roared into the stadium on motorcycles and proceeded to dazzle the audience. Since then, Techno Nazha the Third Prince troupes with body puppets have frequently been invited to perform at international events such as the 2009 Deaf Olympics in Taipei, the 2010 World Expo in Shanghai and the 2010 International Flower Expo in Taipei. Moreover, in January 2010, a performance in the USA was awarded first prize in an international competition at the Pasadena Rose Parade. In August 2010, 11 members of

Taiwan's marathon team took turns running a super marathon through the Sahara Desert dressed in Nazha body puppets. They did so to publicise Taiwan during the week-long event. And in July 2012, while attending a cross-Strait exchange programme, China's leader Jintao Hu accepted an invitation to join in an act dancing with Nazha body puppets. [8]

From February 2011 to the end of 2013, Chien-Heng Wu, a Taiwanese student in his early twenties who was studying Sports Management at National Taipei University, performed in a Nazha giant body puppet weighing 14 kilograms in over sixty countries, including India, Egypt, Kenya, Peru, Argentina, Paraguay, Brazil, the USA and the UK. During his performances he played techno music and danced to a disco beat. However, he also replaced the five flags representing the five directions with ROC national flags decorated with LED lights. Publicity around Nazha reached a high point during the period of the London Olympic Games in summer 2012. Wu, within his giant Nazha body puppet, participated in a demonstration in which 300 overseas Taiwanese (most of them studying in the UK) carried Taiwan's ROC flag through central London. The highlight of the event was street dancing in Regent Street, where for a few days Taiwan's ROC flag hung alongside the flags of the 206 other participating countries. Unfortunately, after a week, Taiwan's national flag was removed at the PRC's insistence and replaced by the Chinese Taipei Olympic flag.[9] However, together with campaigners, Wu's performance of the unruly Nazha brought Taiwan's national flag back to Regent Street, albeit in a temporary action.

Photos of Wu's performance dancing in a Nazha body puppet decked out with ROC national flags while on his global tour have been posted on social media sites such as Facebook and YouTube. The images show him surrounded by groups of local people of different cultural backgrounds in various foreign cities, towns and villages. According to an article posted to the website *Taiwan Insights*, which is run by the Press Division of the Taipei Economic and Cultural Office (TECO) in San Francisco, Wu explained that 'people from many parts of the world have no idea what Taiwan is, and therefore he chose this way to present Taiwan'. He also said that 'those local residents and international tourists in each country would never have dreamt of meeting the Third Prince god Nazha from Taiwan during their life journey'. [10] According to a comment posted under the story:

> Like many in Taiwan, Wu feels frustrated with the island's diplomatic isolation; however, his creative thinking has helped the national flag to be seen on the international arena once again. Nazha the Third Prince, a mythical teenage hero, represents a symbol of youth, bravery, agility and freedom

from conventional bondage, a perfect mascot for grassroots diplomacy engaged by Wu.[11]

It is understandable that young people desire and seek global recognition for their country, Taiwan. In the age of social media, the younger generation expects equal access to communication and equal visibility. However, Taiwan's rights to visibility and to recognition in international relations have been restricted. At the same time, young Taiwanese *individually* have global civic rights and exercise their freedom to travel, to demonstrate and to communicate with other global citizens, as well as use social media. The global tour of the techno Nazha performance was thus conducted in a spirit of civic freedom and mobility, elaborating and extending the capabilities of communication, visibility and connection—young actors hoped that global citizens even living at a distance could 'see' and 'touch' Taiwan as represented by the Techno Nazha and thus give recognition to the existence of Taiwan.

The development of the Nazha tour, both nationally and internationally, has created significant opportunities to mark the presence of Taiwan (as symbolised by the national flag) more prominently in the international world and thus to express Taiwan's right to visibility; by the end of 2013 the number of countries visited by Wu was greater than the number exposed to Taiwanese diplomacy. In addition, videos of the Techno Nazha performance have attracted the attention of hundreds of thousands of internet users. *Want China Times* reported that Chien-Heng Wu 'has earned himself a reputation as a cultural ambassador for Taiwan, as he always dances with the ROC flag'.[12]

Concluding Remarks: Religious Actor and International Recognition

The increasing global nature of Nazha performance tours has intensified the reach of Nazha as a new vehicle for Taiwan's identity. If we want to understand this new form of Taiwanisation, we need to understand the desire for independence and subjectivity as manifested in the myth of Nazha and the solution of his conflict with his father. The mythology of Nazha has been an important constitutive element of the Chinese family system within which a Chinese subjectivity has traditionally been produced.[13] It has always been an issue in the Chinese family, in which fathers have strong patriarchal authority: is a Chinese son to be his own agent or subject, or the instrument or object of his father? The Nazha story embodies the struggle of a young Chinese man to produce and define his own subjectivity while facing his father's authority.

By approaching geopolitics from a perspective of liminality, I have shown that

Taiwan's relation to China is not, or not only and not always, that of a periphery dominated by a centre, and further I have also demonstrated how Taiwan has been turned into a site invested in by human cultural and social projects via the vehicle of religion in a twenty-first century context of geopolitical flows. Via the case study of Techno Nazha performances we see that in Taiwan, identity does not mean a fixed or stable geopolitical identity but rather a plurality of identities formed through symbolic struggle. Nazha's attempt to establish his autonomy is drawn as analogous with Taiwan's sovereignty in relation to China. The unruly god Nazha is thus identified as unruly Taiwan, and Nazha's conflict with his father is an analogy of the conflict of Taiwan with its 'fatherland', China. The Nazha performances suggest that the Taiwanese are simply not interested in voluntary unification with China; instead they are interested in a symbolic exploration of a conflict between Taiwan and China, which they have come to see as inevitable. The performance of Nazha revives local cultural knowledge at a time when all knowledge seem inadequate in the face of complex global problems. Through a local symbol of resistance, Taiwanese people can feel themselves capable of 'resisting' Chinese domination: a parallel with Nazha's resistance to his father's authority. The problem is not conflict and resistance as such, but rather how to ensure that the energies of conflict and resistance do not spill out into actual violence but are constructively contained and directed towards the production of symbolic capital in the post-Cold War era's culture wars.

Notes

1. Stephane Corcuff, 'The Liminality of Taiwan: A Case-Study in Geopolitics', *Taiwan in Comparative Perspective*, 4 (2012) 42.
2. Corcuff, *The Liminality of Taiwan*, 53.
3. Fang-long Shih, 'Introduction to Taiwan and Hong Kong in Comparative Perspective: Centres-Peripheries, Colonialism, and the Politics of Representation', *Taiwan in Comparative Perspective* 5 (2014) 8.
4. Shelley Rigger, *Politics in Taiwan* (London: Routledge, 1999), 221.
5. Sung-sheng Yvonne Chang, 'Representing Taiwan: Shifting Geopolitical Frameworks', *Writing Taiwan: A New Literary History* (London: Duke University Press, 2007), 17.
6. Steven Sangren, 'Power and Transcendence in the Ma Tsu Pilgrimages of Taiwan', *American Ethnologist* 20(3) (1993), 576.
7. De-chung Wa, *Daojiao Zhushen Shuo* 道教諸神說 *Daoist Deities* (Taipei: Yiqun, 1992), 248–251.
8. Chien-Heng Wu, 'Third Prince God, from Temple Fairs to International Stage', *Taiwan Insights*. Accessed at: http://www.taiwaninsights.com/tag/wu-chien-heng/ (Mar 1, 2013).
9. *Want China Times*, 'Taiwanese Students Rally in London to Defend ROC Flag', Accessed at: http://www.wantchinatimes.com/news-subclass-cnt.aspx?id=20120731000072&cid=1101 (Mar 1, 2013).
10. Wu, *Third Prince God*.

11. Wu, *Third Prince God*.

12. *Want China Times*, 'South America Awaits for Prince Nezha and the Tao of Techno', Accessed at: http://www.wantchinatimes.com/news-subclass-cnt. aspx?id=20120122000012&cid=1803 (Mar 1, 2013).

13. Steven Sangren, *Chinese Sociologics: An Anthropological Account of the Role of Alienation in Social Reproduction* (London: Berg, 2000).

14

More Russian than Orthodox Christianity: Russian Paganism as Nationalist Politics

KAARINA AITAMURTO

UNIVERSITY OF HELSINKI, FINLAND

The second half of the twentieth century witnessed the emergence of various new religious movements, reviving ancient, pre-Christian spiritual traditions. These religions typically reject dogmatism and do not have any commonly acknowledged Holy Scriptures or organisational hierarchies. Consequently, these movements are extremely heterogeneous and any description of the various Pagan religions should be supplemented with numerous reservations. Moreover, contemporary Paganism has developed in varying directions in different geographical areas. Thus, while some small Pagan movements already existed in Europe at the turn of the twentieth century, British Wicca is usually considered to be the first contemporary Pagan religion. After the repeal of the English Witchcraft Act in the 1950s, Wicca was introduced to the public by its creator, Gerard Gardner. The first Wiccans were predominantly middle-class people, interested in the occult and politically conservative.[1] However, in the sixties, the religion spread to America and gained significant influences from the counterculture of the time. Even today, Western Pagans generally hold more liberal or even left-wing social values than the average population, and many Pagans are engaged in feminist or ecological social activity.[2] Nevertheless, some Odinist and Asatru groups in Northern America subscribe to racist views.[3]

The collapse of the communist system in Eastern Europe enabled the few small Pagan movements in the region to surface in the public sphere. At the beginning of the 1990s, they gained momentum in virtually all ex-socialist countries. The majority of these groups subscribed to nationalist politics, but naturally the nature of this nationalism varies between countries. Whereas in Central and Eastern Europe native Paganism is often seen as an inherently anti-Soviet and anti-Communist force, Russian Pagans' relationship with their past is more complex. Despite this, Pagans from Slavic countries have cooperated, especially in a yearly assembly, *Veche*, in advocating a pan-Slavic nationalist ideology. However, due to some internal disputes, the activity of the *Veche* has been halted in recent years, and the Ukrainian crisis will undoubtedly further weaken this pan-Slavic solidarity.

Paganism in Russia

In Russia, many adherents of pre-Christian Slavic spirituality reject the word Paganism. Therefore, the established term for the movement is Rodnoverie, which means 'native faith' (*rodnaya vera*). At present, no Rodnoverie organisation is registered as a religious community. This is partly due to the tightened requirements of current Russian legislation, but many groups do not aspire to such a status because they do not wish to give information about their activity to the authorities. The most radical groups even avoid putting any information about themselves on the internet. In conclusion, it is extremely difficult to estimate the number of small, unofficial Rodnoverie communities. On the basis of the number of members in some internet communities and people attending the largest Rodnoverie festivals, it seems safe to say that there are several tens of thousands of Rodnovers in Russia.[4]

Demarcating Rodnoverie as a movement or a religion is extremely difficult. Quarrels are rife among Rodnoveries over who can legitimately present themselves as representatives of the religion. For example, syncretic groups are easily accused of representing New Age spirituality. Authors or organisations making wild historical claims are accused of tarnishing the name of Rodnoverie. For a scholar of the topic, one of the biggest challenges in defining Rodnoverie is demarcating it as a religious movement. For example, within skinhead subculture, Pagan aesthetics and mythology can be used without any deeper commitment to Paganism as a religious identity.[5]

Rodnoverie and Politics

Linking religion with political views is not uncommon in contemporary Paganism, which emphasises the immanence of the sacred. For example, Pagans argue that the ideal of the transcendental and the afterlife in Christianity leads to neglect of our environment and a reluctance to confront social injustice. In Russia, nationalism is the most pervasive and prominent feature of Rodnoverie politics, despite the fact that the movement encompasses both extreme left-wing and extreme right-wing groups.

In the 1990s, the social turbulence of the time manifested itself in the radicalism of various small Pagan parties, which was typical of the period. However, Paganism was not accepted within the official ideology of the largest nationalist movements, such as Russian National Unity. Only in the following decade, undoubtedly due to the increase in the number of Pagans, did the programmes of such organisations as the notorious Slavic Union and the Movement Against Illegal Immigration admit Paganism to be 'the second' of the traditional Russian spiritualties.

The biggest Rodnoverie group is Kontseptsiya Obshchestvennoi Bezopasnosti (KOB), though it is somewhat questionable whether the organisation as a whole can be termed Pagan. In its heyday, the organisation claimed to have over 50,000 members, but it seems unlikely that the majority of its activists identified themselves as Pagan by religion. Paganism can be found in the esoteric, even cryptic teachings of the KOB, but religion is not among its main themes. The KOB propagates a far-leftist, anti-Semitic and socially conservative ideology, celebrating Stalin as its main hero.[6] With its heavy emphasis on Soviet-style rhetoric, the KOB represents somewhat old-fashioned nationalism, and in the present decade its popularity has begun to decrease.

From the outset, anti-Semitism was one of the determining characteristics of the nationalism of Rodnoverie. In *Desionizatsiya* (1979), the first Pagan publication in the Soviet Union, its author Valerii Emelyanov argued that Russians should turn to their native faith because it was a more efficient means of combating 'Zionism' than was Christianity, which is based on Judaism. Yemelyanov insisted that Jews were leading a global conspiracy against other peoples, especially Aryans. The flagrantly anti-Semitic claims of Yemelyanov have since been repeated in various Rodnoverie publications, which also draw material from the anti-Semitic literature of the beginning of the twentieth century and from Nazi Germany. Rodnoverie groups have often been accused of holding Nazi sympathies, and indeed some authors admit their admiration of Hitler and the Third Reich. However, others deny these accusations, even though their ideology has some similarity with German National Socialism. One of the most revealing cases, perhaps, is that of one of the pioneers of the Rodnoverie movement, Viktor Bezverkhy, who was prosecuted for selling *Mein Kampf* at the beginning of the 1990s. Startlingly, he was found not guilty, since he explained that his publishing business had commercial rather than political aims and that *Mein Kampf* was to begin a series of publications written by the 'enemies of Russia', which would include, for example, writings by Trotsky.[7] Lately the Russian judiciary has adopted a stricter line, and in 2009 a Rodnoverie organisation, the Church of Ynglings, was banned because extremism and using the swastika were central tenets of the religion. Nowadays, the majority of Rodnoverie groups use an eight-pointed form of the swastika called the *kolovorot*, undoubtedly partly motivated by the wish to avoid prosecution. However, it should be noted that most Rodnoverie organisations genuinely denounce Nazism, and especially Nazi Germany, for its part in the death of so many Russians.

A decisive factor in the growth of the Rodnoverie movement was its connection to the martial arts scene. At the beginning of the 1990s, the Pagan writer Aleksander Belov introduced a new martial art, 'Slavyano-Goritskaya Borba', which he claimed was based on a unique Russian tradition. Like Yemelyanov, Belov argued that Paganism was the 'religion of the warrior', in contrast to Christianity, which preaches humility and submission. Within sport clubs practising Slavyano-Goritskaya Borba, Paganism effectively spread among the Russian youth and also gained a foothold among skinhead groups.

The size of the radical fringe of Rodnoverie is difficult to estimate because these groups seldom openly display their activity. Some Rodnovers have committed such crimes as attacks on Orthodox churches, synagogues and mosques or violent racist assaults on people of 'non-Slavic appearance'. Perhaps the most repugnant case was revealed in 2009, when a group of three 17-and 18-year-olds, who identified themselves as Rodnovers, were arrested for 12 racist murders and two attempted bomb attacks in Moscow.[8] Although these are individual cases and it seems safe to say that the majority of Rodnovers do not approve of them, they cannot be dismissed as a phenomenon separate from the movement. Even though most prominent Rodnoverie leaders do not openly encourage violence, it is tacitly endorsed by their Manichean worldview and demonisation of the 'other'. Revealingly, while very few Western Pagans support the notorious Norwegian metal musician and neo-Nazi Varg Vikernes or even acknowledge him to be a true Pagan, his translated writings are hugely popular among Rodnovers in Russia. Like Vikernes, younger Rodnovers tend to be less obsessed with anti-Semitic ideology but instead engage in anti-migrant and anti-Islamic activities. Moreover, they do not necessarily see the West as Russia's enemy, as many older Rodnovers do; rather, it is viewed as an ally in the fight by the 'white race' against other peoples.[9]

In the middle of the 2000s, new anti-extremist laws were introduced in Russia, and since then the surveillance and prosecution of ultra-nationalism has intensified. Consequently, some Rodnoverie organisations and especially publications have been banned. Furthermore, mainstream Rodnoverie communities have begun to censor their public statements in order to avoid accusations of extremism—but of course this does prevent many of their members from subscribing to racist values. However, the mainstream of the Rodnoverie movement seems to be gradually moving further away from ultra-nationalist politics. As the movement has matured and the focus has shifted more to gaining an established position as a religion, ritual practices and theology have gained significance. At the moment, one of the biggest Rodnoverie organisations is Rodolyubie, which is known for its elaborate rituals and the numerous publications of its charismatic leader, Veleslac (Il'ya Cherkasov). Significantly, his books contain much less nationalist propaganda than mystical reflection and discussion of the Slavic spiritual tradition.

Conclusions

Though contemporary Eastern European Pagan religions more often subscribe to nationalism and racism than their liberally oriented Western counterparts, this division is somewhat simplistic. There are ultra-nationalist communities in the West and liberal groups in the East, and most importantly, many groups create original combinations of these ideologies. Moreover, despite dramatic differences in the political views of various forms of Paganism, they also share many common features—for instance, their emphasis on freedom of thought and individual responsibility. Moreover, Pagan rituals aim to reconnect the participants not only with the divine but also with nature. Paganism sees nature as sacred, and, consequently, green thinking is associated with Pagan religiosity in both the West and East. Naturally, ecological convictions can be combined both with liberal social views or ultra-conservatism and anti-modernism. Nature can be seen as a reality that unities all human kind, but it can also be understood in the nationalist framework, similar to the German ideology of *blut und boden* (blood and soil).[10]

According to Ronald Inglehart, social instability increases conservative values,[11] and indeed East European Paganism reflects the post-socialist rise of conservatism and nationalism in the region. The economic and social stabilisation of Russia seems to have led to less politicised and radical forms of Rodnoverie. Instead of wishing to find a spiritual basis for their nationalist political convictions, today more often people who convert to Rodnoverie are interested in Paganism as a Green religion or fascinated by its aesthetically lavish rituals, which provide strong emotional experiences and an opportunity to express one's creativity. Yet it is difficult to predict the direction in which Rodnoverie will develop. As an anti-dogmatic religion, it will undoubtedly remain a heterogeneous movement that also encompasses radical forms.

Though the movement is marginal, it continues to grow rapidly—and more importantly it has a wider influence within such youth subcultures as heavy metal music fans, live role-players, fantasy fiction aficionados and martial arts practitioners. Thus, given its intimate connections with these groups, Rodnoverie reflects the values and concerns of Russian youth. Its role in Russian nationalism has followed the wider changes that have occurred in recent decades. First, instead of anti-Westernism and anti-Semitism, a hatred of migrants and Islam has begun to typify ultra-nationalist rhetoric. Secony, the nationalist movement has become increasingly alienated from the state. Among ultra-nationalists, the Russian state is seen as an enemy due to its anti-extremist measures. Less radical nationalist opposition is also disillusioned by the hypocrisy and undemocratic nature of state patriotism. For the Pagan nationalist, the strong alliance between the state and the Russian Orthodox Church seem exclusive and discriminatory. In this respect, the Rodnoverie movement illustrates the versatility of nationalism in contemporary Russia and the difficulty of constructing clear national identities in modern societies, where people have more choices and more overlapping identities, many of which transcend national boundaries.

Notes

1. Vivianne Crowley, 'Wicca as Nature Religion', *Nature Religion Today: Paganism in the Modern World* (Edinburgh: Edinburgh University Press, 1998), 174.
2. Helen Berger, Evan Leach, and Leigh S. Shaffer, *Voices from the Pagan Census: A National Survey of Witches and Neo-Pagans in the United States* (Columbia: University of South Carolina Press, 2003), 55-88.
3. Mattias Gardell, *Gods of the Blood: The Pagan Revival and White Separatism* (Durham & London: Duke University Press, 2003).
4. In comparison, there are over one million Pagans in the United States and over 70,000 in England. 'How many Pagans are there?', *Patheos*. Accessed at: http://www. patheos.com/Library/Answers-to-Frequently-Asked-Religion-Questions/How-many-Pagans-are-there.html (Aug. 14, 2014) 'Release: 2011 Census, Key Statistics for Local Authorities in England and Wales', Office for National Statistics. Accessed at: http://www.ons.gov.uk/ons/publications/re-reference-tables.html?newquery=*&newoffset=25&pageSize=25&edition=tcm per cent3A77-286262 (Aug. 4, 2014)
5. Hilary Pilkington and Anton Popov, 'Understanding Neo-paganism in Russia: Religion? Ideology? Philosophy? Fantasy?', *Subcultures and New Religious Movements in Russia and East-Central Europe* (Frankfurt am Main: Peter Lang, 2009).
6. Serguei Oushakine, *Patriotism of Despair: Nation, War, and Loss in Russia* (Ithaca: Cornell University Press, 2009).
7. Aleksei Gaidukov, 'Sovremennoe slavyanskoe (russkoe) yazychestvo v Peterburge: Konfessional'naya dinamika za desyatileie', *Religioznaya situatsiya na severo-zpade Rossii i v stranakh Baltii* (St. Petersburg: Svetoch, 2005), pp. 42-44.
8. Kaarina Aitamurto, 'Modern Pagan Warriors: Violence and Justice in Russian Rodnoverie' *Violence and New Religious Movements* (New York: Oxford University Press, 2011), p. 235. For a comprehensive account of some other racist crimes committed by Rodnovers, see Victor Shnirelman 'Russian Neopaganism: from Ethnic Religion to Racial Violence', *Modern Pagan and Native Faith Movements in Central*

and Eastern Europe (Durham: Acumen, 2013), pp. 62 – 76.

9. See also Marlene Laruelle, 'The Ideological Shift On The Russian Radical Right: From Demonizing The West To Fear Of Migrants', *Problems of Post-Communism*, Vol. 57 (No. 6. 2010).

10. Adrian Ivakhiv, 'Nature and Ethnicity in East European Paganism: An Environmental Ethic of the Religious Right?' *The Pomegranate*. Vol. 7 (No. 2. 2005).

11. Ronald Inglehart and Wayne E. Baker, 'Modernization, Cultural Change, and the Persistence of Traditional Values', *American Sociological Review*, Vol 65 (No. 1, 2000), 41.

Part Three
Violence and Peace

15

Sociotheology: The Significance of Religious Worldviews

MONA KANWAL SHEIKH

DANISH INSTITUTE FOR INTERNATIONAL STUDIES, DENMARK

In International Relations (IR), religion's ability to provide legitimacy for an end other than religion has been the usual reason to include it in analysis. The instrumental use of religion is arguably a central concern for IR, but not a sufficient one. This chapter is based on the idea that there can be religious reasons behind the behaviour of political actors, and hence religion should not just be treated as a rhetorical gloss over 'real motives' or non-religious goals. The actions and ideas of political actors can be based on hopes for spiritual transformation in this life and the next, and on the longing for salvation and spiritual fulfilment.

In most cases the motivations of political actors who employ religious vocabulary or draw on religious imagery are neither fully religious nor secular. Rather, they represent a blend that challenges any clear-cut division. Research on activists involved in acts of terrorism show that they simultaneously understand their acts in religious terms *and* as part of struggles for peace, justice and a better socio-political order.[1] For them, there is no 'secular' distinction between defending faith and defending a just socio-political order since the latter is part of their religious vision.

Below I focus on the necessity of bringing into IR a focus on religious worldviews—a study object, which has traditionally been confined to the departments of theology. This does not mean that worldviews are only significant when it comes to understanding violent acts committed by adherents of religious traditions. Worldviews are also entry points to understanding 'secular violence' acted out as part of a secular vision of the world, and also relevant for debates that are not about violent behaviour at all. So even though I concentrate on religious violence in this chapter, the applicability of my framework is broader.

Whether we are talking about the suicide bombings of the Pakistani Taliban, the attack on the Hebron mosque by Baruch Goldstein, Timothy McVeigh's bombing of the Alfred P. Murrah Federal Building in Oklahoma City or the shootings of Norway's Anders Breivik, they all represent a culture in which the justifications for violence are coloured by a religious understanding of social reality.

And in this lies the challenge: accounting for religious thinking and rationality is difficult within existing frameworks of thinking within social analysis and IR in particular. Rational choice theory is baffled by choices that do not seem to be rational in worldly calculations but have a far more distant time horizon and a more imaginative sense of rewards than most materialist calculations support. Strategic analyses flounder when the strategies do not seem to yield immediate benefits. Organisational theories falter when the communities of support are diffuse, unstructured, and lack a palpable chain of command. In order to address some of these challenges, I propose the adoption of a 'sociotheological framework' that enables an investigation of how the social reality looks through the eyes of religious activists.[2]

Sociotheology: Combining Faith and Milieu

Militant movements such as the Taliban, messianic Zionists and Christian abortion clinic bombers draw on specific religious myths, doctrines and ideas. Activists in the movements often present themselves as servants of God implementing a divine command. In India, Hindus and Sikhs have justified violence in defence of their religious faiths, and even Buddhism—a tradition for which nonviolence is its hallmark—has been fused with violence in political movements in Sri Lanka, Thailand, Myanmar and Tibet and in the activities of the Japanese Aum Shinrikyo movement. Though often the motives of these movements can be described in non-religious terms— defending social identity, securing justice and obtaining political order—they are simultaneously phrased in pious language and often characterised as having religious goals. Frequently the personal spiritual mission of salvation is fused with a communal longing for a redemptive social order. Thus these phenomena need to be analysed from both theological and social perspectives.

The *interdisciplinary trend* that Mark Juergensmeyer and I have previously labelled sociotheology emerged out of the recognition that politics has a religious side and religion can be an inherent part of public and political life. This insight was in fact part of the thinking of some of the founding figures of social studies—most notably Emile Durkheim, Max Weber and Karl Marx.[3] Most of the sociological work on religion in the first half of the twentieth century, however, tended to be reductionist and unappreciative of the impact of religious ideas and imagery.[4]

Typically social scientists have felt most comfortable by keeping theology at an arm's length, but the representatives of what we labelled a sociotheological approach have provided exceptions.[5] In some instances, the trend of combining a focus on faith with a focus on the social milieu has been a steady though often minority perspective within the disciplines. At times, the scholarly attention on faith and politics has increased due to particular political events. For example, the Iranian Revolution in 1979, the Sikh and Afghan Muslim rebellions in the 1980s, and the rise of a global jihadi movement that culminated in the spectacular aerial assaults on the World Trade Center and Pentagon in 2001 brought along an increased academic as well as public interest in the religious motives for political acts. In recent years, the issue of examining religion and politics together has returned, in part because of the public prominence of movements that blend together religious and political activism. Religious politics also gained focus because it appears to challenge secularism as an ideology, and this has led to an examination of the post-Enlightenment notion that religion is something private and separate from the public secular realm.[6]

For the social sciences and IR, this sociotheological turn means incorporating into social analysis the insider-orientated attempt to understand the reality of a particular worldview. As a result, the social sciences need to recover an appreciation for a field long banished from the halls of secular academe: theology. The insider perspective on a religious worldview is, after all, what the field of theology has classically been about, long before the advent of the modern academic disciplines: attempts to structure the social, ethical, political and spiritual aspects of a culture's ideas and meanings into a coherent whole. It studies what Michel Foucault once designated as an episteme: the structure of knowledge that is the basis of an understanding of how reality works.[7] These structures of knowledge have traditionally been understood in language about ultimate reality that is today regarded as religious; thus theology was—as the name implies—the study of the logic of God. By extension, it is the study of the essential moral and spiritual connections in all aspects of life.

The power of theology as an academic discipline in the early modern period was its comprehensiveness. It attempted to survey the whole range of human activity and belief. For this reason, theology was once regarded as the queen of the sciences.[8] During the latter part of the modern era, theology fell into disrespect among social sciences partly due to the secularisation narrative that represented faith as the opposite to science, and theology became isolated as a field. Partly this was due to three limitations in the way that theology was increasingly practiced: it had only one religious tradition as its frame of reference, it asserted normative truth claims about its analyses, and its analysts often ignored the social context in which the ideas they study emerge and are cultivated.

Theory and Epistemology

The scholars who study contemporary worldviews from the sociotheological approach are different from the theologians described above in that they apply their analytic style to any tradition or worldview. They bracket truth claims asserted by either the subjects in the study or by the analysts studying the subjects' points of view, and they take seriously the social location in which a view of the world emerges and the social consequences of a particular way of thinking about reality. The point is to try to understand the reasoning behind the truth claims, not to verify them.

Sociotheology is based on the realisation that much of the phenomena that modern people since the time of the European Enlightenment have called religion are related to other aspects of society, from economic and political factors to matters of social identity. For this reason, sociotheological analysis is seldom limited to a study of religion in the narrow sense, as if there were a separate cluster of actions and ideas relating to a notion of transcendence and of spiritual transformation that was unaffected by other aspects of public and private life.

A sociotheological framework for analysis is built upon epistemological revolutions across disciplinary borders that lead to a more dynamic view on inside and outside factors driving the individual. One example is the so-called Strong Programme in the sociology of science associated with the Edinburgh School, which holds that all human knowledge and ideas, including religious ones, contain some social components in its formation process. Another relevant methodological revolution has come from within discursive psychology and social psychology that dissolved the concepts of a mind-body dichotomy.[9] The dynamic view on the mind-body relationship is part of what has been called the 'second cognitive revolution' that challenged the idea that mental and psychological entities exist in a self-contained way.

The same sort of bridge building between inside and outside perspectives has taken place within the field of theology. Here one of the pioneers was George Lindbeck, who developed a 'cultural-linguistic' concept of religious doctrines by bridging anthropology and a Wittgensteinian philosophy of language that probed the relationship between language and culture, on the one hand, and experience and belief, on the other. Together, the approximation of the field of psychology and theology (the mind and belief) and sociology (the context) as two poles in the same discursive dynamics has contributed to eroding a stonewall dichotomy between theology and the social sciences and opened a space for sociotheology.

One of the implications of the epistemological basis of sociotheology is that it is more prone to take seriously the words of violent activists than instrumentalist or essentialist approaches to religious violence. Scepticism towards taking the words of one's study object seriously often reflects an image of the individual who has an isolated inner side that cannot be verified by positivist test methods. Statements representing the 'inside' are therefore also regarded as invalid since there is no theorised 'bond' between the inside and outside.

Epistemic Worldview Analysis

When activists who have supported violent actions are accessed from a sociotheological perspective, the main question relates to how they viewed the world in a way that would allow these actions to be carried out. What is being examined by taking a sociotheological approach is a way of looking at social reality that enables certain action: an 'epistemic worldview'. The idea of an epistemic worldview is a marriage between Foucault's concept of episteme—a paradigm of linguistic discourse based on a common set of understandings about the basis of knowledge—and Pierre Bourdieu's notion of habitus, the social location of shared understandings about the world and how it should work.[10] We want to understand their framework for thinking about reality and acting appropriately within a perceived understanding of the world.[11]

To understand a perception of reality—an epistemic worldview—requires the sociotheological tasks of recovering the internal logic of this perception of reality and placing it within its social milieu. It also requires understanding the relation between those people who share a certain worldview and the social and power structures of the world around them. The task is similar to the hermeneutical approach to the interpretation of texts—an approach that has been employed in cultural sociology as well—in attempting to understand the range of ways that statements and social events have been perceived from various perspectives.

Hence epistemic worldviews are conceptual entities, but they are also tied to social realities. Others share these worldviews in a pattern of association that is usually contiguous with other social boundaries, such as a particular ethnic or religious community. This means there are concentric circles of social realities that coalesce with particular epistemic worldviews. For example, among right-wing Christian Protestants in the American rural West and South, some share an even more extremist Christian identity variety. Though the inner levels of these concentric circles are not always socially distinct, there are often social markers—the movement is dominated by economically distressed, heterosexual white men, for example, a social category in which one would find few blacks, Asians or Hispanics, virtually no women in leadership roles, and no openly gay men or women.

The social boundaries of followers of a movement—those who sympathetically agree with the central tenets and narrative story that dominate a particular epistemic worldview—may be more difficult to demarcate. The supporters of the global jihadi movement at the turn of the twenty-first century provide a case in point. If one thinks of the Al Qaeda organisation as the people who worked directly under the leadership of Osama bin Laden before his death in 2011, the numbers were likely to be only in the hundreds. But if one includes all those who were influenced by, and to some extent sympathetic with, the general jihadi perspective that identified the United States as an opponent of Islam and insisted on militant resistance on the part of concerned Muslims, the number was much greater, in the thousands and perhaps even in the millions. In this situation, therefore, the concentric circle approach to epistemic worldviews applies, with a broad population of followers, often engaged through the internet and other forms of electronic social media.

In order to trace the forms of authority that underpin the epistemic worldview, a relevant question to ask is what constitutes the *bases of* authority in the epistemic worldviews. For religious militants, references to religious myths or spiritual dreams, Holy Scriptures or exegesis, or jurisprudential literature based on the interpretations of revelations or the will of God/gods have the same status empirical evidence would have in a scientific discourse—they are used as the basis of authoritative truth claims that can provide legitimacy to acts of violence.

Concluding Reflections

Sociotheology is a new opening for IR scholars and students interested in studying worldviews that set the scene for political violence to be played out. In an earlier contribution, Juergensmeyer and I laid out basic guidelines of how to conduct 'good sociotheology', drawing inspiration from anthropological methodology of getting close to your subjects of study and the ideals of *verstehen*.[12] The sociotheological approach has relevance for larger debates on what determines political behaviour and can be helpful in illuminating the presence of multiple rationalities, authority and legitimacy structures that matters in situations of political conflicts.

To facilitate the development towards a more nuanced understanding of the dynamics between epistemic worldviews and their social location, there is still a need to develop a more systematic research programme for the archaeological reconstruction of epistemic worldviews in their social milieus. In particular, the methodological question of how to measure the impact of a epistemic worldview vis-à-vis other factors that enable violence requires more attention. Another limitation of the approach is that it cannot be used to explain why only some of those who share an epistemic worldview turn to actual violence. It can only point at the places where the rationality for violence is embedded.

The contemporary need to engage scientifically with worldviews is that in politics the enemy is often deprived of having a rationale. In a violent world, entering into the epistemic worldviews of adversaries is crucial both to explain and prevent the escalation of violence. Often spirals of violence emerge from responses to simplified images of 'the enemy' countered by actions also based on stereotypes. Being empathetic is not the same as morally approving of violence but understanding that there can be a political and religious rationale behind 'their' violence just as 'we' have one in war and other situations.

Resistance to taking an empathetic stance towards the subjects' theologically informed worldview can have disastrous consequences. In the case of the Federal Bureau of Investigation (FBI) standoff at Waco, Texas, in 1993 with members of the Branch Davidian sect led by David Koresh, the FBI agents were criticised for having precipitated the fiery ending of the encounter (and the deaths of members of the movement) by not understanding the internal logic of the theological perception of history that was held by Koresh and that led him to take his tragically decisive actions. To the agents, the rationales given by Koresh in their extensive telephone conversations with him during the standoff were just theological gibberish. Later analyses of the conversations revealed that Koresh had a biblically sophisticated view of the eschatological end of history and a vaunted role of his own movement in the end-time conflagration that helped to explain his responses to the FBI's actions.

Notes

1. See e.g. Cynthia K. Mahmood, *Fighting for Faith and Nation: Dialogues with Sikh Militants*, Philadelphia, University of Pennsylvania Press, 1996; Mark Juergensmeyer, *Terror in the Mind of God, the Global Rise of Religious Violence*, Berkeley, University of California Press, 2000; Michael K. Jerryson and Mark Juergensmeyer (eds), *Buddhist Warfare*, Oxford, Oxford University Press, 2010.

2. The present essay is based on the framework put forward in Mark Juergensmeyer and Mona K. Sheikh, 'The Sociotheological Turn in the Study of Religion and Violence', *The Oxford Handbook of Religion and Violence*, edited by Michael Jerryson, Mark Juergensmeyer and Margo Kitts, Oxford, Oxford University Press, 2012.

3. Durkheim attempted to immerse himself in the thinking of tribal societies to understand the socioreligious significance of totemic symbols (Emile Durkheim. [1912] 1915. *The Elementary Forms of Religious Life*. Translated by Joseph Ward Swain. New York: The Free Press.). Weber adopted a posture of verstehen in his social analysis that was sensitive to cultural values; and he integrated both theological ideas and social theory in his studies of the religions of India and China and in developing his understanding of the Protestant ethic (Max Weber [1905]. 2002. *The Protestant Ethic and The Spirit of Capitalism*. Translated by Peter Baehr and Gordon C. Wells. New York: The Free Press; [1915] 1951. *The Religion of China: Confucianism and Taoism*. New York: The Free Press; [1916]. 1958. *The Religion of India: The Sociology of Hinduism and Buddhism*. New York: The Free Press.). Karl Marx took seriously the relationship of ideological frameworks of thought to social structure, especially in his analysis of the role of religion in the German peasant's revolt (Karl Marx and Friedrich Engels. 1939. *The German Ideology*. Ed. R. Pascal. New York: International Publishers.).

4. IR has been more silent about religion, though the mid-twentieth century scholars of classical realism were exceptions. They did actually point to the importance of religion for the discipline of International Relations, however the explicit debates on religion, theory, and International Relations that took place in Europe disappeared from mainstream IR within ten years. Instead, throughout the 1990s concepts like culture and identity found their way into the mainstream of IR research and, in this, religion has occasionally been implicitly involved as a subcategory of the broader concept of identity, or mentioned as part of a specific ethnic heritage, culture or history. See Kenneth Wald and Clyde Wilcox, 'Getting Religion: Has Political Science Rediscovered the Faith Factor?', *American Political Science Review*, 100:4 (2006), pp. 523–9; Daniel Philpott, 'The Challenge of September 11 to Secularism in International Relations', *World Politics*, 55 (2002), pp. 66–95; Carsten Bagge Laustsen and Ole Wæver, 'In Defence of Religion: Sacred Referent Objects for Securitization', *Millennium: Journal of International Studies*, 29:3, pp. 705–39.

5. Within sociology, both Robert Bellah and Peter Berger have been hospitable to theological points of view with social thinkers such as Pierre Bourdieu and Antony Giddens accepting, albeit more reluctantly, the viewpoints from within religious traditions. In the field of political philosophy, Charles Taylor has been consistently congenial to religious perspectives, while John Rawls and Jurgen Habermas came around to seeing the value of taking seriously religious elements of social thought relatively late in their academic careers. Anthropologists by disciplinary habit have been more disposed to take other people's perspectives seriously, and thus have

accommodated more easily religious points of view. This has been true of such anthropologists as Clifford Geertz, Louis Dumont, Mary Douglas, Stanley Tambiah, Talal Asad, and Gananath Obeyesekere. Within the fields of religious studies and the history of religion, religious perspectives are part of the objects of their studies, and some of the scholars who study religion have also been mindful of the social implications of religious ideas. These socially-minded scholars of religion have included many comparativists, including notably Ninian Smart and Wilfred Cantwell Smith. And though theology sometimes appear as a closed system of thought, the political significance of religious thinking has been a theme of scholars from a variety of theological traditions, including such Protestant Christians as Reinhold Niebuhr and George Lindbeck, the Roman Catholic theologian Hans Kung, the Jewish philosopher Martin Buber, the Jewish-Christian writer Simone Weil, the Muslim legal expert Abdullahi An-Naim, the Hindu thinker Rabindranath Tagore, and the Buddhist social activist Sulak Sivaraksa.

6. This issue has been explored by Talal Asad, for instance, in his discussion of the genealogical origins of the separate spheres of religion and politics (Talal Asad, *Genealogies of Religion: Discipline and Reasons of Power in Christianity and Islam*, Baltimore, Johns Hopkins University Press, 1993; *Formations of the Secular: Christianity, Islam, Modernity*, Palo Alto, Stanford University Press, 2003.) Charles Taylor's examination of the post-Enlightenment emergence of "A Secular Age" (Charles Taylor. 2007. *A Secular Age*. Cambridge, MA: Belknap Press.), Jose Casanova's discussion of the revival of public religions in the modern world (Jose Casanova. 1994. *Public Religions in the Modern World*. Chicago: University of Chicago Press.), and the revival of Carl Schmitt's idea of political theology. (Heinrich Meier. 2006. *What is Political Theology?* Munich: Carl Friedrich von Siemens Stiftung.) Recent works on the idea of secularism within the field of political science and international relations theory also reflect this trend. For instance Elizabeth Hurd. 2007. *The Politics of Secularism in International Relations*. Princeton, NJ: Princeton University Press; Craig Calhoun, Mark Juergensmeyer, and Jonathan VanAntwerpen. 2011. *Rethinking Secularism*. New York: Oxford Univ Press; Mona K. Sheikh and Ole Waever. 2012. 'Western Secularisms: Variation in a Doctrine and its Practice', In *Thinking International Relations Differently*, eds. Arlene B. Tickner and David L. Blaney. London: Routledge, 275-98.

7. Michel Foucault. [1966] 1994. *The Order of Things: An Archeology of Human Science*. New York: Random House.

8. Such diverse thinkers in European history as Adam Smith, widely regarded as the father of modern capitalist economic theory, and Charles Darwin, one of the fathers of evolutionary biology, began their intellectual careers studying theology. The same is true of many of the most influential scientists from the Islamic culture such as Ibn Sina (commonly known by his latinised name Avicenna), who is regarded as a father of modern medicine and creator of the concept of momentum in physics; Ibn Hayyan, known as the father of molecular chemistry; or Al-Khawarizmi and Al-Kindi, who invented algebra. A common element in their scientific approach was that they all studied, went into dialogue with, or drew on inspiration from the field of theology.

9. James P. Gee 1992. *The Social Mind*. New York: Bergin and Garvey; Derek Edwards and Jonathan Potter. 1992. *Discursive Psychology*. London: Sage; Horace R. Harre and Grant Gillett. 1994. *The Discursive Mind*. London: Sage.

10. Michel Foucault. [1969] 1972. *The Archaeology of Knowledge*. Translated by A. Sheridan Smith. New York: Harper and Row; Pierre Bourdieu. [1980] 1990. *The Logic of Practice*. Translated by R. Nice. Palo Alto, CA: Stanford University Press.

11. The idea of an epistemic worldview has much in common with the notion of religion as being an awareness of an alternative reality. In a recent book, the sociologist Robert Bellah speaks about religion as one of the "other realities," like poetry and science that "break the dreadful fatalities of this world of appearances". See Robert Bellah. 2011. *Religion in Human Evolution: From the Paleolithic to the Axial Age.* Cambridge, MA: Harvard Univ Press, p. 9.

12. Mark Juergensmeyer and Mona K. Sheikh, 'The Sociotheological Turn in the Study of Religion and Violence', *The Oxford Handbook of Religion and Violence*, edited by Michael Jerryson, Mark Juergensmeyer and Margo Kitts, Oxford, Oxford University Press, 2012.

16

What's God Got to Do with It? Violence, Hostility and Religion Today

LEE MARSDEN
UNIVERSITY OF EAST ANGLIA, UK

While religion might have been largely ignored by a western-centric international relations (IR) discipline throughout the twentieth century, in the third millennium of the Common Era religion occupies centre stage as one of the key issues in global politics today. The return of God to the international arena coincided with an era marked by globalisation and the end of the Cold War. The challenge of cosmopolitan ideals, universal values and market forces on communitarian societies contributed to the emergence of identity politics in which ethnicity and religion became increasingly important signifiers. The transformation of the Manhattan skyline in September 2001 brought the attention of IR scholars to political actions motivated not by political ideology but religion, and particularistic interpretations of religious belief legitimating violence to achieve religio-political ends. Today, the IR community has finally caught up with the reality that for most of the world, most of the time, religion plays a vital role in lives and politics. Open any newspaper or news programme and you are sure to be assailed by a story which has a religious element to it, whether it be the progress of Islamic State between Iraq and Syria, the Iranian nuclear programme, conflict between Israel and Hamas, the immolation of Tibetan monks, war between Christians and Muslims in the Central African Republic, the kidnapping of school children in Nigeria or Buddhist attacks on Muslims in Myanmar. In seeking to address issues of violence and hostility in the name of religion, policy makers have sought to engage and partner with religious actors, develop religious literacy and welcome religious actors into the public sphere. In this chapter we consider the current state of religious hostility in the world before examining the religious dilemma where religion is both a cause of violence, intolerance and hostility and also a potential solution to conflict. In analysing the casual influence of religion on violence the chapter considers the claims of religious actors themselves and how policy makers have sought to work with alternative religious actors in the battle for hearts and minds in a conflictual international order.

Religious Hostility in the World Today

Religious hostility and intolerance of other people's religious beliefs is endemic across much of the world and has significantly increased over the last few years. This hostility and intolerance is enshrined in government legislation and in the levels of social hostility experienced by people of other faiths and those of no faith. A recent Pew Research Center survey[1] on religious hostilities indicates that social hostilities involving religion reached a six-year peak in 2012, with high or very high levels of hostility rising from 20 per cent of countries in 2007 to 74 per cent in 2012. These social hostilities include crimes, malicious acts and violence motivated by religious bias or hatred and were prevalent in 151 countries (over three-quarters of countries in the world) in 2012. The increase in social hostilities involving religion is reflected across all the Middle East and North Africa, Asia-Pacific, Europe and Sub-Saharan Africa. Deaths related to mob violence related to religion occurred in 21 countries, with sectarian or communal violence taking place in 36 countries. Religion-related terrorist groups were active in 73 countries, with deaths or injuries occurring in 40 of these. Fifteen per cent of countries experienced religion-related war or armed conflict in 2012. In 91 countries, organised groups attempted to dominate public life by using force or coercion to advance their religious perspective while preventing some other religious groups from operating. Seventy-eight countries have experienced violence or the threat of violence, including 'honour killings' in order to enforce religious norms. In almost half the countries of the world people have been displaced from their homes for taking part in religious activity disapproved of by the majority faith. Women have been harassed for violating religious dress codes in 63 countries a significant increase from 2007 when only 14 harassed women in this way. When it comes to converting from one religion to another, this led to hostility in 53 countries, including physical violence in 32 of those.

Brian Grim and his team at the Pew Research Center have produced the most comprehensive account of religious hostilities to date and present a picture of a world where religious intolerance is increasing at both societal and governmental level. The campaigns of Islamic State or Al Qaeda may attract news headlines but what the report reveals is a world in which governments are increasingly seeking to restrict and control religious belief and activity and citizens taking it into their own hands to intimidate and harass those of different faiths. In 61 countries the government generally does not respect religious freedom and in 147 countries interferes with worship or other religious practices. Seventy-five countries restrict public preaching, while 45 limit conversion from one religion to another. Government regulates the wearing of religious symbols, including head coverings and facial hair, in 54 countries. Forty-six countries formally ban some religious groups and 27 have attempted to eliminate an entire religious group's presence in 2012. The survey demonstrates a correlation between government restrictions on religion and the propensity for social hostility. The exceptions to this are harassment of Jews and folk religions: governmental harassment of Jews in 2012 occurred in 28 countries while social hostility towards the group occurred in 66; with folk religions the number of countries was 11 and 18 respectively. All religions have both experienced and perpetrated an increased level of harassment across the world compared to the preceding five years. Muslims were harassed in 88 countries, Christians in 83, Hindus in nine and Buddhists in seven in 2012.

Proponents of the Clash of Civilizations thesis[2] correctly identified religion as becoming a source of conflict after the Cold War but underestimated the propensity for clashes to occur not only between civilisations but within civilisations. In particular, conflict between Sunni and Shia within Islam in Iraq, Syria and Pakistan and intra-Sunni conflict between 'true believers' and 'apostates', Islamists and moderate Muslims kills far more people than any Islamic clash with African, Slavic/Orthodox, western (Judeo-Christian), Hindu or Sinic civilisations. While political-security considerations may trump religious motivations for Israel's attacks on Gaza or the Sri Lankan's government's destruction of the Liberation Tigers of Tamil Eelam, religious differences clearly play a role in how the other side is perceived and the value placed on the life of the other. A recent 11-country survey examining Muslim attitudes to Islamic extremism revealed that the overwhelming majority of the respondents expressed their concerns about such extremism. However, in all the Muslim majority countries surveyed, those unconcerned ranged from just 18 per cent in Malaysia and Pakistan to 51 per cent in Turkey. Over a quarter of the respondents in Egypt, Malaysia, Lebanon and the Palestinian territories felt that suicide bombing can be justified, while an average of 13 per cent had a positive view of Al Qaeda.[3] Religious designation, far from encouraging peace and reconciliation, appears to foster significant numbers of believers who express and demonstrate intolerance towards those who hold different views.

The most visible expression of religious hostility today can be found in the campaign of Islamic State to establish a caliphate under Abu Bakhr al-Baghdhadi in the Levant. Islamic State has called upon all Muslims to recognise and support the caliphate and has attracted up to five hundred

British Muslims and many more French and Belgian ostensibly to fight the Assad regime in Syria but more particularly to establish an Islamic state through the introduction and implementation of Sharia law and the extermination of non-believers including Shia, Christians and Yazidis. The British executioner of journalist Jim Foley justified his actions on the same basis as Al Qaeda and other Islamist groups in terms of western attacks on Muslim lands:

> Today your military air force is attacking us daily in Iraq. Your strikes have caused casualties amongst Muslims. You are no longer fighting an insurgency. We are an Islamic army and a state that has been accepted by a large number of Muslims worldwide.[4]

Faced then with increasing religious intolerance, hostility and violence across the world, how have governments sought to address these problems?

Faith-based Solutions to Faith-based Problems

Western governments have become increasingly sympathetic to the view that religious problems can have religious solutions. Rather than maintaining a secular polity, western governments have sought to engage religious actors in diplomatic, counter-terrorism and counter-radicalisation policies. This presents us with the religion dilemma where religion as well as being a source of violence is also a potential source of conflict resolution. Despite their claims to be peaceful, no mainstream religion is inherently peaceful: their sacred texts espouse violence in the name of god. Moderate and liberal versions of mainstream faiths have been able to contextualise violence as time specific or metaphorical but fundamentalist interpretations of the faith have been able to use examples of sacred violence and notions of exclusivity to legitimate hostility and intolerance towards those of other persuasions. And so it is to those moderate and liberal versions of faith that governments turn in order to secure their national interests and security objectives. The neglect of religion by academics, until recently, is replicated in policy circles. In a western secular polity, decision makers have traditionally argued that religious actors should confine their religious beliefs to the private sphere and present their case on the basis of rational argument in the public sphere, unencumbered by the irrationality of religiosity. Jurgen Habermas, whose seminal work on the public sphere[5] failed to mention religion at all, has led the academic re-engagement with religion in what is now a post-secular age.[6] Habermas argues that religious actors should be welcomed into the public sphere as people of faith and are to be respected by their secular counterparts, and in return they should argue their case on the basis of rational argument.[7] This call has been answered by policy makers encouraging greater religious literacy among diplomats, the military and development and law enforcement agencies.

Religious engagement began during the Clinton administration when the State Department established the Office for International Religious Freedom in 1998 at the request of Congress and started producing annual reports on religious persecution around the world. The annual reports examined religious hostility rather than engaging with religious actors, but this soon changed. One of the first acts of the George W. Bush presidency was to introduce the Office of Faith Based and Community Initiatives to encourage faith-based organisations to bid for funding nationally and to deliver overseas aid projects. Often working with local faith-based partners to circumvent government corruption and deliver assistance effectively, this policy has proved effective and has been continued by the Obama administration. The Obama administration also introduced a Religious Advisory Board to advise on key domestic and foreign policies. Under Obama military chaplains have become the first point of contact with indigenous populations and religious literacy has been introduced as part of the training of the armed forces with an Inter-faith Center established at West Point military academy. In 2009 Judd Birdsall set up a discussion group called the Forum on Religion and Global Affairs at the State Department with the specific intention of engaging religious actors to try and overcome the department's reticence in discussing or engaging with religious issues. The discussion group eventually merged into the Strategic Dialogue with Civil Society, which sought to engage with non-traditional partners to improve US standing in the world. Dialogue was established with faith-based actors in six areas, including religion and foreign policy a significant shift in US diplomacy.[8] The new desire to engage constructively with people of faith arises out of the war on terror and the radicalisation of Muslims, in particular, against the west and western-backed authoritarian governments throughout the Muslim majority world. Where opponents claim to be acting in the name of their religion it behoves western policy makers to understand the basis of such claims and work with co-religionists to counter such claims. This has been especially important as part of counter-radicalisation initiatives domestically.

Radicalisation, de-radicalisation and counter-radicalisation are inherently contested in terms of definition and operationally.[9] In the war on terror such terms became synonymous with tackling Islamist extremism and resulted in governments engaging with those purporting to represent or understand such communities and the threat posed to and by young Muslim men supposedly at danger of radicalisation:

As US and European governments have focussed on stemming 'home grown' Islamist political violence, the concept of radicalisation has become the master signifier of the late 'war on terror' and provided a new lens through which to view Muslim minorities. The introduction of policies designed to 'counter-radicalise' has been accompanied by the emergence of a government-funded industry of advisors, analysts, scholars, entrepreneurs and self-appointed community representatives who claim that their knowledge of a theological or psychological radicalisation process enables them to propose interventions in Muslim communities to prevent extremism.[10]

In Britain this led to the Prevent Strategy to combat violent extremism lumping together Islamists, far right, Northern Irish and animal and environmental activists. However, the main focus is clearly on Islamist extremism and engagement with a smorgasbord of academic, political, security and religious actors spearheading a policy which seeks to challenge the ideology that supports terrorism and those who promote it. It aims to further protect vulnerable people and support sectors and institutions where there are risks of radicalisation.[11] In practice this has led to government engaging with other extremists, particularly under New Labour, and also legitimating male religious leaders as the key representatives of their communities to the detriment of women and non-believers within those communities.[12] Rather than contemplate the extent to which government policy contributes to radicalisation, Muslim communities are co-opted to challenge and condemn Islamist extremism and to inform on suspect activity, including those intending to join Britons fighting in Somalia, Syria and Iraq. The difficulty for western governmental policy engaging with religious actors is that the influence of non-sectarian religious actors is increasing in policy-making circles while at the same time declining among those who practice their faith. Engagement with more radical religious actors who might have more influence on potential extremists is also fraught with difficulty:

> Some of the government's chosen collaborators in "addressing grievances" of angry young Muslims are themselves at the forefront of stoking those grievances against British foreign policy; western social values; and alleged state-sanctioned 'Islamophobia'. PVE [Preventing Violent Extremism] is thus underwriting the very Islamist ideology which spawns an illiberal, intolerant and anti-western world view.[13]

In supplanting a secular discourse with a religious discourse, religious actors are engaged on the basis of their faith and as representatives of a perceived religious community. This representation, by definition, identifies religion as the main signifier of group identity, thereby reinforcing division and suspicion between the group and wider society.

Conclusion

This chapter has sought to highlight the religious dilemma whereby western governments are increasingly abandoning secular approaches to religiously inspired violence and hostility in favour of engaging with religious actors as part of a counter-radicalisation strategy. The chapter has demonstrated that religious conflict and hostility is increasing and that western government's engagement with religious moderates and extremists is equally problematic. In the former case, non-sectarian approaches to religion are losing ground to sectarian and extreme positions, and in the latter case, engaging with alternative extremist groups can exacerbate the problem of radicalisation. Recognising largely male religious leadership of sections of society as representatives of the community provides them with legitimation at the expense of women and non-believers within these communities while simultaneously reinforcing separation and division from the rest of society. This chapter has highlighted difficulties without offering specific solutions and further research would throw greater light on the efficacy of faith-based solutions to religion-inspired violence and hostility.

Notes

1. Pew Forum, 'Religious Hostilities Reach Six-Year High' (Washington DC: Pew Research Center, 2014).
2. Samuel Huntington, 'The Clash of Civilizations?' *Foreign Affairs*, June (1993), http://www.foreignaffairs.com/articles/48950/samuel-p-huntington/the-clash-of-civilizations [accessed 22 August 2014]; Samuel Huntington, *The Clash of Civilizations and the Remaking of World Order* (New York: Simon & Schuster, 1996); and Bernard Lewis, 'The Roots of Muslim Rage', *The Atlantic Monthly*, September (1990), http://www.theatlantic.com/magazine/archive/1990/09/the-roots-of-muslim-rage/304643/ [accessed 20 August 2014]
3. Pew Forum, 'Muslim Publics Share Concerns about Extremist Groups' (Washington DC: Pew Research Center, 2013)
4. Alexander Dziadosz and Steve Holland 'Obama condemns killing of reporter, US hits militants in Iraq', *Reuters* 21 August (2014), http://uk.reuters.com/article/2014/08/20/uk-iraq-security-idUKKBN0GJ0S720140820 [accessed 23 August 2014].
5. Jurgen Habermas), *The Structural Transformation of the Public Sphere: An Inquiry Into a Category of Bourgeois Society* (Cambridge, MA: MIT Press, 1991).
6. Jurgen Habermas 'A "post-secular" society – what does that mean?' ResetDOC, 16 September (2008), http://www.resetdoc.org/story/00000000926 [accessed 23 August 2014].

7. Judith Butler, Jurgen Habermas, Charles Taylor, and Cornel West, *The Power of Religion in the Public Sphere* (New York: Columbia University Press, 2011); and Jurgen Habermas and Joseph Ratzinger, *The Dialectics of Secularization: On Reason and Religion* (San Francisco : Ignatius Press, 2007).

8. Amy Frykholme 'Under Hillary Clinton, the State Department Pursued Greater Religious Engagement', Religion and Politics, 8 May (2013), http://religionandpolitics.org/2013/05/08/since-hillary-clintons-tenure-the-state-department-pursues-greater-religious-engagement/#sthash.lSD1Wzdg.dpuf [accessed 23 August 2014].

9. Alex Schmid, 'Radicalisation, De-Radicalisation, Counter-Radicalisation: A Conceptual Discussion and Literature Review', ICCT Discussion Paper, (The Hague: International Centre for Counter-Terrorism, March 2013).

10. Arun Kundnani, 'Radicalisation: the journey of a concept', *Race & Class*, Vol 54, No 2 (2012): 3-25

11. HM Government, Prevent Strategy, (London: The Stationary Office, 2011).

12. Sukhwant Dhaliwal and Nira Yuval-Davis, *Women Against Fundamentalism: Stories of Dissent and Solidarity*, (London: Lawrence and Wishart, 2014).

13. Lorenzo Vidino, *Countering Radicalization in America: Lessons from Europe*, (Washington DC: United States Institute of Peace, Special report No, 262, 2010).

17

The Future of Islamic State Systems in Light of Rising Sectarian Tensions

SHIREEN T. HUNTER
GEORGETOWN UNIVERSITY, USA

Sectarian tensions have been steadily rising in the Middle East and South Asia since the mid-1990s. They were first manifested in South Asia, especially Afghanistan, following the withdrawal of the Soviet troops in 1989 and the onset of the Civil War in that country, and in Pakistan. The worsening sectarian tensions were reflected in the highly sectarian character of the Sunni extremist Afghan group, the Taliban, and their systematic attacks on the Shias of Afghanistan, notably the 1998 massacre of nearly 8,000 Shias belonging to the Hazara ethnic group.[1]

During the 1990s, sectarian relations also became tense in Pakistan. These relations had begun to deteriorate by the early 1980s following legal changes introduced by President Zia-ul-Haq and his policy of Pakistan's further Islamisation according to a stricter Sunni legal system. These changes were viewed as discriminatory towards the Shias, causing protests on their part and leading to the formation of Shia political groups. Since that time, sectarian relations in Pakistan have continued to deteriorate.[2] In Pakistan, too, the Hazaras have been a particular target of attacks by Sunni extremist groups such as Lashkar-e-Jhangvi and Sipah-e-Sahaba, especially in places such as Peshawar, in the North West Frontier, and Quetta, in Baluchistan.[3] However, Shias in Punjab and Sind have also been attacked.

By contrast, during the 1990s the Middle East remained immune from any particularly sectarian-tinged violence. The situation changed following the US invasion of Iraq in March 2003. The US invasion ended the historic Sunni Arab domination of Iraq. Therefore, soon after Saddam Hussein's fall, Iraq's Sunnis organised militias and other armed groups in order to undermine the new Shia-dominated political setup in Iraq. Meanwhile, various Shia militias, such as the Mahdi Army of Muqtada al-Sadr, were also formed. These were, however, largely for the purposes of intra-Shia competition for power.[4] But following attacks by Sunni extremists on the Shia holy shrine in Samara in 2006, other Shia militias, such as Asa'ib Ahl al-Haq and Kata'ib Hezbollah, were also formed.

The US invasion of Iraq and the change in that country's political setup disrupted regional balance of power in Iran's favour, as well as enhanced the position of the Shias in the region. At least, this was the perception of Sunni Arab states such as Saudi Arabia, Qatar, the UAE and others, plus Turkey. In response they became more deeply engaged in Iraq's internal politics and tried to prevent the consolidation of Iran's influence and the Shias' position by recourse to sectarian factors. Iran, meanwhile, tried to establish its influence in country by using its ties to the Shias.

Changes in Iraq also encouraged other Shia minorities in places such as Saudi Arabia, as well Bahrain's Shia majority, to agitate for more rights, thus further intensifying the Gulf Arabs' unease over Iraqi developments and causing them to try and stem the rise of the Shias in Iraq by funding and arming Sunni militants. These efforts further exacerbated sectarian tensions and increased the occurrence of sectarian violence. Sectarian tensions even reached places like Kuwait, which historically had a reasonable record of sectarian coexistence.[5]

The Arab Spring and the Spread of Sectarian Tensions to Syria and Beyond

Nevertheless, until December 2010—when political disturbances which began in Tunisia and later extended to Egypt resulted in the elimination of presidents Zine El Abidine Ben Ali and Hosni Mubarak, respectively, and came to be known as the Arab Spring—sectarian tensions in the Middle East were largely limited to Iraq and places like Bahrain, with a long history of Shia grievance against the ruling Sunni Al-Khalifa family. The Arab Spring eventually reached Syria and impacted its political conditions and, by doing so, extended sectarian tensions to that country, as well to Egypt and Turkey, and further exacerbated conditions in Iraq and Bahrain.

In particular, Shia protests in Bahrain acquired very large dimensions, resulting in violent repression by the government. It even caused Saudi

Arabia, together with the United Arab Emirates, to militarily intervene in that country under the umbrella of the so-called Peninsula Shield arrangement, although this mechanism was intended for dealing with external aggression against the members of the Gulf Cooperation Council (GCC) and not for suppressing internal dissent.

The Bahrain crisis and the brutal suppression of Shia protests, especially Saudi Arabia's military intervention, further inflamed Shia sentiments in Saudi Arabia's Shia-inhabited regions, such as Qatif. It also angered the Shias in Iraq and Iran, and worsened significant sharpening of sectarian animosities throughout the Middle East. However, because of the presence of Western military bases in Bahrain and general Western support for the Al-Khalifa ruling family, neither Iraq nor Iran could help Bahrain's Shias in any meaningful fashion and had to limit themselves to condemnation of Bahrain's governments.

The Syrian Civil War and its Ramifications

Initially, it seemed that the Arab Spring would not reach Syria, but by March 2011 protests had spread to Syria and eventually grew into a full-scale civil war. Unlike the case of Bahrain, which experienced large-scale repression by the Al-Khalifa leadership, soon after the outbreak of protests in Syria, the United States and other major European countries, together with such regional players as Turkey and Saudi Arabia, called for Syrian president Bashar al-Assad's removal from office, as illustrated by President Barak Obama's statement that 'Assad must go.'[6]

However, Assad refused to succumb to regional and international pressures and set upon a strategy of resistance to growing internal and external challenges to his authority. He was supported in this decision by Syria's long-time ally Iran, the Lebanese Shia group Hezbollah, and Russia. China, meanwhile, adopted a position of low-key support for Assad.

The Syrian conflict soon acquired a sharp sectarian dimension, despite the fact that Bashar al-Assad's regime is essentially secular (although the Alawite community forms the basis of its top military and political leadership). The Sunni countries of the region, notably Saudi Arabia and Turkey, plus Qatar, began to form, fund and even train Sunni groups to challenge the Assad regime and counter the influence of countries such as Iran and groups like Hezbollah. These groups included such entities as the Jabhat al-Nusra. Al-Nusra shared the ideological outlook of Al-Qaeda, including a visceral hatred of the Shias, and later officially joined the organisation. It exhibited sectarian hatred hitherto unseen in Syria, as reflected in its attacks on Shia shrines and wholesale massacre of Shia villages. These acts inflamed the passions of Shias in other Shia-majority countries, notably Iraq, and led them to send volunteers to Syria in order to guard Shia holy places, in this way creating a rift among various sectarian conflicts in the Levant and the Persian Gulf region.[7]

Sectarian tensions in Syria and Turkey's growing interference there negatively affected such relations in Turkey, where the Shia and Alevi communities came under increasing pressure from the government.[8] Even in Egypt, anti-Shia sentiments surfaced, as reflected in the brutal killing of an Egyptian Shia cleric by Salafi Sunnis.[9]

The Rise of ISIS, the Call for Khilafat and the Challenge to the Established State System[10]

Despite significant international pressure, the Assad regime proved more resilient than expected. The divided nature of the anti-Assad forces, the conflicting goals of the countries supporting them and assistance from countries such as Iran and Russia enhanced the Syrian regime's staying power.

Consequently, by late 2013, the focus of sectarian conflicts again shifted to Iraq. Partly because the Iraqi government had supported Assad and the Iraqi Shia volunteers had joined Syrian forces, the principal goal became undermining and even replacing Iraq's Shia-dominated government. Such a change would have eliminated Iraqi support for Syria and would have also undermined Iran's position, another supporter of Assad. Failing that, the goal was to block the road linking Iraq to Syria by creating a Sunni entity on the Iraqi-Syrian border.

One instrument used for this purpose was a new Sunni militant group known as ISIS. The ideological and leadership roots of the group were similar to those of earlier Sunni militant groups such as al-Qaeda, al-Nusra, and others in Syria. But the ambitions of ISIS surpassed those of these groups, as it declared that it wanted to create an Islamic caliphate whose borders would roughly correspond to those of the Abbasid caliphs. Earlier, such diverse groups as the Hizb ut-Tahrir and the Taliban had also called for the establishment of an Islamic caliphate, but it was only ISIS that, by gaining control of large swathes of Iraq and Syria, seemed to have any chance of creating the nucleus of such an Islamic entity and thus potentially redrawing the existing map of states in the Middle East.

Moreover, the worsening of political and sectarian crisis in Iraq and Syria also raised the possibility of the territorial disintegration of both states, with the risk of similar disintegrative processes reaching other countries, such as Iran and Turkey.

The Root Cause of Sectarian Problems: Religion or Politics and Inter-state Competition?

The rise of sectarian tensions in the Middle East and South Asia in the past two decades, and especially since the US invasion of Iraq in 2003, has given greater credence to the view that religion is increasingly a more important factor in determining the behaviour of various actors and, hence, in shaping the character of international relations, than the more traditional motivations of behaviour. It has also enhanced the position of those who believe that religion is eroding the foundations of the post-World War II state system by giving rise to transnational, non-state actors organised along sectarian lines.

Clearly, since the late 1970s, religion has become a more significant force in the domestic politics of most states in the Middle East and South Asia. At times it has caused the collapse of old systems, as was the case in Iran in 1979, or their significant transformation, such as Turkey under the AKP. These changes, in turn, have shifted the external behaviour of these states and, thus, have altered the dynamics of regional and, to some degree, international politics. Non-state actors at least partly created under religious impulses and to some degree motivated by them, such as the Taliban, Hezbollah and more recently ISIS, have also significantly impacted the dynamics of regional and international relations.

Similarly, sectarian divides and deep-rooted animosities are real enough, as is the failure of most states in these regions to develop national identities transcending ethnic and sectarian divisions. However, sectarian divisions and dislikes have existed for centuries, and yet at least for the last three hundred years there had not been any significant conflict caused by sectarian differences; certainly nothing of the magnitude of recent events.

What the above means is that it is not correct to assume that religion has replaced other determinants of either state behaviour or those of semi-state actors, such as the Taliban, Hezbollah or ISIS. Nor have these new sectarian actors replaced states as the main players within the international system. Rather, it would be more accurate to say that religion, including in its sectarian version, has increasingly been used as an instrument of state policy and for advancing largely non-religious strategic and political goals. In fact, most of the apparently religious non-state actors, such as the Taliban, Hezbollah and ISIS, have been the creations of states and cannot function without their assistance. For example, Pakistan was instrumental in the creation of the Afghan Taliban.[11] Certainly Pakistan has trained and partly funded the Taliban with the diplomatic and financial support of Saudi Arabia.[12] Similarly, the Saudis have funded many of Iraq's Sunni militant groups and those of Syria, as has Turkey.[13] Meanwhile, Iran has been instrumental in transforming Hezbollah into a formidable political and military force. Moreover, it was a state action, namely Israel's invasion of Lebanon in 1982, that afforded Iran the opportunity to help create Hezbollah. Even today, Hezbollah to a large degree follows Iran's policy directions and, therefore, its behaviour changes according to shifts in Iran's foreign policy priorities.[14] In short, the main non-state actors of the category of the Taliban and Hezbollah are, in reality, proxies for states; although, as in any relationship between the sponsor and the proxy, the latter could manipulate the former, or the sponsoring state could, in time, lose control over its proxy.

Furthermore, these types of actors do not want to dismantle the state. Instead, they want to gain control over it, reshape its character, or replace it with a new one. In short, the state is still the principal unit of international system.

If the above thesis—that religion has not been the main cause of rising sectarian tensions and new religious formations are not about to replace the state—is accepted, then the question becomes what has triggered the recent sectarian conflicts. The answer lies in the systemic changes, at both international and regional level, caused by the USSR's collapse, the US military interventions in Afghanistan and Iraq, the American policy of reshaping the politics and governments of the region and, in particular, the US policy of containing Iran. In other words, politics and quests for security and influence by states have been behind rising sectarian conflicts.

The Soviet Collapse, the Struggle for Eurasia, Dual Containment and the Rise of the Taliban

The USSR's dismantlement produced significant changes in the character of the international system and the dynamics of regional sub-systems. At the international level, by eliminating the Soviet counterweight to the NATO power it encouraged more interventionist and transformative policies on the part of America, especially in regard to the Middle East and South Asia.

At the regional level, by eliminating the common Soviet threat and opening up the Muslim-inhabited regions of the USSR to new actors, it intensified the competitive and conflictive aspects of regional relations, including those between Iran and Pakistan, Iran and Saudi Arabia, and Iran and Turkey. The impact of this factor is clearly reflected in Pakistan's decision to create the Taliban.[15] This development prompted these regional rivals to more systematically exploit each other's sectarian fault lines.

The US policy of containing Iran, under President Bill Clinton, and, later, President George W. Bush's policy of regime change in that country contributed both to the worsening of regional relations and to sectarian tensions. For example, until 1998, when US embassies in Africa were bombed by the Taliban's ally al-Qaeda, the US saw the group as a counterweight to Iran because of its anti-Shia, and hence anti-Iran, tendencies. In fact, America did not object to the Taliban's obscurantist version of Islam and remained silent in the face of atrocities committed by them. The Bush administration, as part of its strategy of regime change, not only did not prevent Pakistan and Saudi Arabia from manipulating Iran's Sunni minorities, especially in its Baluchistan province, but might have done so itself.

Reshaping Middle East Politics

US policies of reshaping the Middle East further exacerbated sectarian tensions. The most consequential was the invasion of Iraq, which, by disrupting the regional balance of power, intensified regional rivalries, notably those between Iran and Saudi Arabia, and involved Turkey more deeply in Middle East rivalries. Similarly, US efforts to reshape Lebanon's politics through the Cedar Revolution, partly to weaken Hezbollah and thus Iran's influence there, and later efforts to eliminate the Assad government worsened sectarian tensions. Here it is important to note that opposition to the Assad regime by some Arab states, notably Saudi Arabia, was not because of its Alawite character but rather because of its alliance with Iran, which was based on political considerations. This view is supported by the fact that until 2010 Saudi Arabia was courting Assad in the hope that he would abandon his ties to Iran.

After its invasion of Iraq in 2003, as part of its strategy of containing Iran and preferably changing its regime, the US encouraged and supported a Sunni-Israeli alliance against Iran. Gary Sick, in 2007, noted that 'an emerging strategy is developing that brings the United States, Israel and Sunni Arab states in an informal alliance against Iran'.[16] The intention might not have been to cause sectarian conflict, but that is what happened.

Conclusions

Despite a widespread belief to the contrary, the rise of sectarian tensions in the Middle East and South Asia is not solely or even principally attributable to religious factors, although the existence of religious differences creates a receptive environment for the emergence of such conflicts. Rather, politics and conflicting security and other interests of international and regional actors and their competition for power and influence are the principal culprits. What has happened is the increased use of religion as an instrument of policy, as secular ideologies were used in the past. However, the use of religion has not meant that states have stopped manipulating their competitors' other vulnerabilities, such as ethnic divisions.

Moreover, despite the rise of non-state actors ostensibly motivated by religion, the main impetus behind their emergence has been state action, and they cannot easily function without continued state support. Therefore, these actors are unlikely to supplant states, although they might form new state governments.

Nevertheless, religion has become a far more important factor in the domestic politics of regional actors, and since external behaviour of international actors is partly determined by the nature of their domestic politics, religion has become a more significant, albeit not determinant, factor in shaping the character of internal relations. Similarly, the rise of religious non-state actors has been added to other sources of stress on the states.

Notes

1. "UN Report Derails 'Taliban Killing Frenzy'", *News International*, 6 November 1998, at http://www.rawa.org/killing.htm
2. For more details, see Shireen T. Hunter, 'The Regional and International Politics of Rising Sectarian Tensions in the Middle East and South Asia', ACMCU Occasional Papers, May 2013.
3. Syed Fazel Haider, 'Nowhere Is safe for Pakistan's Hazaras', *Asia Times*, 20 February 2013, at http://www.arimes.com/atimes/South Asia/SOU-04-200213.html
4. On the Mahdi Army and Muqtada al-Sadr, see Nimrod Raphaeli, 'Understanding Muqtada Al Sadr', *The Middle East Quarterly*. Vol. XI, no.4, Fall 2004, at http://www.meforum.org/655/understanding-muqrada-al-sadr
5. Mona Kareem, 'Shiaphobia Hits Kuwait', *Jadaliyya*, 17 May 2011, at www.jadaliyya.com/pages/index/1603/shiaphobia-hits-kuwait
6. Scott Wilson & Joby Warrick, 'Assad Must Go, Obama Says', *Washington Post*, 18 August 2011, at http://www.washingtonpost.com/politics/assad-must-go-obama-says/2011/08/18/gIQAelheOJ_story.html
7. For more detail, see 'The Regional and International Politics of Rising Sectarian Tensions in the Middle East and South Asia'.
8. Gareth Jenkins, 'Turkey's Beleaguered Alevis', *The Turkey Analyst*, vol.7, no.11, 11 June 2014.
9. 'Egypt: Mob Attack Kills Four Shia Muslims', BBC News/Middle East, 24 June 2013,

at http://www.bbc.com/news/worlld-middle-east023026865. Among those killed was Hassan Shehata, a leader of the Shia community.

10. The group changed its name to IS, standing for Islamic State, in August 2014.

11. Amin Saikal, *Modern Afghanistan: a History of Struggle and Survival*, London: I.B. Tauris, 2004, pp.220-221.

12. Anthony Davies, 'How the Taliban Became a Military Force', in William Maley (ed.), *Fundamentalism Reborn: Afghanistan and the Taliban*, New York: New York University Press, 2001, p.74.

13. Ahmed Rashid, 'Pakistan and the Taliban', in Ibid., p.74.

14. Fred Halliday, 'A Lebanese Fragment: Two Days with Hezbullah', *Open Democracy*, 20 July 2006.

15. Amin Saikal, *Modern Afghanistan*, p.221.

16. 'Sick: Alliance against Iran', Council on Foreign Relations, 23 January 2007, at http://www.cfr.org/israel/sick-alliance-against-iran/p12477

18

The Geopolitics of Religious Liberty

NILAY SAIYA

STATE UNIVERSITY OF NEW YORK, USA

Introduction

The world is currently witnessing three trends related to religion.[1] The first is the so-called 'global resurgence of religion'. Recent scholarship has shown that religion is gaining in strength worldwide and is more politically engaged today than it has ever been. Thanks to processes like modernisation, globalisation and democratisation—the very developments that the secularisation thesis predicted would kill off religion—the major world religions have experienced newfound relevance in today's world.[2] The second trend involves the concurrent attempts on the part of states to restrict religious practice in the face of this resurgence. A 2011 report by the Pew Research Center found that between 2006 and 2009, one-third of the world's population experienced rising restrictions on religion, and over two-thirds of the population lived in countries characterised by 'high' or 'very high' religious restrictions. Incredibly, the report also found that only 1 per cent of the world's population lived in countries where religious liberty was increasing.[3] A follow-up report issued in 2014 revealed that religious persecution had reached its highest point in six years.[4] The convergence of these two antithetical trends—religion's revival and simultaneous regulation—has given rise to a third development: resistance. Religious believers who find the practice of their faith stifled by government actions are likely to resist those efforts. Sometimes this resistance takes the form of non-violent protest, as in Eastern Europe following the collapse of the Soviet Union. At other times, the reaction to repression can turn violent, even to the point of tearing countries apart and threatening the stability of their neighbours.

When one thinks about geopolitics, religious liberty (or religion more generally) is probably not the first thing that enters the mind. Guided by the 'secularisation thesis', the field of international relations has been slow to recognise religion's growing importance and, until recently, tended to ignore it altogether. For this reason, little attention has been paid to the effect of religious factors, including religious liberty, on conflict and political stability. Some might see religious liberty as a normatively good idea but not centrally related to power politics. This chapter argues that this conventional wisdom is incorrect; religious liberty is connected to political stability in profound ways. Where religious liberty is threatened, the chances of a state experiencing sectarian violence increases, as does the likelihood that violence will spread to neighbouring countries.

Religious Liberty and Geopolitics

Religious liberty encompasses both the *religious* rights of individuals or communities to manifest religion or belief in teaching, practice, worship and observance and the *political* rights of these persons to run for office and otherwise participate in politics. This freedom has long been recognised as a central human right and been enshrined in various international laws, charters, treaties and national constitutions.[5] How, then, does religious liberty help shape geopolitics? Because religion is such an innate component of human identity, efforts to restrict its legitimate manifestation understandably meet with resistance from believers. If this resistance turns violent, it can have an effect on domestic and international security.

Religious repression commonly stems from state leaders who fear an independent and active religious citizenry.[6] Such leaders often attempt to control religious bodies that could potentially threaten the state's official ideology, public order, cultural identity or the regime itself. Depending on the context, these leaders may attempt to suppress religion across the board, as in the case of countries that are officially atheist like the former Soviet Union or China, or they may form an alliance with a particular (usually dominant) religious group in the cause of enhancing political stability, domestic legitimacy and ideological amenability, while suppressing the other (usually minority) religious groups in society that do not abide by the dominant state-endorsed religious framework. States often do this in response to intense social and religious pressures from their populations.[7] In fact, in certain countries, religious regulation arises from social persecution and a general climate of religious intimidation that emanates from the general populace as much as from the government. Such patterns can be seen today in Iran, Saudi Arabia and Russia.

Repressive environments like these that choke religious liberty and independent thinking serve as a natural breeding ground for extremism.[8] In addition to suppressing the positive contributions that religion can make to society, they also silence the voices of liberalism and moderation and empower the narrative of extremists who claim that the state is acting unjustly towards people of faith.[9] Violence occurs because religious restrictions both create grievances on the part of targeted groups and sometimes encourage dominant religious groups to undertake violence themselves against religious communities not favoured by the state. In the former case, embattled religious communities strike out against those perceived to be responsible for their marginalised and suppressed status as happened in Egypt, Algeria and Tunisia.[10] Religious militants may also attack government targets or citizens of another state believed to be complicit in their subjugation: witness the terrorist strikes of 11 September 2001. The state may use the threat of violence as a pretext for further repression and, in the process, invite more retaliatory violence.[11] In the latter pathway, groups that are empowered as a result of governmental repression against other faith communities seek to impose their worldview throughout society and eradicate alternative religious voices. This may even happen with the active support or non-interference of the state, as seen during the 2002 pogroms in Gujarat, India.[12] It is not uncommon for religious bloodshed to spread to neighbouring countries as civil or military leaders leverage extremist organisations as part of their foreign policies, as in the cases of Iran and Pakistan.[13]

Conversely, religiously free countries allow for the development of a wide range of diverse perspectives, religious practices and cross-cutting cleavages.[14] The freedom of thought and exchange of ideas part and parcel of religious liberty serve to create a marketplace of views that can empower liberal and moderate voices who challenge the claims made by religious extremists, thus diminishing the prospects of religious strife. In such countries, individuals belonging to different religious communities tend to see each other as legitimate, even if they disagree on matters of faith and practice.[15] Freedom thus has the effect of levelling the playing field among the different religious groups in society. Furthermore, the political openness part and parcel of religious liberty allows potential extremists to work through alternative and legitimate channels—electoral participation, grassroots activism and civic engagement—by which they can seek to shape religion, politics and society.[16] Finally, regimes tolerant of religion promote stability through the social activities in which they allow religious bodies to engage. Religious groups can use their energies towards the betterment of their societies: running schools, hospitals, orphanages and charities; reducing poverty; and promoting faith-based reconciliation practices. Illiberal religious groups holding radical theologies may well exist in religiously free countries, but the environment of freedom can serve to deprive fringe groups of the legitimacy they need to thrive.[17]

All this has tremendous implications for political stability. Where religious liberty does not exist, the potential for domestic stability and freedom will be greatly compromised. In other words, religious restrictions induce the very conflict they aim to thwart. Take, for example, the issues of religious persecution and terrorism. In their path-breaking work *The Price of Freedom Denied*, sociologists Brian Grim and Roger Finke found that government regulation of religious practice was the strongest predictor of religious persecution. At times, persecution of people of faith resulted in displaced or exiled faith communities, assaults on physical integrity rights and refugee crises. Recent work has also shown that countries restrictive of religious liberty are far more likely to experience religiously motivated terrorism. My analysis of religious terrorism since the end of the Cold War, for instance, shows that religiously restrictive countries are about nine times more likely to experience religiously motivated terrorism than countries that are religiously free. Furthermore, virtually all religious transnational terrorist organisations originate from religiously restrictive places.[18] Contrariwise, Grim and Finke have unearthed powerful evidence indicating that the relaxation of religious restrictions and protection of religious liberty nurtures peaceful competition between religious groups in society, thus contributing to a wide array of positive externalities that come from widespread freedom.

The Case of Iraq

Iraq is a prime case regarding the intersection of religious liberty and geopolitics. In 2014, Iraq descended into a new round of religious violence and terrorism. Nearly three years after American troops left the country, the radical Islamist terrorist group ISIL (Islamic State in Iraq and the Levant), a terrorist group believed to be more extreme and powerful than Al Qaeda, made rapid progress in gaining control over Iraqi territory, armoured vehicles and weapons stockpiles that had been abandoned by the Iraqi armed forces. ISIL's goals involved a fundamentalist Islamic takeover of Iraq and Syria and the setting up of an Islamic caliphate in the broader Middle East. In early July, the group announced the official creation of a new religious state in Iraq and Syria, and has even been able to establish some institutions of governance in the areas under its control.[19] The recent violence in Iraq is reminiscent of the cycle of violence that gripped the country 2006–2008 and saw a brutal sectarian war between Sunni extremists who targeted Shiite sacred spaces and equally ruthless Shiite militias who responded by torturing and executing Sunnis.

How did this state of affairs come to be? One could point to a number of factors: the bungled American occupation, the collapse of the Iraqi security forces, the civil war in Syria, and the backing of Sunni militants by certain Gulf States. Perhaps the greatest blame lies, however, with the brutal and arbitrary treatment of Iraq's minority religious communities by the state.

The American-led invasion and occupation of Iraq unleashed two processes, both centrally related to the issue of religious liberty, which ultimately led to a sectarian war along religious lines. The first process, 'de-ba'athification', was the official policy adopted by the George W. Bush administration and involved the forced disbanding of the Iraqi army, the dismantling of the bureaucracy, and the general purging of Ba'athism from Iraqi society. In one fell swoop, hundreds of thousands of Sunni Iraqi civil servants who had been nominally aligned with Saddam Hussein's Ba'ath Party found themselves jobless and barred from holding any government position in the future. Systematic discrimination along religious lines served to create a sense of desperation and angst among Sunnis who believed they would have no place in the new Iraq. Indeed, the government of Shiite strongman, Nouri al-Maliki, pursued a punitive policy towards Iraq's Sunni community, including using the security forces to suppress opponents and bully rivals. For example, when peaceful Sunni protests broke out in the Anbar province in 2012, Maliki responded with an intense crackdown, leading to the shelling of villages and the arrests of hundreds of Sunnis. This, the second process—what I call 'Shiaification'— witnessed the Shiite takeover of the state; the systematic discrimination and persecution of religious minorities via the army, police and militias; and the refusal of hardline Shiite parties to enter into a power sharing agreement with Sunnis that would bring them into the structure of the government.

These twin processes of de-ba'athification and Shiaification unleashed a religious and sectarian civil war between militant Shiite groups who had long been repressed under Saddam (but now had an opportunity to gain unilateral control over the new Iraq) on one side, and angry, dispossessed and armed Sunnis on the other. Maliki's authoritarian turn directly fuelled the insurgency by creating an environment of impunity, continuing to marginalise the Sunni population and fostering a sense of fear among the country's minority religious populations. Threatened and insecure, Iraqi Sunnis turned to extremist groups for protection. The Iraqi civil war not only worked to tear that country apart but also spread into the neighbouring states of Syria and Lebanon, producing a humanitarian nightmare. Nearly two million refugees fled Iraq after 2003; half of Iraq's Christian population left the country, never to return.[20] Moreover, Sunni co-religionists in neighbouring Syria also became radicalised and joined the Iraqi insurgency. For his part, Maliki was more than willing to allow his country to become a corridor for thousands of Shiite warriors to enter Syria and fight on behalf of the embattled Syrian regime. It is unlikely that the situation in Iraq will lead to an official redrawing of borders, though for all intents and purposes the border between Iraq and Syria has all but disappeared.

Some might argue that the case of Iraq shows precisely why straightforward repression of religion works. These individuals might claim that though Saddam was an undeniably brutal tyrant, at least his heavy-handedness was able to keep the forces of religious extremism at bay. Two points are worth mentioning. First, repression may provide the illusion of order but only fuels the underlying rage among the people. Eventually, the brewing discontent under the surface can no longer be contained. Second, the stability of regimes such as Saddam's is far less certain than once believed. Just 15 years ago it seemed unthinkable that the firmly entrenched Arab dictatorships in Libya, Iraq, Egypt and potentially Syria could be overthrown. Yet when the regimes of Muammar Qaddafi, Saddam Hussein and Hosni Mubarak fell, the groups which filled the power vacuum were highly illiberal ones that had been suppressed or banned for decades.

Conclusion

The relationship between religious liberty and political stability is of particular importance as pro-democracy revolts and religious violence continue to wash over large swathes of the Arab world. Governments in the Middle East and North Africa have historically used the potential for social conflict as a justification for restricting religious rights. Indeed the conventional wisdom has been that restrictions on a wide range of freedoms—including religious liberty—may be a necessary evil in order to realise the goals of order and stability. The result has often been the exact opposite of that which was intended: more sectarian strife and violence.

This chapter has argued that religious liberty and security are not mutually exclusive categories. In fact, religious liberty *is* a security issue. There are steps that governments can take to lessen the likelihood that ordinary religious individuals will subscribe to the narrative of extremism. Such steps might include allowing religious groups to carry out activities distinctive to their faith including establishing houses of worship, publishing literature, fundraising, building hospitals and schools, and celebrating holy days. Furthermore, states in which religious organisations also enjoy full political rights such as voting, lobbying and staging protests will also experience less religious conflict. The denial of such rights only serves to create resentment and increase the appeal of radicalism. Though some might argue that repression serves to quash extremism, this tends to be only a short-term gain that hardens opposition to the state. The international community therefore ought to pay greater attention to religious liberty both as an important value in its own right and as an important instrument in countering extremism.

Notes

1. By 'religion' I mean the sets of beliefs, practices, or rituals that seek knowledge of and harmony with supernatural realities.

2. See Josè Casanova, *Public Religions in the Modern World* (Chicago: University of Chicago Press, 1994); Peter L. Berger, *The Desecularization of the World: Resurgent Religion and World Politics* (Grand Rapids, MI: William. B. Eerdmans Publishing Company, 1999); Monica Duffy Toft and Timothy Samuel Shah, 'Why God is Winning'', *Foreign Policy* July/August (2006): 39-43; Monica Duffy Toft, Daniel Philpott, and Timothy Samuel Shah, *God's Century: Resurgent Religion and Global Politics* (New York: W.W. Norton, 2011).

3. Pew Research Center, 'Rising Tide of Restrictions on Religion', *Pew Forum on Religion in Public Life*, available at http://www.pewforum.org/2011/08/09/rising-restrictions-on-religion2/, accessed June 1, 2014.

4. Pew Research Center, 'Religious Hostilities Reach Six-Year High', *Pew Forum on Religion in Public Life*, available at http://www.pewforum.org/2014/01/14/religious-hostilities-reach-six-year-high/, accessed June 1, 2014.

5. For example, Article 18 of the United Nations Declaration on Human Rights asserts: 'Everyone has the right to freedom of thought, conscience and religion. This right includes freedom to change his religion or belief, and freedom…to manifest his religion or belief in teaching, practice, worship, and observance'.

6. Ani Sarkissian, *The Varieties of Religious Repression: Why Governments Restrict Religion* (New York: Oxford University Press, 2015).

7. Brian J. Grim and Roger Finke, *The Price of Freedom Denied: Religious Persecution and Conflict in the Twenty-First Century* (Cambridge: Cambridge University Press, 2011).

8. William Inboden, 'Religious liberty and National Security', *Policy Review* 175 (2012): 55-68.

9. This is not to suggest, of course, that religious extremists strive for religious tolerance, but that such radicalism is often incubated in environments of religious repression. Lisa Anderson, 'Fulfilling Prophecies: State Policy and Islamist Radicalism', in *Political Islam: Revolution, Radicalism, or Reform?*, ed. John L. Esposito, (London: Lynne Rienner Publishers), 17-31.

10. Mohammed Hafez, *Why Muslims Rebel: Repression and Resistance in the Islamic World* (London: Lynne Rienner, 2003); Gilles Kepel, *Jihad: The Trail of Political Islam* (London: I.B. Tauris, 2006).

11. Max Abrahms, 'Why Democracies Make Superior Counterterrorists', *Security Studies* 16(2): 223-253; James I. Walsh and James A. Piazza, 'Why Respecting Physical Integrity Rights Reduces Terrorism', *Comparative Political Studies* 43(5): 551-557.

12. Parvis Gassam-Fachandi, *Pogrom in Gujarat: Hindu Nationalism and Anti-Muslim Violence in India* (Princeton: Princeton University Press, 2012).

13. Husain Haqqani, *Pakistan: Between Mosque and Military* (Washington: Carnegie Endowment for International Peace, 2005).

14. Chris Seiple and Dennis R. Hoover, 'Religious liberty and Global Security', in *The Future of Religious liberty: Global Challenges*, ed. Allen D. Hertzke, (New York: Oxford,

2013): 315-330.

15. Anthony Gill, *The Political Origins of Religious Liberty* (New York: Cambridge University Press, 2008).

16. Alfred C. Stepan, 'Religion, Democracy, and the 'Twin Tolerations', *Journal of Democracy* 11(4): 37-57.

17. Thomas Farr, *World of Faith and Freedom: Why International Religious Liberty is Vital to American National Security* (New York: Oxford University Press, 2008), 243-272.

18. Nilay Saiya, *The Roots of Religious Terrorism* (PhD dissertation, University of Notre Dame, 2013).

19. Michael Crowley, 'The End of Iraq," *Time*, June 19, 2014, available at http://time.com/2899488/the-end-of-iraq/, accessed July 1, 2014.

20. Aryn Baker, 'Unholy Choices', *Time*, April 10, 2014, available at http://time.com/57277/unholy-choices, accessed June 26, 2014.

19

Is There a Religious Diversity Peace Dividend?

DAN G. COX

SCHOOL OF ADVANCED MILITARY STUDIES, FORT
LEAVENWORTH, USA

Several years ago, John Falconer, Brian Stackhouse and I began researching the relationship between democracy, economics, identity and regime stability on the one hand and terrorism on the other. We published a book, *Terrorism, Instability, and Democracy in Asia and Africa*, with the findings of our research in 2009. We found that states containing significant diversity (of ethnicity and religious belief) experienced more stability and fewer acts of terrorism that their more culturally homogenous counterparts. We referred to this as an 'apparent diversity dividend' for those countries called home to three or more significant religious or ethnic groups. This chapter considers some of this evidence and places it into the context of Thomas Farr's theoretical work on the United States' religious freedom policy.[1]

In our research we analysed the effects of regime type, ethnicity, religion, economic stability and political stability against incidents of terrorism in African and Asian states. When compiling our data on religious affiliation and ethnicity, we only coded significantly sized groups for examination. This meant that a group had to comprise 10 per cent or more of the total population to be considered a significant group in our study. While 10 per cent is an admittedly arbitrary barrier for inclusion, it is one of the standard delimiters used in many past scholarly research studies. We also felt the threshold had to be significantly high in order to prevent smaller, less significant religious and ethnic groupings from unfairly biasing the results towards no or spurious correlations.

We were initially surprised to find an apparent peace dividend in states with significant religious diversity. These states showed significantly fewer terrorist incidences compared to more monolithic religious societies. We did not know how to explain this finding theoretically and were forced to speculate as to why this correlation existed. As I explain later, we relied on theories of coalition-building and conciliation to explain what we observed.

In a novel way, this chapter is an attempt to place our empirical findings into a broader body of evidence and theory that has developed or at least gained notoriety since our research was first published. Much of the new thinking on religion and stability is correctly attributed to the work of Thomas Farr, the first director for the State Department's Office of International Religious Freedom. Since Farr is at the vanguard of this relatively new theoretical examination of the possible link between religion and stability, it seems appropriate to summarise some of his relevant assertions prior to relating them to what I am now dubbing the 'religious peace dividend'.

Religion and Stability: Thomas Farr and Other Recent Evidence

Thomas Farr is arguably the most notable voice espousing the benefits of a US foreign policy that places primacy on spreading religious freedom. Farr defines religious freedom as the 'right protected in law, to engage in the religious quest, either alone or in community with others, in private and in public'.[2] Citing Samuel Huntington's *Third Wave of Democratization*, Farr notes that in many Catholic colonies and states, the Second Vatican Council's adoption of religious liberty for all triggered a movement towards greater freedoms that eventually cascaded into the expansion of democracy. Further, Farr argues that any state that offers religious liberty necessarily begins to limit its own authority.[3] This is an important assertion because it relates directly to another recent seminal work on social revolutions by Misagh Parsa. Specifically, Parsa finds that, as authoritarian rulers consolidate power, they intervene in the economic, political and social lives of their citizenry to compensate for the narrowness of their actual base of support. Outside of this base of support, only harsh coercion kept the masses of people from rising up against the ruler and his or her supporters. Eventually, the state oppression tended towards the overly indiscriminate, which Stathis Kalyvas notes is often a driver for insurgency.[4] Such violence also eventually emboldens the masses to build coalitions against the oppressive state and bring about social revolutions.[5] Therefore, it is within this broader theoretical discussion that Farr's assertions are properly and powerfully placed. Expansion of religious freedoms is either an indication of increasing domestic stability or a *driver* of such stability.

Farr tends to embrace the driver thesis and therefore is completely consistent in insisting that conservatives in America are off base in their global condemnation of fomenting religious freedom to its fullest extent, even if this means that some states will produce Sharia-driven or other fundamentalist religious parties. Farr argues that over the long term, allowing 'religious freedom in those [Muslim] countries will reduce violent extremism, including the terrorism that has reached our shores, while also increasing the chances for stable democracy and economic growth'.[6] Farr is quick to note that actual religious extremism should not be tolerated but that since so many peoples and groups are religious, some way to accommodate religion in the political sphere must be found.[7] Further, Farr notes that Muslim minorities are often at risk even in states where Islam, in general, is dominant. In Saudi Arabia, Shiite minorities suffer, while the Ahmadis are bearing the brunt of minority discrimination in Pakistan. These persecuted minorities often serve as fertile ground for recruitment from extremist groups. Farr argues that extending religious freedom to all sects within a society will actually counteract religious extremist tendencies.[8]

Despite these cogent arguments, movement towards a foreign policy that emphasises religious freedom has been slow. Farr notes, 'In 1998, President Bill Clinton signed the International Religious Freedom Act, which mandated that the freedom to practice religion, a founding tenet of the United States, become a foreign-policy priority.'[9] Still, movement to actually embrace such a policy was slow during both the Clinton and George W. Bush administrations. Worse still, the current president has failed to appoint key foreign policy officials which might help foster a foreign policy emphasising religious freedom despite two high-profile reports—one by the Chicago Council on Global Affairs and the other by the president's own Advisory Council on Faith-Based and Neighbourhood Partnerships—which both recommend just such a foreign policy initiative.[10]

In short, the theory and some early evidence suggest that great stability benefits flow from states' embrace of religious tolerance and freedom. Despite presidential rhetoric extolling the virtues of pushing religious freedom abroad, little movement in that direction has actually occurred. What we add to the debate is some deep empirical evidence that corroborates what Thomas Farr and others have been saying for years.

A Religious Diversity Peace Dividend in Asia and Africa

To begin, there are a few caveats regarding the generalisability of our findings. First, we only examined states in Asia and Africa so our findings may not apply to states outside of these areas. This is a particularly important point given the turmoil in the Middle East. Hopefully, this will spur on further research expanding our study to new areas. Second, we focused mainly on terrorism which is a tactical tool used by insurgent groups so our findings may not apply to incidences of violence that are either interstate in nature or non-insurgent-based, such as genocide.

In *Terrorism, Instability, and Democracy in Asia and Africa*, we broke down our examination of terrorist incidences into separate examinations of international and domestic terrorism. In both cases we found a religious diversity peace dividend that supports Farr's contentions, among others. Our examination was exhaustive. Not only did we examine religion and terrorism using advanced statistical techniques aggregating the results across Asia and Africa, we also dived deeper into each major case of a state experiencing terrorism through the use of micro-case study analysis. In this way, we hoped to gain a broad and somewhat deep view of the causes of terrorism.

We were somewhat surprised by our international terrorism results. States containing only one dominant religion experienced the greatest incidence of terrorism. This was not overly surprising as the clash of civilisations between states, if one existed, might be sharper between mono-religious societies. What was surprising was the precipitous rate at which international terrorist incidences dropped off when there were two or more major religions present within the state boundaries. In fact, international terrorism was almost non-existent in states with three or more major religious groups. We speculated at the time that this finding might be

> due to the fact that it becomes more difficult for one religion to seize power and abuse the human or economic rights of the out-group. In other words, when power is distributed such that no single group can exploit its political or economic position in society, a more consociation or conciliatory outcome might be produced.[11]

While this is not an exact duplication of Farr's reasoning, it is very close. What was particularly amazing was that when we added an interactive variable combining religion and ethnicity, the results only increased in favour of a religious diversity peace dividend.

When we examined domestic terrorist incidences, we found a religious diversity peace dividend as well. However, the states with the greatest number of terrorist incidences were ones that comprised both a monolithic religious supermajority and states with two dominant religions. We fully expected states with two dominant religions to experience more terrorism, but again, we were surprised to find that states with one dominant religion experienced such high levels of terrorist violence.[12] Also, states with three or more major religions experienced almost no terrorism. We were again forced into the realm of speculation at this peculiar finding. We noted:

> There are several reasons that may explain this finding. First, societies with one dominant religion may be abusing the political and economic rights of very small religious minorities within society that feel their only recourse is to last out with terrorism. Another possibility is that there may be a shared religion in society with two or more dominant ethnic groups and that this religious bond is not enough to stop ethnic conflict manifesting in terrorism.[13]

The first line of reasoning conforms nicely with Thomas Farr's assertion that small minorities are suffering mightily at the hands of central governments in Saudi Arabia and Pakistan. The second assertion is partially refuted by our own work, as we found no statistical increase in terrorism when we factored in both religion and ethnicity.[14]

Even when we found cases of terrorism in countries with a deep religious split, the case study examination still bore out Farr's central theoretical thesis that extending religious freedoms and perhaps economic freedoms as well, would have gone a long way towards quelling the violence. In the Philippines, for example, a hundreds-of-years-old conflict between the Christian Catholics in the northern islands and the Muslim minority population located mainly on the southern island of Mindanao and the southern Sulu Island archipelago draws its roots from perceived and actual religious intolerance, a lack of meaningful inclusion of the southern Muslims in the political process, and a lack of economic opportunity and development there. So even in a case that seems to at least partially disprove the religious freedoms argument on the surface, ends up supporting the thesis when one examines the situation in more detail.

Bringing It All Together: The Religious Diversity Peace Dividend

Thomas Farr has been arguing coherently for years now for a US foreign policy based at least in part on the premise of extending religious freedoms in as many nations as possible. He argues that religious tolerance leads to an erosion of state monopoly on the means of coercion, empowers people in many different ways, prohibits exclusionary treatment of minority sects and religions, and brings stability and perhaps even economic development in its wake.

Our work provides some empirical evidence to support such assertions. It appears that states which contain three or more dominant religions have to act in a conciliatory manner, are likely sharing power and resources and have developed a consociational form of governance that does not overly favour one group over the other. In retrospect, knowing what Farr and others have asserted, I wish we had added a variable for religious freedom in our statistical analysis. I speculate that societies with three or more major religious groups have been forced to offer more religious and other freedoms than societies with one or two dominant religious groups. This becomes a cogent idea for further research. Additionally, our research did not cover the globe, nor did it examine all forms of violence. This, then, is another avenue of pressing future research.

In the final analysis, we found a religious diversity peace dividend. One cannot force the formation of new religions so the next best thing might be to encourage religious tolerance and respect for religious freedoms which should end up approximating the religious diversity peace dividend we observed. Still, more research is needed to ascertain if there is a religious freedom peace dividend that is as strong as the religious diversity peace dividend we originally observed.

Notes

*Opinions, conclusions, and recommendations expressed or implied in this chapter are solely those of the author, and do not represent the views of the U.S. Army School of Advanced Military Studies, the U.S. Army Command and General Staff College, the U.S. Army, the Department of Defense, or any other U.S. government agency.

1. Dan G. Cox, John Falconer, and Brian Stackhouse, *Terrorism, Instability, and Democracy in Asia and Africa* (Hanover, New England: University Press of New England, 2009).
2. Thomas Farr, 'Is Religious Freedom Necessary for Other Freedoms to Flourish?' *Big Questions Online* (7 August 2012). First accessed 31 July 2014. http://berkleycenter.georgetown.edu/rfp/essays/is-religious-freedom-necessary-for-other-freedoms-to-flourish.
3. Ibid.
4. Stathis N. Kalyvas, *The Logic of Violence in Civil War* (New York: Cambridge University Press, 2006), 151.
5. Misagh Parsa, *States, Ideologies, and Social Revolutions* (New York: Cambridge University Press, 2006).
6. Thomas F. Farr, 'American Conservatives, Islam, and Religious Realism in U. S. Foreign Policy', *National Review Online* (9 July, 2013). First accessed 31 July 2014, http://berkleycenter.georgetown.edu/rfp/essays/american-conservatives-islam-and-religious-realism-in-u-s-policy.
7. Ibid.

8. Thomas Farr, 'The Trouble with American Foreign Policy and Islam', *The Review of Faith and International Affairs* (2011), 65.

9. Thomas F. Farr, 'Undefender of the Faith: After 15 Months in Office, Why Hasn't Obama Even Nominated A Candidate for the Position of Ambassador at Large for International Religious Freedom?' *Foreign Policy* (5 April 2010). First accessed 14 August 2014 at http://www.foreignpolicy.com/articles/2010/04/05/undefender-of-the-faith?page=0.

10. Ibid.

11. Cox, Falconer, and Stackhouse (2009), 62.

12. Cox, Falconer, and Stackhouse (2009), 78-9.

13. Cox, Falconer, and Stackhouse (2009), 80.

14. Cox, Falconer, and Stackhouse (2009, 81.

20

Inter-Religious Work for Peace through Globalised Transnational Civil Society

PAULINE KOLLONTAI
YORK ST JOHN UNIVERSITY, UK

Introduction

During the latter part of the twentieth century the view that religion had been eclipsed by modernisation and secularisation has been challenged by the realities of the world in which we live. Scott Thomas argues there is a global resurgence of religion and one of the areas through which religions have re-entered the political spheres, foreign and domestic, is through Transnational Religious Actors (TRAs).[1] Recognition of this is seen in the work of scholars such as Rudolph and Piscatori and also Haynes.[2] Petito and Hatzpoulos argue religion must be given serious consideration in the study of international relations because it can be both a positive and negative force within and across borders.[3] Studies on TRAs demonstrate this dual capacity within religion by looking at the role of such groups and organisations as the Roman Catholic Church; the Christian Right in the USA (known as the Moral Majority); Al-Qaeda; Sikhs United; and the Organisation of Islamic Conference.

Less work has been done on the work of Inter-Religious Transnational Actors (IRTAs) such as the United Religions Initiative, World Council of Religious Leaders, Council for a Parliament of the World's Religions and Religions for Peace. One of the important aspects of these actors is that they are already modelling working together across religions to manifest the principles and values associated with peace and justice which are present in the fabric of all religious teachings. This chapter focuses on the work of the inter-religious transnational organisation, Religions for Peace, to examine its peace-building work under the aegis of globalisation. One of the areas of its work is Women, Community Development and Peace-Building which is looked at here to identify methods and approaches and the potential of this work to constitute an embryonic globalised transnational civil society.

The Exile and Return of Religion from International Relations

The exiling of religion from the foreign policies of states began in Europe during the seventeenth century following the Peace of Westphalia in 1648 because religion had been the cause of numerous religious wars and each religion's claim to have the absolute truth was considered by political leaders as potentially detrimental to embodying more of a spirit of co-operation in international relations. The superiority of secular power and authority, first in Europe and then across the globe, became the dominant operating principle for international relations. Religious voices—their ideas, values and principles—became marginalised in this area of state policy and governance. An interesting question to ask is whether the exiling of religion in this sphere meant that international relations proceeded to develop more co-operatively. The growth of imperialism and colonialism which were a central part of the foreign policies of most European states during the 300 years following the Peace of Westphalia normally involved some form of exploitation, aggression or even full-scale war. This appears to suggest that the exiling of religion made little difference to the behaviour of European leaders towards countries they wanted to conquer. Secular authority, as history shows, is also potentially prone to bouts of constructing policies that minimise human rights and in some cases destroy not only these rights but also innocent human life. Such authority in its more extreme expressions of power has oppressed religions; has failed to see that religion has the ability and capacity to contribute to the building of a more just and peaceable world; and has certainly not understood or misunderstood that ignoring religious leaders and their communities either in domestic or foreign policies assists in feeding the extremist elements in all religions.

The return of religion into IR was inevitable partly because of the points raised above but also because of the role that aspects of globalisation have played in assisting religious communities to connect more efficiently and on a greater scale. The growth in the transnational activity of religious actors (individuals groups and organisations), both negative and positive, has woken up the political leaders and their establishments to the reality that religion is a serious player in the affairs of states. The resurgence of religion and intensification of its presence in many parts of the world is a characteristic of postmodernism. For many people, modernity with its scientific rationalism, emphasis on meta-narratives and rejection of absolute unquestioning ways of speaking truth has caused a search for the transcendent, for new ways of understanding the human condition and for ways to change and improve human existence. Haynes states, 'Overall the postmodern condition offers opportunities for various religious actors to pursue a public role in a variety of areas.'[4] This activity expresses the spectrum of religious adherents and their interpretation of religious teachings—from conservative to liberal to fundamentalist—which then are translated in words and actions that seek either to nurture or destroy human societies. The return of religion to international relations reflects the view that 'religion is older than the state, and its aims encompass not just politics but all of life',[5] and this return reminds us that 'religion pre-dates the field of international relations, it has been and will always be integral to human identity'.[6]

Religion: The Dynamics of Co-operation and Conflict

Religion for many is considered authoritarian, parochial, exclusivist and intolerant. In the past decade, this one-sided view of religion has undergone some change as a more open-minded approach has been applied on the part of those working in the political and social sciences. Turner is one such individual who has done does this in his work, which shows that religion can operate in ways that do not promote the difference of others in a negative and confrontational way. He gives examples where religion has promoted concern, empathy and a sense of responsibility for others and seen every person as worthy of equal moral concern. For Turner, globalisation has challenged change within 'these traditional (religious) systems of inclusion and exclusion through hybridisation'.[7]

Arguing the case that indeed religion can promote and support pluralism and democratic values is explored through the paradigm of the dual nature of religion. Boulding speaks of 'the holy war and peaceable garden culture' in religion[8], while Galtung says, 'every religion contains, in varying degrees, elements of the soft and the hard'.[9] This dual nature of religion is described by Scott Appleby: 'Religion is a source not only of intolerance, human rights violations and extremist violence, but also of non-violent conflict transformation, the defence of human rights, integrity in government, and reconciliation and stability in divided societies.'[10] This presents religion as having a dual potential. This is argued by Appleby to result from the fact that most religions are by nature internally pluralistic.[11] For many people across the globe religion is a means of trying to understand life and the human condition and, for many, religion becomes the inspiration and a tool for peace-building. But, returning to the dual nature of religion argument, what must be recognised is that religions, 'while providing many valuable tools for peacebuilding, can also contribute to perpetuating cultures of violence.'[12]

Religion has the capacity and power to create and promote various worldviews, but fundamentally these express variations on one or other of two main models: (i) closed and exclusivist; or (ii) open and inclusivist/ pluralist. Many religions, because of their claim to a universal truth, are naturally constructed in their ethos and approach to work across territorial boundaries and state borders. The interaction of religion with globalisation can be experienced negatively and positively.

Case Study: Religions for Peace

The transnational, inter-religious organisation Religions for Peace (RfP) was set up in 1970. The global organisation consists of a world council made up of senior religious leaders from all regions of the world, four regional bodies, over seventy national bodies and the Global Youth and Global Women of Faith networks. RfPs origins are in the 1960s when a meeting took place between religious leaders from the major religious traditions who believed there was an urgent need to have an international religious summit for people of faith to focus their efforts of working towards achieving world peace. The first meeting of RfP took place in Kyoto, Japan in October 1970 and produced *The Kyoto Declaration of the First World Assembly.* Its opening statement sets out clearly the role of the meeting as 'an historic attempt to bring together men and women of all major religions to discuss the urgent issue of peace'.[13] In grave terms it identifies the challenge as humanity being faced with 'cruel and inhuman wars and by racial, social and economic violence', as well as the threat of nuclear extinction.[14] What then follows in the Declaration is an identification of seven principles of belief that can unite the world religions in action for world peace. These seven principles provide a starting point for a perspective that sees all of humanity as one family, thereby articulating the equality and dignity of all human beings. An explicit challenge to those who abuse and sometimes destroy the lives of people and a counter way of behaving in the world is then clearly established with the statement that 'love, compassion, selflessness, and the force of inner truthfulness and of the spirit have ultimately greater power than hate, enmity, and self-interest'.[15] Evident from the Declaration is the fact that RfP is not just a discussion forum but has an ethos of praxis, presenting religions as providing a meta framework to challenge both in word and action those ideologies and their adherents that deny rights, needs and life to people. The Declaration makes clear that RfP aims to be an organisation that transcends religious and political differences and challenges governments and other organisations that violate human dignity and life. This is evidenced on the final page of the *Kyoto Declaration:*

> We pledge ourselves to warn the nations who citizens we are
> that the effort to achieve and maintain military power is the

road to disaster. It creates a climate of terror and mistrust; it demands resources for the meetings of the needs of health, housing and welfare; it fosters the escalation of the arms race; it sharpens differences among nations into military and economic blocs; it regards peace as a truce or a balance of terror; it dismisses as utopian a truly universal concern for the welfare of all humankind.

To all this we say 'No!'[16]

The work advocated in this statement operates on three levels: nationally, regionally and internationally.

RfP is a transnational religious actor but has the added advantage of being specifically inter-religious in its membership and model of working. The organisation is thus truly 'global' in terms of the mixing and sharing of cultures, practices, ideas and values which certain aspects of globalisation, in particular communication via technology and travel, have helped to facilitate. Its practical and policy work shows that while its principles are rooted in the concept of a global human family underpinned by a fundamental unity, the organisation recognises that work undertaken has to be contextualised. In order to explore this we will look at RfP's work with women on community and peace-building. This involves multi-religious partnerships that support and mobilise the social and moral resources of people to work together on specific issues. This is certainly an area of RfP development work significantly enhanced by those aspects of globalisation that expedite inter-personal and inter-group communication.

Women, Community Development and Peace-building

In 2001, under the auspices of RfP, the Global Women of Faith Network (GWFN) was established. At the time of writing, this network consists of over a thousand local and national religious women's organisations and also regional networks in Africa, Asia, Europe, South America and the Caribbean and North America. All regional networks are inter-religious, led by representatives of religions within each region. These networks aim 'to provide a platform for cooperative action throughout the different levels of religious communities, from grassroots to the most senior level'.[17] Based on the recognition that many women of faith across the world are involved in activities of community development and peace-building, GWFN's role is to support such women in their work whether through small grants, micro-finance and economic enterprise services, training in leadership and advocacy, or educational services. This support is also intended to increase the visibility of these women as agents of building sustainable and peaceful localities and thus as role models within their communities and societies. The work of the African Women of Faith Regional Network (AWFRN) is explored to show the approaches and methods used.

The AWFRN'S plan of action for 2007–2012 gives special attention to conflict transformation, peace-building and sustainable development. It states that this plan is grounded in women's experiences not only in Africa but across the world and that

> It is woven around women's aspirations and desire for an African continent and global family that cherishes and enjoys equality of women and men, enjoyment of human rights for all; and a world safe and secure, free from poverty, violence and disease.[18]

It also makes clear that this work seeks to push forward the commitment made by African government leaders in their adoption in 2003 of the *Protocol to the Charter on Human and Peoples' Rights on Women's Rights in Africa* and in 2004 of the *Solemn Declaration on Gender Equality by African Heads of States.*

The priority is to facilitate the work of women in Africa, with support from women in other parts of the globe, 'to coordinate strategies and pool resources and capabilities for interfaith action to achieve results that would be difficult for any single member to accomplish alone on the issues of: network building; peace and security; conflict transformation; and gender, poverty and health'.[19] The methods and approaches of the AWFRN is illustrated in the case of Uganda, where it is working with women on issues of sustainable development in small towns and villages to provide and/or improve heath and care services for HIV/AIDS sufferers and their family members; to review the appropriateness of educational policies with regard to orphans and vulnerable children having access to primary education; and to support the development of local economic services through setting up village loan associations and micro-finance initiatives in villages. The work with women involves capacity-based training on such things as psychosocial support for vulnerable people; leadership and advocacy; understanding and reviewing government policy and law concerned with child protection, rights of the child in terms of education and employment of children; and economic and business skills to run small enterprises designed to benefit individuals and their communities. The work relating to the rights and protection of orphans and vulnerable children and access to primary education involves both practical and policy work. On the practical side, the AFNRW worked 2006–2011 with local women in three districts (Kamuli, Luwero and Tororo) to support access to formal education for 6,782 orphans and vulnerable children. Regarding advocacy for change in government policy, this involved working with religious leaders in Uganda on a review of educational policy and legislation to identify the barriers to orphans and vulnerable children accessing education. These advocacy initiatives are reported as having 'resulted in the enactment of bylaws and follow-up mechanisms for accountability and reporting, government banning of employment of children, and school visits by government officials and religious leaders to monitor implementation of education'. [20]

As the AWFRN shows, the GWFN and its member organisations have a transnational role which aims to build bridges and partnerships in all areas of its work 'between faith-based women's organisations, secular partners, international agencies and the United Nations'.[21] It is clear that the central aim is threefold: (i) for women to be supported and further enabled to work on the practical realities of the issues they face; (ii) to build networks and form strategic multi-stakeholder partnerships and alliances; (iii) to educate and raise awareness throughout their localities of ways to respond to issues in a way that can make changes and provide choices for women and men with regard to living with a sense of worth and dignity. And underpinning this is articulated the right for people to freely organise, discuss and take action on issues that government and other official bodies are seen not to be making sufficient progress in rectifying.

Conclusion

The work of the GWFN reflects the overall work of RfP, which emphasises the importance of civil society and the expression of collective action representing shared interests, concerns, purposes and values. RfP therefore operates in the intermediate space between the individual and government, providing the opportunity for communities to find ways to improve situations. However, RfP is not only helping to develop civil society within localities but is also a catalyst for this development across immediate and regional borders and from one side of the world to the other. In this case, as Haynes argues, globalisation is facilitating 'the growth of transnational network of religious actors which, feeding of each other's ideas and perhaps aiding each other with funds, form bodies whose main priority is the well-being and advance of their transnational religious community'.[22] While Haynes is making this argument in his research on religions working transnationally on issues within their own religious communities, his argument of globalisation facilitating such work also appertains to these inter-religious transnational actors.

RfP, from its world council to its regional, national and local organisations, is made up of people from different religions and different social, cultural and political contexts, and it is the sharing of experience, strategies and practice which has the ability to transplant expressions of civil society and help shape new models. In the process of this transplantation, a more globalised or transnational civil society is shaped, as the building of social capital, trust and shared values transcends borders and boundaries. According to Lipschutz, transnational civil society is 'the self-conscious constructions of knowledge and action, by decentred, local actors that cross the reified boundaries of space as though they were not there'.[23] The interconnectedness of peoples and their societies then becomes more explicit and the potential becomes greater for religions working in an inter-religious framework to influence national and international government policies. In this sense RfP is assisting in the creation of global civil society. If civil society within nation-states is an essential aspect of a functioning democracy, even more than is global civil society central to the global politics of peace.

Notes

1. Scott Thomas, *The Global Transformation of Religion and the Transformation of International Relations* (New York: Palgrave Macmillan, 2005).

2. Suzanne H. Rudolph and James Piscatori, (eds), *Transnational Religion and Fading States* (Boulder, CO: Westview Press, 1997); Jeffrey Haynes, 'Transnational Religious Actors and International Politics', *Third World Quarterly* 22:2 (2001), 143-158.

3. Fabio Petito and Parlos Hatzpoulous, *Religion in International Relations: The Return from Exile* (New York: Palgrave, 2003).

4. Jeffrey Haynes, *An Introduction to International Relations and Religion* (2nd edition, Harrow: Pearson Education Ltd, 2013), 3.

5. Timothy Samuel Shah and Daniel Philpot, 'The Fall and Rise of Religion in International Relations: History and Theory', *Religion and International Relations Theory* (New York: Columbia University Press, 2011), 24.

6. Chris Seiple, 'From Ideology to Identity: Building a Foundation for Communities of the Willing', *Religion, Identity and Global Governance: Ideas, Evidence and Practice* (Toronto: University of Toronto, 2011), 292.

7. Bryan S. Turner, *Religion and Social Theory* (CA: Sage, 1991), 148.

8. Elise Boulding, 'Two Cultures of Religion as Obstacles to Peace', *Zygon* 21:4 (December 1986), 508.

9. Johan Galtung, 'Religions, Hard and Soft', *Cross Currents* 47:4 (Winter 1997-98), 3.

10. R Scott Appleby, *The Ambivalence of the Sacred: Religion, Violence and Reconciliation* (New York: Rowman & Littlefield, 2000), 821.

11. Appleby, *The Ambivalence of the Sacred*, 30-32.

12. Anna Halafoff and Melissa Conley Tyler, 'Rethinking Religion: Transforming Cultures of Violence to Cultures of Peace', *Responding to Fundamentalism and Militancy – Education for Shared Values for Intercultural and Interfaith Understanding* (Paris: UNESCO, 2005), 365.

13. Religions for Peace, The Kyoto Declaration of the First World Assembly. Accessed at: http://religionsforpeace.org (March 25, 2014), 1.

14. Religions for Peace, The Kyoto Declaration of the First World Assembly, 1.

15. Religions for Peace, The Kyoto Declaration of the First World Assembly, 1.

16. Religions for Peace, The Kyoto Declaration of the First World Assembly, 3.

17. Religions for Peace, Religions for Peace: Mission. Accessed at: http:// religionsforpeace.org/vision-history/mission (May 4, 2014), 1.

18. African Women of Faith Network, National Women of Faith Networks, Accessed at: http://religionsforpeaceinternational.org/who-we-are/global-women-faith-network (May 6, 2014), 1.

19. African Women of Faith Network, National Women of Faith Networks, 2.

20. African Women of Faith Network, National Women of Faith Networks, 2.

21. Katherine Clark, Rori Picker Neiss, Angela Oliver, Elisa Levy and Valeri Getti, *A Guide for Building Women of Faith Networks* (New York: Religions for Peace Publications, 2009), 29.

22. Haynes, 'Transnational Religious Actors and International Politics', 144.

23. Ronnie D. Lipschutz, 'Reconstructing World Politics: The Emergence of Global Civil Society', *Millennium Journals of International Studies* 21:3 (1992), 390.

Part Four
Human Rights and Institutions

21

Faith-Based Organisations at the United Nations

JEFFREY HAYNES
LONDON METROPOLITAN UNIVERSITY, UK

What do faith-based organisations (FBOs) at the United Nations (UN) seek to achieve? This chapter[1] seeks to answer this question, focusing on the activities of selected FBOs at the UN, the most significant inter-governmental organisation (IGO) with a global public policy role. For the UN, a feature of recent years has been increasing regularity and institutionalisation of interactions with selected FBOs. This is partly because the UN now regularly engages with civil society organisations, both faith-based and secular, and partly because the UN is aware that the 'values' that FBOs bring to global governance are something it needs to factor into its own concerns. For their part, many religious believers from many religious traditions see such FBOs as significant actors in trying to influence public policy in relation to various public issues at the UN.

FBOs at the UN: From Marginalisation to Significance

> As a secular organization, the UN has no common religion. But, like all the major faiths, we too work on behalf of the disadvantaged and the vulnerable. ... I have long believed that when Governments and civil society work toward a common goal, transformational change is possible. Faiths and religions are a central part of that equation.[2]

In what follows, I examine selected FBOs'[3] attempts to influence public policy formation and execution at the UN. I make two main arguments. First, I contend that the UN has over time consolidated policy-making structures and processes, with strongly secular preferences. Led by publicly accountable officials, the UN makes decisions based on its long-term and institutional secular preferences, which traditionally exclude religious concerns—or at best regard them as marginal to the organisations' policies. Recently, however, publicly accountable officials at the UN have begun to engage with increasing regularity with selected FBOs in the context of a more general increase in relations with civil society organisations. The outcome has been that at the UN, selected FBOs have seen their significance increase, an arrangement conducive to improved ability to engage with public officials in the IGOs, with the goal to encourage them to make policy according to FBO preferences.[4] Second, FBOs are in competition with each other at the UN. This is manifested in two ways. First, it can imply an inter- or intra-religious competitiveness. In addition, competiveness can also relate to ideological issues, including schisms between 'conservative' and 'liberal' (or 'progressive') FBOs.[5] As a consequence, Berger notes, FBOs may compete with each other, pushing 'for change from both liberal and conservative platforms'.[6] In addition, in order to pursue their ideological goals, Petersen notes, many FBOs regularly engage in alliances with various secular actors—including, states and other sources of power and authority, such as secular non-governmental organisations.[7]

Increasingly, the UN accepts that FBOs may have something useful to contribute to various issues that have recently risen in importance, especially in the context of deepening globalisation and its impact upon people's lives, welfare and employment. Regularised or institutionalised involvement of FBOs in the activities of the UN is quite recent, although not *de novo*. Nevertheless, Hurd[8] recounts a recent conversation at the UN between Father Bryan Hehir, Secretary for Health Care and Social Services in the Archdiocese of Boston, and John Ruggie, the UN Secretary-General's Special Representative for Business and Human Rights, whose job it is to propose measures to strengthen the human rights performance of the business sector around the world.[9] According to Hurd, Hehir said to Ruggie: 'Where is religion at the UN?' Ruggie replied: 'There is none.' In the quotation above, the UN Secretary-General, Ban Ki-moon, claimed in 2009 that the UN is 'a secular organisation, the United Nations has no common religion'.

The comments of Ruggie and Ban seem inherently problematic, even contrary, in highlighting the secular orientation of the UN when, as we shall see below, the UN is a focal point for hundreds of transnational FBOs. Their statements do, however, suggest that traditionally the UN has had problematic relationships with 'religion'. As the quotations also indicate, the UN has a *raison d'être* traditionally involving pursuit of 'liberal' or 'progressive' 'secular' goals, including inter-state cooperation, democracy, peace and the rule of law, while religion was traditionally pejoratively characterised as both conservative and prone to conflict.[10]

How then to explain an additional thrust of the quotation from Ban: religion can be part of the solution, not necessarily an integral aspect of the problem? Ban points to common ground between the UN and 'major faiths', which 'work on behalf of the disadvantaged and the vulnerable', implying that 'religion' has something to contribute in this regard. Ban's comment also highlights public policy concerns at the UN that are today significantly informed by both moral and ethical issues, often with an identifiable religious component. More generally, today's changed international environment provides FBOs with a new or enhanced role in global public policy. This centres on 'values' and, more generally, encourages a shift from an exclusively secular approach to dealing with problems to one that is informed by ideas deriving from religious values that may be quite beneficial for inter-group and inter-community relations. As a result, selected FBOs—that is, those that publicly adhere to the fundamental values of the UN, including, human rights, democracy and the rule of law—are now increasingly seen as credible interlocutors in relation to various moral and ethical issues, which can validly inform global public policy via debates, discussions and 'fact-finding' initiatives.

Before briefly looking at current involvement of FBOs at the UN, it is useful to trace their involvement at the organisation over time. As is well known, the UN was founded just as World War II ended and the organisation's worldview was strongly moulded by the events of 1939–45. The UN was established with the primary goal of building international peace, security and cooperation. Today, the UN is the only near-universal IGO, with 192 member states.

In the context of its work, the UN has long engaged with selected non-state actors, including (secular) NGOs.[11] In recent years, as previously noted, the UN has considerably developed its dealings with selected FBOs, that is, those that share the organisation's core values. This also reflects, first, the fact that many FBOs active at the UN are transnational in orientation, with expanded activities in recent years. Focusing on national, regional and global contexts, many seek to influence public policy in relation to various issues, typically centring on an array of human rights concerns.[12] Second, it also suggests that the UN is keen to be seen to be interacting with FBOs, in the context of what is often claimed to be a widespread—or even universal—religious resurgence, a generalised search for improved 'values' to inform global public policy and a comprehensive desire to engage more closely and consistently with 'civil society' organisations, including, in some cases, those with a strong faith perspective.[13]

Third, today's post-secular international environment is characterised by the expansion of many FBO concerns from primarily theological issues to concerns traditionally understood as 'secular'. These include: human, including women's, rights, conflict resolution and problems of international development.[14] In relation to the latter, for example, many FBOs now express interest in how poor and undeveloped countries can develop both economically and in terms of their human capital, an issue whose focal point is currently the UN-derived Millennium Development Goals (2000–2015). Increasingly, the issue of international development and how to achieve it is regarded as not simply improving economic output and hoping that this will somehow 'trickle down' to the poor to improve their living standards; it has also become a burning moral concern. And, as Lynch notes, when FBOs ponder 'international development', they may well shift from a perusal of the moral dimensions of the issue to focus on 'neoliberal competition of the "market" [in] international development'.[15] From there it is an easy jump to think about how post-Cold War globalisation encourages an unjust and polarised world, with the rich appearing to benefit disproportionately compared to the poor. It is also often noted that increasing globalisation has coincided with what is judged to be a global religious revival, with religious ideas assuming increased significance and relevance in national and international ethical and moral debates, suggesting to some the existence of a post-secular international environment. In short, today 'religious' views and opinions expressed by FBOs often reflect and draw on and feed into 'secular' controversies, including not only international development but also 'climate change, global finance, disarmament, inequality, pan-epidemics and human rights'.[16] The result is that questions about the focus, values and content of global public policy are increasingly influenced 'by the moral resources that "religions" offer and agencies of global governance need an awareness of what religious actors are doing and sensitivity to religious difference'. [17]

Liberal and Conservative FBO Tensions

> Conservative religious groups have for years engaged in clashes over family policy. Much of their activism aims to preserve traditional families against what they decry as an *onslaught of feminism, abortion and gender politics* (emphasis added).[18]

> While health policy is usually framed as a part of the secular political domain, it touches upon combustible religious values and engages powerful alliances across religious divides. *Catholics and Mormons; Christians and Muslims; Russian Orthodox and American fundamentalists find common ground*

> *on traditional values and against SRHR issues at the UN* (emphasis added).[19]

Since its inception in 1945, the UN has had an institutionalised relationship with numerous NGOs, while in recent years hundreds of selected FBOs have also established access and in some cases achieved institutionalised status with the UN's central agencies, including the Economic and Social Council (ECOSOC). More generally, UN engagement with selected NGOs is rooted in Article 71 of the UN Charter, established in 1945. Article 71 states that the UN will 'consult' with NGOs in order to carry out its work, especially via ECOSOC. In addition, the UN Declaration of Human Rights (1948) recognises that religious belief is a fundamental aspect of human rights and human freedom[20]. Three decades after the promulgation of the UN Charter, the UN agreed to the establishment of a 'Committee of Religious NGOs' in 1972, followed in 2004 by the formation of the 'NGO Committee on Spirituality, Values, and Global Concerns'.[21] In addition, recent years have seen both increased numbers of FBOs and greater day-to-day FBO involvement at the UN, with regular contributions to UN committees in both New York and Geneva. In this context, many FBO representatives are very active, enjoying institutionalised involvement with many UN Committees and UN Commissions, including, for example, the UN Commission for Social Development.[22]

Today, there are around 320 FBOs at the UN registered by ECOSOC, with regularised access and involvement in the UN system, including the General Assembly and in relation to specialised agencies, including the United Nations Population Fund and World Bank. A few years ago, Petersen[23] identified 58 per cent of FBOs at the UN as Christian, while Carrette and Miall's recent survey identifies fully three-quarters of UN FBOs as *both* Christian and northern-based. Muslim FBOs at the UN are greatly in the minority, with only one-sixth of 'officially' registered FBOs at the UN. On the basis of these numbers, Christians (30.8 per cent of people in the world) are 'over-represented' at the UN: Christian FBOs are between 58–75 per cent of total ECOSOC-registered FBOs at the UN, while less than 31 per cent of the world's population are Christians. On the other hand, Muslims (23.3 per cent of global population) are significantly 'under-represented', with just 16 per cent of ECOSOC-registered FBOs. In addition, at the end of 2012 there were an estimated 13.76 million Jews in the world, less than 2 per cent of the global population, whereas Jewish FBOs accounted for 7 per cent of the total number of ECOSOC-registered FBOs at the UN; thus, Jews too are over-represented at the UN compared to their global numbers, while, not only Muslims, but also Hindus (14 per cent of global population/2 per cent of ECOSOC-registered FBOs) and Buddhists (7 per cent/4 per cent), are significantly under-represented.

In this section, I briefly examine a particular issue involving FBOs at the UN. I am selective in this regard both because of the large number of FBOs active at the UN and because of the wide range of topic and issues with which they are concerned (for an overview of these issues, see Haynes, 2013a).[24] Here, I focus on the issue of women's sexual and reproductive health rights (SRHR). As one of the most controversial of the issues regularly engaging the attention of FBOs at the UN, it pits 'conservative' FBOs against 'liberal' FBOs. Both kinds of FBO seek to enlist allies—both religious and secular—to try to advance their goals. The key point is that a shared 'conservative' outlook brings activists together and it does not seem important in this respect what their religious outlook is. For example, campaigns at the UN in pursuit of 'family values' brings together 'conservative' Christian actors from a variety of Christian faiths—Mormons, Catholics, Protestants and the Russian Orthodox Church—as well as traditionalist Muslims. This inter-faith conservative bloc constitutes an influential grouping at the UN, projecting a distinctly traditionalist social agenda (Bob, 2012). [25]Secular and religious 'liberals' regard the conservatives as motivated by 'pre-modern' ideas about gender issues, family politics and women's health, and believe that they work in pursuit of the denial of the advance of women's sexual and reproductive health rights. For the liberals, the conservatives work

> ceaselessly to contest, obstruct and delay the development of relevant UN agendas. Their influence does not reflect their number but is largely due to a striking ability to build alliances across religious boundaries as well as elicit the support of religious communities around the world.[26]

Why should it be that FBOs rely on non-religious arguments to make their case at the UN in relation to issues related to women's sexual and reproductive health rights? As a secular forum, debates at the UN necessarily 'take place in the context of a secular global public policy sphere'. This produces norms, values and expressions which strongly influence potential 'non-liberal' ideas by 'causing' them to 'align [their] frame to match the dominant [liberal] discourse'.[27] Thus, conservative FBOs seeking to oppose what they regard as liberal SRHR policies at the UN do not believe it appropriate or feasible if they want to make progress to express their arguments in terms of their religious values (based on community, personal responsibility and traditional patriarchal understandings of the family and women's place within it). Instead, they couch their concerns in religiously neutral concerns with an ambiguous notion—that is, 'family values'—enabling them to overcome what openly expressed conservative religious values would produce: 'limited access to discursive and institutional opportunities at the UN.'[28] Consequently, if anti-SRHR groups wish to be successful they find it necessary to 'concentrate on countering the pro-abortion'—that is, liberal—

groups' agendas and declarations through blocking or weakening the pro-choice language in UN documents. They also adjust the frame of their discussions by arguing for concepts like the 'natural family' and referring to God as the 'creator' in order to bypass theological differences and find non-Christian language.

Conservative groups' strategy in relation to SRHR has developed over two decades. The starting point for their campaign was two UN conferences in 1994 and 1995: Cairo (population growth) and Beijing (women and gender). At the 1995 Beijing conference, conservatives claimed that lesbians had launched a 'direct attack on the values, cultures, traditions and religious beliefs of the vast majority of the world's peoples'.[29] These conferences marked the beginning of a concerted anti-liberal campaign in relation to SRHR, initially led by the Pope, the Holy See (Vatican) and, more generally, the Catholic Church. As Chao notes, at this time 'the Catholic Church became a leading actor on the conservative wing'.[30] This propelled then-Pope John Paul II to overall leadership of the global conservative faith-based struggle. This is not to imply however that to be Catholic is *necessarily* to be conservative. Instead, we can note a polarisation between 'conservative' and 'liberal' Catholics, a competition played out at the UN. For example, Catholic NGOs with ECOSOC range from the pro-choice *Catholics for choice* to the pro-life *American Life League*.[31]

Conservative Catholic campaign leadership was added to by supportive involvement of mainly US-based Protestant evangelicals and conservative Muslims from various countries. Bob[32] refers to this alliance as the 'Baptist-burqa' link.[33] The augmentation of the conservative Catholic campaign from additional conservative religious sources highlights the entities' shared conservative ideological orientation and their dispersed geographical locations. Conservative Catholics from Italy were joined by traditionalist Muslims from Egypt and Pakistan (among others), while right-wing evangelical Protestants joined the campaign from their bases in the US. These people were united not by a shared religious worldview but by an ideological agreement of the necessity of weakening or, better, blocking pro-women's choice language in UN documents.

Conclusion

Several overall conclusions emerge from this brief examination of FBOs at the UN. First, the UN has a strongly 'liberal' secular agenda, whose concerns, exemplified by the Universal Declaration of Human Rights (1948), focuses on a range of justice and human rights concerns. As a result, the UN's liberal-secular focus compels all actors at the UN, including FBOs which wish to influence debates and discussions, to adopt 'appropriate' UN-sanctioned language in their engagements with UN bodies.

We have also seen that FBOs compete with each other primarily on ideological—not theological—grounds. This implies that, for example, socially conservative FBOs may well work not only with theologically conservative FBOs but also socially conservative secular state and non-state actors at the UN. On the other hand, 'liberal' FBOs are likely to work not only with other liberal FBOs but also with 'liberal' NGOs and governments, in pursuit of shared goals. In addition, FBOs wishing to maximise their influence at the UN typically seek to link up with allies—including, other FBOs, secular NGOs, and friendly governments—which share their ideological—not necessarily theological—norms, values and beliefs. Some FBOs active at the UN manage to achieve persistent influence, via regularised and/or institutionalised access to opinion formers and decision makers located in friendly governments and IGOs. Finally, some FBOs are less favoured, without consistent capacity to enjoy such access and associated potential of building influence with significant players at the UN.

Notes

1. This study derives from a much longer by me, entitled: 'Faith-based organisations at the United Nations', RSCAS 2013/70, Robert Schuman Centre for Advanced Studies/RELIGIOWEST, (Florence: European University Institute, September 2013). Available at: http://cadmus.eui.eu/handle/1814/28119;
2. Secretary-General SG/SM/12585 (200) Press Release, 'You Can – and Do – Inspire People to Change', Secretary-General says, Encouraging Summit of Religious, Secular Leaders on Climate Change to "Make Your Voices Heard"' Available at http://www.un.org/News/Press/docs/2009/sgsm12585.doc.htm Last accessed 10 June 2013.
3. At a minimum, a FBO must be connected with an organised faith community. According to Scott (2003), these connections occur when an FBO 'is based on a particular ideology and draws staff, volunteers, or leadership from a particular religious group.' See Jason D. Scott, *Exploring the Funding Relationships Between Community Foundations and Faith-Based Social Service Providers,*(New York: The Roundtable on Religion and Social Welfare Policy/The Rockefeller Institute of Government/State University of New York, 2003). Other characteristics that qualify an organisation as 'faith-based' include: religiously-orientated mission statements, support from a religious organisation, or being founded by a religious institution. See Haynes 2013.
4. Michael D. McGinnis (2010) 'Religion policy and the faith-based initiative: Navigating the shifting boundaries between church and state', 'Forum on Public Policy.' Available at http://forumonpublicpolicy.com/vol2010.no4/archive.vol2010.no4/mcginnis.pdf Last accessed 12 June 2013.
5. Clifford Bob, *The Global Right Wing and the Clash of World Politics* (Cambridge: Cambridge University Press, 2012)
6. Julia Berger, 'Religious Non-Governmental Organizations: An Exploratory Analysis', (Harvard University, September 2003).

7. Marie Juul Petersen (2010) 'International religious NGOs at the United Nations: A study of a group of religious organizations', *The Journal of Humanitarian Assistance*, November. Available at http://sites.tufts.edu/jha/archives/847 Last accessed 29 May, 2013.

8. Elizabeth Shakman Hurd (2011) 'International politics after secularism', *Review of International Studies*, Vol. 38, pp. 943-961. p1

9. Hehir is also Parker Gilbert Montgomery Professor of the Practice of Religion and Public Life at Harvard University, while Ruggie is Berthold Beitz Professor in Human Rights and International Affairs at Harvard's Kennedy School of Government and Affiliated Professor in International Legal Studies at Harvard Law School. Ruggie served as United Nations Assistant Secretary-General for Strategic Planning from 1997 to 2001 (http://www.hks.harvard.edu/m-rcbg/johnruggie/index.html).

10. Jeffrey Haynes, 'Faith-based organisations, development and the World Bank', *International Development Policy/Revue Internationale de Politique du Devéloppement*, No. 4 (Special issue on 'Religion and Development' 2013), pp. 49-64. Also published in French as 'Les organisations confessionelles, le développement et la Banque mondiale', available at http://poldev.revues.org/1376

11. Defined here as private, not-for-profit, non-governmental groups, with specific delimited concerns and interests.

12. Ronan McCrea 'Religious contributions to law- and policy-making in a secular political order: the approach of European institutions', in L. Leustean (ed.), *Representing Religion in the European Union. Does God Matter?*, (London: Routledge, 2013) pp. 217-235.

13. Böllman, F. 'How many roads lead to Brussels?: the political mobilisation of religious organisations within the European public sphere', in L. Leustean (ed.), *Representing Religion in the European Union. Does God Matter?*, (London: Routledge, 2013) pp. 201-216.

14. Lynch, C. 'Religious Humanitarianism in a Neoliberal Age', *The Religion Factor Blog*, September 12. 2013 Available at http://religionfactor.net/2012/09/12/religious-humanitarianism-in-a-neoliberal-age/ Last accessed 29 May, 2013.

15. Jeremy Carrette and Hugh Miall 'Big Society or Global Village? Religious NGOs, Civil Society and the UN'. Briefing Paper. 2012.

16. Ibid 3

17. Ibid

18. Clifford Bob, *The Global Right Wing and the Clash of World Politics* (Cambridge: Cambridge University Press 2012).

19. NORAD (Norwegian Agency for Development Cooperation) (2013) 'Lobbying for Faith and Family: A Study of Religious NGOs at the United Nations', Oslo: NORAD. 1.

20. The Universal Declaration of Human Rights 1948 Available online at http://www.un.org/en/documents/udhr/

21. The NGO Committee on Spirituality, Values and Global Concerns, United Nations, New York, Website: http://www.csvgc-ny.org/

22. Jeremy Carrette and Hugh Miall 'Big Society or Global Village? Religious NGOs, Civil Society and the UN'. Briefing Paper. 2012.

23. Marie Juul Petersen (2010) International religious NGOs at the United Nations: A study of a group of religious organizations', *The Journal of Humanitarian Assistance*, November. Available at http://sites.tufts.edu/jha/archives/847 Last accessed 29 May, 2013.

24. Jeffrey Haynes (2013a) 'Faith-based organisations at the United Nations', RSCAS

2013/70 , Robert Schuman Centre for Advanced Studies/RELIGIOWEST, Florence: European U Haynes, J. (2013a) 'Faith-based organisations at the United Nations', RSCAS 2013/70 , Robert Schuman Centre for Advanced Studies/RELIGIOWEST, Florence: European University Institute, September 2013. Available at: http://cadmus. eui.eu/handle/1814/28119niversity Institute, September 2013. Available at: http:// cadmus.eui.eu/handle/1814/28119;

25. Clifford Bob, *The Global Right Wing and the Clash of World Politics* (Cambridge: Cambridge University Press 2012).

26. NORAD (Norwegian Agency for Development Cooperation) 'Lobbying for Faith and Family: A Study of Religious NGOs at the United Nations', Oslo: NORAD, 2013).

27. Turan Kayaoğlu, (2011) 'Islam in the United Nations: The liberal limits of postsecularism', Paper presented at the Conference: *The Postsecular in International Politics*, University of Sussex, 27-28 October. 17.

28. Ibid.

29. Clifford Bob, (2010) 'Globalizing the Culture Wars: The United Nations Battle over Sexual Rights'. Paper prepared for the American Political Science Association annual meeting, September 2. Human Rights Watch (2005) World Report, New York: Human Rights Watch.

30. Chao, J.K.T. (1997) 'The evolution of Vatican diplomacy', *Tamkang Journal of International Affairs*, Vol.1, no. 2, pp. 35-63.

31. NORAD (Norwegian Agency for Development Cooperation) (2013) 'Lobbying for Faith and Family: A Study of Religious NGOs at the United Nations', Oslo: NORAD. 11

32. Clifford Bob, *The Global Right Wing and the Clash of World Politics* (Cambridge: Cambridge University Press, 2012). 6.

33. Seeing mutual benefit in working together via a shared concern with 'pro-family values', the 'Baptist-burqa' coalition has endured such setbacks as 9/11, whose impact otherwise was to divide the Christian and Muslim worlds from each other.

22

National Religions: How to be Both Under God and Under the European Union?

FRANÇOIS FORET

UNIVERSITÉ LIBRE DE BRUXELLES, BELGIUM

When looking at the geopolitics of faith in international affairs, Europe appears as a specific spot on the map for several reasons. First, it is an island swept by waves of secularisation (understood as the decline and mutation rather as the disappearance of religion) in a world where gods still hold strong positions. Second, it is a bastion of institutional separation between spiritual and temporal matters in contrast to other regions where the two domains are intimately intertwined. Third, Europe has experienced the most advanced process of regional integration. The rise of the European Union (EU) as a full political system and a level of governance salient in almost all policy fields may question the historical national arrangements between churches and states, and more largely between the sacred and the political. Though they incorporate their religious heritages in collective identity, memory and ethics, European nations, in short, may be less 'under God' than they used to be, but they are more and more 'under Brussels'. The question is then to know to what extent religions remain national and/or are reworked by European institutions, public action and power games. This chapter browses several levels of analysis (the distribution of competences to regulate religious affairs; religion in European politics in interactions with other political belongings; religion and the legitimisation of the EU) with references to more in-depth scholarship on each point to go further. The conclusion is that European integration interacts with the contemporary evolution of religion but does not command it. The EU is rather a structure of opportunity to foster societal trends, sometimes to resist them, and frequently to reformulate traditional discourses mixing religious and political repertoires in tune with present times. To a certain extent the European context reinforces the national character of religions, first by comparisons with the different practices of other member states, which highlights national specificities, and second by its use as a symbolic resource to express the national Self within the supranational and transnational arenas.

Extent and Limits of the Europeanisation of Religion

Two opposite discourses collide regarding the place and influence of religion in European politics and how it is altered in return by European public action. On the one hand, 'Vatican Europe' would be dominated by Christian forces, mostly Catholic. European institutions would be besieged by religious lobbies, turning the EU into a 'Christian club'. On the other hand, the EU would be a soulless and materialistic political system giving no place to values and crushing traditional morality.

Both discourses have this in common, that they are frequently developed without much empirical grounding. European studies have been reluctant to deal with identity and cultural—not to say religious—matters since their beginning, as European integration was supposed to be all about interests and economic issues. Nevertheless, the extension of EU competencies and its painful 'democratic deficit' have brought more and more legitimacy issues onto the agenda. The failed attempt to give a constitution to the EU fuelled the debate on the nature and limits of the European political community and what constitutes 'Europeanness'. Religion has been part and parcel of this search for roots and substance.

Interactions between the EU and religions should be conceived in the broader setting of political and spiritual changes at work at all territorial and functional levels, from the local to the global. According to the treaties, the EU has no specific competences regarding the regulation of faith. It 'respects and does not prejudice the status under national law' of churches, religious associations or communities (as well as philosophical and non-confessional organisations) in the member states. The implementation of the principle of subsidiarity means that every country remains its own master at home. The European Court of Human Rights has confirmed this national rule on religious matters by recognising the 'margin of appreciation' left to states within the implementation of the core principles at the heart of European integration (through both the EU and the Council of Europe).

In European arenas, religious actors and references must submit to pluralism and relativism. To be heard, it is necessary to use the repertoire of fundamental rights and to enter into coalitions with other religious and non-religious actors. In other words, religion has to play by the rules of European multi-level governance and participatory democracy. It is not very different from what happens in member states, simply with more diversity and more pluralism. The more influential denominations at the national level are also the big players at the supranational level.

Religious and National Belongings: In Congruence, Tension or Conflict?

To know how religions and national loyalties may be articulated in EU politics and policies, the best thing is to directly interrogate European political actors. This was the purpose of the survey, Religion at the European Parliament (RelEP), the first attempt of its kind to document what members of the European Parliament (MEPs) believe, and what they do with these beliefs. The purpose was to offer objective data on the role of religion in decision-making, coalition-framing and political socialisation in supranational parliamentary politics. One hundred and sixty-seven MEPs of multiple party and national belongings were interviewed between 2010 and 2013.

The first acknowledgement of MEPs is that the way to relate to faith business differs according to the country of origin. There is near unanimity (82.8 per cent) among interviewees in stressing that religion does indeed have a particular importance, depending on nationality. Religion is often said to create notable differences between representatives of new and old member states, the former being more religious than the latter. Differences between old member states are also perceptible according to the place of religious issues on their own domestic agendas. German Catholics are more focused on economic issues related to religion to protect the fiscal status of German churches; Italian Catholics are particularly involved in debates on how religion is handled in the public sphere in the wake of the controversy over religious signs in classrooms that raged after the ruling of the European Court of Human Rights on the Lautsi case.[1]

This path-dependence relating to the national way of addressing religion is not really altered by the experience of politicians in European institutions. Almost half of MEPs (45.4 per cent) consider that the place of religion at the EP is different from their experience of it in national politics. This perception is especially acute for the representatives who come from very secularised and/or secular (separating strictly religion and politics) backgrounds and who are shocked by the views of religious lobbyists and the occasional priest in a cassock in the corridors of the assembly. However, 31.6 per cent of interviewees—especially those coming from systems with a tradition of denominational diversity and cooperation between religious and political powers—are less surprised by what they see in Brussels and Strasbourg. But surprised or not, there is a consensus (84.7 per cent) among MEPs that their experience at the EP has not changed their views on the links between religion and politics. Their national conceptual frameworks to deal with spiritual matters still prevail.[2]

What may evolve a little is the form of expressing their religious or philosophical beliefs, in order to comply with a multicultural environment where idiosyncratic references rooted in a national memory are less likely to make sense. Religious discourses have to be qualified in intensity to respect all sensibilities, including secular ones, and have also to manage tensions between national memories. A religious figure considered as a virtuous proselyte by Catholics may be seen as an oppressor by Protestant or Orthodox Christians. This resentment of minority denominations against the influence of majority faiths is a constant in European integration.[3]

What is true for MEPs is also true for religious interest groups. Politicians and lobbies have to enter into multi-national and multi-faith coalitions and therefore comply with the rule of moderation coming with the Brussels' territory. But MEPs still have privileged connections with national and even local religious communities. Some MEPs adopt strong postures to defend radical religious views at the cost of marginalisation by mainstream political forces at the EP and exclusion from the cooperative mechanisms of the assembly based on compromise. But the purpose of these outsiders is less to act as European legislators than to display their loyalty to their domestic constituencies.

The example of religion at the EP shows how such a normative resource may collide with the usual European policy-making based on rationalisation and bargaining. By definition, a discourse referring to an absolute truth and claiming an authority rooted in the sacred will not be a natural player in a game where virtually everything has to be negotiable. But the EU is also a polity in the making, and religion has been constitutive in the building of all political systems in the history of humanity. It has been to various extents a matrix of national identities for member states and it is now mobilised to legitimate an EU in search of a founding narrative. So the challenge may be to find a place for Europe between the 'nations under God' and God himself, without mentioning other competing geopolitical 'roofs' such as Christianity or the West.

The Religious Heritage of Europe as a Possible Unifying Background

Religion may serve in different ways to justify the project of European integration. It may be used as material in the production of a discourse on

European identity; to highlight a similarity of values between European societies; as religious networks and actors to pass the European message. But in these three functions (as content, normative cleavage and go-between), religion may as well be instrumentalised to oppose European integration. The everlasting debate on the Christian heritage of Europe is the best illustration of the dilemma of religion torn between national and supranational belongings.

A controversy has raged since the 1990s on the appropriateness of referring to God and/or to the legacy of Christianity in the preamble of a European constitution and later in various attempts to institutionalise a European memory through museums or other achievements. Religion is then a resource to reinvent a European tradition which existed prior to the nation-state and thus to give primacy to European unity. It also aims at connecting individual beliefs and affiliations with an abstract and alien supranational project.

The motivations for activating a European memory with Christian connotations are of various types. They can be understood at the level of the EU as a political system; in the articulation of the national and the European; and in the to and fro of everyday politics. At a systemic level, the main objective is to endow the EU with a founding myth which is distinct from national histories and which predates them, thus justifying an autonomous European political system. There may also be an attempt to define the historical criteria for belonging to a European cultural community. Societies and populations can be placed in a hierarchy on the basis of these criteria: as longstanding or new member states which have undergone or avoided subjection to communist, atheistic materialism; their historical roles as central heartlands or advanced bastions of Christianity; their level of religiosity/ secularisation and/or their dominant religious denomination. They may also be excluded. In articulating the national and the European, religion can serve as an adjustment or resistance variable when adapting national identity to the context of European integration. France, with its secular tradition, opposes any mention of the Christian heritage in European treaties in the name of Enlightenment principles, which are the foundation of its Republican identity.

In contrast, during the Lautsi affair, Italy defended the cultural meaning of crucifixes displayed in classrooms as symbols of national identity. Finally, at the level of the Brussels political game, the churches' demand for recognition of the primacy of Christian values over time aims at more than an acknowledgement of a historical fact. If one subscribes to the idea that the Rights of Man derive from Christianity, the next stage is to recognise a preponderant place for church guardians of the Christian tradition in deliberations over the public good, while also granting special influence over public policy choices to collective preferences informed by Christian values. Finally, religion can also be used to criticise European integration in part or in its entirety. Invoking the Christian foundations of European civilisation confers an authority with which to challenge the excessive materialism or cultural liberalism (on abortion, homosexuality, etc.) of Community policies as a betrayal of common European origins. This may provide an argument for justifying or disqualifying the candidature of an accession state or for solidarity with a population elsewhere in the world that is being persecuted for its convictions.[4]

The failure to achieve any mention of the Christian heritage in the European constitution and the treaty of Lisbon has not marked the end of the symbolic struggle around the reference to religion. Several episodes show that the question is still a live one and is likely to remain so. The main arena for this debate is the European Parliament, which reflects the cultural diversity of European societies and which allows for initiatives by political minorities and NGOs. In 2005, Polish MEPs campaigned to name new Parliament buildings after Karol Wojtyla, Pope John Paul II, to honour his contribution to the fall of communism. Secular forces rejected the promotion of a moral leader hostile to abortion and homosexuality; Protestant and Orthodox Christians resented the grip of Catholics on European symbols, a permanent concern for minority Christian denominations threatened by a Christian Europe turned Catholic.[5] The most recent memory endeavours, such as the 'House of European History' supported by the European Parliament, meet the same temptations and problems in mobilising religion as identity material.[6]

Conclusion

Religion may appear elusive in a European Union which is itself frequently criticised for its abstraction. The addition of two transparent entities is not the most likely solution to create substance. Even when one shifts from domestic to external politics, the diagnosis is not very different. The 'Christian' nature of Europe may be more frequently emphasised by non-Christian parts of the world than by European themselves. But during a traumatic event such as the crisis created by the publication in the Danish newspaper *Jyllands Posten* of cartoons depicting the prophet Muhammad in 2005–2008, the US and not the EU was the main scapegoat of furious Muslim crowds.[7]

However, religion in Europe is nowadays defined less by a specific content and more as an ethical source irrigating normative choices and as a symbolic marker of identity. As such, beliefs and observance may be less important than the way of relating to religion. Religious heritages can be understood as public goods submitted to inventories according to the needs and tastes of collective and individual actors. Countries are distinguished from others according to the way they exercise this selective relation. Within countries, social groups are differentiated according to their approach to religiously loaded questions rather than in strictly religious terms. So religion keeps marking European societies with its footprint. The divine canopy has many holes, exists in multiple colours and fabrics to accommodate all preferences and overlaps with several other man-made skies, but European nations are still under gods, and the stars of the European flag add simply a little more complexity and variety to the firmament.

Notes

1. François Foret, *Religion and Politics in the European Union: The Secular Canopy* (Cambridge, Cambridge University Press, 2015), 237-240.
2. François Foret, 'Religion at the European Parliament: an overview', *Religion, State & Society 2014, Vol 42, Nos 2-3, 130-147.*
3. Brent F. Nelsen and James L. Guth, *Religion and the Struggle for European Union: Confessional Culture and the Limits of Integration* (Washington, Georgetown University Press, 2014).
4. For an extensive development, see François Foret and Virginie Riva, 'Religion between nation and Europe. The French and Belgian 'no' to the Christian heritage of Europe', *West European Politics,* (July 2010 33/4) 791–809.
5. Andrew Rettman, 'Polish MEPs push for Papal plaque in Brussels', *Euobserver,* (14/4/2005)
6. Committee of Experts, 'Conceptual Basis for a House of European History' report, (October 2008), pp. 11–13.
7. Jytte Klausen, *The Cartoons that Shook the World*, New Haven, (Yale UP, 2009).

23

Religion in the European Union: The Forgotten Factor

BRENT F. NELSEN & JAMES L. GUTH
FURMAN UNIVERSITY, USA

What does religion have to do with European integration? The major approaches to explaining the remarkable success of the European project usually stress economic interests, strategic motivations or institutional forces in the growth of continental unity since 1945. And although constructivist scholars have insisted on a role for ideas and beliefs in the integration process, few have said very much about religion.

Indeed, any argument that European religion matters politically today or in the recent past is immediately suspect. The majestic churches that still dominate urban skylines sit all but empty. Few attend services and even fewer accept traditional dogmas. Scholars may debate whether religion is dying or just transmuted into less recognisable—and less politically salient—'spiritualties'. But no one can deny that organised religion has lost influence everywhere, even in Catholic strongholds such as Poland and Ireland.

A decline in traditional religion does not mean, however, that religion no longer matters in Europe. Religion shapes cultures in deep and lasting ways. Lives are marked by ceremonies, celebrations and ancient holidays—all filled with emotional power, if drained of theological content. Individual worldviews, once shaped by understandings of God, creation, humanity and revelation, persist in more secular guises from generation to generation. Religion as a social marker still shapes identities by drawing dark lines around 'us' and 'them'—even among those with few ties to organised faith. Thus, religion shapes a 'confessional culture' that lingers long after the vibrancy of faith has diminished.

We see religion's impact in both the history and contemporary politics of European integration. Many journalists have observed that the most enthusiastic proponents of 'ever closer union' have been the predominantly Catholic countries of continental Europe, while the Protestants of Britain and the Nordic regions have been much more guarded about shifting power towards Brussels. Although most scholars explain away this religious divergence, it reflects fundamental differences in confessional culture: Catholics and their church never really accepted the legitimacy of the Westphalian nation-state system, remembering the 'unities' of Rome, Charlemagne's empire, and medieval Christendom. For Protestants of the North (and many in the Netherlands and Germany), the nation-state was the protector of national liberties, and their specific religion became a central aspect of national identity. Of course, these ideals often succumbed to the reality of power politics, but they maintained a tenacious hold on religious leaders, politicians and mass publics alike.

The post-war European project was born out of the concerns of Catholic statesmen, preoccupied with creating permanent peace among the warring tribes of Europe. Robert Schuman of France, Konrad Adenauer of Germany, Alcide de Gaspari of Italy and a host of lesser Christian Democratic politicians saw the creation of supranational European institutions as a way not only to restore prosperity to a devastated continent but also to create a new Europe 'deeply rooted', as Schuman put it, 'in Christian basic values'. Many of these leaders had become acquainted in the 1920s and 1930s and quickly established intricate Catholic and Christian Democratic political networks after the war, opening channels of communication on nascent proposals for new institutions to safeguard peace and prosperity and, more importantly, reconcile former enemies in a process of Christian forgiveness. Although there were some 'secular' figures, such as Paul-Henri Spaak, who played significant roles in creating these new European institutions, their ideological rationale had deep Catholic roots.

The institutional developments leading up to the Treaties of Rome in 1957 similarly drew their most enthusiastic support from Christian Democratic parties. To an extraordinary extent not often remembered today, governments in the six nations experimenting with new forms of unity were dominated by Christian Democrats, either governing alone or in coalition. Indeed, European integration went from being an interesting, if unrealistic idea in interwar Catholic circles to a central tenet of Christian Democracy and a vital element of movement identity, so much so that Etienne Borne claimed for the French MRP in 1954: 'We are the party of Europe.'[1] The centrality of European federalism to the post-war Christian Democratic vision is easily understood in light of the movement's core tenets: a personalist view of society, concern for the well-being of the family, and reconciliation among former enemies, all of which required new political forms.

The European project also had strong backing from the Vatican and national Catholic hierarchies. Although the Vatican usually refrained from attempting to direct the activity of Christian Democratic parties, the Catholic church still had a powerful moral influence over a continent undergoing a post-war religious resurgence. Pius XII said that he was 'instinctively drawn' to the 'practical realization of European unity'[2] and had repeatedly backed the goal of a united Europe from the earliest days of the war.[3] Catholic organisations, even as far away as the United States, followed his lead and called for 'some kind of voluntary European union'.[4] After the war, in the afterglow of the Hague Conference (1948), Pius again called for a European union.[5] In a Catholic Europe not yet experiencing the onset of secularisation, the church's vocal support for unity provided strong encouragement to Catholic statesmen and publics alike.

In fact, one of the most critical contributions of religion to integration was the support provided by grassroots Catholics. Whether taking cues from Christian Democratic politicians or church leaders, Catholic laity were by far the most enthusiastic backers of European unity—and the more devout the Catholic, the stronger the pro-unity views. Although Europe-wide polling on such questions begins with the prototype Eurobarometer in 1970, there is little doubt that the strong support that Catholics exhibited for the project in the 1970s and 1980s was at least as vigorous during the early years of integration. While such public attitudes did not necessarily dictate the action of politicians, it did provide a broad permissive consensus in which national leaders might create supranational institutions. Both the strength and duration of Catholic public support for European unity have been quite impressive.[6]

The 'Protestant' reaction to the developing integration process was quite different. Protestant states have consistently resisted handing sovereignty to federal institutions. Britain has always been an 'awkward' European partner, but so have others. Denmark, Sweden and Finland also joined the EU late and have resisted deeper integration. Iceland, Norway and Switzerland are natural EU members but each refuses to join. Historically, these countries have taken a route independent of the continental powers; each was deeply shaped by the Protestant side of the Reformation. Britain and the Nordics feared the very notion of an *ever closer union* and stayed out of the Community as long as their economic and strategic interests allowed. Once inside the house, they proved to be perpetually grumpy family members. After discovering the cost of membership, Britain demanded money back; Denmark's voters nixed the Maastricht Treaty, then reversed course after securing opt-outs from all the significant parts; among Protestant countries only Finland has joined the Eurozone; and other members with large Protestant populations, including Germany and the Netherlands (currently led by Protestants), have vetoed or watered down every attempt to solve the recent Eurozone crisis by giving federal institutions more control over national economies.

And just as support from the Catholic church, Christian Democratic politicians and grassroots Catholics provided the support base for the integration project, 'Euroscepticism' in its earliest forms dominated their Protestant counterparts. The national churches in Protestant countries, whether Lutheran or Anglican, exhibited very little enthusiasm for integration in the years after World War II. Indeed, most remained tied closely to their national regimes and were quite suspicious of what they perceived to be a 'Catholic project'. Although these sentiments began to soften somewhat after Vatican II, it was hard to find much organised Protestant enthusiasm for the European project, even after several Protestant nations finally joined. Even today, their institutional lobbying presence in Brussels pales beside that of the Catholic church. The stances of more sectarian Protestant churches in Britain, the Nordic countries and the Netherlands never wavered at all: they remained adamantly opposed to yielding sovereignty to supranational institutions, still fearing encroachment on religious liberty and in some cases, exhibiting ancient anti-Catholic prejudices.

These attitudes have characterised Protestant politicians and publics as well. Although the systematic study of religion's influence among European elites is rare, we have some evidence. Some of the most intriguing is biographical: we can look at the fascinating contrast in attitudes towards integration exhibited by the Methodist grocer's daughter who became the Eurosceptic prime minister of Great Britain—Margaret Thatcher—and the devout French Catholic politician and bureaucrat—Jacques Delors—who was the architect of the European Union's programmatic growth and territorial expansion in the 1980s and 1990s.[7] Even today, it is instructive to observe that the national leaders resisting deeper economic and political integration are Protestants from Britain, Sweden, the Netherlands, Denmark and even Germany.

More systematic analysis also confirms religion's influence among elites. Foret's work on the European Parliament finds relatively few differences between Catholics and Protestants but notes that Catholics feel much more comfortable in EU institutions and less likely to identify religion as a source of conflict. A survey of national parliamentary elites also found minimal differences by religious identity of members, but showed that the religious composition of their societies influenced attitudes towards integration. Contrary to the authors' expectations (but consistent with ours), elites in Catholic countries (regardless of their own affiliation) showed the strongest support for integration, with those in Orthodox countries next, followed by those in 'mixed' nations, with elites in Protestant nations bringing up the rear. In a multivariate analysis including many potential influences (economic wealth, regional location and historic experiences), Protestant country elites were still significantly less likely to support further integration; indeed, the coefficient for 'majority Protestant' obtained a higher level of statistical significance than any other variable.[8]

The impact of confessional culture may sometimes be subtle, but that culture continues to shape the functioning of national institutions. A good test case is presented by the EU practice of allowing opt-outs during treaty negotiations and a more recent policy of 'enhanced cooperation'.[9] Enhanced cooperation allows any group of EU states to pursue deeper integration (usually in a specific policy area) beyond that acceptable to other members. Combined with the many opt-outs allowed by treaty, this has created a multi-speed Europe with members participating in a varying number of integration formations. Thus, the number of formations in which a country participates is a reasonable measure of enthusiasm for integration. And, as we would expect, the more Protestant a country, the less often it joins efforts to integrate more deeply. Even controlling for national wealth and the timing of accession to the EU, Protestant countries are much more reluctant to engage in *voluntary* integration.

Work by other scholars suggests additional ways in which confessional culture influences national elite behaviour. Ivy Hamerly found that Protestant confessional culture encourages stronger national oversight of decisions taken in Brussels. If Protestant parties are members of coalition governments when parliaments create European oversight committees, those committees are much more likely to scrutinise Brussels closely than are oversight bodies established by governments that include Catholic or mixed confessional Christian Democratic parties. In other words, the presence of sceptical Protestants produces more scrutiny by parliamentary committees protecting the national interest.[10]

Not surprisingly, the attitudes of Protestant politicians (and of others representing Protestant constituencies) mirror those of Protestant publics. From the very beginning of the Eurobarometer surveys, Protestant citizens have been much less supportive of the European Union (and its predecessors), less likely to prefer more policymaking in Brussels, and less inclined to evaluate EU institutions favourably, even under rigorous controls for other factors more often identified as determinants of such support (nationality, party identification, ideology, political engagement, European identity, economic situation, gender, class and education).[11] Qualitative evidence strongly suggests that church-attending sectarian Protestants are far less supportive of integration than their mainline co-religionists. Eurobarometer affiliation measures are not usually precise enough to identify the small numbers of sectarian Protestants, but where they are, we find them to be fiercely anti-integration.

One final piece of evidence deals with the critical question of 'European' identity. For many advocates of an 'ever closer union', a crucial requisite is the development of a European 'demos', a large group of citizens who think of themselves as 'Europeans' and identify with European institutions and symbols. Religion matters here as well: in Eurobarometer data there is a strong positive correlation between the proportion of a nation's citizens who think of themselves only as 'nationals' and the proportion who are Protestants ($r=.419$), a relationship that persists in multivariate analysis.

Unfortunately, the Eurobarometer does not permit a direct test of the individual-level relationship between confessional culture and European identity: no survey includes both types of question. But Eurobarometer 65.2 (Spring 2006) permits an indirect approach. That survey asked about an important symbol of European unity, the EU flag: (1) did the respondent identify with the flag, and (2) should the flag be flown next to the national flag on all public buildings? The results are instructive: Catholics are significantly more likely than Protestants to identify with the flag, and even more likely to want it flown. Catholics vary little by their national religious location, but Protestants do. Protestants in the religious majority are quite negative towards the EU flag, while those living in majority Catholic countries are more favourable. Thus, Catholics act as though the EU flag is *their* flag: they identify with it and want to see it flying, but Protestants identify with the flag only when a religious minority. When in the majority, they want nothing to do with it.[12]

Thus, despite the purported secularisation of European politics, we find that confessional culture still affects the movement towards European unity. Of course, that influence has shifted with changes in the religious environment and in the European Union itself. The declining number of observant Catholics and Protestants has weakened religious influences on both pro- and anti-EU sides. The growing ecumenism of Catholic and Protestant churches may explain a recent tendency for the dwindling number of observant Protestants to exhibit more positive attitudes towards integration. The EU's expansion into Eastern Europe has diversified its religious composition, bringing in more Eastern Orthodox and Muslims, often more sceptical about the project. And in recent years the social liberalism of Brussels institutions and the failure to acknowledge religious influences in the proposed unsuccessful Constitution have antagonised traditionalist Catholics from Ireland to Poland, threatening the old pro-EU Catholic consensus.

Why do such changes matter? Put most broadly, the erosion of one of the historic sources of support makes the integration project much more subject to the vagaries of public reactions to the current economic performance of the EU and its member nations—shifting ground indeed compared to the old bedrock of Catholic supranationalism. Will the EU develop a new ideational basis for a renewed 'permissive consensus' on integration? Perhaps, but the task will prove daunting in a deeply divided Europe.

Notes

1. Quoted by Wolfram Kaiser, *Christian Democracy and the Origins of European Union* (Cambridge: Cambridge University Press, 2007), 189.
2. Pius XII, 'European Union: An Address of Pope Pius XII to the Congress of Europe, June 14, 1957', *The Pope Speaks* 4 (Summer 1957): 201.
3. Jacqueline Stuyt, 'Pius XII and European Unity', *Catholic International Outlook* 18, no. 212 (1962): 9.
4. Catholic Association for International Peace, 'America's Peace Aims', Paulist Press, 1941 as cited in *Plans for European Union in Great Britain and in Exile, 1939-1945*, vol. 2 of *Documents on the History of European Integration*, ed. Walter Lipgens (Berlin: Walter de Gruyter, 1986), 726-727.
5. Pius XII, 'Address to the European Union of Federalists', quoted in Edward A. Conway, 'Catholics and World Federation', *America* 80 (4 December 1948): 233.
6. Brent F. Nelsen, James L. Guth and Brian Highsmith, 'Does Religion Still Matter? Religion and Public Attitudes toward Integration in Europe', *Politics and Religion* 4, no. 1 (2011): 1-26; Brent F. Nelsen and James L. Guth, 'Religion and Youth Support for the European Union', *Journal of Common Market Studies* 41, no. 1 (2003): 89-112; Brent F. Nelsen, James L. Guth and Cleveland R. Fraser, 'Does Religion Matter? Christianity and Public Support for the European Union', *European Union Politics* 2, no. 2 (2001): 191-217; Brent F. Nelsen and James L. Guth, 'Exploring the Gender Gap: Women, Men, and Public Attitudes toward European Integration', *European Union Politics* 1, no. 3 (2000): 267-91.
7. For an extended comparison of Thatcher and Delors, see Brent F. Nelsen and James L. Guth, *Religion and the Struggle for European Union: Confessional Culture and the Limits of Integration* (Georgetown University Press, in press), Chapter 8.
8. François Foret, *Religion and Politics in the European Union: The Secular Canopy* (Cambridge University Press, forthcoming); Wolfgang C. Müller, Marcelo Jenny, and Alejandro Ecker, "The Elites-Masses Gap in European Integration," in *The Europe of Elites: A Study into the Europeanness of Europe's Political and Economic Elites*, ed. Heinrich Best, György Lengyel, and Luca Verzichelli (Oxford: Oxford University Press, 2012), 167-191. In the multivariate analysis of national legislators, those in Orthodox and mixed religion states are not significantly less supportive of unification than those in Catholic countries, although the mixed category comes fairly close to statistical significance (Mladen Lazić, Miguel Jerez-Mir, Vladimir Vuletić, and Rafae Vázquez-Garcia, 'Patterns of Regional Diversity in Political Elites' Attitudes', in *Europe of Elites*, 147-166, esp. 160-163). Finland, the Netherlands and Sweden were not included in the sample.
9. For a discussion of the policy of flexibility, see Alexander C-G. Stubb, *Negotiating*

Flexibility in the European Union: Amsterdam, Nice, and Beyond (Houndmills: Palgrave, 2002).

10. See Ivy Hamerly, 'Christian Democratic Parties and the Domestic Parliamentary Response to European Integration', *Journal of Church & State* 54, no. 2 (2012): 214-239.

11. See the sources cited in note 6 above.

12. For more details, see Nelsen and Guth, *Religion and the Struggle for European Union*, Chapter 10.

24

Religious Movements and Religion's Contribution to Global Civil Society

PAUL S. ROWE
TRINITY WESTERN UNIVERSITY, CANADA

Introduction

Global civil society has become an important theme of investigation for scholars of global politics. The expansion of globalisation over the past decades through technological innovation has intensified the influence and impact of global civil society. Religious organisations are natural participants in this global civil society, articulating their members' concerns to global society. The expansion of their independence since the end of the Cold War has been identified as an explanation for their seeming resurgence as political actors in the past twenty years, according to many scholars. Though the expanded influence of religious actors is viewed by many as a dangerous development, this reflects the way in which anti-social activities of radical religious movements dominate media headlines. When we assess the day-to-day activities of global religious movements, we find a wide array of actors involved in development and peace advocacy and contributing to the cultural vitality of global society. The normative power of religious movements to shape global civil society is an important theme of inquiry for political science into the future.

Religion among Global Communities of Purpose

The increasing pace of social change and its spread to the four corners of the globe have led many political scientists to emphasise globalisation's role in bringing change to international politics. One of the key features of globalisation is the way in which people relate to one another in new ways mediated by new information technologies as well as improved transportation links. Step by step since the early 1990s, computerisation, satellite communication, the fax machine, the internet and social media have created new platforms on which politics plays out in transnational space. They challenge the extent to which politics is local and they create new communities of purpose, including religious movements. Everyone in the world seeks purpose and meaning in some way, and religious communities provide fundamental answers to the larger proportion of the world's population. These communities in turn relate to states and to one another. As globalisation links humans in more complex ways, these communities of purpose create a new political geography. Issues of religion and politics are no longer confined to one locality: they become items of global concern.

One does not need to look very far to see ways in which religious matters have become global issues. During the late 1990s, the Jubilee 2000 campaign, largely spearheaded by Christian groups in the United Kingdom, inspired a larger campaign for Third World debt relief that eventually featured prominently at the 2005 G8 Summit in Gleneagles, Scotland. In late January and early February 2006, violent protests gripped several Middle Eastern capitals after concerned Muslims learned about the publication of a series of cartoons depicting the Prophet Muhammad in the Danish newspaper *Jyllands-Posten*. In July 2010, Terry Jones, the pastor of a small radical Christian congregation in Florida, also created a global furore with his plan to burn the Quran in a symbolic trial against the Muslim scriptures. The plight of the Rohingya Muslim minority population, subject to violence and discrimination at the hands of Buddhists in Myanmar, grabbed headlines in 2013. In June 2014, the eyes of millions of Christians worldwide turned to northern Iraq, where a militant Islamist group known until then as the Islamic State of Iraq and al-Sham (ISIS) conquered northern Iraqi cities and forced indigenous Christians to flee, convert, or pay an extortionate tax. Tens of thousands worldwide converted their Facebook profile picture to the Arabic letter nun, in solidarity with the displaced who had been forced to self-identify as *nasiri*, the Quranic term used for Christians.

The principal communities of purpose in each of these cases—whether advocacy groups calling for action in defence of human rights, vigilante groups that target other sects, movements of Facebook users, or religious groups seeking recognition of their concerns—are not states but sub-state groups, what political scientists refer to as organisations of 'civil society'. Prominent sociologist of religion Peter Berger describes civil society as the independent sphere in which people organise themselves into groups: it exists somewhere between the individual and the state, in what we might call 'the tertiary sector'. Politically, it is 'the ensemble of institutions that stand *in between* the private sphere (which notably includes the family), on the one hand, and the macro-institutions of the state and the economy, on the other hand'.[1] Because of the ascriptive quality of many religions—which can seem much like ethnic groups rather than self-directed organisations—some question the extent to which religion is part of civil society. But religious groups in the twenty-first century tend to be malleable and fluid, contributing a great deal to the construction of a larger society in which personal choices shape the politics of the day.

Almost all religions become social phenomena through self-constituted sects, groups, or organisations. Buddhism has been spread over the centuries by the *sangha*, the community of monks. Christians organise themselves into churches, parishes, monastic and lay orders, missions and parachurch movements. Muslims participate in their faith through involvement in neighbourhood mosques, *da'wa* organisations and Sufi orders. Jewish synagogues and community centres provide social networking sites that support the work of charitable groups pursuing *tikkun olam* (healing for the world). This panoply of organisations is increasingly innovative and responsive to the needs of individual believers, seeking to capture a larger 'market share' by presenting new and exciting ways to participate, even in the case of ancient traditions.[2]

Religion as a Feature of Global Civil Society

In the early 2000s, Mary Kaldor argued that the emergence of sub-state actors at the transnational level signalled the creation of 'a new form of politics', a global civil society.[3] The nature of this society was constantly evolving based on the interactions of people within the system. Civil actors became the motors of change, propelling the system forward and determining what issues would be significant to the politics of the future. Over the next few years, many political changes underscored the importance of these civil society actors. Small groups brought attention to the AIDS crisis and the ongoing civil war in many parts of Africa. Others lobbied governments to take action to ban the use of landmines and cluster munitions. Dictatorial regimes in Tunisia, Egypt, Libya and Yemen were overthrown during the so-called 'Arab Spring' of 2011, set in motion by young activists who often spread their message via Facebook and Twitter, a message later broadcast via al Jazeera to a world audience.

The role of religion in this global civil society is controversial. Numerous books have been published over the past several years that point to the growth of religion as an influence on political behaviour, contrary to the predictions made for many decades by secularisation theorists. In one groundbreaking work, Mark Juergensmeyer argued that with the collapse of ideological polarisation during the Cold War, religious nationalism emerged to fill the gaps left by disillusionment with capitalism and communism.[4] Later, Scott Thomas identified multiple ways that religion had made a resurgence twenty-first century politics.[5] More recently, Monica Duffy Toft, Daniel Philpott and Timothy Shah have addressed the way in which the independence of religious groups from state authority enhances their importance to global politics. They challenge the presumption that the state's embrace of religion is the most important way in which religion becomes 'political'. Instead, they present the case that religion's resurgence as a political force has more to do with the relative independence and autonomy of religious actors, which thrive in liberal democratic societies and oppose authoritarianism that limits their free exercise.[6] Religious actors survived the repression of modernist and communist regimes and thrived as liberty expanded in the wake of the Cold War.

Not all viewed the expansion of religion in the post-Cold War world as a positive development. The late Christopher Hitchens, in particular, articulated the view that the role of religious movements was consistently negative.[7] Indeed, one might assume that the increasing salience of religion to global civil society is inherently divisive. Religious organisations often present exclusive claims to truth. They often stand behind conflict, motivating the faithful to lay aside compromise and to give up even their own temporal existence in the pursuit of a more ultimate and transcendent goal. Wouldn't a religious resurgence be dangerous to global society, causing it to be more 'uncivil'?

It is true that religious resurgence has often emphasised the fundamental differences between religious groups. Often this occurs because of pent-up stresses related to the repression of religion in the past. For example, the modernist White Revolution instituted in Iran in the 1960s and 1970s led revolutionaries to enshrine Islamic guidance in the Iranian constitution of 1979. The Soviet-led government of Afghanistan had introduced numerous secular reforms in the 1980s that became the primary targets of the Mujahedeen (and later the Taliban) regimes of the 1990s. In other cases, religious movements make instrumental use of religious difference as a means of political gain. India's Bharatiya Janata Party (BJP) was able to make use of a controversy over the existence of a mosque at the legendary birthplace of the Hindu god Ram to slingshot to the top of the polls in the early 1990s. Their supporters went on to target Muslims and their shrines in numerous incidents over the following decade.

Religion's 'Normative Promise'

However, in spite of the common complaint that religious organisations pursue divisive political action, it would be inaccurate to assume that the reactionary and instrumental use of religion in global conflict is its most common form. For every headline that describes the violent and reactionary actions of religious radicals, there are thousands of unreported activities that arise out of the pro-social intentions of religious devotees. The quotidian efforts of religious people do not capture wide public interest but they contribute to the normal functioning of the majority of the world's societies.

The work of many scholars shows that the expanded role of religion in civil society helps to reflect natural divisions in society even as it supports liberalism and pluralism in those states that embrace religion's independence. Toft, Philpott, and Shah observe that religion has had an extremely important role in the expansion of democratisation over the past few decades: 48 out of 78 cases of 'substantial democratisation' were influenced by religious actors, such that '[i]n most of the cases where democracy was on the march between 1972 and 2009, freedom had a friend in religion'.[8] Robert Putnam and David E. Campbell analyse the role that religion plays in modern American society. They argue that even though religion divides Americans, the very connections that religion encourages among human beings also help to mitigate conflict among the American people.[9] Religious pluralism in civil society therefore both reflects our divisions over fundamental values and provides the key for living with those divisions. John Coleman, a Jesuit scholar, presents the case that religious organisations provide numerous social goods that encourage the formation of social capital: they promote volunteerism and a communitarian vision of the world, they address major social problems including poverty, crime and health issues, they provide opportunities to build civic skills and promote economic justice.[10] What is more, such religious organisations by definition work within a global orbit, as most religious traditions are confined not to one country but to several.

Reflecting on the work of the World Council of Churches in bringing down the apartheid regime in South Africa in the 1980s, Kevin Warr speaks of the 'normative promise' of religious organisations in contributing to a more peaceful, harmonious, and democratic world. Religious organisations are uniquely powerful actors in civil society because

> they have the ability to change peoples' worldviews, based on a shared version of ultimate truth. Therefore, these organs of global civil society are able to foster social capital transnationally in a manner that travels well.[11]

What this means is that religious organisations transcend national boundaries and speak deeply to the hearts of people, in a way that facilitates cultural and social change.

Today, global civil society is enriched by the participation of religious actors. Some of the world's largest relief and development organisations are rooted in religion, including World Vision, Caritas, the Aga Khan Foundation and Compassion International. Many other religious organisations present the case for action on behalf of relief and development at the state level. Religious actors promote human rights and freedom of conscience: for example, the International Justice Mission, a global advocacy group based in Washington, DC, promotes the freedom of modern-day slaves in the sex trafficking industry.[12] Peace movements seek alternative means of promoting political change: Soka Gakkai, a peace movement rooted in Nichiren Buddhist philosophy, works to promote peaceful enjoyment of culture and personal enrichment through the actions of committed 'engaged Buddhists' throughout the globe. The experience of Baha'i, many of whom have been persecuted for their faith, contributes to the active participation of Baha'i throughout the world in promoting peaceful development and human rights. Concerned about the way in which religious polarisation has affected Western politics since the terror attacks of 11 September 2001, numerous small initiatives have arisen in the past decade throughout North America and Europe that bring together people of many faiths to promote interfaith understanding.[13] One of these, the Interfaith Youth Core, was the brainchild of interfaith activist Eboo Patel and works on college campuses throughout the United States and abroad.[14]

Religious actors have long been important influences on the domestic politics of states. Today, they are increasingly working on the global stage: interacting with one another, with intergovernmental organisations, development organisations, and foreign actors. As the politics of religion globalises, it puts more and more believers in dialogue with one another and it transforms and expands our knowledge of one another. Religious organisations articulate the basic normative assumptions of most of the world's population and thereby contribute to authentic interaction between people. Religious traditions have withstood the test of time and respond to the inner lives of believers and as such it is unlikely that religious organisations will disappear any time soon. Although religious organisations may do so in a way that is uncompromising or even violent, in most cases they simply take action on issues and problems that are common to all the world's peoples. A world of many religions, all of which make a contribution to global civil society, can be both daunting and thrilling. Global politics into the future will increasingly reflect the pluralism of a world where spiritual voices provide deeper meaning to our common experience as human beings. As such, political science will need to grapple with the influence of religious organisations as important actors in global civil society.

Notes

1. Peter Berger, 'Religion and Global Civil Society', in Mark Juergensmeyer, *Religion in Global Civil Society* (Oxford: Oxford University Press, 2005), 12.
2. Ted G. Jelen and Clyde Wilcox, eds., *Religion and Politics in Comparative Perspective: the one, the few, and the many* (Cambridge: Cambridge University Press, 2002), 11-15.
3. Mary Kaldor, *Global Civil Society: an answer to war* (Cambridge: Polity Press, 2003), 2.
4. Mark Juergensmeyer, *The New Cold War? Religious nationalism confronts the secular state* (Berkeley: University of California Press, 2003).
5. Scott Thomas, *The Global Resurgence of Religion and the Transformation of International Relations: the struggle for the soul of the twenty-first century* (London: Palgrave Macmillan, 2005).
6. Monica Duffy Toft, Daniel Philpott, and Timothy Shah, *God's Century: resurgent religion and global politics* (New York: W.W. Norton, 2011), 81-85.
7. Christopher Hitchens, *God is not Great: how religion poisons everything* (New York: Twelve, 2007).
8. Toft, Philpott, and Shah, *God's Century*, 93-95, 98.
9. Robert Putnam and David E. Campbell, *American Grace: how religion divides and unites us* (New York: Simon and Schuster, 2010), 4-5.
10. John Coleman, 'Religious Social Capital: its nature, social location, and limits', in Corwin E. Smidt, *Religion as Social Capital: producing the common good* (Waco: Baylor University Press, 2003), 34-36.
11. Kevin Warr, 'The Normative Promise of Religious Organizations in Global Civil Society', *Journal of Church and State* 41, no.3 (1999), 522-523.
12. The story of IJM and a larger network of religious human rights organizations is told in Allen D. Hertzke, *Freeing God's Children: the unlikely alliance for global human rights* (Lanham, MD: Rowman & Littlefield, 2004).
13. Jean Idleman Smith, *Muslims, Christians, and the Challenge of Interfaith Dialogue* (Oxford: Oxford University Press, 2007).
14. Eboo Patel, *Acts of Faith* (Boston: Beacon Press, 2007).

25

Whose God? A Human Rights Approach

J. PAUL MARTIN
COLUMBIA UNIVERSITY, USA

Introduction[1]

This chapter argues (a) that secularism, understood as the range of theories and practices calling for the separation of state and religion, has become too amorphous and culture-bound a concept to guide religion-related policies in contemporary domestic and international affairs; (b) that secularism needs to be replaced by the more widely accepted and tested standards and institutions of the modern international human rights regime that define substantial legal obligations and practices developed and accepted through treaties by the world's states; and (c) that the human rights framework calls not merely for state neutrality but also for state engagement with religion and thus for national and international institutions able on a systemic basis both to protect the rights associated with freedom of religion and to minimise inter-religious discrimination and conflict.

The Limits of Secularism

When Bismarck set about building a unified Germany in the middle of the nineteenth century, he found he had to work with numerous small political entities in which rulers and citizens generally espoused common religions, typically Lutheranism, Calvinism or Catholicism. This fragmentation reflected the solutions adopted in the 1648 treaties of Westphalia that had ended the Thirty Years War. Through these treaties, the principle *cujus regio, eius religio* was established, that is, that citizens should share the religion of their ruler, although the treaties also provided some protection for minority religions. Two hundred years later Bismarck sought to unify these diverse, still religion-conscious, entities into a single German state without arousing religious animosities. With the exception of the Catholics, he achieved his goal through pragmatic devices and motivations, short conflicts and individualised negotiations with the different parties. In each he pointed out the political and economic benefits of the union as well as the ideals associated with German nationalism and culture. His biggest challenge was incorporating Catholic Bavaria, for which he developed more aggressive policies under the rubric of *Kulturkampf or culture fight.*[2] The core of his strategy was to insist that all schools be without a religious presence and that the state control clergy education and ecclesiastical appointments.[3] In fact, state control of clergy appointments was not achieved as Bismarck soon found it necessary to seek as an ally in the legislature the large Catholic Centrum party. Nevertheless as German chancellor from 1871 to 1890, the separation of religion and the state was a consistent component of his strategy to unite Germany. His answer to the God question was simple: 'No one's God in the public sphere!'

Theories and practices of secularism have had a long history in the West as a political paradigm to define separation of religion and state.[4] Within Christianity its roots can be traced back to Jesus' words: 'Render to Caesar the things that are Caesar's and to God those that are God's'.[5] A form of separation of civil and religious powers was formalised politically in the fourth century of the Common Era under the Roman Emperor Constantine.[6] However, separation and pure secularism have never been fully implemented. With the exception of a few states committed to atheism such as North Korea and for periods, other communist states, virtually all other political systems retain signs of their respective religious heritages.[7] The continuing signs of these heritages include physical artefacts, national calendars and official holidays as well as the forms of national observance enforced by the civil authority that have roots in religion. This blurring of the lines between civil and religious elements is now being undermined by the growing presence in the West of Islamic communities. Islamic patterns of religious observance challenge traditional Western customs in ways that expose the former's bias in favour of the West's Christian heritage. One example which has received much media attention is the way in which France, which has long valued its form of secularism as part of its shared national identity, has engaged in debates about the legality of Muslim women wearing one or other form of the veil. In question is to what degree France's national identity and public culture retain Christian characteristics and, thus, whether a new consensus is called for. These challenges highlight the degree to which an erstwhile assumed common identity and practices might not give equal status to those of new or other minority citizens. Either way, such conflicts undermine the presumption that official secularism in the West assures, and even can ensure, a neutral state and equal treatment for all religions.

Bismarck's experience is important because it was a classic application of the concept of secularism as a necessary means to build unity among communities with strong but different religious affiliations. His approach provides a useful contrast for those now seeking to address religious diversity in our increasingly religiously plural societies. On the one hand, Europe has seen the increasing secularisation of its societies in the sense that religious observance among Europeans has diminished substantially during the course of the last hundred years.[8] On the other hand, many of these same communities have been challenged by the increasing presence within them of Muslim immigrants turned citizens whose faith and its religious observances are critical to their social identity. In the process, traditional conceptions of the secular state have been called into question both by the degree to which Islamic communities are not part of the dominant *modus vivendi* and by the need for states to put in place institutional arrangements that enable them to deal directly with tensions between religious communities.[9]

While Bismarck dealt easily with states that had allegiance to one or other of the Protestant traditions and met greater resistance from Catholic Bavaria, they were all Christian communities, sharing many common roots, beliefs and practices. While Christianity and Islam are both monotheistic religions and share many beliefs and traditions, fifteen centuries of political, cultural, military and economic interaction have sculptured many wounds and mental constructs. Today the communities are no longer so segregated geographically and politically. The explosions in communications and worldwide migration have created new patterns of interaction between them. This is both a global and a local phenomenon. In Nigeria, for example, the multiple patterns of past interaction between the largely Islamic north and the largely Christian south have been disturbed by an increasing awareness of differences, especially in access to wealth, between the two regions and by the aggravation of these tensions by the militant Islamists, notably Boko Haram, who have adopted violence as the way to achieve their religious and political goals. In question is the ability of existing Nigerian public and private institutions to minimise the violence and assure peaceful relations between the two, roughly equal in size, religious communities in a nation of around 170 million people. This and similar problems point to the urgent need for states to develop the national policies and the institutions needed to assure peaceful and non-discriminatory relations among its citizens of different faiths. Traditional forms of secularism, such as that implemented by Bismarck, which rely on separation of religion and the state do not provide an adequate theoretical basis for the state actions and institutions needed to assure peaceful relations among religious communities as diverse as Christianity and Islam.

This brief overview of new social conditions, combined with the findings of many recent academic studies,[10] shows that secularism, understood as the range of theories and practices calling for the separation of state and religion, has become too amorphous and culture-bound a concept to guide religion-related policies in contemporary domestic and international affairs. Its answer to the God question was: 'No one's God—but states have and continue to tolerate some of the relics.'

Recent Changes

Today, the various conflicts that arise between Islamic communities and the West draw on many more elements than religious beliefs. One fundamental principle of Islam is the unity of civil politics and religion, enabling Muslim civil leaders to link specific political goals with religious and moral imperatives. Muslim fundamentalists, for example, frame their mission as a jihad, a fight to bring the rest of the world into the Muslim Ummah or community under the guidance of Sharia, namely the complex of Muslim beliefs and practices based on the Quran and the Hadith or sayings of the Prophet. Within this perspective the West is not necessarily defined as Christian. Rather it is defined as evil, anti-Islamic and exploitative. This political and cultural dichotomy is reinforced by the Islamic tradition that eschews any division between the religious and political in public affairs. Both in principle and practice, political (religious or civil) authorities incorporate their (Shia, Sunni, etc.) interpretation of Sharia into public life. This perspective does not exclude human rights but it redefines human rights by placing their interpretation exclusively within the parameters of Sharia. This is well illustrated in the 1990 Cairo Declaration on Human Rights in Islam developed by the Conference of Islamic States. This and other statements seeking to incorporate human rights into Islamic thought and practice preclude a secularist approach to civil life by insisting on the primacy of the 'civilizing role of the Islamic Ummah which God made the best nation and has given mankind a universal and well-balanced civilization ... .'[11] Similarly, throughout the Declaration's 25 articles there is the frequent repetition of principle that 'all the rights and freedoms are subject to Islamic Sharia'. Thus, the good news is that this document accepts the notion of human rights. However, Islam's answer to the God question is: 'Allah's law is supreme in the public sphere.'

In the face of such a strong position, the question facing the rest of the international community is to what degree is there space for a new shared or common future enterprise defining human rights.[12] The problems arising between religions and the state in the public sphere are both vertical—that is, between the state and religion—and horizontal—that is, relations between religions within the state. Bismarck and most other Western political systems found solutions to both dimensions through the privatisation of religion and religious differences. in the West, common educational and health systems, for example, have been successfully developed on this basis without infringing individual religious liberties. As indicated above, the model is now being challenged in at least two ways by the growing Islamic presence in the West. Moreover, Islam's model for multi-religious communities—that is, relations between different religious communities living within the same spaces—is one based on the primacy of Sharia and the Muslim community's laws and practices, which define a reduced status for *dhimmis*, people of the book, namely Jews and Christians, and an even more reduced status for those professing other beliefs and religions.[13] In comparison, the Western tradition has accepted secularism as an adequate principle to assure peace among different communities. The secularist and separation paradigms, however, have not historically provided the institutional forms and tools necessary to address tensions among religions.

In the modern world, states like Nigeria with serious tensions between religious communities are obliged to engage the parties and devise institutional provisions that assure peaceful inter-religious relations over time. In other words, they need solutions that are systemic and acceptable to both communities. Within the international human rights tradition they must be committed to non-discrimination on all grounds. Moreover, this is an urgent agenda as a number of regional conflicts have strong religious characteristics, such as those between the north and south of Nigeria and in different parts of the Middle East. In other words, religious affiliation has become a strong component of threats to international and regional security. In such situations where one of the two largest religious communities in the world defines itself and all its public domestic and international politics as God-given, the answer to the God question is truly problematical.[14]

Human Rights Standards and Institutions

The modern international human rights movement offers an alternative to secularism because it establishes specific standards and institutions that have been crafted and refined by the world's community of states, including most Islamic states, at both a global level under the auspices of the UN and through regional level treaties and inter-governmental organisations. In addition to Article 18[15] of the Universal Declaration of Human Rights (UDHR), religious freedom is supported by other articles in the same document and in subsequent covenants. Among the most notable are those prescribing non-discrimination (Article 2), inequality before the law (Article 7) and arbitrary arrest and exile (Article 9), and those promoting privacy (Article 12), freedom of movement (Article 13), the right to marry and found a family (Article 16), and freedom of expression and opinion (Article 19). These rights and freedoms have been incorporated into treaties that have in turn been ratified by many of the world's states[16] and incorporated into their national constitutions and legal systems. The Convention on the Rights of the Child, for example, which has been signed and ratified by all but three of the world's states, specifically protects the right of parents to determine the religious education of their children.[17] Another example, Article 27 of the International Covenant on Civil and Political Rights states that persons belonging to minorities 'shall not be denied the right, in community with other members of their group, to enjoy their own culture, to profess and practice their own religion, or to use their own language'.[18] As a result of subsequent practice and problems, various UN entities, notably the Human Rights Committee, have helped to build and apply a body of international case law governing religious practice.

At first sight these international standards and institutions appear to have followed a secularist approach to religion in public affairs. There is, for example, no international treaty on religious freedom, only a UN Declaration or general statement of values without any legal force, although the related individual articles noted above have acquired legal obligation through subsequent treaties. The 1976 UN Covenant on Civil and Political Rights, for example, protects religious belief as one of a select few non-derogable rights that those that must be protected even in states of emergency. Together with gender, ethnicity and other such criteria, in treaties and legal documents religious affiliation and practice are identified as illegitimate and thus proscribed grounds for discrimination.[19] Moreover, the practices and interpretations associated with religion by the different states are increasingly being scrutinised by international bodies committed to international standards of non-discrimination.[20] In question is not so much religious freedom as whether a given state favours one religion over another. The human rights perspective calls for the state to be neutral but also to take positive action to assure non-discrimination and freedom of religion to all its citizens, rather than simply separate itself from religion. In fact, unlike in theories of secularism, state neutrality may often call for positive state actions such as providing the equitable support to all educational and health institutions run by religious agencies within its jurisdiction. The human rights perspective calls for equal treatment, but also for states to take all actions necessary to ensure non-discrimination and freedom of religion for all its citizens, rather than simply to separate itself from religion as implied in the secularist tradition. This approach assumes that religious institutions are legitimate social entities that deserve treatment equal to that enjoyed by other social entities, whether God enters the picture or not. The human rights perspective does not address the question 'Whose God?' but asks whether citizens' and communities of citizens' religious and belief rights are protected.

Within the human rights framework the answer to the God question is first of all to provide criteria by which to identify all forms of discrimination and any social consequences for those who wish to believe and practice their beliefs, whether a God is involved or not. Second, the human rights regime is shown to promote changes in a given society's culture by providing an alternative set of norms requiring actions that ensure equality among religions. Success is not guaranteed. It depends on both the internal logic and persuasiveness of the principles and institutions and the ways in which it encourages people suffering from discrimination to organise themselves and redress the balance. Whereas in the initial years of the human rights movement, especially in the 1960s and 1970s, the emphasis was on experts developing the principles and practices and outsiders coming to the aid of victims, since then the emphasis has been on empowering the victims to become agents of their betterment. In the specific case of religion and its various social forms and problems, human rights principles and practice offer criteria and institutions to identify and define all forms of discrimination such as persecution, coerced conversion or hate speech. The current regime also offers still limited avenues to remedies as they depend heavily on relevant institutional powers and encounter popular resistance to social and culture change. One of the most important of these remedies is popular human rights education through both schools and other informal educational mechanisms. This is important because unless people know their rights they cannot claim them and mobilise to get them.

Human rights principles may not answer the God question, but they do provide rules of engagement that focus more on the rights and freedoms of citizens. In doing so, the treaties and principles define obligations on the state to protect those rights and freedoms of all citizens—Christians, Muslims and others. They place the God question and its responses within a protection framework but refrain from judgement with respect to the object or content of those beliefs. Human rights protect the right to hold those beliefs but not the beliefs themselves, provided they do not impinge on the rights of others. It also protects the subsequent actions of believers provided the beliefs and actions do not infringe those of others or cause other forms of social disorder. In this sense it spells out the obligations of states to ensure religious tolerance among its citizens. Thus the role of the state is not only to avoid it or its agents infringing the religious beliefs and related actions of its citizens but also to ensure that those rights are known by all and not impinged upon by any social forces within its jurisdiction.

Engaging Religions

In international human rights law, the state has special obligations to protect minority religions.[21] There are two especially difficult problems in the context of religion, namely proselytism and the hate speech to persecution spectrum. These concern relations between religion and other members of the society rather than actions by the state.

While each of the three main monotheistic religions believe in a single, all-powerful God who is active in human history, many in each tradition are reluctant to discourse on whether it is the same (i.e. shared) God. The single 'common' monotheistic God is portrayed in culture-bound images, defined by each community's interpretation of its history and its interpretation of the ongoing mission that God has assigned to them. Thus, any answer to the question 'Whose God?' is culture-specific. For Muslims, Christians and Jews, their respective images of God are of one who actively guides the lives of their community. In both the Islamic and Christian traditions in particular there is a God-ordered proselytising mandate to win converts to one's faith.[22] Most traditions of Islam also strictly forbid leaving the faith but welcome those leaving other faiths. These practices and any related sanctions are typically enforced by the civil government in Islamic states. They have become increasingly problematical in regions where Muslims and Christians are mixing more and thus making intermarriage and changing one's faith more likely. Conditions in the resulting newly mixed communities vary from those created by Pakistani immigrants in England and Algerians in France to the situation of migrant workers in the construction and domestic servant industries in the Middle East. If the building of mosques is resisted in England and France, the construction of churches is completely forbidden in Saudi Arabia. While not so tangible as the physical relocations, modern communications, by increasing the flow of information across communities, have also enabled an undetermined amount of religious proselytization and propaganda. These new conditions place a real strain on prior policies and practices with regard to peaceful co-existence.

The other challenge faced by the human rights regime is that of hate speech. This is especially challenging for human rights on account of its historical commitment in the West to free speech.   However, even with the rules and some enforcement mechanisms, the human rights regime is not a stand-alone system. It needs enabling institutions and practices in both the international and domestic fora. Thus, from the point of view of the question 'Whose God?', the human rights regime offers rules for fair and just action and interaction but it does not determine the outcome. In order to protect such rights as freedom of expression, assembly, belief and movement where the need is greatest, international and domestic regimes need supportive national and international institutions.

Whose God?

If we agree that neither secularism nor human rights theory and practice answer the question 'Whose God?' while at the same time religions remain powerful if very different political forces, it is incumbent on each jurisdiction to develop the institutions and personnel necessary to assure peaceful relations among the different religious communities. However, while I have argued that religious communities ought to possess the same rights as other organisations within civil society, at the same time states must recognise the degree to which religious communities are composed of members espousing comprehensive worldviews and social loyalties to which all else, including their own life and death, are subordinated. Moreover, these loyalties often extend to worldwide systems whose events or decisions can also demand responses on the part of individual members. This characteristic separates religious and some other ideology-based communities from most other members of civil society whose loyalties are less comprehensive or demanding.

These dimensions have to be understood by the state and at the same time the state needs institutions and qualified personnel with the capacity to assure peaceful relations among potentially hostile communities, such as between Muslims and Christians in Nigeria. Such institutions might (a) monitor all forms of discrimination and social animosity on religious grounds, (b) identify emerging problems and tensions as well as design early-warning systems, (c) maintain a database covering both domestic relations and information about remedies that have worked elsewhere, (d) prepare and monitor curricula[23] which address religious issues, and (e) develop specialised public officials able to work closely with religious groups. The forms and size of such institutions will depend on a state's history, culture and current problems. This leads to the final conclusion, namely that the human rights framework calls not merely for state neutrality but also for state engagement with religion and thus for national and international institutions able both to protect the rights associated with freedom of religion and to minimise inter-religious discrimination and conflict.

Notes

1. This chapter builds on earlier articles by the author, notably 'Re-Thinking Secularism: A Paradigm based on Non-Discrimination', in Jaime Contreras and Rosa Maria Martinez de Codes, Eds., *Trends of Secularism in a Pluralistic World,* (Madrid, Iberoamericana/Vervuet, 2013), 145-162; and 'Religions in a Globalizing World', in William A Barbieri Jr., Ed. *At the Limits of the Secular, Reflections on Faith and Public Life* (Grand Rapids Eerdmans 2014), 331-360. In the first he argued that there are no continuing reasons to exclude religion from public spaces and in the second that

international human rights offers a needed alternative normative framework to move beyond outdated uses of concepts of secularism and the separation of religion and the state. This chapter seeks to define the civil/shared norms and institutions needed to assure both religious freedom and peaceful inter-religious relations in modern pluralistic societies.

2. Jonathan Steinberg, *Bismarck, a Life*, (Oxford, Oxford University Press 2013), 320.

3. The last provision illustrates how secularism's vaunted 'separation' is rarely perfect. Seeking state control of clergy appointments is hardly separation of state and religion.

4. Charles Taylor, *A Secular Age* (Cambridge, Belknap, Harvard, 2007) .

5. Gospel of Mark 12, 17.

6. Pierre Lanares, Constantine, *Worldwide Human Rights and Religious Liberty*, Vol. I, (International Association for the Defence of Religious Liberty, Bern Switzerland, 2013), 134-139.

7. Alfred Stepan, *Arguing Comparative Politics*, Oxford, Oxford University Press, 2001) Chapter 13, 'The World's Religious Systems and Democracy'.

8. This analysis is disputed by scholars such as in Peter Berger, Ed., *The Desecularization of the World* (Grand Rapids Eerdmans, 1999).

9. Stepan, ibid.

10. In addition the works of Charles Taylor, Alfred Stepan and William Barbieri listed above: Jose Casanova, *Public Religions in the Modern World* (Chicago, University of Chicago Press, 1994), *Secularisms*, Janet R. Jakobsen and Ann Pellegrini Eds. (Durham and London, Duke University Press 2008); *Varieties of Secularism in a Secular Age*, Michael Warner, Jonathon VanAntwerpen and Craig Calhoun, eds (Cambridge, Harvard University Press, 2010).

11. Organization of the Islamic Conference, 1990, Preamble to the Cairo Declaration.

12. See Michael Freeman, 'The Problem of Secularism in Human Rights Theory', *Human Rights Quarterly*, 26 (2004), 375-400; J. Paul Martin, 'The Three Monotheistic World Religions and International Human Rights', *Journal of Social Issues*, 61, 4 (2005), 827-845.

13. A more detailed discussion can be found in Adnan Aslan, *Religious Pluralism in Christian and Islamic Philosophy, The Thought of John Hick and Seyyed Hossein Nasr*, (Richmond Curzon 1998).

14. A survey of the Muslim/Christian landscape in Africa can be found in *Tolerance and Tension: Islam and Christianity in Sub-Saharan Africa*, (Philadelphia, Pew Forum on Religion and Public Life, April 2010).

15. Article 18, 1, reads: 'Everyone shall have the right to freedom of thought, conscience and religion. This right shall include the freedom to adopt a religion or belief of his choice, and freedom, either individually or in community with others, and in public or private, to manifest his religion or belief in worship, observance, practice and teaching.'

16. The right to change one's religion, found in the UHDR Article 18, was omitted in the subsequent Covenant of Civil and Political Rights.

17. Article 28, UN 1989 Convention on the Rights of the Child. It also includes other articles affirming freedoms and rights shared with all human beings.

18. A similar article protecting minority rights is to be found in the Convention on the Rights of the Child, Article 30.

19. 'Religions in a Globalizing World', Chapter XIII in William Barbieri.

20. Notably in Europe. See Peter G. Danchin and Elizabeth Cole Eds., *Protecting the Rights of Religious Minorities in Eastern Europe* (New York, Columbia University Press,

2002).

21. See 'Introduction', Danchin and Cole.

22. Tad Stahnke, 'Proselytism and Freedom to Change Religion in International Human Rights Law', *Brigham Young University Law Review,* 1 (1999). 251-350.

23. See, for example, *Toledo Guiding Principles on Teaching about Religions and Beliefs in Public Schools* (OSCE, Office of Democratic Institutions and Human Rights, Madrid, 2007).

26

Global Christian Networks for Human Dignity

ALLEN D. HERTZKE
UNIVERSITY OF OKLAHOMA, USA

Introduction[1]

Christianity carries in its DNA the radical notion of universal human dignity, rooted in the theological view that all are made in the image and likeness of God (*Imago Dei*). To be sure, Christians and Christian-influenced societies fall short of this ideal, sometimes egregiously so. But the idea of the surpassing worth of all persons loved by God can serve as a powerful challenge for Christians to address affronts to human dignity.

Today, we see notable global campaigns against slavery, violence, exploitation, poverty and disease—all heavily infused by Christian actors and institutions. The reason is this: the momentous globalisation of Christianity marries the idea of dignity with the growing capacities of transnational networks focused on global poverty, AIDS, human trafficking, religious persecution, displacement and war. These Christian networks, as we will see, play an invaluable if unheralded role on the global stage in human rights advocacy, humanitarian succour and peacemaking.

The idea of universal human dignity came into prominence in the late Roman Empire when Christianity began to offer a broad critique of common practices that we now see as unjust, cruel, or exploitative—such as slavery, sexual coercion and indifference to the poor. It was in these arenas that the gulf between Christian dignity and societal practices seemed most glaring and demanded a response, however haltingly.[2] Today, this Christian DNA reaches across the globe, magnified by considerable resources and unparalleled transnational linkages.

One of the driving factors in the emergence and clout of international Christian networks has been the tectonic shift of the Christian population to the developing nations of the Global South. Whereas in 1900, 80 per cent of Christians lived in Europe and North America, now at least 60 per cent of all Christians can be found in Asia, Africa, and Latin America.[3] This continuing trend nests the church amidst poverty, exploitation, war, persecution and displacement. International mission and development networks, in turn, channel awareness of these conditions to lay believers and policy makers in the West.

Another development is the expansion of global communication and travel, which draw grassroots constituencies into international engagement. Lay Americans meet visiting foreign religious leaders in their churches; they communicate via e-mail with counterparts around the world; and over a million believers a year travel on mission trips to work on humanitarian projects, often side by side with fellow believers in poor nations.[4]

What Western mission travellers discover is that they are not sent to spread the gospel among the heathen but to work alongside fellow Christians whose depth and vibrancy of faith inspires them. Wanting to support their suffering brothers and sisters in Christ, they become advocates for public policy initiatives to address poverty, disease and exploitation. They become contributors to NGOs, form campus groups to fight trafficking or write their members of Congress about AIDS funding or debt relief.

With this framework in mind, let us examine illustrations of how the Christian concept of dignity becomes instantiated through modern global networks.

Christian Development Networks and Global Poverty

As historian Kyle Harper remarked, 'On no other social issue does the Christian gospel provide such complete and unambiguous marching orders' as the problem of poverty. Jesus begins his ministry by proclaiming good news to the poor and liberty for the oppressed, and his parable of the Good Samaritan demands that his followers see any hurting person as a neighbour they are called upon to love. The Christian mandate reaches its pinnacle in Matthew 25's depiction of the Day of Judgment, in which the blessed inherit the kingdom because they succoured the hungry, the thirsty, the naked, the stranger and the prisoner. Indeed, the faithful are called upon to see Christ himself in the faces of the poor, the marginalised and the exploited.

For those engaged in Christian humanitarian ministries, this mandate breathes with special urgency as they work among the world's most destitute people—vulnerable to famine, disease, violence, exploitation and displacement. Indeed, extensive interviews with leaders of Christian non-government organisations (NGOs) and indigenous local staff reveal how deeply animated they are by Matthew 25 and the Good Samaritan.[5] The gospel mandate also calls forth the formidable lay generosity that generates multi-billion dollar resources for the growing network of Christian NGOs that support emergency relief, health care, education, agricultural initiatives and economic advancement.

An enumeration of the major Christian NGOs suggests their range and depth: Adventist Relief and Development Agency, American Friends Service Committee, Caritas International, Catholic Relief Services, Church World Service, Compassion International, Habitat for Humanity, Jesuit Refugee Services, Lutheran World Relief, Mennonite Central Committee, Mercy Corps, Samaritan's Purse, World Concern, World Hope International, World Relief and World Vision, among others.

While initiated in the United States and Europe, these Christian NGOs have become truly global enterprises, with international boards, operations through regional and national affiliates in a hundred-plus countries and international staffs of up to 10,000. In addition, these organisations have undergone what Andrew Natsios describes as decolonialisation, the process of turning over control of field programmes to people in the beneficiary countries.[6] Today, the vast bulk of the personnel of Christian NGOs are indigenous people living amidst suffering or exploited people.

Impressive in scope, sophistication, on-the-ground reach, these groups fill a crucial niche in global development. Indeed, the major development programs operated by the United Nations, the United States Agency for International Development (USAID), and the European Union routinely contract with Christian NGOs to implement local projects or deliver famine relief.[7]

This strategic position enables Christian NGOs to exercise creative leverage in high-level policy circles. With some of the best indigenous networks in developing nations, they generate valuable information on emerging problems and possible remedies. In turn, their global linkages and elite governmental access equips them to convey information to high-level policy makers.

Global Christian networks, for example, have propelled the ongoing effort to relieve debts burdening impoverished nations. Taking inspiration from the 'Year of Jubilee' in Hebrew scripture in which debts were forgiven, Christian leaders and NGOs provided theological inspiration and practical lobby muscle in the campaign to write off debts by lender nations, the International Monetary Fund and the World Bank. In 2000, when the Jubilee campaign sought funding from the US Congress to leverage further action by international institutions and other nations, Christian lobbyists persuaded conservative legislators normally sceptical of foreign aid to back the appropriation.[8]

The nexus of global Christian networks and US foreign policy also came into play in the development of the president's Emergency Plan for AIDS Relief (PEPFAR), which was launched in 2003. Christian development organisations such as World Vision and Catholic Relief Services saw the devastating impact of HIV/AIDS first-hand, especially in Africa, and had begun developing their own relief programs in the 1990s. In addition, many lay members learned about the AIDS crisis in Africa as a result of the growing number of mission trips sponsored by American congregations. Employing the access they enjoyed with President George W. Bush, evangelical leaders joined with Catholics and Jewish groups to lobby the president on AIDS, and he ultimately made it a signature issue. From the launch of the PEPFAR initiative in 2004, AIDS funding more than tripled. The program succeeded in delivering antiretroviral treatment to more than two million HIV-positive Africans by 2008 (up from just 50,000 before PEPFAR), saving many lives and contributing to economic development.[9]

Global Christian Networks, Trafficking and Slavery

Modern slavery—the sexual exploitation of trafficked women and children, forced labour, debt bondage, chattel birth and other forms of servitude—represents a clear threat to human dignity. The wide scope of modern slavery and trafficking—encompassing over 20 million people[10]—is due in part to the involvement of dangerous organised criminal syndicates that specialise in trafficking and labour exploitation. They employ intricate systems to move individuals within countries and across borders, and employ violence and intimidation to keep them in bondage.[11]

Because traffickers purposefully take advantage of weak governments and ineffective law enforcement, transnational Christian NGOs have provided some of the best documentation, rescue, rehabilitation and justice advocacy for trafficking victims.[12] A prominent example of this anti-trafficking movement is the work of the International Justice Mission, founded and led by Gary Haugen. Haugen's searing experience documenting atrocities in Rwanda motivated him to create a Christian organisation devoted to the international fight against injustice.[13] Haugen, an evangelical Christian, sees the fight for global justice as a central tenant of the Christian faith.[14] With a network of investigators and attorneys around the world, IJM directly frees victims, educates law enforcement officials, exposes corruption and presses for more effective national and international laws and policies. In successfully elevating the problem of trafficking and modelling successful law enforcement strategies to attack it, Haugen was recognised by US State Department as a Trafficking in Persons 'Hero'.

Another organisation that demonstrates the link between Christian theology and anti-trafficking efforts is the Catholic women's organisation Talitha Kum: The International Network of Consecrated Life Against Trafficking in Persons. Talitha Kum draws inspiration from the biblical stories of Ruth and the Samaritan woman to inspire solidarity with female victims of trafficking.[15] Sponsored by the International Union of Superiors General, Talitha Kum draws on this vast network of women in Catholic religious orders to respond to human rights abuses globally. It recently partnered with the US State Department in combating human trafficking at the 2014 World Cup.[16]

Transnational Christian networks have been crucial to establishing a new global regime to attack trafficking. Christian NGOs and lobby groups anchored the coalition behind the US Trafficking Victims Protection Act of 2000 and subsequent strengthening legislation.[17] The law created a major State Department office on trafficking with real enforcement teeth. This focus helped spark expanded attention by other governments, the United Nations, and international law enforcement agencies. By placing human dignity at the centre of their advocacy, religious actors helped catalyse non-religious actors and organisations to this global cause.

Christian Peacemaking Networks

Contemporary wars and violence disproportionately afflict the world's poor and call forth Christian peacemaking impulses, from mediation of active conflicts to facilitation of peaceful transitions to democracy to post-conflict reconciliation. In nearly every Christian peace effort, a strong emphasis on human dignity shines through as a prerequisite to negotiations, mediations or reconciliation. Inspired by biblical teachings, such as the 'The Sermon on the Mount', Christian actors and organisations have played an active and creative role in a number of situations.

The most successful involve the ability to cultivate trust-based linkages between all sides of a conflict. Christian groups also employ expansive human networks to promote peacemaking. From the hierarchal Catholic Church to the more decentralised pacifist denominations, diverse Christian use humanitarian and evangelistic connections to respond to conflicts across the globe.

Christian organizations are not the only religious groups to engage in peacemaking—Buddhist, Islamic and Jewish actors also press for mediation, call for policy changes and take active roles in post-conflict resolution. But an examination of modern religious peacemaking efforts demonstrates the prevalence of Christian actors. The authors of *God's Century* provide the most comprehensive and systematic documentation of religious-based mediation over the past three decades.[18] Of the 21 disputes they identified in which religious actors played a role, 16 involved Christian groups exclusively. Moreover, of the conflicts where religious actors played a strong mediating role, *all involved Christian actors.* Thus Christianity plays a disproportionate role in faith-based conflict mediation. The global size and span of Christianity, its ethic of peacemaking and its robust international networks combined to produce this striking pattern.

Illustrative of this role is the Community of Sant'Egidio, an organisation of peacemakers nested in the larger Catholic world. In the *God's Century* study, this one group engaged in seven of the mediation cases, five of which involved strong mediation. The intensity and scope of the community's involvement in mediation efforts demonstrates the power of focused efforts connected to global Catholic networks. While their extraordinary efforts span activities from prayer to peace conferences, they seem to have an ability to bring disparate violent factions to the table in such diverse nations as Mozambique, Algeria, Uganda, Kosovo, Guatemala and Liberia.[19] In contrast to traditional methods of engagement, Sant'Egidio stress multi-polar, synergistic efforts that incorporate actors at all levels, from the grassroots to the international. This strategy offers responsiveness to local needs and guarantees of international organisations.

Pacifist Christian denominations, such as the Quakers and Mennonites, offer a distinct doctrinal and practical expression of the biblical call to be peacemakers. [20] Though small in size, they have cultivated transnational networks that capitalise on their ethic of non-violence. As credible third-party actors they have been prominent mediators in a number of civil wars and insurrections— delivering messages between combatants, offering neutral venues for negotiations and fostering environments for post-conflict conciliation.[21]

Conclusion

Each instantiation of Christian dignity is notable in its own right. But collectively we see the broad scope and weight of this witness in the world. Christian networks, while not always successful,[22] play an expansive and invaluable role on the global stage in human rights advocacy, humanitarian efforts and peacemaking. At a more theoretical level, what we observe is the emergence of a genuine global system, in which a theological ideal serves as a central organising principle. Unlike governmental structures or even UN institutions, this system is more organic and nimble in upholding human dignity. This system links local actors and congregations with international mission, development and denominational structures that magnify the collective Christian witness in policy circles. Perhaps we stand at a hinge point of Christian history as the faith's contribution to dignity and freedom becomes more fully manifest and global.

Notes

1. This chapter is taken from a larger piece: Mark Brockway and Allen D. Hertzke, 'Christianity, Globalization, and Human Dignity', in *Christianity and Freedom: Contemporary Perspectives*, edited by Allen D. Hertzke and Timothy Samuel Shah, for the Religious Freedom Project, Georgetown University, under review.

2. Kyle Harper, 'Christianity and the Roots of Human Dignity in Late Antiquity', in *Christianity and Freedom: Historical Perspectives,* edited by Timothy Samuel Shah and Allen D. Hertzke, 'Religious Freedom Project', Georgetown University, under review.

3. Philip Jenkins, *The Next Christendom: The Coming of Global Christianity*, Revised and Expanded Edition (New York: Oxford University Press, 2007).

4. Robert Wuthnow, *Boundless Faith: The Global Outreach of American Churches* (Berkeley, CA: University of California Press, 2009).

5. As director of the Pew Research Center's 2011-2012 study, 'Lobbing for the Faithful', Allen Hertzke interviewed a number of the advocacy directors of international relief and development organizations, and during field research in South Sudan in August of 2014 he interviewed country officials and indigenous staff of these organizations. The invocation to see the face of Christ in those they serve came out routinely and naturally in these conversations. See 'Lobbying for the Faithful', Pew Research Center: http://www.pewforum.org/2011/11/21/lobbying-for-the-faithful-exec/

6. Andrew S. Nasios, 'Faith-Based NGOs and US Foreign Policy', in *The Influence of Faith: Religious Groups & US Foreign Policy*, edited by Elliot Abrams (Lanham, MD: Rowman & Littlefield, 2001).

7. Stephen V. Monsma, 'Faith-based NGOs and the Government Embrace', in *The Influence of Faith: Religious Groups & US Foreign Policy,* ed. Elliott Abrams (Lanham, MD: Rowman and Littlefield, 2001).

8. Joshua William Busby, 'Bono Made Jesse Helms Cry: Jubilee 2000, Debt Relief, and Moral Action in International Politics', *International Studies Quarterly* 51 (2007), 247–275; 'Religious Leaders Cheer Debt Relief', *Christian Century*, November 2000.

9. Scott Baldauf and Jina Moore, 'Bush Sees Results of His AIDS Plan in Africa', *The Christian Science Monitor*, February 20, 2008, 7.

10. This is the figure given by the 2014 State Department's Trafficking in Person's report http://www.state.gov/j/tip/rls/tiprpt/2014/index.htm. Kevin Bales estimates 27 million persons in conditions of slavery. Kevin Bales, *Disposable People: New Slavery in the*

Global Economy (Berkeley: University of California Press, 2000).

11. UNODC Global Report on Trafficking in Persons 2014; Bales, *Disposable People*.

12. Allen Hertzke, *Freeing God's Children: The Unlikely Alliance for Global Human Rights (*Lanham, MD: Rowman & Littlefield, 2006), Chapter 8.

13. Quentin Hardy, 'Hitting Slavery Where It Hurts (Gary Haugen of International Justice Mission)', *Forbes* 172, no. 14. 2004: 76.

14. As Haugen writes, the 'good news' about injustice is that God is against it, which mandates that believers must fight against it as well. See Gary Haugen, *The Good News About Injustice* (Downers Grove, Il: InterVarsity Press, 1999).

15. See Talith Kum's website for more information and mission statement. Accessed May 24, 2014. www.talithakum.info.

16. US Embassy to the Holy See Conference on Building Bridges of Freedom, May 18, 2011, http://vatican.usembassy.gov/news-events/launch-talitha-kums-countering-trafficking-in-persons.html, accessed June 16, 2014; Elise Harris, "Anti-Human Trafficking Effort Launched ahead of World Cup," accessed June 21, 2014. http://www.catholicnewsagency.com/news/anti-human-trafficking-effort-launched-ahead-of-world-cup/.

17. Hertzke, *Freeing God's Children*. For text of the act and subsequent reauthorizations see the state department office website http://www.state.gov/j/tip/laws/, accessed May 28, 2014.

18. Monica Duffy Toft, Daniel Philpott, and Timothy Samuel Shah, *God's Century: Resurgent Religion and Global Politics,* (New York: W. W. Norton & Company, 2011) Chapter 7.

19. *God's Century*, Chapter 7 and Table 7.1.

20. For a historical and analytical look at Christian pacifist religions see Cecil John Cadoux. *Christian Pacifism Re-Examined* (New York: Oxford University Press, 1940).

21. Michael Norton Yarrow, *Quaker Experiences in International Conciliation* (New Haven, CT: Yale University Press, 1978); Adam Curle, *True Justice: Quaker Peace Makers and Peace Making* (Philadelphia, PA: Quaker Books, 2007); Cynthia Sampson and John Paul Lederach, *From the Ground Up: Mennonite Contributions to International Peacebuilding* (New York: Oxford University Press, 2000).

22. Christian solidarity networks championed the cause of the African peoples of southern Sudan, who for two decades were engulfed in a brutal civil war with the Islamist-dominated regime in Khartoum. The campaign led to the creation in 2011 of South Sudan, but that new nation was not equipped for self government and has been rent by factional violence and looming famine.

27

Islam and Human Rights in Pakistan

ISHTIAQ AHMED
STOCKHOLM UNIVERSITY, SWEDEN

Introduction

Although ideas of rights and dignity of human beings can be traced to antiquity, modern human rights originated in the wake of the European Enlightenment. The American Declaration of Independence and the French Revolution ushered in processes that some 150 years later culminated in human rights being proclaimed as universal entitlements of all individuals. Contemporary human rights theory is based on three axioms: one, that human rights are universal and belong to all individuals, irrespective of their religion, ethnicity, gender or sexuality; two, that human rights are absolute and innate, not grants from states or some metaphysical authority; three, that they are the properties of individual subjects who possess them because of their capacity for rationality, agency and autonomy.[1]

The 1945 UN Charter and the 1948 Universal Declaration of Human Rights (UDHR) obliges states to protect the human rights of their populations and provide redress of their violation through appropriate judicial procedures. However, since the UN system recognises states as sovereign entities, the concomitant non-interference principle has, in practice, meant that the human rights situation varies from country to country, and even those countries that have formally ratified UN treaties on human rights can get away with violation of those commitments with formal protests from UN monitoring agencies. Moreover, some treaties permit partial derogation. Historical, cultural and developmental factors are usually invoked to justify the derogations. Consequently, discrepancy between formal acceptance of UN human rights instruments and the actual practice of states is more of a rule than an exception.

Islam and Human Rights

Claiming to be heirs to Islam, a divinely ordained universal, inclusive civilisation which welcomes conversions of all peoples of the world, contemporary Muslim states have invoked cultural relativistic arguments to justify modifications of, and derogations from, UN-based international human rights norms and standards. Typically, human rights are recognised as necessary for individuals to live free and dignified lives, but subjected to Islamic standards which presume that if God's will and sovereignty are enforced through the all-embracing Islamic law, the Sharia, in all departments of life by the Islamic state—individual, collective, private and public—then and only then will true equality, freedom and justice accrue to all individuals.

The model of an ideal Islamic polity is traced back to the seventh century CE, when the Prophet Muhammad and his immediate successors ruled at Medina. Classic Islamic political theory dichotomised society into two distinct categories: Muslims and non-Muslims. In accordance with Quranic rulings, non-Muslim religious communities, called *dhimmis*, paid the *jizya*, or protection tax, and were entitled to internal autonomy. Originally only a special category of non-Muslims, the people of the Book—that is, Christians, Jews and an extinct group called Sabeans—were accorded the status of *dhimmis*. The same principle was extended later to include the Hindus of India.[2] Both tolerant and intolerant forms of this principle have existed, but both Muslims and non-Muslims remained subjects of the sultan and not proper citizens enjoying inalienable human rights.[3] From early times, segregation of men and women was taken for granted in Islamic society. Within the Muslim Umma (community), sectarian divisions resulted in the state privileging the dominant sect or sub-sects.[4]

Considered in this light, the notion of an inclusive, undifferentiated citizenry and equal rights, as upheld in the UDHR and subsequent treaties and conventions, is not consonant with Islamic political values and norms. This point was set forth bluntly in 1981 by the Iranian representative to the UN, who rejected the UDHR by asserting that it was 'a secular understanding of the Judeo-Christian tradition' and therefore its adoption would result in trespassing Islamic law.[5] The main international forum of Muslims countries, the Organisation of Islamic Conference (OIC), issued a Universal Islamic Declaration of Human Rights in 1981. It recognised almost all the rights laid down in the UDHR, but added the rider that these were to be enjoyed within limits imposed by the Sharia. It was followed by the Cairo Declaration on

Human Rights in Islam (CDHRI) of 1990.[6] The CDHRI's last two articles unequivocally reiterate that all rights are to be enjoyed in accordance with the rules laid down by the Sharia:

> Article 24:
>
> All the rights and freedoms stipulated in this Declaration are subject to the Islamic Sharia.
>
> Article 25:
>
> The Islamic Sharia is the only source of reference for the explanation or clarification of any of the articles of this Declaration.

Such a disposition can be described as the 'clawback' approach which, on the one hand, accepts human rights, but, on the other, hedges them with restrictions which nullify their purpose and meaning. Thus, for example, the Sharia does not permit a Muslim to convert to another religion, a Muslim female cannot marry a non-Muslim, a Muslim male can marry up to four wives simultaneously, and the laws of inheritance confer a greater share to male descendants.

Pakistan and Human Rights

The last official census of Pakistan, from 1998, gave the total population of Pakistan as 132 million. Muslims (Sunnis and Shias) made up 96.28 per cent of the total population; Christians, 1.59 per cent; caste Hindus, 1.60 per cent; scheduled castes, 0.25 per cent; Ahmadis (known also as Qadianis), 0.22 per cent; and the rest, including Sikhs and Buddhists, a mere 0.07 per cent. The current estimated Pakistan population is close to 200 million. As a member of the United Nations, Pakistan accepts the human rights obligations under the UN Charter. It has ratified several UN treaties and conventions on human rights, including the International Covenant on Civil and Political Rights (1966) and the Convention on the Elimination of All Forms of Discrimination Against Women (1979), but with reservations on both so that Sharia laws pertaining to freedom of belief and freedom to enter marriage have precedence.

Pakistan emerged on 14 August 1947 as a separate state, when British rule in the Indian subcontinent ended and India was partitioned to establish two states based on religious majorities: Hindus in India and Muslims in Pakistan.

The partition proved to be one of the bloodiest upheavals in history, however. An estimated one million Hindus, Muslims and Sikhs were killed in violent riots, while 14–18 million crossed the international border between the two states to escape violence, discrimination and persecution. Yet, religious minorities remained on both sides.[7] Constitutional and legal development in Pakistan pertaining to human rights has oscillated between modernist and Islamist interpretations. Both standpoints derive from the phantasmagoria that the All-India Muslim League and its supreme leader, Mohammad Ali Jinnah, successfully projected a vision in which Muslims of all sorts of ideological persuasion and sectarian affiliations were given diverse and conflicting promises were given in order to mobilise their support for a utopian polity. Thus, for example, the ulema were given a free hand to project future Pakistan as an Islamic state, while to the British, the rival Indian National Congress, and modern educated Muslims, it was painted as a democracy. More importantly, the point that Jinnah hammered down with great flourish was that Hindus and Muslims were two separate nations who could under no circumstance live in peace in one state.[8]

Constitutional Vagaries and Human Rights

A complete reversal on the definition of nation was proffered by Jinnah on 11 August 1947, three days before Pakistan became independent. He said famously:

> You are free; you are free to go to your temples, you are free
> to go to your mosques or to any other place of worship in this
> State of Pakistan. You may belong to any religion or caste or
> creed—that has nothing to do with the business of the State …
> . We are starting with this fundamental principle that we are all
> citizens and equal citizens of one State … . I think we should
> keep that in front of us as our ideal and you will find that in due
> course Hindus would cease to be Hindus and Muslims would
> cease to be Muslims, not in the religious sense, because that
> is the personal faith of each individual, but in the political
> sense as citizens of the State.[9]

Jinnah died on 11 September 1948. His close lieutenants in the Muslim League discarded the inclusionary vision on Pakistani nationalism, since the stand taken by Jinnah on 11 August 1947 completely contradicted the underlying ideology upon which the support of the Muslim voters and masses had been solicited to create a separate Muslim state. The Islamic underpinnings of Pakistani nationalism had been written in blood by the violent division of India and, notwithstanding the founder of Pakistan's about-turn, such a state could not be separated from its foundational ideology. Prime Minister Liaquat Ali Khan moved the Objectives Resolution in the Pakistan Constituent Assembly on 7 March 1949, which proclaimed that sovereignty over the entire universe belonged to God Almighty, in which the elected representatives of the people would enjoy delegated powers within limits imposed by Him. In the same vein, he went on to say that democracy will be practised and minorities will enjoy their legitimate interests and religious freedom within 'Islamic limits'. The non-Muslim members of the Pakistan Constituent Assembly expressed their apprehensions and objections to the notion of God's sovereignty limiting the powers of the elected representatives of the people, as it would create a bias in favour of the Muslims, but such concerns were described as unfounded.[10]

The Islamist Challenge

The Islamist ideologue Syed Abul Ala Maududi argued that, since Pakistan had been won in the name of Islam, it was immanently an Islamic state. In 1951, he compiled a 22-point political programme in favour of an Islamic state. Although elections were accepted as the basis of legitimate government, Western democracy, female equality and equal rights for non-Muslims were rejected. Maududi was able to secure the signatures of the leading Sunni and Shia clerics to that document.[11] Things came to a head when the ulema launched the *Khatam-e-Nabuwat* (finality of the prophet-hood of Muhammad) movement in 1953. The roots of the conflict went back to the early twentieth century, when Mirza Ghulam Ahmad (1835–1908), born at Qadian in the Punjab, began to claim that he was a prophet who received revelation from God. Mirza also claimed to be carrying the attributes of Jesus and of the Hindu god Krishna. Moreover, he rejected *jihad* (holy war) against the British. Such claims were unacceptable to the Sunni and Shia ulema, who denounced him as an imposter and his teachings as heretical. In 1912, his son, Mirza Bashiruddin Maumud Ahmad, made a statement to the effect that those Muslims who had not converted to Ahmadiyyat were outside the pale of Islam.[12] Nevertheless, Jinnah had made a prominent Ahmadi, Sir Muhammad Zafrulla Khan, Pakistan's first foreign minister. In 1953, mainstream ulema demanded that, since Pakistan was an Islamic state, only Muslims could hold key positions in the state. Therefore, since Ahmadis held beliefs that were irreconcilable with Islam, they should be removed from key positions. On that occasion, the central government acted forcefully and the agitation was crushed.[13]

Constitutional Development and Human Rights

The first constitution of Pakistan was adopted in 1956. It described Pakistan as an Islamic Republic. It was laid down that all laws should be brought into conformity with the Quran and Sunnah. The president, envisaged as a titular head of state, was required to be a Muslim. A bill of rights was included which upheld human rights, and all Pakistanis were given the right to vote without any reference to religion. The Islamists hailed the constitution as an authoritative commitment to Islamise Pakistan. However, a military coup brought Field Marshal Mohammad Ayub Khan to power. Khan drew up a second constitution in 1962. The constitution reiterated the commitment to bringing all laws in consonance with the Quran and Sunnah, and the condition that the president should be a Muslim was retained. Pakistani citizens, in principle, continued to enjoy the same fundamental rights and freedoms, without discrimination based on religion or sect. However, the epithet 'Islamic' was dropped and Pakistan became simply the 'Republic of Pakistan'. Immediately protests and demonstrations took place, and the first amendment reinserted the epithet 'Islamic'.[14]

Military rule ended in December 1971, after Pakistan broke up and East Pakistan became a separate state in the wake of a bloody civil war. Zulfikar Ali Bhutto, whose Pakistan People's Party had won the most seats in the December 1970 election in West Pakistan, formed the government in the truncated Pakistan. A third constitution was adopted in 1973 by the Pakistan National Assembly, which not only required the president but also the prime minister to be Muslim. Further, they had to take an oath testifying to the finality of the prophet-hood of Muhammad. In 1974, the Pakistan National Assembly declared the Ahmadis non-Muslims after listening to the arguments of the caliph of the Ahmadis, Mirza Nasir Ahmad, as well as mainstream Sunni and Shia ulema.[15]

In July 1977, Bhutto was overthrown by General Muhammad Zia-ul-Haq. Zia declared the establishment of an Islamic order a prerequisite for the country. In 1979, his government announced the imposition of the Hudood Ordinances, i.e. punishments laid down in the Quran for the offences of adultery, fornication, false accusation of adultery, consumption of alcohol, theft and highway robbery. In 1983–1984, the Ahmadis were forbidden to use Islamic nomenclature for their worship, places of worship, and so on.[16] In 1982, a Blasphemy Law was introduced, which criminalised any insult to Prophet Muhammad and other prophets and laid down life imprisonment as maximum punishment for such an offence. In 1986, the Blasphemy Law was reformulated and capital punishment was prescribed as the maximum punishment. Thus, Section 295-C of the Penal Code established explicitly:

> Use of derogatory remarks etc. in respect of the Holy Prophet:
> Whether by words, either spoken or written, or by visible representations, or by any imputation, innuendo or insinuation,

directly or indirectly, defiles the sacred name of the Holy Prophet (peace by upon him) shall be punishable with death, or imprisonment for life, and shall be liable to fine.[17]

The blasphemy law was further brutalised when, through a constitutional amendment in 1991, 'imprisonment for life' was deleted; in the future, individuals proven guilty of blasphemy were to be awarded only the death penalty. The amendment passed during the government of Prime Minister Nawaz Sharif (1990–1993). However, it was adopted as law proper during the government of Prime Minister Benazir Bhutto (1993–1995).[18]

The Human Rights Commission of Pakistan (HRCP) has been reporting that, most of the time, the accusations of blasphemy have been fabrications.[19] On several occasions, fanatics have taken the law in their own hands and killed the alleged blasphemer. With regard to the judicial procedure, while the lower courts have typically found the accused guilty, at the higher levels the sentences have either been turned into long imprisonments or the accused have been set free and allowed to seek humanitarian asylum in the West. It is doubtful if assassins of alleged blasphemers have not been tried in court, punished, and the sentence carried out. The HRCP, Amnesty International, Asia Watch, and other such organisations have been critiquing Pakistan for extensive human right violations.

Women

The military government of Field Marshal Mohammad Ayub Khan made a special effort to reform Sharia law pertaining to personal affairs of marriage, divorce, and inheritance. On 15 July 1961, the Muslim Family Laws Ordinance (MFLO) was passed, which made polygamy conditional. The husband had to give a convincing reason to contract a new marriage. Only when permission was granted by the arbitration council, in consultation with the wife or wives, could a man marry another wife. The MFLO also fixed 16 as the legal age of marriage for girls. The ordinance was assailed by the ulema as a great transgression of the Islamic system. Such protests were rejected and the MFLO became law, which, despite recurring calls for its repeal, remains in force.[20]

General Muhammad Zia-ul-Hoq, however, introduced cultural and legal changes that weakened the status and human rights of women. The law pertaining to rape was recast in traditional Sharia terms. It required evidence given by four pious Muslim male witnesses to prove the offence. Failure to provide such evidence could result in 80 lashes. Several women who claimed they were raped were unable to establish the crime due to the lack of four pious male witnesses. The military government of General Pervez Musharraf tried to revive the modernistic approach, and in 2006, the four-witness condition was discontinued.[21]

The HRPC annual report, *The State of Human Rights in Pakistan*, gives a long list of injustices and violent crimes committed against women. These include increasing trends towards honour killings among Muslims and forcible conversions and marriages of kidnapped non-Muslim women to Muslim men. In 1998, the heads of the United Nations agencies in Pakistan issued a statement in which Pakistan was reminded that, since it had ratified the Convention on the Elimination of all Forms of Discrimination Against Women (though a proviso 'subject to the provisions of the Constitution' was added), gender discrimination and gender-related violence contravened its commitments, and it must take substantive measures to prevent them.[22]

Conclusion

This chapter demonstrates that the constitutional and legal relationship between citizens and the Pakistani state is mediated by the founding ideology of the state: Muslim nationalism. The two main strands of Muslim nationalism—the liberal-modernist and Islamist—seek legitimacy from the Sharia. In practice, it means that a logical and necessary link exists between membership in the Islamic community and citizenship. Such disposition is premised on the assumption that the true believer has to be differentiated from the non-believer, the heretic, and the hypocrite. It is further compounded by gender criteria favouring men. One need not labour the point that Pakistan's human rights theory and praxis deviate from contemporary international standards and norms.

Notes

1.   Darren J. O'Byrne, 'Theorising Human Rights', *Human Rights: An Introduction* (London: Pearson Education Limited, 2003), 27.
2.   S. M. Ikram, 'Interaction of Islam and Hinduism', in Toheed Ahmad (ed), *A Large White Crescent, Readings in Dialogue Among Civilizations: The Pakistan Experience* (Lahore: Apa Publications, 2011), 201-25.
3.   Will Kymlicka, *Multicultural Citizenship: A Liberal Theory of Minority Rights*, (Oxford: Clarendon Press, 1996), 156-8.
4.   Ishtiaq Ahmed, *The Concept of an Islamic State: An Analysis of the Ideological Controversy in Pakistan* (London: Frances Pinter, 1987), 61-2.
5.   David Littman, 'Human Rights and Human Wrongs: Sharia can't be an exception to international human-rights norms', *National Review* (online, 19 January 2003), http://www.nationalreview.com/articles/205577/human-rights-and-human-wrongs/david-g-littman.

6. *The Cairo Declaration on Human Rights in Islam* (5 August 1990), http://www.fmreview.org/en/FMRpdfs/Human-Rights/cairo.pdf.

7. Ishtiaq Ahmed, *The Punjab Bloodied, Partitioned and Cleansed: Unravelling the 1947 Tragedy through Secret British Reports and First-Person Accounts* (Karachi: Oxford University Press, 2012), xxxvii-xxxviii.

8. Ibid, 81-90; Ishtiaq Ahmed, *Pakistan: The Garrison State – Origins, Evolution, Consequences 1947-2011* (Karachi: Oxford University Press, 2013), 31.

9. Ibid, 104.

10. *The Constituent Assembly of Pakistan Debates, Volume 5, 1949* (Karachi: Government Printing Press, 1949), 1-102.

11. Syed Abul Ala Maududi, *The Islamic Law and Constitution* (Lahore: Islamic Publications Ltd, 1980), 332-6.

12. K. W. Jones, *The New Cambridge History of India: Socio-Religious Reform Movements in British India* (Cambridge: Cambridge University Press, 1989), 200.

13. *Report of the Court of Inquiry constituted under Punjab Act II of 1954 to enquire into the Punjab Disturbances of 1953* (Lahore: Government Printing Press, 1954), 187-200.

14. Y. V. Gankovsky and V. N. Moskalenka, *The Three Constitutions of Pakistan* (Lahore: People's Publishing House, 1978), 29-86.

15. Muhammad Mateen Khalid (compiler), *Qadyaniat: In the Eyes of the Law* (Lahore: Ilm-o-Irfan Publishers, 2008).

16. Ishtiaq Ahmed, "Religious Nationalism and Minorities in Pakistan: Constitutional and Legal Bases of Discrimination", in Ishtiaq Ahmed (ed), *The Politics of Religion in South and Southeast Asia* (London: Routledge, 2011), 90-91.

17. Ishtiaq Ahmed, 'The Politics of Group Rights in India and Pakistan', in Ishtiaq Ahmed (ed.), *The Politics of Group Rights: The State and Multiculturalism* (Lanham, Maryland: University Press of America, 2005), 203.

18. I. A. Rehman, 'The Blasphemy Law', *Dawn*, (Karachi: 25 November 2010).

19. *State of Human Rights in Pakistan* (Lahore: The Human Rights Commission of Pakistan, see annual reports available online), http://hrcp-web.org/publication/book-genre/annual-reports/.

20. Ishtiaq Ahmed, 'Women under Islamic Law in Pakistan', in Ishtiaq Ahmed (ed), *The Politics of Religion in South and Southeast Asia* (London: Routledge, 2011), 106-8.

21. Ibid, 108-16.

22. Ishtiaq Ahmed, 'Globalisation and Human Rights in Pakistan', in *International Journal of Punjab Studies*, (Vol. 9, No. 1, January-June 2002), 57-89.

28

Building a Reform Movement: Could Muslims Emulate Nineteenth Century Judaism?

JONATHAN BENTHALL
UNIVERSITY COLLEGE LONDON, UK

A Crisis of Authority

Let us start from the premise, though not all social scientists would agree, that religious doctrines generate their own ideological dynamic distinct from the markers of language, ethnicity and class —albeit often overlapping with them. The oldest religions have accreted over many centuries through the deployment of potent symbolic power by means of the communication media of their day. It has been convincingly argued that the Islamic tradition is particularly conducive to politicisation, and a crisis of authority within Islam has been diagnosed.[1] Dispassionate debate on this topic is made harder by the long history of domination of the Muslim world by colonial powers, by current geopolitical conflicts and tensions, and by the anti-Muslim prejudice (usually characterised as 'Islamophobia' despite the objections to this word as implying a passive, quasi-medical condition) which has been exacerbated in the West by economic stress and probably by the collapse of Communism as a bugbear. I hope to show that, whereas a tradition of progressive Islamic thought can be traced back for at least a century and includes some highly articulate personalities today, it has not yet coalesced into a movement. Thus a vacuum is left that can be filled by more ambiguous religious leaders claiming to occupy a 'middle ground'—in Arabic, *al-wasatiyya*. Sheikh Yusuf Al-Qaradawi, the Egyptian scholar born in 1926 and now resident in Qatar, was the most prominent claimant to this ground in 2014, though recently he appeared to be losing his influence after pressure was applied by Saudi

Arabia on the rulers of Qatar to reduce the support they had given to the Muslim Brotherhood, of which he is the spiritual leader.[2]

Over forty countries with Muslim majorities were ruled in the past by European powers (including Russia), while a few others such as Iran and Afghanistan belonged to what has been called an 'informal empire'. It is possible to apply towards Islam the same kind of decentring, or deprovincialisation of the West, that social anthropologists have been used to apply towards 'indigenous' societies, except that the Islamic tradition has been as universalising and proselytising as Christianity. Classical Islamic political thought had assumed an expansion of Muslim rule (*dar al-islam*) rather than its contraction. For some five to ten centuries an Islamic 'world system' was at the centre of world civilisation and hegemony; now, as Abelwahab Meddeb has written, Islam is 'unconsolable in its destitution'.[3] Muslims responded to their domination by Europe in various ways: through military resistance, through exodus or opting out of politics, and through accommodation.[4] The current geopolitical crisis in the Middle East is of unprecedented complexity, as a result of the rise of the petrodollar states, the 'Islamic resurgence' with its violent extremist edge, the fall of Communism, the tragic and apparently irresolvable Israeli–Palestinian conflict, the 'war on terror' with its squandering of American military power, the return of Russia to its previous global role, the deepening of the Sunni–Shia divide, the retaliatory spirit provoked in the Muslim tribal periphery by heavy-handed repression,[5] and intensified anti-Muslim prejudice in the West. Here, I will focus only on the contribution that interpretations of Islamic doctrine make to the present-day imbroglio.

We may discard the theory that the Islamic scriptures lead inevitably to bigotry. It is part of the genius of the great religions that they are able to give an impression of immobility while continuously changing, and Islam like Christianity has been capable of extensive accommodation with diverse local circumstances while also inspiring great achievements in intellectual life and the arts. However, a scrupulous comparison by the historian Michael Cook between Sunni Islam, Hinduism, Buddhism and Christianity (mainly Catholic) as resources for political engagement in the Global South has provided persuasive evidence that, whereas no tradition is a reliable predictor of the behaviour of those who inherit it, just as surely traditions are not interchangeable.[6] All Third World populations, Cook argues, need to choose between defiance towards the richer nations and cooperation with them; also between conservation of heritage and adoption of Western institutions and values. He finds that the Islamic heritage provides a wider choice of political possibilities than the others that he has analysed. Extreme rejectionism and absolutism come to the fore in some parts of the Muslim world. But there is another form of Islamism that is much more eclectic and modernising—

stressing for instance opportunities for women outside the home, egalitarianism as an Islamic principle, and scriptural authorisation of peaceful relations with non-Muslims. Reviewing the possible future of Islamist movements, Cook sees little chance of their dying out, at least in the short term, though he thinks it conceivable that large numbers of Muslims may gradually be attracted by a less politicised version of their religion.

Possible Precedents: European 'Renaissance', Christian 'Reformation' and Jewish Reform

Can we envisage an Islamic renaissance? With a qualified nod of recognition to Arnold Toynbee, the anthropologist Jack Goody has argued that there have been many renaissances in history as well as the standard European example.[7] Islam experienced over the centuries a number of temporary and local efflorescences, including the rediscovery of Greek scientific literature under the Baghdad-based Abbasid caliphate and the magnificent mosque architecture still to be seen in Cairo and Istanbul. Ibn Khaldun (1332–1406) has been hailed as a founding father of the social sciences. But Goody leaves us to come to our own judgment about the present day.

The word 'renaissance' is indeed often used to translate the Arabic term Al-Nahda, a period of modernisation and reform that began in Egypt in the late nineteenth century and continued into the twentieth. But the geopolitical crisis of the Arab Islamic world today is partly explained by the problem diagnosed in the Arab Human Development Report 2003: '[The] Arab world must turn outwards and immerse itself in the global knowledge stream.'[8] Despite energetic steps to strengthen research and education in the decade since publication of that report, the social sciences in particular remain weak throughout the heartlands of Islam; and without help from the social sciences, religious adherents run the risk of having access only to an insider's view of their faith. A full-blown renaissance seems far off at the moment—with due respect to the many thoughtful and talented Muslim *individuals* working in every walk of life, including some impressively articulate intellectuals.[9]

But what about a reformation comparable to that which created the Protestant churches in the sixteenth century? The call for an Islamic reformation has been voiced for over a hundred years, more recently by (among others) the social anthropologist Dale Eickelman, who has written about Muhammad Shahrur's widely circulated *The Book and the Qur'an: A Contemporary Interpretation* (1990) that 'it may one day be seen as a Muslim equivalent of the 95 Theses that Martin Luther nailed to the door of the Wittenberg Castle church in 1517'.[10] Eickelman's cautious prediction may well be proved correct in time, though in fact the Protestant Reformation set off forces of intolerance that led to bloodshed as heavy as what we now see in Iraq or Pakistan, so this is not the most encouraging parallel.

A more apposite exemplar for Islam is the rise of Reform Judaism, which began in Germany in the early nineteenth century when progressive synagogues found they had interests in common and decided to cooperate. In the 1840s, rabbinical conferences brought the modernist rabbis together, and the movement spread to the United States. In 1885, the Pittsburgh Platform was agreed by the Reform movement, merging its German and American wings, as a formulation of principles that included acceptance of other religious perspectives, rejecting dietary restrictions and discarding the idea of a Jewish nation in favour of that of a 'religious community'.[11] The World Union for Progressive Judaism was founded in 1926. The Columbus Platform, agreed in 1937, adapted the principles of the movement to the mid-twentieth century, especially in responding to the persecution of Jews as a people and the threats to their survival.[12] Today, Reform Judaism has a recognised position together with the Orthodox and Conservative movements, allowing space for degrees of organised dissent and solidarity within the wider faith community.

Individuals and Institution Building

There has been no shortage of individual Islamic modernists, of whom one of the first and most influential was Muhammad Abduh (1849–1905), who sought as grand mufti of Egypt to reverse the inertia of his country's religious and cultural habits through introducing the values of the European Enlightenment—scientific enquiry, moral development and education—while remaining committed to the Quran as the source of governmental legitimacy. He aimed at an alternative Islamic modernity to that disseminated from the West: Europe was an obstacle, because of its machinations in the Middle East, but also a conduit for progressive principles.[13] It has been argued by Ahmad Moussalli that the reason why the trend set by Abduh, and the many intellectuals inspired by him, did not solidify into a movement is that 'the Arab reform remained superficial and did not penetrate basic social fabrics. [It] blindly and unconditionally adopted Western thought and generalised its suitability to the Arab world.' Hence the liberation movements of the twentieth century were linked to the very doctrines used to exercise and justify Western domination.[14]

One of the most promising legacies of the twentieth century for Islamic reformism was that of the Sudanese religious leader Mahmud Muhammad Taha (1909–85), who set out to synthesise liberal socialist ideas with Sufi interpretations of Sharia, distinguishing the Quran's universal revelation, transmitted during the Prophet Muhammad's early period in Mecca, from the rigid legalism of the later Medinan chapters. Taha was executed for apostasy under the military regime of Jaafar Nimeiri. Since his death his ideas have become widely known among Muslim intellectuals; but Taha is far less well remembered than the founders of the more hard-line and well-organised Muslim Brotherhood.[15]

Current turmoil in the Middle East is driving thousands of disaffected young Muslims to sympathise with violent jihadis. There is a widespread consensus in the West that Islamic reformism should be encouraged—but how? Western-inspired initiatives, such as that embarked on briefly by the RAND Corporation in 2004, to intervene in the theology of another religion may have unintended consequences, one of which is that progressive *ulama* are exposed to allegations that they are tools of Western intelligence services.[16] To be successful, a reform movement would need not only a new generation of accredited individual Islamic opinion-formers but also decisive efforts at institution building.[17]

Islamic Charities as Autogenous Institutions

Several successful Islamic overseas aid agencies have grown in Britain—encouraged by the Charity Commission and successfully surmounting the political and financial obstacles put in the way of Islamic charities since 11 September 2001, most notably by the US government.[18] These NGOs demonstrate that Muslims in the West are fully capable of building autogenous institutions that harmonise and cooperate in practical ways with the non-Muslim mainstream, and make constructive use of media opportunities, while also being faithful to their own religious traditions: in this case, the strong injunctions to charitable giving that are found in the Quran. Islamic Relief Worldwide, the leading British Muslim overseas relief and development charity, was founded in Birmingham, England, by medical students in 1984.[19] But there is no nationwide institution in Britain, or any other Western country, comparable to Muhammadiyah in Indonesia. This progressive religious network manages many thousands of educational, health and welfare institutions, and celebrated its centenary in 2012 with a conference where not only its achievements but also its internal ideological divisions were discussed with the utmost openness.[20] An affiliated women's organisation, Aisyiyah, was founded as long ago as 1917. Muhammadiyah is marked by a high degree of internal democracy and administrative rationalisation. Unlike the Muslim Brotherhood (founded in Egypt in 1928, but later becoming a Pan-Arab network) it refrained from adopting a concerted oppositional stance. While Indonesia does have its own problems with violent Islamist extremism, it has escaped the hyper-politicisation of all aspects of life which has held back human development in the Middle East, and which intrudes on the everyday life of Muslims in many places elsewhere.

The precedents of Islamic Relief Worldwide in Britain, and Muhammadiyah in Indonesia, should inspire Muslims everywhere not only to think creatively about how to adapt their religious practices to modern exigencies but also to crystallise their new thinking in durable institutions. A vast Muslim public must be hoping for the emergence of alternatives to that religious conservatism whose loyalties to the *umma* (or global Muslim nation) the jihadis attempt to exploit. Sheikh Yusuf Qaradawi attained his dominant influence not only by means of his seductive oratory but also through a lifetime of building up institutions in different spheres—academic, financial, judicial, educational and charitable—as well as his media profile. Yet though he is opposed to violent offensive jihadism and though he claims (as noted above) to occupy a middle ground, Qaradawi's rhetoric is essentially authoritarian.[21] A commitment to institution building as strong as his will be needed if reinterpretations of Islamic doctrine, more compatible than Qaradawi's with the spirit of free enquiry, are to compete effectively with the traditionalist views. The message should be 'Don't agonise, organise.'[22] Determination and courage— sometimes physical as well as moral—will be needed to graduate from individual advocacy to the founding and expansion of new associations and media outlets; but the need and demand are certainly in place, and the reward could be epoch-making.

Current Reformist Movements

Efforts are indeed being made in the Islamic world to cultivate reformist institutions. Fetlullah Gülen, an Islamic intellectual and activist born in Turkey but now resident in Pennsylvania, has built up a major transnational movement including educational institutions and media resources.[23] It has encountered strong opposition in Turkey from both Islamic and secular political leaders. In September 2014, President Tayyip Erdogan accused the movement of setting up what he called a 'parallel state' within the country, and asked the USA to deport him to Turkey for questioning.[24] Meanwhile, in July the senior Islamic cleric in Turkey, Sheikh Mehmet Görmez, convened a meeting in Istanbul of over one hundred 'World Islamic Scholars for Peace, Moderation and Common Sense Initiative', arguing in his opening speech that, rather than pin all the blame for violence in the Muslim world on others, 'those who really have any sense of responsibility would care to look inside their own fold and make an analysis and come up with evaluations'.[25] Reportedly, Görmez attracted a large Iranian delegation, tapping into the Turkish traditions of Sunni and Shia coexistence by attracting Sufis from both sides; but two dominant Islamic nations, Egypt and Saudi Arabia, were not represented.[26] In March 2014, a rival 250-strong gathering was held in Abu Dhabi: the Forum for Promoting Peace in Muslim Societies, which led to the launch in July of the Muslim Council of Elders, presided over by the Grand Imam of Al-Azhar in Egypt, Sheikh Ahmed Al-Tayeb. This consortium is critical of both Wahhabism and the Muslim Brotherhood, favouring a 'political Sufism' which is also promoted by the Zaytuna College based in California, and which has elicited a sympathetic response from some American foreign policy experts.[27] Added to this mix, the possibility that Saudi Arabia may find ways to liberalise Wahhabism, the rigorist form of Islam that legitimates the royal house and its aged leaders, tempted to retreat into a moneyed theological laager, is one of the unknowns whose outcome will shape the future of the religion worldwide.

So, the challenge for Islamic reformers today is vastly more politically complicated than that which leaders of an ethno-religious minority responded to in the nineteenth century. But this surely makes the task all the more urgent.

Notes

1. Michael Cook, *Ancient Religions, Modern Politics: The Islamic case in comparative perspective* (Princeton: Princeton University Press, 2014).

2. See Jonathan Benthall, 'Qara□āwī, Yūsuf al-', *The Oxford Encyclopedia of Islam and Politics* (New York: Oxford University Press, 2014), vol. 2, 295–7.

3. Abdelwahab Meddeb, *Islam and its Discontents* (London: William Heinemann, 2003).

4. James Broucek, 'Colonialism and the Muslim World', *The Oxford Encyclopedia of Islam and Politics* (New York: Oxford University Press, 2014), vol. 1, 195–207.

5. Akbar Ahmed, *The Thistle and the Drone: How America's war on terror became a global war on tribal Islam* (Washington, DC: Brookings Institution Press), 2013.

6. Cook, *Ancient Religions, Modern Politics* (2014).

7. Jack Goody, *Renaissances: The one or the many?* (Cambridge: Cambridge University Press, 2013).

8. "Building a knowledge society", UNDP Arab Fund for Social and Economic Development, 2003, i.

9. For a useful anthology of articles by reformist Muslim thinkers, see Mehran Kamrava, ed., *The New Voices of Islam: Rethinking Politics and Modernity, A Reader* (Berkeley: University of California Press, 2006). Well-known contributors include Mohammed Arkoun, Fetlullah Gülen, Muhammad Shahrour, Nasr Abu Zaid, Leila Ahmed, Amina Wadud and Fatima Mernissi.

10. Dale Eickelman, 'Inside the Islamic Reformation', *Wilson Quarterly*, 22.1 (Winter 1998), 80–9, available online: http://www.l.u-tokyo.ac.jp/IAS/HP-e2/papers/eickelman.html. I asked Professor Eickelman recently whether he stood by his prediction, and he said yes, with emphasis on the 'one day' and a possible timeframe of three or four decades from now.

11. See: http://www.jewishvirtuallibrary.org/jsource/Judaism/pittsburgh_program.html Also Encyclopaedia Judaica, 1971, vol.14, 213–27. The suggestion that Islamic institutions might emulate the example of nineteenth century Reform Judaism was

advanced by Emanuel de Kadt at a seminar on religion and development at the University of Sussex in c. 2003. See his *Assertive Religion: Religious intolerance in a multicultural world* (New Brunswick: Transaction Publishers, 2013).

12. See: https://www.jewishvirtuallibrary.org/jsource/Judaism/Columbus_platform.html

13. Scott Morrison, 'Abduh, Mu☐ammad', *The Oxford Encyclopedia of Islam and Politics* (New York: Oxford University Press, 2014), vol.1, 9–14.

14. Ahmad Moussalli, p.593, 'Islamic Reform', *The Oxford Encyclopedia of Islam and Politics* (New York: Oxford University Press, 2014), vol.1, 592–4.

15. See Abdullahi Ahmed An-Na'im, *Islam and the Secular State: Negotiating the future of Shari'a* (Cambridge, MA.: Harvard University Press, 2008); George Packer, 'The moderate martyr: a radically peaceful vision of Islam', The New Yorker, 11 September 2006, http://www.newyorker.com/magazine/2006/09/11/the-moderate-martyr

16. See also Saba Mahmood, 'Secularism, hermeneutics, and empire: the politics of Islamic reformism', *Public Culture,* 18.2, 2006, 323–47.

17. I have argued elsewhere that Tariq Ramadan, one of the best-known Islamic intellectuals in Europe and the USA, is committed less to Islamic reformism than to reconciling his loyalty to Islamic orthodoxy with the humanities as they are understood in the West (for instance, in his refusal to totally condemn stoning of women convicted of adultery in certain countries such as Nigeria, despite there being no authority for lapidation in the Quran). As importantly for the argument of the present chapter, Ramadan has shown no talent for institution building. "Splits at the seams", review of Tariq Ramadan, *The Arab Awakening: Islam and the new Middle East, Times Literary Supplement*, 12 October 2012, 24–25. (This review also defended Ramadan against unfair criticism and saluted his personal courage.)

18. Cf. 'Blocking Faith, Freezing Charity: Chilling Muslim charitable giving in the war on terrorism financing' (New York: American Civil Liberties Union, 2009).

19. Jonathan Benthall, '"Cultural proximity" and the conjuncture of Islam with modern humanitarianism', in *Sacred Aid: Faith and Humanitarianism* (ed. Michael Barnett and Janice Stein, New York: Oxford University Press, 2012), 65–89. See also Jonathan Benthall, 'Islamic Relief Worldwide', *The Palgrave Dictionary of Transnational History* (Basingstoke: Palgrave Macmillan, 2009), 605–6. An umbrella group, the Muslim Charities Forum, was founded in Britain in 2007: https://www.muslimcharitiesforum.org.uk/

20. Muhammadiyah was founded by Ahmad Dahlan (1869–1923), under the influence of Egyptian religious reformers including Muhammad Abduh. See Claire-Marie Hefner, Report on International Research Conference on Muhammadiyah, Malang, Anthropology Today, 29:11, 2012, 27–28; Mitsuo Nakamura, *The Crescent Arises over the Banyan Tree: A Study of the Muhammadiyah Movement in a Central Javanese Town, c. 1910s–2010*, 2nd edition (Singapore: Institute of Southeast Asian Studies, 2012).

21. See Jacob Høigilt, *Islamist Rhetoric: Language and culture in contemporary Egypt* (London: Routledge, 2011).

22. The slogan is attributed to the American lawyer Florynce Kennedy (1916–2000), founder of the National Black Feminist Organization.

23. See M. Hakan Yavuz and John L. Esposito, eds, *Turkish Islam and the Secular State: The Gülen Movement* (Syracuse, NY: Syracuse University Press, 2003).

24. World Bulletin, 19 September 2014. Available at http://www.worldbulletin.net/media/144734/erdogan-accuses-gulen-movement-of-coup-attempt

25. http://www.diyanet.gov.tr/en/content/world-islamic-scholars-meet-for-peace/17095

26. Islam Affairs online magazine, 9 October 2014, 'The scramble for religious authority', http://islamaffairs.com/blog/scramble-religious-authority/

27. Islamopedia online, 5 September 2014, http://www.islamopediaonline.org/fatwa/ muslim-council-elders; Islam Affairs, 4 November 2014, http://islamaffairs.com/blog/ zaid-shakir-identity-reason-political-sufism/mu. See also Zeyno Baram, 'Understanding Sufism and its potential role in US policy', March 2004, World Organization for Resource Development and Education, available at http://www.worde.org/publications/ commentary/empowering_asj__sufi_muslim_networks/understanding-sufism-and-its-potential-role-in-u-s-policy/

29

The Religion Agenda: The Sahrawi Refugees and the Politics of Tolerance

ELIZABETH SHAKMAN HURD
NORTHWESTERN UNIVERSITY, USA

Introduction

In recent years, religion has moved from being considered marginal to the study of international relations and global order to assuming an increasingly prominent role in the discipline. The fragile consensus that states were to deal with religion internally began to crumble in the 1990s, and fell apart entirely after 9/11, as experts turned to religion as simultaneously a central problem to be resolved (the agenda of surveillance) and as its own solution (the agenda of reassurance). This is new religion agenda. Tony Blair has described it as the 'two faces of faith'.[1] This agenda has gained a prominent foothold in contemporary international public policy circles. Good religion should be restored to international affairs, it suggests, while bad religion should be reformed or eradicated. This approach privileges religion as the basis from which to formulate foreign policy, develop international public policy, and orientate human rights campaigns. It organises expert knowledge production and informs government and non-governmental decision-making in contemporary international affairs. It structures the global governance of religious diversity and shapes fields of social, political and religious practice and possibility in particular ways.[2] Following a brief introduction to this framework, this chapter examines the effects of the religion agenda in a specific context, that of Sahrawi refugees living in south-western Algeria, one of many contexts in which the global dynamics of good religion/bad religion have been brought to life. In the process, it introduces an approach to religion and world politics, developed in my forthcoming book , that interrogates the distinction between religion as construed for reasons of power, including the good/bad religion framework, and a broader field of social and religious practice of those without it.[3] This juxtaposition offers a glimpse of the politics of global advocacy for religious toleration by revealing the mixed consequences for many Sahrawi refugees of the representation of their camps as 'ideal spaces' occupied by religiously tolerant individuals.

The Two Faces of Faith and the Religion Agenda

The two faces of faith serves as shorthand for an interpretive frame, form of expert knowledge, and normative orientation that has provided the discursive scaffolding for much of the so-called return of religion to international affairs over the past two decades.[4] This template pre-structures the field in which many scholars and decision-makers, particularly in Europe and North America, approach and respond to questions involving religion and international public life in scholarly discussions, media conversations, and public policy debates. It serves as a reliable, easy to access language in which to speak about religion that provides a shared point of departure for public policy debates and discussions. It is now often taken for granted in such debates and discussions that irenic religion should be restored to international public life: cementing the moral foundations of international order, providing depth and moral sustenance to claims for international human rights, facilitating the spread of freedom, and promoting human flourishing through advocacy for inter-faith understanding. The return of peaceful religion is lauded as an overdue corrective to secularist attempts to quarantine benevolent religious actors and voices. In the words of Canadian Ambassador of Religious Freedom Andrew Bennett,

> In Canada and I'd say the liberal western democracies, we've pushed any expression of faith so far into the private sphere in the last half-century or so that we've sometimes forgotten how to have that faith-based discourse, and engage faith.[5]

Bennett and other advocates for the religion agenda seek to persuade their listeners that religion and religious actors are especially relevant to global politics because they are uniquely equipped to contribute to relief efforts, nation building, development, and peace building. Good religion is an agent of transformation. It is important and necessary for politics and public life to unfold democratically and for religious freedom to flourish globally. Religion 'done right' is an international public good. Tolerant faith-based leaders and authentic religious texts are said to be waiting expectantly in the wings, biding their time while they wait for the public authorities to come to their senses and grant religious voices and actors their proper place in international public life. Religious goods and actors are celebrated as contributors to global justice campaigns, engineers of peace building, agents of post-conflict reconciliation and countervailing forces to terrorism. With a little help from the authorities, the story goes, peaceful religion will triumph over its intolerant rivals.

This conciliatory side of the two faces narrative is reflected in international political projects of striking reach and variety. Global public policy areas subject to this framing include transitional justice efforts, human rights advocacy, development assistance, nation and public-capacity building efforts, religious engagement, humanitarian and emergency relief efforts, and foreign and military policy. Religion appears in this rendering as a potential problem and its own solution, insofar as interfaith cooperation, religious freedom and tolerance can be engendered and institutionalised and extremists marginalised. A proliferating number of generously funded projects are occupied with discerning and engaging peaceful religion and projecting it internationally through states, international tribunals, and international and non-governmental organisations. As this global infrastructure is put in place, a is taking shape.

Other global projects, and sometimes the same ones, are consumed by equally pressing efforts to identify and reform intolerant religion and ensure that it is not projected internationally. This less euphemistic side of the 'two faces' narrative is concerned with surveilling and disciplining intolerant and divisive religion. When it assumes such forms, it is claimed, religion becomes an object of securitisation and a target of legitimate violence. States are expected to work together with international authorities to contain or suppress dangerous and intolerant manifestations of politicised religion.[6] This fearful, restive religion is associated with the violent history of Europe's past and much of the rest of the world's religious present, including the wars of religion during the European Reformation and afterwards, and the intolerance and fanaticism associated with certain forms of what today is often named as religious extremism. Bad religion is understood to slip easily into violence, unlike peaceful religion, which curbs it. Bad religion is sectarian religion, and associated with the failure of the state to properly domesticate it—or, in some cases, of religion to properly domesticate itself.

The two faces of faith reproduce a number of conventions for conceptualising religion that have been discussed and deconstructed in recent years in an impressive literature that spans academic disciplines. Yet it is also distinctive, in some sense, in that religion is not only no longer private—as José Casanova argued in the 1990s—but also takes on specific new forms of publicity, demands new kinds of partnerships and presses forward new agendas with a surprising alacrity and remarkable degree of self-assurance. Initiatives pairing religious institutions and leaders with government offices are being launched, mandates for moral and spiritual reform are drafted and centres for interfaith understanding are built, all with great fanfare.[7] A small army of international public authorities with significant financial means and unflagging political will is awaiting an answer to the question of how to locate and promote tolerant, free religion.[8] Purveyors of the two faces narrative have an answer that has proven compelling to many concerned donors, governments, and other actors: certain religions, and certain forms of certain religions, need to be recognised, reorganised and rescued without delay from secularist condemnation and marginalisation.

Religious inputs and religious actors need to be named, promoted and propelled into the international public spotlight to serve as global problem-solvers. Others need to be disciplined, shunned, or reformed. In this view, religions and religious actors are identifiable. It is obvious who they are. They are inherently different and distinguishable from secular actors. And, importantly, they have allegedly been excluded. My own work questions these claims in favour of an alternative approach to contemporary religion in relation to global politics, law, and society. I have argued, for example, that religion has not been excluded but has assumed different forms and occupied difference spaces in different regimes of governance, often understood as secular.[9] I have suggested that religion might be approached as part of a complex and evolving, shifting series of fields of contemporary and historical practice that cannot be singled out from other aspects of human activity but also cannot be merely reduced to them. I have sought to resist the adoption of any singular, stable conception of religion, instead acknowledging the vast, diverse and shifting array of practices and histories that fall under the heading of religion as the term is used today.[10]

Yet the two faces model retains a certain appeal. It is easy to understand. It provides structure and simplicity for academics, advocates, bureaucrats, journalists, and others struggling to understand a world in which religious leaders, institutions and traditions appear to be gaining significance. It reduces complex social and historical fields, dizzying power relations and diverse and shifting fields of religious practice into a one-size-fits-all policy prescription that meets the needs of those with limited background or interest in religion. The recipe is simple: identify and empower the peaceful moderates and marginalise or reform the intolerant extremists. Many governments, think tanks, foundations, foreign policy pundits and self-proclaimed religion experts traffic in the baseline assumption that when religious moderates are identified and empowered—and fundamentalists identified and reformed—then the problems posed by extremist forms of religion will fade and religious freedom, rights, and toleration will spread unimpeded across the globe. This logic is being institutionalised, to varying degrees and in accordance with local elite sensibilities, in governments around the world, including the US State Department's Office of International Religious Freedom and, most recently, Office of Faith-Based Community Initiatives. The Europeans and Canadians are not far behind.

An important assumption underlying the two faces discourse is often overlooked in the excitement over the so-called return of religion. The two faces embodies the presumption that academic experts, government officials and foreign policy-makers, especially 'religious' ones, know more or less what religion is, where it is located, who speaks in its name, and how to incorporate 'it' into foreign policy and international public policy decision matrices. This questionable assumption enables academics, practitioners and pundits to leap straight into the business of quantifying religion's effects, adapting religion's insights to international problem-solving efforts, and incorporating religion's official representatives into international political decision-making, public policy and institutions. And this is precisely what they are doing. Governments, international organisations and even much of the academic literature on religion and international relations treat religion as a relatively stable, self-evident category that is understood to motivate a host of actions, both good and bad.

My book suggests that religion is not an isolatable entity and should not be treated as such, whether in an attempt to separate it from law and politics or to design a political response to it. Any attempt to single out religion as a platform from which to develop law and public policy inevitably privileges some religions over others, leading to what Lori Beaman and Winnifred Sullivan have described as 'varieties of religious establishment'.[11] Scholars and practitioners working internationally and comparatively need to consider the implications of this critique, and work to embed the study of religion in a series of more complex social and interpretive fields. This requires disaggregating and complicating the category of religion in relation to politics, culture, law and society. It requires considering what the world looks life after we move beyond the ideology of separation. It involves exploring the disjuncture between the forms of official religion that are sanctioned by expert knowledge and produced through specific acts of legal, constitutional and governmental advocacy for religious freedom, tolerance and rights, on the one hand, and the various forms of religion lived by ordinary people, on the other. While these fields overlap and are always entangled with each other, and also with institutional religion, in complex formations, they cannot be collapsed entirely, as is often the case in contemporary international scholarly and policy discussions on religion and politics.

Legal and political advocacy for specific conceptions of religious freedom, tolerance and the rights of religious minorities shape both religion and politics in context-specific and variable ways. These efforts stand neither outside history nor above politics. At the same time, and critically, local practices often work outside of, exceed and confound the utopian legal, political and religious imperatives associated with the ambitious aspirations of the religion agenda. Exploring the consequences of distinguishing in specific contexts between religion as construed for reasons of power, and religion as lived by those without it, calls into question the stability of the category of religion that anchors both the agenda of reassurance and the agenda of surveillance. Attempts to realise religious freedom, religious tolerance and religious rights both shape and constrain religious possibilities on the ground.

The Good Sahrawi and the Politics of Religious Tolerance

Located in Tindouf province in south-western Algeria, the Sahrawi refugee camps were established in the mid-1970s to accommodate Sahrawis fleeing Moroccan forces during the Western Sahara War. Situated on a flood-prone desert plane known as 'The Devil's Garden' with limited access to water and scarce vegetation, and governed by the Polisario Front, the camps depend almost entirely upon foreign aid. In this context, European and North American constructs of good religion, bad religion, progressive Muslims, religious freedom and inter-faith dialogue—all constructs associated with the religion agenda—have shaped both transnational and intra-Sahrawi politics.

According to Elena Fiddian-Qasmiyeh, the Polisario has

> successfully projected the Sahrawi camps as 'ideal' spaces inhabited by 'good' refugees, in part by reflecting mainstream European and North American normative preferences for the development of a 'good' and 'progressive' Islam.[12]

In interactions with non-Sahrawi audiences and potential donors, particularly those from Europe and North America, she explains, Polisario leaders make reference to notions of secularism and religious tolerance in an effort to represent the ideal nature of the camps and their inhabitants to audiences that are presumably primed to react positively to these terms. Yet this projection is only one among several different representations of the refugees in the leadership's repertoire, and which representation is utilised in any given interaction depends on the audience. This strategy enables the Polisario leadership to tap into a substantial and diverse array of political and financial support both inside and outside the camps. Supporters provide material aid and engage in lobbying campaigns in their home countries on behalf of the Polisario's political objectives. The latter involves most notably the attempt to reclaim a degree of sovereign authority over Western Sahara from the Moroccan government, which has controlled the disputed territory for four decades. From the late 1800s until the mid-1970s, when the Polisario Front launched an armed rebellion, the territory was occupied by Spain and known as the Spanish Sahara. Under pressure from Morocco and the US, Spain reneged on its promise of independence and in 1975 agreed to a joint Moroccan and Mauritanian occupation, later exclusively Moroccan. Half the Sahrawi population subsequently fled into Algeria and became the refugees they remain today. The US continues to support Morocco's refusal to hold a referendum on independence, while the UN formally recognises Western Sahara as a non-self-governing territory—Africa's last colony.[13]

From the perspective of the global politics of religious tolerance, the strength of Fiddian-Qasmiyeh's account lies in her focus on a triangular set of relationships that have evolved between evangelical humanitarian groups (the Defense Forum Foundation, Christ the Rock Community Church and Christian Solidarity Worldwide-USA) that are active in the camps, Polisario leaders and the Sahrawi people.[14] There is a particularly tight connection linking the Polisario and the evangelical humanitarian groups. As Fiddian-Qasmiyeh explains, 'the Polisario's determination to activate not only evangelists' humanitarian assistance but also their political support is arguably, at least in part, as a result of these organations' proven dedication and efficiency in so prominently lobbying on behalf of "the Sahrawi people"'.[15] The Sahrawi's purported 'religious tolerance' is a critical ingredient in this alliance. Fiddian-Qasmiyeh observes, for example, that Defense Forum Foundation representative and pro-Sahrawi activist Suzanne Scholte:

> has widely transmitted accounts of the Sahrawi's receptivity to Christianity and overarching religious tolerance in the international arena, including before the US Congress and the UN Decolonization Committee on numerous occasions since 2002. ... Several other evangelists have lobbied for the Polisario on Capitol Hill and before the UN Decolonization Committee, including (in October 2009) Dan Stanley, senior pastor from RockFish Church, who reportedly led the first prayer session in the camps, and Cheryl Banda and Janet Lenz from Christ the Rock Community Church.[16]

This supportive relationship between the Polisario and their foreign humanitarian supporters also generates particular forms of intra-Sahrawi politics. As Fiddian Qasmiyeh explains, 'the international celebration of the Sahrawi refugee camps' success is ... directly associated with and even dependent upon the concealment, or discursive minimisation, of everyday Muslim identity, practice and institutions'.[17] Maintaining the appearance of 'religious tolerance' depends upon what she describes as a 'tyranny of tolerance'—or 'system of -entation, which purposefully centralises certain groups, identifiers and dynamics while simultaneously displacing and marginalising those which challenge official accounts of the camps.'[18] Journalist Timothy Kustusch's description of a 2008 interfaith dialogue session in the camps confirms this, noting that 'to avoid potential tension, only a few political leaders from the Polisario Front (the independence movement of the Sahrawi people), local religious leaders and volunteers from Christ The Rock were invited'.[19] As Fiddian-Qasmiyeh explains, 'the Sahrawi 'audience' was restricted to those who had already officially demonstrated their allegiance to the official script of "tolerance"'.[20] Dissenting, unofficial scripts were inadmissible. Janet Lenz, founder of Christ The Rock's Sahrawi project, observed of the session that, 'while a few of the attendees at the inaugural session did attempt to debate, the proceedings were for the most part peaceful and cordial'. For Lenz, the achievement of tolerance and peacefulness hinge on what Fiddian-Qasmiyeh identifies as 'the repression of "debate" or contestation on-stage, recreating the camps as spaces of unequivocal acceptance of the religious Other'.[21]

There is an interesting tension between religious tolerance as construed by the Polisario-evangelical axis of cooperation, on the one hand, and those Sahrawis whose 'individual, familial and collective priorities and concerns may be irrevocably different from those of Polisario and evangelical actors alike' on the other.[22] This Polisario–international humanitarian axis of cooperation leaves little or no space for dissenting Sahrawi voices to be heard, not only when confronted with non-Sahrawi audiences but also, and critically, within the Sahrawi community itself:

> Although the Polisario has the potential to 'ingratiate themselves' with their supporters through representations of the camps as unique spaces of religious freedom and tolerance and of 'the Sahrawi people' as inherently welcoming of evangelical groups, these performances equally have the potential to create an irreconcilable rupture not only with other, non-evangelical donors (including 'secular' Spanish 'Friends of the Sahrawi'), but also between the Polisario and the very refugees which this organization purports to represent. The enactment of such debates and contestations, however, is suppressed in the camps via strategies of entation which limit the audibility, visibility and very presence of those actors whose individual, familial and collective priorities and concerns may be diametrically opposed to those of key donors and the Polisario alike.[23]

These particular Sahrawi refugees' lack of voice and agency in these circumstances illustrates who and what is excluded when international religious freedom, tolerance and inter-faith dialogue—and the material benefits that follow in their wake for those in a position to claim them— capture the field of emancipatory possibility as unchallengeable political and social goods in a particular context.[24] These dynamics are central to the politics of the religion agenda, which is distinguished by a strong commitment to the global realisation of these purportedly universal goods and goals.[25]

The diverse experiences and complex power relations uncovered by Fiddian-Qasmiyeh speak to the potential of discriminating analytically between religious tolerance, freedom, and rights as construed by those in power and the practices of ordinary people who are subjected to these techniques of governance. Doing so reveals a gap or tension between expert and 'governed' religion—heuristics described in more detail in my book—and the practices of ordinary people who often experience complex and shifting relationships to the institutions, orthodoxies and authorities that allegedly represent them, whether understood as secular, religious or neither. The Sahrawi case also speaks to the transformative effect of a particular conception of 'religious tolerance', cemented in a political partnership between external supporters and local Polisario leaders, on the lives of potential dissenters and others not in power, in this case the average refugee. Finally, it attests to the value of attempts to apprehend Sahrawi practices and histories on their own terms, even or especially to the extent that they appear as unintelligible or illegible to legal and normative frames such as religious tolerance or religious freedom, rather than seeking to assimilate them into these templates. This may be, in part, what Markus Dressler and Arvind Mandair are referring to when they call for releasing the 'space of the political from the grasp of the secularisation doctrine'.[26] Doing so allows us to bring international human (and religious) rights advocacy back into history,[27] acknowledging its debts to particular histories and conceptions of secularity, tolerance, subjectivity and religion. To fail to do so is risk remaining within, and reproducing, the specific discourses of religious tolerance, freedom and rights purveyed by those in power. It risks losing sight of diverse aspects of Sahrawi, and many other histories and experiences, beyond religious freedom.

Notes

1. Tony Blair, 'Taking Faith Seriously' *New Europe Online*, January 2, 2012.
2. As Courtney Bender observes, 'insofar as religious "freedoms" appear to operate outside of the articulation of various state powers in social scientific models of religious pluralism, they emerge as free-floating tools, strategies, and "capacities" that can be exported or that can be used to judge the religious lives of individuals and groups in

other parts of the world.' Bender, 'Secularism and Pluralism', unpublished paper, June 2012.

3. Elizabeth Shakman Hurd, *Beyond Religious Freedom: The New Global Politics of Religion* (Princeton: Princeton University Press, forthcoming 2015).

4. Elizabeth Shakman Hurd, 'International Politics after Secularism', *Review of International Studies* 38, Issue 5, Special Issue, 'The Postsecular in International Relations' (December 2012): 943-961.

5. Olivia Ward, 'Meet Canada's Defender of the Faiths', The Toronto Star, February 14, 2014.

6. See for example the Report of the Chicago Council on Global Affairs, 'Engaging Religious Communities Abroad: A New Imperative for US Foreign Policy', Report of the Task Force on Religion and the Making of US Foreign Policy, Scott Appleby and Richard Cizik, co-chairs (Chicago: February 2010). Peter Danchin sums up the Report's recommendations: 'the strategy proposed in the report is thus to continue to kill religious extremists while simultaneously engaging Muslim communities through all possible bilateral and multilateral means—through, e.g., the machinery brought into existence by the International Religious Freedom Act of 1998 (IRFA) or international organizations such as the UN and its specialized agencies.' Danchin, 'Good Muslim, Bad Muslim', *The Immanent Frame*, April 21, 2010.

7. An example is the KAICIID Dialogue Centre (King Abdullah Bin Abdulaziz International Centre for Interreligious and Intercultural Dialogue), located in Vienna, which according to its website 'was founded to enable, empower and encourage dialogue among followers of different religions and cultures around the world'. The Centre describes itself, rather improbably, as 'an independent, autonomous, international organisation, free of political or economic influence'.

8. In some sense, Casanova's *Public Religions in the Modern World* (Chicago: University of Chicago Press, 1994) may be seen as having opened the floodgates for public consumption and eventual acceptance of this narrative.

9. Elizabeth Shakman Hurd, *The Politics of Secularism in International Relations* (Princeton: Princeton University Press, 2008).

10. Elizabeth Shakman Hurd, 'The Specific Order of Difficulty of Religion', *The Immanent Frame*, May 30, 2014.

11. Lori G. Beaman and Winnifred Fallers Sullivan, eds., *Varieties of Religious Establishment* (London: Ashgate, 2013).

12. Elena Fiddian-Qasmiyeh, 'The Pragmatics of Performance: Putting "Faith" in Aid in the Sahrawi Refugee Camps', *Journal of Refugee Studies* Vol. 24, no. 3 (2011): 537.

13. Stephen Zunes, 'The Last Colony: Beyond Dominant Narratives on the Western Sahara Roundtable', Jadaliyya, June 3, 2013.

14. Working in the camps since 1999, Christ the Rock provides US summer host families for Saharawi children, teaches English in the Smara camp, and develops programs to 'build bridges between people in the United States and Saharawis forced to live in the arid Saharan Desert'. Timothy Kustusch, 'Muslim Leaders and Christian Volunteers Host Religious Dialogues in Saharawi Camps', UPES, April 2, 2009.

15. Fiddian-Qasmiyeh, 'Pragmatics of Performance', 539.

16. Ibid., 539.

17. Ibid., 537.

18. Ibid., 542.

19. Kustusch, 'Muslim Leaders and Christian Volunteers Host Religious Dialogues'.

20. Fiddian-Qasmiyeh, 'Pragmatics of Performance', 542.

21. Ibid 542.

22. Ibid 544.

23. Ibid., 544, citing Barbara Harrell-Bond, 'The Experience of Refugees as Recipients of Aid', in *Refugees: Perspectives on the Experience of Forced Migration*, edited by Alastair Ager (London: Pinter, 1999): 136–168.

24. Wendy Brown makes a related argument in *Regulating Aversion: Tolerance in the Age of Identity and Empire* (Princeton: Princeton University Press, 2008). For a perceptive attempt to rethink and refashion the theory and practice of tolerance in western democracies see Lars Tønder, *Tolerance: A Sensorial Orientation to Politics* (Oxford: Oxford University Press, 2013).

25. For a reconsideration of these efforts see the publications of the Luce Foundation-supported project, Politics of Religious Freedom: Contested Norms and Local Practices, including the forthcoming volume *Politics of Religious Freedom*, edited by Winnifred Fallers Sullivan, Elizabeth Shakman Hurd, Saba Mahmood and Peter Danchin (Chicago: University of Chicago Press, 2015).

26. Markus Dressler and Arvind Mandair, 'Introduction: Modernity, Religion-Making, and the Postsecular', in *Secularism and Religion-Making*, edited by Markus Dressler and Arvind-Pal Mandair (Oxford: Oxford University Press, 2011), 18. Dressler and Mandair describe three distinct trajectories in the critique of secularity: '(i) the socio-political philosophy of liberal secularism exemplified by Charles Taylor (and to some extent shared by thinkers such as John Rawls and Jürgen Habermas); (ii) the postmodernist critiques of ontotheological metaphysics by radical theologians and continental philosophers that have helped to revive the discourse of political theology; (iii) following the work of Michel Foucault and Edward Said, the various forms of discourse analysis focusing on genealogies of power most closely identified with the work of Talal Asad'. Ibid., 4.

27. Samuel Moyn, *The Last Utopia: Human Rights in History* (Cambridge: Belknap Press, 2010).

Conclusion

'Nations under God': Problems of Meaning in Contemporary Rhetoric

TIMOTHY FITZGERALD
UNIVERSITY OF STIRLING, UK

Introduction[1]

The title of this collection was well chosen by the editors, because it invites consideration of the many problematic terms and images commonly deployed in Anglophone discourse and amplified throughout the media. Given that so much of the media is, understandably, preoccupied at this historical moment with the turbulence occurring in states with large Muslim populations, many readers will immediately if not exclusively think of 'Islam'. The expression, 'nations under God', immediately conveys vivid images that the reader might involuntarily imagine: TV images of 'the Middle East' full of sand and violence; 'failed states'—Iraq, Libya, Iran, Egypt, Palestine and Syria; incessant turbulence and war; of presumably oppressed women wrapped in the allegedly dehumanising burqa; and of strange, bearded men shouting 'Allah' while shooting guns.

I am not saying that these images are necessarily confined to Islamic contexts. They arguably represent a more basic discourse that legitimates rational liberal modernity against all perceived forms of backwardness and irrational barbarity. Whether the topic is occasioned by Muslim or some other militancy, there is a discourse on 'religion' or 'faith' and 'its' propensity to irrational violence, a discourse that tacitly constructs our rational, liberal civility compared to their medieval barbarity, and our secular, logical reasonableness compared to their wild inability to settle their differences through negotiation, free market relations and respect for private property.[2] Whereas we are modest, peace loving and only reluctantly violent, they are lost in superstition and the authors of their own misery.

Liberal journalists and academics, in our largely sincere attempts at factual reportage, tend unconsciously to reproduce these ancient 'us and them' narratives. Recently, such a wide and deep stream of Europhone media propaganda received stimulation by the 'revival' of the 'medieval Caliphate' by a group called ISIS (the Islamic State of Iraq and the Levant). The idea that the contemporary declaration of a new caliphate straddling the Iraq-Syria border is a 'medieval revival' feeds into the wider discourse sketched above. In Europhone discourse, the medieval is the pre-modern, and the opposition between the modern and the medieval, like that between modernity and tradition, is a conceit that derives from the European enlightenment assumption. We are modern and progressive; they are traditional, medieval and backward.

But this self-serving presumption about the progress of nations is an illusion that has become transformed by various rhetorical devices into common sense reality. There is no neutral observational data from which we can infer that Euro-American ideas, goals or policies represent progress or enlightenment. It is as much an unfounded belief or act of faith as the Millenarian belief in the second coming.

This problem of the habitual reproduction of collective self-delusion is not confined to International Relations (IR). 'Nations', 'God', 'Geopolitics' and 'Faith' are all typically deployed in academic discourse and public rhetoric as though their meanings are self-evident, universal and ahistorical. This problem stems in part from the Enlightenment assumption that European secular rationality, classification systems, and science of political economy are (or ambiguously *ought to be*) universal in their application. Arguably this kind of claim to universal truth already existed in both Catholic and Protestant discourses and self-representations, exemplified in the belief that pagan peoples must be converted to save their souls and teach them proper governance and how to be civilised. Such a disposition seems to have found its way into the narrative of Euro-American enlightenment and progress.

Colonial and neo-colonial power has always been as much about cognitive and linguistic imposition as military. In the interests of global communication, it might be held that all languages ought to be translatable into a universal language, which just happens to be European. But the 'just happens to be' is itself part of our problem.

Arguably, however, there is also a more general process at work. There is a tendency for abstract categories with a very general application to become attributed with misplaced concreteness, transformed into reifications, things that seem to exist objectively beyond their conventional (and contested) deployment. Imaginaries that are useful to think with become transmuted into common sense reality that it is eccentric or even irresponsible to question. While we need general categories to think with, some are invested with a priority that reflects the dominant interests of powerful institutions and classes. The literate male elites that governed the Roman Catholic Church for centuries have invested specific concepts with huge importance, and these have been policed and violations punished. This theme can presumably be extended widely and globally, because all power formations need to appear legitimate to those with and to those without power. Hegemonic imaginaries in all their varieties are presumably identifiable in situations of actual or potential conflicts of interest. We can describe this tendency as the transformation of imagined orders of power into the self-evidently real, of desired forms of domination into unquestionable legitimacy.

Categories that today sustain our own myths of the modern—such as the distinction between religion (either irrational or merely non-rational 'faith') and the nonreligious secular (rational science and realistic politics)—are policed by a range of agencies, not only the media, politicians and the academics, but also including constitutions and the courts. It is surely dangerous when foreign policy experts, diplomats and military leaders uncritically internalise our myths about what is good for everyone.

The problem with these general categories and their conscious or unconscious representation as neutral and universal goes well beyond International Relations. One can even find the problem in Edward Said's groundbreaking work, *Orientalism*, and the postcolonial and subalternist paradigms that it ably helped to generate. Said and postcolonial theorists hardly deconstruct secular reason in its dichotomous relation to religion, though this step seems perfectly compatible with their position and would represent a legitimate extension of their work.[3]

IR is a crucially important discipline, being concerned with global communications and understandings and having a fairly direct influence on the thinking of powerful agencies in the international arena. In this sense, IR is a potent agency for the reproduction of hegemonic discourse. In Althusser's terms, it is an ideological state apparatus. Yet an IR critical of the kind that will perhaps be welcomed in this book might contribute powerfully to its unravelling.

Nations under God

To unravel hegemonic liberal discourse requires us to pay critical attention to the disguised ideological functions of some of our most widely deployed categories in their apparent innocence. We can begin in the title with the problematic term 'God' in the expression 'Nations under God'. This word, 'God', is not innocent and cannot provide us with a neutral category for describing or analysing anything. It is an empty signifier that acts as the binary opposite of 'the world', which is also a metaphysical imaginary with no essential content. The rhetorical illusion that this binary generates is that, whereas God is purely imaginary, the world is empirically encountered in our everyday experience. However, we do not encounter 'the world' in our everyday experience. For 'the world' is *everything* in empirical experience, and therefore nothing.

This God–World binary oscillates along the same axis as 'the supernatural' in binary opposition to 'the natural', 'faith' in opposition to 'knowledge', and 'religion' in opposition to non-religious secular reason. One empty binary stands in for all the rest, protects the whole series from critical deconstruction, and holds us in circular reasoning.

In Anglo-American and Europhone Enlightenment discourse more widely, 'God' has historically been derived from Christian theology(ies). Within the history of Christian theology the meaning of 'God' has been contested bitterly between different confessional states and has entailed extreme punishment for what the powerful have considered heretical misrepresentation. We cannot know what it means to say that some person or group has belief in God, or belongs to a faith community, unless we are clear about the meaning of the key terms both for us and for them. The authoritative transmission of the true meaning of God understood as monotheistic, Trinitarian and Christological has been the central topic of many of the controversies throughout the history of the Catholic Church, the Orthodox Church, and the various churches founded since the Reformation. The true meaning of God has required persuasive argumentation, creedal and liturgical definition and policing by various authorities, and does not offer a ready-made, neutral descriptive and analytical concept. In fact we could say that there is no true meaning of 'God' outside someone's (or some community's) assertion that there is.

I am not an expert on Islam, but my understanding is that for at least some important Muslim theologians, Trinitarian doctrine is polytheistic and thus an error, a kind of paganism. If this is the case, then Christian monotheistic belief in God (even if there were any one meaning attributable to these terms) would not be the same as what many Muslims understand by Allah.

Restriction of the use of the term God to monotheism or monotheistic systems does not solve the problem but further extends it, requiring an agreed understanding of what does and does not constitute a monotheistic idea—as distinct from a polytheistic, pantheistic, monistic, deistic or henotheistic one. Beliefs that the Catholic and Protestant authorities have deemed to be pantheistic, or those that deny the ontological identity of God the Father and God the Son, have been proscribed as pagan heresies. Given the history of bitter contestations around the term 'God', it is difficult to see how it could ever be considered useful as a neutral descriptive or analytical concept.

God, Gods and Goddesses

Use of the term 'God' as if it is a neutral descriptive concept generates further problems when one considers the related term 'gods' and 'goddesses' in the plural. Even in Anglophone discourse, it is difficult if not impossible to know quite what these terms can mean. What is a god? So much can be included that the term is rendered vague at best and at worst incoherent. Virtually anything that someone or some group somewhere deems special, sacred or of deep significance in their life or lives can be and has been termed a god. Our liberal secular gods are self-interest, capital, private property and money.[4] Durkheim and many since him have argued that the Individual is the dominant modern 'sacred'.[5] These are all abstractions transformed into objects of faith, the hope of salvation and striving for generations of believers, collective imaginaries transposed into sacred realities and policed by various agencies. The illusions of Euro-American progress and development are other objects of devotion; so is the sacred nation-state and its territory.[6] However, where there is no limit to the content of a concept, and where 'religion' is used to encompass belief in a constitutionally 'secular' state, then the point of making the distinction at all seems to get lost and becomes questionable if not vacuous.

Natural, Unnatural and Supernatural

One strategy that is evident in much contemporary rhetoric on God or gods has been to fall back on the distinctions between the 'supernatural' and the 'natural'. This move does not solve the problem, because nobody can claim to know definitely what either of these terms means or how to distinguish between them.

To take the term 'nature' or 'natural', one might ask what is *not* natural? There does seem to be a useful distinction to make between the natural and the artificial, for in many contexts it is important to know if there is a conscious human intention behind an occurrence. However, this would not typically be taken to mean that an artificial, consciously produced factor is *unnatural*. For biologists and other scientists (I suppose) everything is natural and can be explained in naturalistic terms. Even those scientists that accord a degree of explanatory autonomy to 'society' would be likely to give the final reduction to nature, understood as evolutionary adaptation for the purposes of survival and reproduction of the genes. But then in this case the term 'nature' and 'natural' appears to encompass everything that can be known.

To some people, homosexuality is an *unnatural* act, but this is a moral judgment and typically depends on a specific tradition of value judgments. On the other hand, a biologist might claim that homosexuality is natural and can be given a factual, naturalistic explanation—in terms of genetic inheritance, for example. Many biologists might be committed to the view that not only homosexuality but everything can be given a naturalistic interpretation, at least in principle. But if this is the case, then the terms 'natural' and 'naturalistic' seem to become less useful. If everything can in the final analysis be explained as part of nature, then why would a biologist or physicist need to refer at all to nature or the natural? What more is being tacitly asserted by the propensity to refer to nature?

Another person might answer the same question—what is not natural? —by claiming that some events are *supernatural*. But such a claim itself depends on a specific theory of the supernatural, often conveyed in a theological or philosophical system, and representing a specific and contested viewpoint. The meaning of terms like supernatural and natural, and the supposed relations between them, have been conceived in radically different ways in Thomist-Aristotelian, Deist, and empiricist or positivist systems respectively. In Thomist-Aristotelian thought, the supernatural is the ultimately real, and nature is encompassed at a lower level of creation. In modern secular empiricist and positivist thought, the secular is *essentially* different from the religious, as faith is to knowledge, etc.

Many peoples reportedly make no such distinction. Scholars in religious studies, anthropology, philosophy and the social sciences, in their attempts to formulate a neutral descriptive concept, have been unable to agree on the meaning of supernatural (as with so many other critical terms) and some have consequently played with alternatives such as superhuman. But such a move requires a clear understanding of what 'human' means and how far beyond is 'super'. In ordinary language a nuclear explosion could be described as a force that is superhuman, but we wouldn't typically describe it as beyond nature. If we cannot give a clear answer to the question about the meaning of supernatural, then the meaning of natural is also indeterminate.

When biologists and physicists deny the existence of God, how do they or we know what they are denying? Or what anyone is affirming by claiming such an existence? How to articulate a clear and universal distinction between the natural and supernatural is thus deeply problematic, and attempts to define God or gods in terms of supposed distinctions between natural and supernatural lead to an endless circularity.

God, Gods and Problems of Translation

The concepts of God, gods and goddesses also involve accompanying problems of translation. Deployment of the term is often assumed without argument to indicate an essential meaning that can be translated into different formulations in non-European languages. Some well-known examples of this are the uses of God or gods/goddesses for Allah in Arabic, Yahweh in Hebrew, Brahman in Sanskrit, deva/devi and devata in Sanskrit, kami in Japanese, and so on.

Any intended or unintended importation of Christian, Trinitarian, monotheistic, incarnational meanings of 'God' into non-European and non-Christian contexts is likely to distort what other people want to say and believe and mean. If we take the Japanese term kami as one example of a non-European term that is frequently translated as god or gods, in different contexts it can refer to mythical persons, living human persons, ancestors, enlightened beings, shamanistic spirits, entities such as trees, waterfalls, mountains and rivers, the sun and the moon, and so on.[7] Much the same can be said about the vast range of what might be called deva and devi in India or South Asia more widely. Only sustained contextual analysis can hope to determine what meaning is being attributed to such multivalent terms in any specific and relevant situation.

It is highly problematic to attribute a belief in the supernatural to people who use such terms as kami or devi. Is *ganga*, the goddess who is also the river Ganges, supernatural or natural? One would need to enter complex debates between Hindu pilgrims and natural scientists (often the same people) about the meaning of a claim that the Ganges is a goddess—or what it would mean to call it part of nature. If we cannot find a clear meaning for supernatural in our own discourses, then the problem of translating the term and its supposed opposite 'natural' into Sanskrit (or Tamil, Chinese, Japanese, etc.) seems even more unlikely.

Geopolitics of Faith

The 'Geopolitics of Faith' referenced in the title may trip off the tongue in some circles, but even a cursory examination renders it hard to understand.

Are people who are attributed by self-confessing secularists with 'faith' really in a different category from people with faith in secular reason? Is the secular science of economics based on knowledge rather than faith? Or is economics itself a form of faith, even when economists proclaim themselves to be scientists in an empirical field of research? Liberal faith in free markets, which are aspirations and not observable facts, is not essentially different from faith in the providential designs of the Christian triune Godhead. Yes, they are different, but they can both be legitimately described in ordinary language as acts of faith in unobservable postulates.

In much of today's public and academic rhetoric, faith is in binary opposition to knowledge, just as religion is to secular political economy. The people who charge others with having 'faith', or living in a faith community, also may want to tacitly convey that they themselves do not, because moderns don't live by faith but by science. This may not be an intended implication, but it can easily be read as such because it forms part of a discourse with a long history: they have religion but we have science, they are backward whereas we are progressive, they have the medieval caliphate but we have modern nation-states, they are not yet fully rational but we are. This faith-knowledge binary, when challenged or elaborated, is substituted by others such as religion and science, supernatural and natural, God and the real world, myth and fact, blind belief as against empirical observation. These binaries form a self-perpetuating, self-referential, and circular system that ensures the ongoing viability of the rhetorical construct in the face of any possible challenge. Thus, all of these terms are parasitic on each other in one way or another and are protected from exposure as empty postulates.

One of the effects of these binary, either–or formulations (it is either faith or it is knowledge, it is either religion or it is science, it is either their uncomprehending fanaticism or it is our reasonable and measured defence of our own interests) is to create essentialising distinctions. Yet it is hard to see in ordinary language how we could imagine any science without acts of faith being involved, or any belief that does not involve a claim to knowledge.

Arguably, all systems of thought are dependent on categories that are themselves not based on empirical observation. Has anyone actually seen a nation-state? Or a society? Or a self-regulating market? Or a religion? These are all abstract constructs with specific histories of emergence since the Enlightenment. What constitutes knowledge has been deeply contested historically, even among self-identifying scientists, and is the matter of unresolved epistemological debate. To assume that there is a world of faith, or several systems of faith, from which secular science or liberal political economy are excluded is to presume too much.

The term 'geopolitics' attempts (very roughly speaking) to link and analyse conflicts of power to specific geographical spaces and control of specific areas of land, air and sea. Maps are presumably important representations of geopolitical knowledge, but maps are contested, because there is an issue about who draws them and who controls their authoritative interpretation.

In the general formulation 'geopolitics', the term politics takes on a universal and ahistorical meaning such as power struggles or conflicts of interest. It strikes a tone of realism, facing the actual ongoing conditions of scarce resources in rational and pragmatic ways.

However, the public and academic discourse on politics enfolds beneath its appearance of universal neutrality a very different and more historically and ideologically specific nuance. The English term politics is not ahistorical or universal. It was invented as a consistent discourse in the seventeenth century to demarcate a domain of governance or 'political society' essentially distinct from 'religion'. In this myth, religion ought to be kept out of governance because religion (in contradistinction to what was, at that time, the normal and orthodox understanding of religion as encompassing Christian truth) is a private affair of men's hearts and consciences (I use the gendered language deliberately) and has (or ambiguously ought to have) nothing to do with the public arena of policy. In developing his own myth of man in the state of nature and the rational accumulation of private property, Locke introduced an either–or binary that has become an habitual part of our own thinking: it is either rational politics concerned fundamentally with the protection of natural rights—especially the right to private property, and thus in the domain of elected representation; or it is religious faith that is essentially private and divorced from power. Locke's myth had an elective affinity with the interests of powerful white male property owners in North America and found its way into the US Constitution.

Even if the reader wishes to question the precise historical origin of the religion–politics binary, what cannot be doubted is that the term politics today includes the highly contestable assumption that it is non-religious secular, which implies that in its 'real nature' (the nature of politics) it is separate and separable from a distinct domain of religion. Religion in turn and in its 'real nature' has nothing to do with power. Religions and faith communities do not, or ought not to have, political agendas. Religion and politics don't mix. Irrational violence results if they become confused. One of the marks of western progress and reasonableness is that we keep religion out of politics, but unfortunately others have not yet become sufficiently intelligent to understand this, and our tutelage must continue until they do.

As with so many of the other categories discussed in this chapter, politics and the state, and their distinction from something called religion, is imaginary, yet it is proclaimed by written constitutions, policed by the courts, the media, by prominent politicians and scientists, and reproduced in the disciplinary structures of the universities. This is the ambiguous content of politics: on the one hand it is a neutral and universally valid term for human conflict and its resolution, or power in general; yet it is also a key category in a historically specific power formation, a dominant discourse of liberal secular civility and rationality. These two faces give the term marvellous resonance and flexibility. All interventions by the US and other western powers that are deemed as well-meaning, pragmatic attempts to reduce violence in various regions and introduce the rational techniques of problem-solving and good governance turn out also to be impositions of alien values and language categories on peoples who are just as intelligent as us, and who have their own resources for dealing with their own problems, if only the self-serving western powers would end our interminable and misread interventions in their affairs.

The Internalisation of Anglophone Discourse

One other complicating factor that ought to be mentioned is that the Anglophone formulations and vocabulary, along with their concealed ambiguities, have been internalised in different ways and to different degrees by the elites of other countries. To communicate to the US government or other US and international agencies requires deployment of English (or French) language categories This could mean that the elite in question to some extent agrees with the US ideals and demands, or it could mean that they are forced by translation problems to say one thing to the Americans and another to their own and neighbouring people. The Americans and their acolytes then accuse the elite in question of hypocrisy.

A good example of this problem is when a mullah or the Dalai Lama is first categorised as a 'religious' leader and then accused of illegitimately dabbling in 'politics'. Or alternatively he is described as a political leader pretending to be a religious one. This inscribes without any argument the assumption that needs to be questioned. Recently the Dalai Lama has adopted these very categories for self-description (I am a religious leader, not a politician) and has proclaimed the need for Tibet to have a constitution that separates religion from the secular state.[8] This is probably not a cynical move but a bid for survival by a revered leader of Tibetan people in a power game in which he holds little power. When invited to Taiwan to perform Buddhist rites for the dead, the Chinese tried to stop him on the grounds that he is not a 'pure religious leader' but someone who dabbles in politics—a troublemaker. This was all reported in English in the *Japan Times* whose sources were East Asian news agencies[9].

Yet, despite the high stakes for millions of ordinary lives, these terms have little clear meaning in English. Written constitutions such as the US, Indian or Japanese (and many others) provide a right to freedom of religion but also seek to protect the secular state from religion. The problems for the courts in making decisions about whether or not a belief or practice is religious or secular are very great indeed. For example, the US Constitution insists that there must be a distinction, but a review by a constitutional expert of Supreme Court interpretations since 1790 fails to establish any clear and consistent criteria for making it[10].

Is our own seeking for justice in secular courts of law essentially different from the desire for justice under Sharia or any other system of legal representation? My point here concerns the representation of legal systems as either secular or religious. One can argue that secular courts of law are sacred spaces replete with ritual, taboo, solemnity, special spatial layout, hierarchy and so on. These are where we go to realise Justice in our lives. Is Justice less of a transcendent value to us than devotion to various 'gods'? Secular courts of law are not essentially different from 'religious' institutions themselves, except in the discursive either–or construction that proclaims that they are.

The challenge would be to try to translate these Anglophone or more widely Europhone terms and the supposedly intelligible distinctions that are intended to be made into Tibetan, Arabic, Urdu, Chinese, Swahili, or whatever. If the distinctions are not fully intelligible in English in the first place, then this seems to be a recipe for global miscommunication.

Inconclusive Conclusion

This has been a brief exercise in deconstructing some of the common Anglophone categories of everyday public life that appear in this collection's title, attempting to indicate how they conceal (largely unconscious) rhetorical devices that allow abstract and rather empty terms to appear persuasive, objectively real and inevitable. I will finish by anticipating some of the objections to the arguments I have outlined here. We need general categories to think with. What would you put in their place? Why would alternative formulations and terms not bring their own inherent confusions? The whole argument is negative; what positive and constructive suggestions do you have? If there is as little clear content as you claim to such significant concepts as religion, politics, God, and so on, then from where do they derive their rhetorical power? I have made suggestions about this here and in other places, but I am sure that the question will surface again.

Notes

1. This is a highly compressed argument, and as such cannot be comprehensive. I hope it might provoke critical thought. The arguments are given a more extensive airing in several publications. A good starting place for anyone who is interested in following them up is my book *Religion and Politics in International Relations: the Modern Myth* (Continuum, 2011). This book also includes references, which are few here for purposes of length. I am at present working on a book provisionally titled *Abolishing Politics and Other Felicities*.

2. A typical and influential version of this mythical discourse can be found in Christopher Hitchens, *God is Not Great: How Religion Poisons Everything*. See my discussion, side by side with more academic texts that reproduce much the same propaganda, in *Religion and Politics in International Relations* (op.cit)

3. See William D. Hart, *Edward Said and the Religious Effects of Culture*, CUP, 2000. See also Jil Anidjar, 'Secularism', *Critical Inquiry*, 33, Autumn 2006, pp52-77 for an interesting discussion of the religion-secular distinction in Said's texts.

4. 'God is dead but has been resurrected as "Capital"'; Jeremy Carrette & Richard King, *Selling Spirituality: the Silent Takeover of Religion* (Routledge, 2005), p1.

5. Paul Heelas, 1992, 'The Sacralization of the Self and New Age Capitalism', In Nicholas Abercrombie and Alan Warde (eds), *Social Change in Contemporary Britain*. Cambridge: Polity Press (pp. 139-166)

6. Bellah, Robert N. (1967). 'Civil Religion in America', *Dædalus* 96 (1):1-21; (1991). *Beyond Belief: Essays on Religion in a Post-Traditionalist World*. Berkeley: University of California Press. Carolyn Marvin and David Ingle, (1996) 'Blood Sacrifice and the Nation: Revisiting Civil Religion', *American Academy of Religion* 64(4), Winter, 1996; available at http://www.asc.upenn.edu/usr/fcm/jaar.htm

7. The many possible deployments of the term *kami* were brought out by D. C. Holton, (1940) 'The meaning of kami', *Monumenta Nipponica* 3:1-27. The complexity of the term is well brought out in Kuroda Toshio [Trans. Fabio Rambelli] (1996). 'The Discourse on the "Land of Kami" (Shinkoku) in "Medieval Japan: National Consciousness and International Awareness', *Japanese Journal of Religious Studies*, 23, pp353-385.

8. "The Dalai is definitely not a pure religious figure. He is using the cloak of religion to engage in long-term activities to separate China, he is a political exile." Official representative of Chinese Government commenting on President Obama's meeting with the Dalai Lama, reported by Roberta Tampton & Sui-Lee Wee, 'Obama meets with Dalai Lama despite China warnings', *Reuters*, Fri Feb 21, 2014, <http://uk.reuters.com/article/2014/02/21/uk-usa-china-tibet-idUKBREA1K1HA20140221> See also *Charter of the Tibetans in Exile*, adopted on 14 June 1991, Central Tibetan Administration, <http://tibet.net/about-cta/constitution/

9. I have discussed this issue more fully in *Religion and Politics in International Relations: The Modern Myth*, Continuum, 2011

10. See Micah Schwartzman, (2012). 'What if Religion Isn't Special?', Virginia School of Law: Social Science Research Network Electronic Paperw Collection. http://ssrn.com/abstract=1992090 [accessed on 20 August 2014].

Contributors

Ishtiaq Ahmed is Visiting Professor, Lahore University of Management Sciences (LUMS); Professor Emeritus of Political Science, Stockholm University; and Honorary Senior Fellow, Institute of South Asian Studies, Singapore.

Kaarina Aitamurto received her doctoral degree from the University of Helsinki. Her dissertation analysed Russian contemporary Paganism and nationalism. In her post-doctoral studies she has also focused on populism and hate speech in Europe and Muslim minorities in ethnically Russian areas. She has a postdoctoral researcher position at the Aleksanteri Institute and is a member of the Finnish Centre of Excellence in Russian Studies—Choices of Russian Modernization, funded by the Academy of Finland. She is the editor of *Modern Pagan and Native Faiths in Central and Eastern Europe* and a member of the editorial board of the *Journal of Religion and Violence*.

Jonathan Benthall is an Honorary Research Fellow in the Department of Anthropology, University College London and former Director of the Royal Anthropological Institute, where he founded the journal *Anthropology Today*. His publications include *The Best of* Anthropology Today (editor, 2002), *The Charitable Crescent: Politics of Aid in the Muslim world* (with Jérôme Bellion-Jourdan, 2003, new edition 2009), *Returning to Religion: Why a Secular Age is Haunted by Faith* (2008) and *Gulf Charities and Islamic Philanthropy in the 'Age of Terror' and Beyond* (co-edited with Robert Lacey, 2014). He reviews regularly for the *Times Literary Supplement*.

Ruy Llera Blanes is a Spanish anthropologist, who is currently working at the University of Bergen, Norway as a postdoctoral researcher. He is also Associated Researcher at the Institute of Social Sciences of the University of Lisbon, Portugal, where he received his PhD (2007). His current research site is Angola, where he investigates religion, mobility (diasporas, transnationalism, the Atlantic), politics (leadership, charisma, repression, resistance), temporalities (historicity, memory, heritage, expectations), knowledge and gender. He is currently Project Leader of the Collaborative Research Project Currents of Faith, Places of History: Diasporas, Connections, Moral Circumscriptions and World-making in the Atlantic Space, funded by the HERA consortium. He is Co-editor of the journal *Advances in Research: Religion and Society* and Associate Editor of the journal *HAU—Journal of Ethnographic Theory*.

Mark S. Cladis is the Brooke Russell Astor Professor of the Humanities in the Department of Religious Studies at Brown University. He is the author of *Public Vision, Private Lives* (Oxford University Press, 2003; paperback edition, Columbia University Press, 2006) and *A Communitarian Defense of Liberalism* (Stanford University Press, 1992), and over fifty articles and chapters in edited books. After receiving his doctorate from Princeton University, where he studied philosophy and social theory as they relate to the field of religious studies, he taught at the University of North Carolina, Stanford University, and at Vassar College where he served as chair for six years. Since 2004, he has been at Brown, where he has served as chair. He is the editor of Emile Durkheim's *Elementary Forms of the Religious Life* (Oxford University Press, 2001) and of *Education and Punishment: Durkheim and Foucault* (Oxford: Centre of Durkheimian Studies, 1999). Currently he is completing the book *In Search of a Course: Reflections on Pedagogy and the Culture of the Modern Research University*. He is also working on a new book project, *Radical Romanticism: Religion, Democracy, and the Environmental Imagination*.

Dan G. Cox is Associate Professor of Political Science at the School of Advanced Military Studies, Fort Leavenworth, Kansas. His current research interests are identity/human terrain and conflict, armed nation-building, counterinsurgency (especially the indirect approach), terrorism, strategy and military planning, operational art, and futures.

Stephen Dawson works at the intersection of religious studies, philosophy and the social sciences. His current research focuses on the Thomist understanding of religion as a virtue embedded in a disciplinary program. Currently he is Assistant Professor of Religious Studies at Lynchburg College in Lynchburg, Virginia. He holds a BA in English from George Mason University and a PhD in Religious Studies from Boston University.

Gertjan Dijkink currently works as Associate Professor of Political and Cultural Geography at the University of Amsterdam. He is the author of *National Identity and Geopolitical Visions: Maps of Pride and Pain* (Routlegde, 1996). He obtained his PhD in social sciences in 1987, with a thesis on geographical information and crime fighting in Amsterdam.

Timothy Fitzgerald is Reader in Religion at the University of Stirling. He is the author of *Religion and Politics in International Relations: The Modern Myth* (Continuum, 2011); *Discourse on Civility and Barbarity: A Critical History of Religion and Related Categories* (OUP, 2007); and *The Ideology of Religious Studies* (OUP, 2000).

François Foret is Professor of Political Science at the Free University of Brussels (Université Libre de Bruxelles—ULB) and Jean Monnet Chair ('Social and Cultural Dimensions of European Integration', SocEUR) funded by the European Commission. He is also Director of Political Research at the Institute for European Studies—ULB and a researcher at the CEVIPOL. His research interests include: European integration: institutions, politics and policies; European identity and memory; symbolic politics; the role of culture in the legitimization of political orders; interaction between religion and politics. Among his recent publications are: *Religion and Politics in the European Union; The Secular Canopy* (Cambridge University Press, 2015); 'Religion and Fundamental Rights in European Politics: Convergences and Divisions at the European Parliament', *Human Rights Review*, 15: 1 (2014), 53–63; and 'Religion at the European Parliament', *Religion, State & Society*, special issue, 3 (September 2014).

Jonathan Fox is Professor of Political Science at Bar-Ilan University in Ramat Gan, Israel. He specialises in the influence of religion on politics, using both quantitative and qualitative methodology to analyse the impact of religion on domestic conflict, international relations.

James L. Guth is William R. Kenan, Jr. Professor of Political Science at Furman University, Greenville South Carolina, USA. Guth has taught at Furman since 1973. He has served as chair of the University Faculty (1987–89) and of the Political Science Department (1988–91), as well as on many faculty committees and task forces. A specialist in American politics, his recent work has assessed the impact of religion on the electoral process and on public policy in the Clinton, Bush and Obama administrations.

Don Handelman is Sarah Allen Shaine Professor Emeritus of Anthropology and Sociology, Hebrew University, Jerusalem, and a member of the Israel Academy of Sciences and Humanities. His research interests focus on cosmology, religion, ritual and what he calls 'bureaucratic logic'. His research locales are in Israel and South India. Among his books are *Nationalism and the Israeli State: Bureaucratic Logic in Public Events* (Berg, 2004), and *One God, Two Goddesses, Three Studies of South Indian Cosmology* (Brill, 2014).

Allen D. Hertzke is David Ross Boyd Professor of Political Science, University of Oklahoma and Faculty Fellow in Religious Freedom for OU's Institute for the American Constitutional Heritage. He is also Distinguished Senior Fellow for the Institute for Studies of Religion at Baylor University and Senior Scholar for Georgetown University's project on Christianity and Freedom. He is author of *Representing God in Washington*, an award-winning analysis of religious lobbies, which has been issued in a Chinese-language translation, *Echoes of Discontent*, an account of church-rooted populist movements, *Freeing God's Children: The Unlikely Alliance for Global Human Rights,* and co-author of *Religion and Politics in America*, a comprehensive text now in its fourth edition.

Scott W. Hibbard is an Associate Professor in the Department of Political Science at DePaul University. He has also taught at the American University of Cairo and at Swarthmore College. Hibbard received his PhD from Johns Hopkins University and holds master's degrees from the London School of Economics and Political Science and Georgetown University.

Shireen T. Hunter is a Visiting Professor at Georgetown University's School of Foreign Service. She directs a project on Reformist Islam funded by the Carnegie Corporation Of New York. She is also a Distinguished Scholar at CSIS where she directed the Islam Program from 1998 to 2005. She is the author of seven books and three monographs and the editor and contributor of seven books and three monographs. She has contributed to more than 35 edited volumes and written forty journal articles. Her publications include, *Reformist Voices of Islam: Mediating Islam and Modernity* (M.E. Sharpe, forthcoming in June 2008); *Islam And Human Rights: Advancing A US–Muslim Dialogue* (ed.) (CSIS Press, 2005); *Modernization, Democracy and Islam* (co-editor and contributor) (Praeger, 2004); *Islam In Russia: The Politics of Identity And Security* (M.E. Sharpe, 2004); *Islam: Europe's Second Religion* (ed.) (Prager, 2002). Her latest book is *Iran Divided: Historic Roots of Iranian Debates on Identity, Culture, and Governance in the 21st Century* (Rowman & Littlefield, 2014).

Elizabeth Shakman Hurd is Associate Professor of Political Science and holds a courtesy appointment in Religious Studies at Northwestern University in Evanston, Illinois. She is the author of *The Politics of Secularism in International Relations* (Princeton, 2008), which won an APSA award for the best book on religion and politics published 2008–2010. Her latest book is *Beyond Religious Freedom: The New Global Politics of Religion* (Princeton, 2015). She is co-organiser of 'Politics of Religious Freedom: Contested Norms and Local Practices', a collaborative research project funded by the Luce Foundation, and consults on academic, media and foundation projects involving religion and international affairs. Her opinion pieces have appeared in *Boston Review*, *Public Culture*, *The Atlantic*, *Chicago Tribune*, *Globe* and *Mail*, *Foreign Policy* and *Al Jazeera America*.

Pauline Kollontai is a Professor of Higher Education in Theology and Religious Studies in the Faculty of Education and Theology of York St. John University and the Associate Director for the Centre for Religion in Society.

She worked previously at the University of Leeds in the School of Adult Education and at the University of Bradford in the Department of Peace Studies. Her academic qualifications are in the disciplines of peace studies and theology and religious studies and this is reflected in her teaching and particularly in her research on religion in social context with a particular focus on religion, peace and reconciliation.

J. Paul Martin is Director of Human Rights Studies at Barnard College, Columbia University. Professor Martin's professional experience has been built around his 29 years as Executive Director of Columbia's Center for the Study of Human Rights, of which he was a co-founder, along with Law and University Professor Louis Henkin. Previously, and later simultaneously, he was Director of the Earl Hall Center at Columbia University; a lecturer in the School of International and Public Affairs; and Adjunct Professor at Teachers College. He has also served as Director of the Human Rights and Humanitarian Affairs concentration at the School of International and Public Affairs, as well as Academic Advisor for the human rights concentration in the master's program of the Graduate School of Arts and Sciences. Professor Martin's early publications were on moral education. More recently he has focused on human rights and human rights education. He has edited three collections of human rights documents and contributed to the *Oxford Encyclopedia on Political Science* and *Encyclopedia of the Modern Middle East*.

Lee Marsden is Professor of International Relations, School of Political, Social and International Studies, University of East Anglia. He is also editor of the Ashgate Series on Religion and International Security. His key research interests lie in the area of religion and security, religion and international relations, religion and politics and US foreign policy.

Brent F. Nelsen is Professor of American Political Science at Furman University in Greenville, South Carolina. He serves as chair of the South Carolina Educational Television Commission, having been appointed to the position by South Carolina Governor Nikki Haley in 2011. In 2010 he was a Republican candidate for the position of South Carolina State Superintendent of Education. On Thursday, April 25, 2013, US President Barack Obama nominated him for confirmation by the US Senate to be a member of the Board of Directors of the US Corporation for Public Broadcasting, for a term expiring Sunday, January 31, 2016. He was confirmed by the Senate on August 1, 2013.

Fabio Petito is Senior Lecturer in International Relations at the Department of International Relations at the University of Sussex. He joined the

Department of International Relations in 2007, having previously taught at the School of Oriental and African Studies (SOAS) in London. He has also taught in recent years at the ESCP-EAP in Paris and at 'L'Orientale' University in Naples. Fabio holds a *Laurea* in Economic and Social Disciplines (DES) (*magna cum laude*) from Bocconi University, Milan, Italy and he undertook his MScEcon in International Politics at the University of Wales, Aberystwyth and his PhD in the department of International Relations at the LSE, where he was also editor of *Millennium: Journal of International Studies*.

John A. Rees is a research specialist in religion and international policy. He is Associate Professor of International Relations and Convener of the Religion and Global Affairs Program, Centre for Faith, Ethics and Society at the University of Notre Dame Australia (Sydney) He is the author of numerous publications on religion and world politics, including *Religion in International Politics and Development: the World Bank and Faith Institutions* (Edward Elgar, 2011).

Paul S. Rowe is Associate Professor of Political and International Studies at Trinity Western University and coordinator of the Political and International Studies programmes. He completed his PhD in Political Science at McGill University in 2003. He teaches in the areas of international and developing world politics with a specialty in the Middle East and South Asia. He has lived and worked in the Middle East and travels frequently throughout the region. His research interests lie in the politics of religion in the Middle East/South Asia and at the global level. He is the author of *Religion and Global Politics* (Oxford University Press, 2012).

Nilay Saiya is Assistant Professor of Political Science and Director of International Studies State University of New York, Brockport. His research focuses on the intersection between religion and international relations, including its role in American foreign policy making and international security.

Mona Kanwal Sheikh is a Senior Researcher at the Danish Institute of International Studies, where she specialises in issues of religion and secularism in international relations. She is currently a Visiting Research Scholar at the Orfalea Center for Global and International Studies at UC Santa Barbara. Relevant publications include 'Sacred Pillars of Violence: Findings from a Study of the Pakistani Taliban' (*Politics, Religion, Ideology*, 2012), 'How Does Religion Matter? Pathways to Religion in International Relations' (*Review of International Studies*, 2012), 'Western Secularisms: Variations in a Doctrine and its Practice' (in *Thinking International Relations Differently*, eds Arlene B. Tickner and David L. Blaney, Routledge, 2012) and 'A Sociotheological Approach to Understanding Religious Violence' (in *The*

Oxford Handbook of Religion and Violence, eds Michael Jerryson, Mark Juergensmeyer and Margo Kitts, Oxford University Press, 2012).

Fang-long Shih is a former Co-Director of Taiwan Research Programme and a Research Fellow at the London School of Economics Asia Research Programme. She has published on religion and the state in Taiwan, focusing in particular on state-led guidelines in the areas of ritual and tourism that have direct and indirect impact upon popular religious practices. She has further published on the so-called 'Red Tide' anti-corruption protest, focusing on the socio-cultural significance of the colour red. Her work considers questions of translation, context and location in the writing and re-writing of religion in Taiwan. She is currently writing a chapter on 'Feminisms and Religions' for the *New Blackwell Companion to the Sociology of Religion,* and her current research interest is on religious practice in relation to environmental discourse.

Brendan Sweetman is Professor of Philosophy and Chairman of the Department of Philosophy at Rockhurst University, Kansas City, Missouri, USA. He is the author or editor of ten books, including *Religion and Science: An Introduction* (Continuum, 2010); *The Vision of Gabriel Marcel: Epistemology, Human Person, the Transcendent* (Rodopi Press, 2008); *Why Politics Needs Religion: The Place of Religious Arguments in the Public Square* (InterVarsity, 2006); *Contemporary Perspectives on Religious Epistemology* (Oxford University Press, 1992); *A Gabriel Marcel Reader* (St. Augustine's Press, 2011); and, most recently, *Philosophical Thinking and the Religious Context* (Bloomsbury, 2013). He was consulting editor for the *New Catholic Encyclopedia Supplement: Ethics and Philosophy* (Cengage Gage, 2013, four vols.). He has published more than a hundred articles and reviews in a variety of journals and collections.

Jodok Troy is a Project Leader and Lecturer at the Department of Political Science at the University of Innsbruck, Austria. His most recent publications on this religion include *Christian Approaches to International Affairs* (Palgrave Macmillan, 2012) and (with Alan Chong) 'A Universal Sacred Mission and the Universal Secular Organisation: The Holy See and the United Nations', *Politics, Religion, and Ideology*, 12: 3 (2011).

Linda Woodhead is Professor of Sociology of Religion in the Department of Politics, Philosophy and Religion at Lancaster University. She was Director of the £12m AHRC/ESRC Religion and Society Programme 2007–13 and is Chair of the Theology and Religious Studies REF sub-panel and a member of the ESRC. Her books include *Christianity: A Very Short Introduction* (2nd ed., 2014), *Prayer in Religion and Spirituality* (with Giuseppe Giordan, 2013),

Everyday Lived Islam in Europe (with Nathal Dessing and Nadia Jeldtoft, 2013), Religion *and Change in Modern Britain* (with Rebecca Catto, 2012), *A Sociology of Religious Emotions* (with Ole Riis, 2010), *Religions in the Modern World* (2009), and *The Spiritual Revolution* (with Paul Heelas, 2005).

Note on Indexing

E-IR's publications do not feature indexes due to the prohibitive costs of assembling them. However, if you are reading this book in paperback and want to find a particular word or phrase you can do so by downloading a free e-book version of this publication in PDF from the E-IR website.

When downloaded, open the PDF on your computer in any standard PDF reader such as Adobe Acrobat Reader (pc) or Preview (mac) and enter your search terms in the search box. You can then navigate through the search results and find what you are looking for. In practice, this method can prove much more targeted and effective than consulting an index.

If you are using apps such as iBooks or Kindle to read our e-books, you should also find word search functionality in those.

You can find all of our e-books at: http://www.e-ir.info/publications

www.ingramcontent.com/pod-product-compliance
Lightning Source LLC
Chambersburg PA
CBHW060029030426
42334CB00019B/2239